THE MEDIEVAL WORLD

The twelfth century in Europe was a time when a "Christendom" of flexible ideas prevailed rather  dogma and th of Islam enr when Russia Europe and t During the alien race, creed, or opinion was widespread; political boundaries were nebulous and open, and the ruling aristocracy had not yet become the iron, closed caste of later centuries.

Friedrich Heer's incisive history describes how the buoyant, fluid society of twelfth-century Europe solidified into the medieval world—a fourteenth century of religious and intellectual intolerance, fortified frontiers, and bitterly competitive states. He discusses the Crusades; the alienation of Rome and Byzantium; the rising power of the Church and the aristocracy; the life of the peasant, the town dweller, and the tradesman.

Along with vivid sketches of medieval personalities, Professor Heer analyzes art and science, Gothic architecture and courtly literature, and shows how they reflect the character of the age. His richly exuberant style captures the exciting color and contradiction of a little-known period of European history.

THE
MEDIEVAL
WORLD

EUROPE 1100-1350

by *FRIEDRICH HEER*

Translated from the German
by *JANET SONDHEIMER*

A MENTOR BOOK from
NEW AMERICAN LIBRARY

Published by arrangement with Harry N. Abrams, Inc.

The Medieval World was first published
in Germany, 1961, under the title *Mittelalter*

MENTOR TRADEMARK REG. U.S. PAT. OFF. AND FOREIGN COUNTRIES
REGISTERED TRADEMARK—MARCA REGISTRADA
HECHO EN WINNIPEG, CANADA

SIGNET, SIGNET CLASSIC, MENTOR, PLUME, MERIDIAN AND NAL
BOOKS are published *in the United States by*
New American Library,
1633 Broadway, New York, New York 10019,
in Canada by The New American Library of Canada Limited,
81 Mack Avenue, Scarborough, Ontario M1L 1M8

13   14   15   16   17   18   19   20   21

PRINTED IN CANADA

CONTENTS

LIST OF ILLUSTRATIONS

(between pages 128 and 129)

ACKNOWLEDGEMENTS

Acknowledgement is made to the following for translations used in the text: pp. 157-8, Verse by Philippe de Thaun: translation by A. Kelly in *Eleanor of Aquitaine and the Four Kings* 1952 (Cassell & Co.); pp. 175-6, King Richard's verses: translation in B. H. Adam's *Mont Saint Michel and Chartres* 1930 (American Institute of Architects, Boston and New York); pp. 228, St. Francis' Hymn of Praise: translation by N. Wydenbruck in O. Karrer's *St. Francis of Assisi: The Legends and Lands* 1947 (Sheed and Ward); pp. 228-9, Canticle of the Sun: translation by F. C. Burkitt in *The Song of Brother Sun, in English Rime* (S.P.C.K.).

FOREWORD

PEOPLE who can write about Europe from the outside have the advantage of being able to take an objective view. A degree of detachment may even be possible for Englishmen, who from early medieval times have been in the habit of thinking of their country as an *alter orbis,* a world in itself, distinct from continental Europe. The writer of this sketch of European civilisation between 1100 and 1350 has had no such advantages. This is a book written by a European living in central Europe, where much that was medieval is still contemporary, and this may have been something of a handicap.

But a still greater handicap has been the need to summarize important historical developments in a few lines or even in a single phrase. Thus many problems and controversial areas have been left unexplored and in several cases even their existence has had to be ignored. And not only important personalities, such as William of Ockham, and large issues, such as the varying status of the peasantry at different periods, have suffered; details which are apparently trivial but which are in fact full of significance have also had to be neglected. The life of the Middle Ages as it was lived, let alone the hypotheses historians have constructed around it, is fraught with contradictions. But in the drastic simplification imposed by the limited space available much of this complexity has disappeared, and the portraits of individuals have had to be sketched in a few strokes, in an effort to present their salient characteristics in a distinct and colourful form.

The most that can be hoped for is that this sketch, with all its imperfections, will entice the reader to explore further for himself those complex processes of medieval life and civilisation which here are often presented in deliberately provocative terms. This, in fact, is to be interpreted as an 'open' book, in keeping with one of its main themes. Its purpose is to lead the reader to the work or other writers, whose treatment of these great themes may be different, and to a closer study of the material. If such study leads to a deeper personal involvement in the life of this past age, the author's main aim will have been achieved. Anyone who becomes immersed in the great conflicts of the Middle Ages and in the contemporary controversies which have grown up round them cannot fail to find himself enriched by the experience.

CHAPTER 1

EUROPE 1100-1350

OUR contemporary European societies, both Western and Eastern, in many ways continue to live on their medieval inheritance. History is the present, and the present is history. When we look more closely into the crises and catastrophes, the hopes and fears of our own day, whether we know it or not we are concerned with developments whose origins can be traced back directly or indirectly to their source in the high Middle Ages.

During this period Europe underwent some far-reaching transformations. The continent which in the twelfth century was open and expanding by the mid-fourteenth century had become closed, a Europe of internal and external frontiers, where nations, states, churches (i.e. the various regional "Gallicanized" churches) and intellectual systems already confronted one another—often in uncompromising and hostile attitudes—in the forms they were to retain at least until the mid-nineteenth century or even into the twentieth.

In the twelfth, and to a large extent still in the early thirteenth century, Europe had the characteristics of an open society. The frontiers, later to become barriers, "iron curtains" delimiting separate worlds, were still open, even fluid. There were open frontiers on Europe's eastern borders. Until the time of the Mongol onslaught and the Fourth Crusade (1204) Russia was still accessible to the West, linked to Western Europe and Germany by commercial and economic ties and by aristocratic intermarriage. In the eleventh and twelfth centuries an international trade route running from Scandinavia to Byzantium passed through the centre of Russia, by way of Novgorod. The magnificent twelfth-century doors of Novgorod cathedral, of German workmanship, still stand as witness to this link.

Whilst it was still open, Russia was a bridge across another of Europe's frontiers, that between Byzantium and Rome, between the churches of the East and West. The antithesis between medieval Rome and Byzantium was as ancient as that between Latin and Greek; the two confronted one another as opposites, like the Old Testament prophets and apostles face to face on the façades of medieval cathedrals. Since the eighth century there had been a steady increase in ecclesiastical rivalry between Rome, the city of the Popes, and Constantinople, the city of the Emperor Constantine, "equal of the Apostles". Byzantium, that is to say the Eastern Roman Emperor and the Eastern Church, was highly suspicious of the new Frankish Empire and the support it received from the Papacy. What lay in the balance was the conversion to Christianity of the newly emerging nations of Eastern Europe: whoever achieved it would become the decisive influence in the formation of their political, social and intellectual traditions.

Although in the eleventh century a serious breach occurred in the relations of the Latin and Greek churches, nevertheless the open Europe of the twelfth century still gave scope for friendly intercourse, as the art of Western Europe impressively bears witness. The real break came with the Fourth Crusade and its aftermath. It was this final rupture between the Greek and Latin churches that set Eastern and Western Europe at odds with each other for the next seven centuries. The sight of swarms of Franks ("barbarians", "brigands", "war-mongers" are among the terms used to describe them) marching into the Holy Land led by their princes and bishops aroused the cultivated Greek intelligentsia, clerical and lay, to loathing and despair. To the Byzantines it seemed the Franks could have only one objective: the destruction of the world's greatest political and cultural masterpiece, the great Empire of the Rhomaioi, that marvellous and multi-national empire which had so long defended itself against so many enemies.

The third frontier of this open Europe of the twelfth and early thirteenth centuries, that with Islam, was also fluid. True, there was fighting in Spain, which meant that here the aristocracies of the two cultures were constantly in combat. But even so, old friendships prospered and new ones were formed, Islamic and Hispano-Christian families intermarried, and even the Cid Campeador, the greatest Spanish hero in the war with Islam, whose exploits are celebrated in the national epic, spent most of his life in the service of Islamic rulers.

In this expanding Europe of the twelfth century there was such curiosity and so great a thirst for knowledge that the intellectual and cultural treasure Islam had to offer exerted an immense attraction. This treasure was nothing less than the intellectual wealth of Greek antiquity, augmented by the glosses and commentaries of Islamic scholars from the Near East and the Mediterranean, masters in a vast and flourishing "empire of learning" which stretched from Persia and Samarkand by way of Baghdad and Salerno to Toledo. Arab (and Jewish) translators and commentators helped to make the heritage of philosophical and scientific writings left by Plato and Aristotle and their disciples and successors available to the West. Not only in Spain, but also in southern France, Sicily and southern Italy, there were men who welcomed these contacts and kept the lines of communication with Islam open.

If there was room for manoeuvre on these three "external" frontiers of Europe in the twelfth century, there was a corresponding internal flexibility: learning was liberal, popular piety took many forms, the Church itself stood open. Learning was becoming more broadly based. The young clerks who in growing numbers frequented the cathedral schools of France and Germany and the municipal schools of Italy brought with them curiosity, freshness and open minds. The culture they acquired there had many elements derived from pagan antiquity and the non-Christian world of the Orient, strands which threaded themselves into a brightly-coloured tissue to adorn not only the humanism of Chartres but also the courtly culture of the Angevin Empire. This was no mere flash in the pan. The poets and natural philosophers of the Italian Renaissance of the fifteenth and sixteenth centuries had their predecessors in the humanists, Platonists, natural philosophers, poets and theoretical exponents of the *ars amandi* (the art of loving in the courtly, civilized fashion, governed by strict rules) of the twelfth century, who had shown themselves so readily receptive of such alien material. Similarly, in the sixteenth and seventeenth centuries, when the foundations of modern scientific thought were being laid, philosophers and natural scientists (Nicholas of Cues, Leibnitz, Galileo, Isaac Newton, Boyle and Locke) constantly looked back to what had been learned in the open Europe of the twelfth and early thirteenth centuries.

This widely-ranging eclecticism was only possible because of the open-mindedness prevailing in the Church and in religious life as a whole. It is sheer prejudice which condemns the entire Middle Ages as a Dark Age, based on the hackneyed assumption that the medieval mind was narrow, dominated by a fanatical clergy, strait-jacketed by a rigid set of dogmas. Reality presents quite a contrary picture. True, no medieval century (any more than any modern century) was entirely free from intolerance; there were always people full of hatred and mistrust of their neighbours and of anyone who did not conform, there were always people whose hearts and minds were narrow and fearful. But what is important for a proper appreciation of the twelfth and early thirteenth centuries, and of the perspectives then opened up, is to realize that both the pious common folk and the spiritual élite accepted with great readiness, in all the robust and wholesome simplicity of young peoples and young minds, a truly "catholic" religion, compounded of a great variety of elements. It was only when the world turned puritanical that this synthesis was broken, subjected to analysis by purists who sorted out its various components and dug deep chasms to keep them apart. This open religion of the earlier Middle Ages was a satisfying blend of ingredients taken from pre-Christian "pagan" folk religions with others that were certainly Christian but which had acquired an exotic flavouring from their intimate association with contrasting and non-Christian material. This religion, which was the religion of the people and also in some cases that of the ruling classes and of eminent personalities, will be more fully discussed later. All that needs to be stressed here is that it could be accommodated, together with an open culture, within the broad bosom of an equally open Church, in a way which later filled the men of the Reformation and Counter-Reformation with fear and disgust.

The open Church of the open twelfth century permitted liberties that were inconceivable to later generations. This was a living Church, alive in body and members, buoyant, pliable and colourful. The number of the sacraments had not yet been fixed at seven, nor had the Mass reached its final form. Many articles of faith were still without definition as dogmas; they were to be debated by the Schoolmen in the thirteenth century and ultimately defined by the Council of Trent. It was not until the middle of the twelfth century that the Church as an entity was even mentioned. Up to that time people thought rather in terms of Christendom; no-one wrote theological or religio-political treatises on "the Church" ("church" meant the building, the House of God), nor was there much talk of theology. It was the audacious Abelard who introduced theology in its modern sense, both as a word and as a concept, into Europe. As a word it had been avoided for its associations with pagan antiquity; and men were fully conscious of its dangers as a concept, feeling that attempts to "understand" God, to imprison Him within the rigid vice of theology, was a form of temptation. The theological speculations of this older, more open Europe moved instead about the great mysteries of faith, in an attitude of reticence, reverence and love. This faith, like all ultimate realities, could ultimately only be experienced, never comprehended.

The open Church of the older Europe was a living union of mighty opposites: Heaven and Earth, matter and spirit, living and dead, body and soul, past, present and future. Reality was seamless, there was no chasm separating created from redeemed mankind; all men were of one blood, from the first man to the last, and inhabited a single hemisphere, at once natural and "supernatural". It was not until the thirteenth century that theology was invaded by the concept of the "supernatural". This open Church was served by bishops and lower clergy who led boisterous, cheerful lives, accepting tears and laughter as they came; they were full of *savoir vivre* and very independent in their relations with each other, which were sometimes amicable, sometimes acrimonious. Rome was very remote; so, often, was a man's immediate superior, his bishop or abbot.

Several political and social frontiers which would later be closed still stood open. The long boundary between France and Germany, for centuries one of Europe's worst danger-spots, was in many places nebulous; lordships intermingled there, since many magnates held fiefs and estates both from the French monarchy and the Empire. Within the Empire, Italy only started to pursue its separate interests after its ecclesiastical organization had been disentangled from that of the Empire by the Concordat of Worms in 1122. Europe's eastern frontiers were still quite fluid. The German colonizers and the native East European nobility (Slavs, Poles, Prussians, Lithuanians and Magyars) were between them bringing Eastern Europe increasingly closer to Central and Western Europe, until together they became a unit, though expansion still continued eastwards into the Baltic lands until the furthest point was reached with the settlement of Riga, Revel and Dorpat in the early thirteenth century. The first systematically fortified frontiers were those erected by the Plantagenet rulers of England as a defence against the Welsh and Irish, and, later, the Scots. But even here there was a constant passage to and fro, especially since there were close family ties between the nobility on both sides.

For this open Europe had also its open aristocracy. Admittedly, it might be said that by the beginning of the twelfth century the higher aristocracy were a single "clan". The commanding position of the Norman nobility, with its offshoots spread over France, Sicily and England, was a conspicuous example of the growing tendency towards the formation of a "closed caste", sharply distinct both from the subordinate peasantry and from the free and unfree inhabitants of the towns. Further, in the twelfth century there were significant advances in the direction of making the aristocracy yet more exclusive. However, the rise in the social scale during the twelfth and thirteenth centuries of the *ministeriales*, originally an unfree "aristocracy of service" within the Holy Roman Empire (they were mostly in the direct employ of the German monarchy, in the German parts of the Empire) shows that social barriers were still not insurmountable. There is further evidence of this from the wide areas of Europe which had a substantial lesser aristocracy, living on the land in close proximity to the peasants, their social inferiors, and open to penetration from below. The evolution of the English governing class from the time of the Norman Conquest onwards is a tribute to the wisdom of the Normans: originally a small and exclusive group, they succeeded in preserving their identity whilst admitting to their ranks a stream of able and successful recruits from the lower classes, who became eminent in Church and State and were further reinforced from the wealthy patrician families of London.

An open aristocracy: and an open clergy, too. Most twelfth-century clerics were outward-looking, accessible to their people and to their own kindred, at all levels of society. There were few of those rigid barriers which were later to separate clergy and people, when the Church became increasingly sacerdotal, bureaucratic and scholastic in complexion, as it did from the thirteenth century onwards. Even the higher, indeed the very highest, clergy were culturally speaking often

on a level with their people, sharing their faith and superstitions, closely associated with them in their feasts and festivals and daily life. Although the government of the Church
continued to become more and more aristocratic (this was a
legacy from late antiquity), there was a certain relaxation
following the reform movements of the eleventh and early
twelfth centuries; men of low rank and very obscure origin
rose to be princes of the Church and to occupy the highest
offices in Church and State.

But there were clouds even in the open sky of the twelfth
century; well before it was ended there was already more than
a hint of the changes which would make the Europe of the
thirteenth and fourteenth centuries a closed Europe, fore-
shadowing in many respects the Europe of our own time.
These ominous developments must now be described, but
first it is worth remarking on the survival into this later
period of qualities brought to life and fostered in the womb
of that older, more open Europe: the roistering humour of a
Chaucer or a Shakespeare, the breadth of mind of the
Christian humanists, as represented by Thomas More and
his friend Erasmus of Rotterdam; the satisfying combination
in a single way of life, whether that of an individual or of a
community, of contradictory and conflicting elements (this
has been especially characteristic of England, but is not
unknown on the Continent). Thus in describing the Europe
of the thirteenth and fourteenth centuries as "closed" it must
first be understood that this is a simplification. This "closed"
continent retained much of the open character of early
twelfth-century Europe, the "old" Europe, just as the conflicts of the eleventh and twelfth centuries had prepared the
way for the rigid divisions characteristic of the later period.

A few well-known facts will suffice here to illustrate the
growing internal and external isolation of Europe in the
period 1200–1350. The Mongol deluge cut Russia off from
Europe for centuries, a separation which in many respects
still endures. The Latin Crusaders' capture of Constantinople
by force and the foundation of Crusading states on Byzantine
territory inevitably brought about the separation of East and
West, the division of Christendom into Greek and Latin
spheres of influence. The armed presence in Spain of small
Arabic-Moorish states and the emergence of a new Muslim
power, the Turks, as a threat to the Balkans and the Mediterranean created rigid frontiers between European Christendom and Islam which still exist. The three powerful and con-

tiguous cultures, Western Christendom, Byzantium and Islam, were now drawing further and further apart, and this despite the facts that basically they had much in common and that there had been considerable intercourse between them in the early Middle Ages: now all three tended to revert to what is usually considered a typically "medieval" condition—they became closed societies, withdrawn into their separate worlds.

This growing external isolation was matched by the development inside European society of sharply differentiated specialist institutions and groupings. The two universal powers of the early Middle Ages, the Papacy and the Empire, succeeded in humiliating each other. The Papacy achieved the degradation of the Empire, only to succumb to the power which was formerly its staunchest ally, the French monarchy. The emerging nation states of the later Middle Ages kept their churches and bishops on a tight rein; these churches were the prototypes of the Erastian and national churches of the Reformation and Counter-Reformation, and it is interesting to see them in a setting both medieval and catholic.

The emergence of the nation state, a phenomenon of unusual complexity, first attracts attention in its religious-political aspect: Wyclif and Hus stand on the boundary of the period under review. The religious upheaval was inseparably linked with the rise of the vernacular languages and of national literatures. The peoples sought and found their inner strength in their own native tongues. Only the vernacular seemed adequate to explore and describe the hills and valleys in the landscape of the popular soul and mind, to sing the people's hopes and fears, and, not least, to sound the call to battle.

Latin, the language of the Church and of the clerically educated intelligentsia, now lost its pre-eminence as the universal language of Europe. It was retained as the language of the universities and the governing élite in both Church and State, surviving in parts of Germany and Eastern Europe into the eighteenth or nineteenth centuries (it was the language of Hungarian officialdom until 1848).

The two most powerful estates, the nobility and the clergy, cut themselves off from the masses and became closed societies; so did the intelligentsia, jealous of their university learning and privileges. These three groups were becoming distinct and separate bodies within the nations; and the nations themselves were also becoming conscious of their separate identities, largely as a consequence of their joint and acrimonious participation in the Crusades. The anti-Semitism of the later Middle Ages was part of the same trend: the Jews were expelled from England in 1290 and other nations followed suit. Higher education was becoming narrower and more specialized, and the bureaucratic Church, entrenched behind the Inquisition and Canon Law and intent on theological refinement, was becoming increasingly remote from the laity and the "people". The Church was in fact becoming clericalized, a process hastened by the shocking discovery (*circa* 1200) that the whole of south-western Europe and western and southern Germany was riddled with "heresy", heresy which in some places was so extreme that it led to the establishment of an opposition church. The Church's answer was to erect a huge administrative machine, to establish new religious orders (soon to become mutually antagonistic), to develop a more rigorous theology, and to intervene directly in the external and internal affairs of the nations.

It is important to realize the magnitude of this initial shock as a key to the fragmentation of Europe in the thirteenth century, and the standardization which began to take the place of rich diversity. The shock consisted in the realization that Christendom, an indivisible unit, had suddenly become permeated and undermined by sects whose views on religion, the world, and sometimes also on politics, differed totally from those of the Church and its people. This realization set off a chain reaction: it led to internal "Crusades" against the heretics, the setting up of the Inquisition, censorship of thought and belief on the part of Church and State, and a rigid definition of ecclesiastical dogmas and secular knowledge.

In the later medieval centuries, when one might say men lived in a perpetual state of shock, the tolerance often extended in "open" Europe to persons of alien race, creed or opinion was superseded by a mounting tide of prejudice, of xenophobia, which grew higher with each fresh wave of fear. After the heretics came the Turks. They struck almost simultaneously with the Hussites, whose armies marched all over central Europe. Joan of Arc, the Maid of Orleans, was willing to oppose them; yet to her French and English foes Joan was herself a "heretic", close kinswoman to the Hussites.

The sudden outbreaks of epidemics, known in the Middle Ages under the general description of "the plague", served to spread and intensify the general feeling of crisis endemic towards the end of the medieval period. The "Black Death" (*circa* 1350), by depopulating large areas, confirmed the condition of internal shrivelling which was generally characteristic of Europe's development in the later Middle Ages. In the twelfth and early thirteenth centuries there had been expansion, internally and externally, accompanied by a striking increase in population. As Europe contracted the population correspondingly declined and the economy became stagnant.

Stagnation, the shock to Christendom, national antagonisms, social arrogance and exclusiveness all found their reflection in the intellectual and spiritual life of the time. This was the period when nominalism triumphantly invaded the universities and theology, a victory for those who would sharply distinguish faith from knowledge, spirit from matter, God from man, and the natural from the supernatural; this philosophy, like mysticism, was expressive of the doubts and despair which troubled the age. Both nominalism and mysticism were attempts at building inner kingdoms of the mind and soul whilst outside the peoples of Europe remained locked in a state of permanent civil war.

The enclosed Europe of the later Middle Ages provided a stage for the unrolling of two great epics, both of them momentous for Europe's future. It was in this period that England and France were growing to maturity side by side; they fought each other over the Angevin Empire, lived amiably together through the long years of truce in the thirteenth century, fought again through the still longer years of war in the fourteenth and fifteenth centuries, and between them laid the foundations of the "West". The "West" as an entity, distinguished by its own ideals of humanism, its own concepts of political and social order and religion, cherishing its own hopes and faced with its own realities, had here its nucleus, its primitive cell, from which life proliferated in a process of continuous formation and deformation. It was the contacts made between the British Isles and France from the twelfth to the fifteenth centuries, on whatever footing—political, religious, social or belligerent—which created the unit that later, with the addition of the Netherlands and of North America, was to extend far beyond Europe and become the Atlantic Community, the model for the "free world".

While the "West" was being created on the Atlantic seaboard, another process was at work in the heart of the continent. With the decline of the Empire the Germans concentrated their energies on expanding eastwards, an advance in which soldiers, missionaries and settlers all played their part. From that time Eastern Europe lived in a state of permanent unease, keeping a cautious eye on everything German: the towns, which were German enclaves in non-German territory, the peasant-farmers, the nobility and higher clergy, even the "German God" and Christianity. Brandenburg-Prussia and Hapsburg Austria, the two states which grew in the East from the ruins of the Holy Roman Empire and which from the seventeenth to the twentieth centuries disputed for hegemony in the German-speaking lands, first struck root in the contentious soil of the thirteenth and fourteenth centuries.

This enclosed Europe had thus its own "East" and its own "West", a division which provoked serious internal tensions and discords that could, and did, lead to East–West conflicts within Europe itself. Under the shock of crisis "Westerners" were ready to see their nearest Eastern neighbours as the "wicked East" incarnate. This was the French view of the Germans, the German view of the Poles, the Polish view of the Russians, the universal view of the Mongols when they appeared in the early thirteenth century, and later of the Turks.

The "closed" Europe of the thirteenth and fourteenth centuries was in fact rich in explosive material; all the political, social, intellectual and religious questions which were to be of lasting significance in European history were already present in basic form. In all the modern history of Europe, right down to the outbreak of the second world war, there was no crisis, no war, no catastrophe, no calamity which was not in some way prefigured in the happenings of that period of medieval Europe which saw the conflict and overthrow of Empire and Papacy, the emergence of an "East" and "West" within the confines of Europe itself, the rise of nation states and of exclusive social groupings within the nations.

But there is much to attract and admire even in a Europe apparently so forbidding. From this area of combat arose an art and a culture; and political institutions were born which are still used as foundation-stones for building free societies of free men. The Gothic cathedrals are inseparably linked with the initial struggles of the French kings to maintain themselves in the tiny portion of France which was all they could call their own. In the same way, European intellectualism, the universities, and the humanistic education of the schools were all inseparably linked with the rivalries between Popes, kings, bishops, secular and regular clergy, and with the battles over whether alien intellects, the great masters of the ancient, Islamic and non-Christian worlds, should be treated as allies or enemies in the common front against the heretic and the heterodox. Intellectualism throve on conflict, fire gave it a keener edge; and if the fire was often fed by flames licking round the stake, it could also burn with the softer glow of an inner light, kindled in the more peaceable setting of a learned disputation.

This culture was also a culture of the emotions; courtly society disciplined the passions and instructed in the arts of love and of refined manners. The conventions of civility observed in the eighteenth and nineteenth centuries—in England the age of the gentleman, in France of the abbés and salons, in Germany of the Enlightenment, "sensibility" and the youthful Goethe—still drew nourishment from the fount of courtoisie, the Provençal and Hispano-Islamic civilization laid low by the northern onslaught which exterminated the Albigensians and their culture.

Until well after the time of Shakespeare and the early prose romances, European writers continued to draw on that treasure-house of tales, folk-legends, romances and "romantic" themes first opened up in the twelfth and thirteenth centuries for the benefit of an eager public, avid for new matter. Medieval art and civilization reached one of its summits with Dante, who mirrors all the religious and political aspirations of his medieval world. Dante created the *Divine Comedy* and brought all his wrath, his smart, his sorrow and his ecstasy to his vision of his fellow-travellers on their voyages to Heaven and Hell. His medieval masterpiece is the work of an exile, banished for life from his native Florence. None could hate so well as Dante, but for all his spleen he is still one of the noblest exponents of love, earthly and divine.

This period of the Middle Ages was volcanic territory, with the threat of eruption always just below the surface: not a year passed, not a day, without outbreaks of war, feud and civil conflict. But this same volcanic soil could sustain the Gothic vine; poetic laurels flourished in it and the myrtle of mysticism grew sturdily. German mysticism had its beginning in the crumbling Empire, at a time when lay and ecclesiastical princes were wrangling over the spoils and men, women and children were being burnt as heretics at Strasbourg and Cologne. The influence of Meister Eckhart, Tauler, Suso and their sisters and daughters in religion flowed into two channels, an emotional and an intellectual, and both were far-reaching and fruitful. The one fertilized the Neo-Platonism and Enthusiasm of sixteenth and seventeenth century England, with effects on the culture of the emotions which lasted until well after the time of Shaftesbury; the benefit of the other was felt in the Spain of Loyola and Teresa of Avila, in the France of Fénélon and in early nineteenth-century Russia.

Roman Catholicism, in violent reaction to the effluvia of these new eruptions, hardened into a set of crystalline forms of thought and into institutions continuously purified and perfected under the stress of ambition and anxiety in later centuries. And this great edifice of power and dominion stirred up in its turn further resistance, among the masses, among the learned clerks of the universities, and in the monasteries, a resistance both emotional and intellectual; the protection offered by some of the nobility to people persecuted for heterodox religious views may be mentioned as an example. It has often and justly been said that the Reformation (and the Counter-Reformation too, for it had its origins in the Albigensian Crusade) was born in this period of the Middle Ages. All the ingredients are there: vociferous criticism of the clergy and of Rome, waves of religious frenzy among the masses ("enthusiasm" and a popular brand of mysticism), monarchical and civic governments who undertook the reform of their "own" churches and exerted an ecclesiastical authority so comprehensive that it foreshadows their ultimate assumption of complete power at the time of the Reformation. Moreover, there was a deep rift within the Church itself, separating the higher orders from the lower. To the lower orders belonged the village priests, virtually serfs, living among their flocks of fellow-villagers in poverty and ignorance, and the clerical proletariat of the towns, unbeneficed clerks who made a living by saying Mass for well-endowed incumbents, and a host of footloose friars. On the other side of the gulf stood their superiors, the higher clergy, sharply conscious of being distinct from this clerical riff-raff through the possession of aristocratic connections and, equally important, a university education. Lutheranism, Calvinism, the Church of England, the nonconformist Protestant sects of Europe and America all spent their infancy in this medieval cradle.

The institutions and principles which lie at the root of our existing legal and political systems also reach back into the later Middle Ages. "Injustice stalks the high-roads." In these words Walther von der Vogelweide, the greatest German political poet of the Middle Ages, sums up his own bitter experience, and it may also fairly be reckoned as the common experience of common people throughout the Middle Ages. Every day the law was being broken, every day the law was being encroached upon by magnates great and small. Injustice as flagrant as this was too painful to be borne, and evoked a belief in law unique in the history of the world; this medieval attachment to law is the foundation and core of all free and democratic political and social principles and institutions. "God is Himself the law": and men are called to the duty of discovering the law, guarding it and fighting for it. Barons, burgesses, peasants, even serfs (whose unfreedom varied greatly in degree and who cannot be compared with the slaves of antiquity) all lived by the conviction that they had their law; all fought as best they could to preserve the law proper to their order, their town, or their house.

From quite an early date this trust in law demanded a practical legal knowledge at a level which seems to us astonishingly high. The individual had to be much more legally-minded and far better educated in legal matters than is necessary today: in town and country alike he battled every day to maintain his right. This belief in law and in the efficacy of litigation is at the root of the jury system, of courts of royal and popular jurisdiction, of the English Parliament; it produced charters of liberties such as the English Magna Carta and its Spanish, Hungarian and Polish counterparts, by which the crown confirmed the rights of the various estates. Once won, these were all priceless possessions, the nucleus of future democratic development.

The law was a contract which imposed binding obligations on both partners: God and man, king and people, king and barons, king and estates. Resistance to a ruler who broke the law was permissible, even mandatory. The right of resistance as exercised in medieval Europe lies behind every act of resistance offered to "tyrants" wherever and whenever they have tried to impose a totalitarian and absolutist rule.

There are echoes of medieval legal theory and practice in the constitution of the United States of America.

All in all, there seems sufficient reason to devote our attention to a detailed discussion of the high Middle Ages.

CHAPTER 2

ARISTOCRACY AND PEASANTRY

MEDIEVAL Europe abounded in castles. Germany alone had ten thousand and more, most of them now vanished; all that a summer journey in the Rhineland and the south-west now can show are a handful of ruins and a few nineteenth-century restorations. Nevertheless, anyone journeying from Spain to the Dvina, from Calabria to Wales, will find castles rearing up again and again to dominate the open landscape. There they still stand, in desolate and uninhabited districts where the only visible forms of life are herdsmen and their flocks, with hawks circling the battlements, far from the traffic and comfortably distant even from the nearest small town: these were the strongholds of the European aristocracy.

The weight of aristocratic dominance was felt in Europe until well after the French Revolution; political and social structure, the Church, the general tenor of thought and feeling were all influenced by it. Over the centuries, consciously or unconsciously, the other classes of this older European society—the clergy, the bourgeoisie and the "common people"—adopted many of the outward characteristics of the aristocracy, who became their model, their standard, their ideal. Aristocratic values and ambitions were adopted alongside aristocratic manners and fashions of dress. Yet the aristocracy were the objects of much contentious criticism and complaint; from the thirteenth century onwards their military value and their political importance were both called in question. Nevertheless, their opponents continued to be their principal imitators. In the eleventh and twelfth centuries, the reforming Papacy and its clerical supporters, although opposed to the excessively aristocratic control of the Church (as is shown by the Investiture Contest) nevertheless themselves first adopted and then strengthened the forms of this control. Noblemen who became bishops or who founded new Orders helped to implant aristocratic principles and forms of government deep within the structure and spiritual life of the Church. Again, in the twelfth and thirteenth centuries the urban bourgeoisie, made prosperous and even rich by trade and industry, were rising to political power as the servants and legal protégés of monarchy. These "patricians" were critical of the aristocracy and hostile towards it. Yet they also imitated the aristocracy, and tried to gain admittance to the closed circle and to achieve equality of status. Even the unarmed peasantry, who usually had to suffer more from the unrelieved weight of aristocratic dominance, long remained tenaciously loyal to their lords, held to their allegiance by that combination of love and fear, *amor et timor*, which was so characteristic of the medieval relationship between lord and servant, between God and man.

The castles and strongholds of the aristocracy remind us of the reality of their power and superiority. Through the long warring centuries when men went defenceless and insecure, the "house", the lord's fortified dwelling, promised protection, security and peace to all whom it sheltered. From the ninth to the eleventh centuries, if not later, Europe was in many ways all too open. Attack came from the sea, in the Mediterranean from Saracens and Vikings, the latter usually in their swift, dragon-prowed, easily manoeuvred longboats, manned by some sixteen pairs of oarsmen and with a full complement of perhaps sixty men. There were periods when the British Isles and the French coasts were being raided every year by Vikings and in the heart of the continent marauding Magyar armies met invading bands of Saracens. The name of Pontresina, near St Moritz in Switzerland, is a memento of the stormy tenth century; it means *pons Saracenorum*, the "fortified Saracen bridge", the place where plundering expeditions halted on their way up from the Mediterranean.

It was recognized in theory that the Church and the monarchy were the principal powers and that they were bound by the nature of their office to ensure peace and security and to do justice; but at this period they were too weak, too torn by internal conflicts to fulfil their obligations. Thus more and more power passed into the hands of warriors invested by the monarchy and the Church with lands and rights of jurisdiction, who in return undertook to support their overlords and to protect the unarmed peasantry.

Their first concern, however, was self-protection. It is almost impossible for us to realize how primitive the great majority of these early medieval "castles" really were. Until about 1150 the fortified houses of the Anglo-Norman nobility were simple dwellings surrounded by a mound of earth and a wooden stockade. These were the motte and bailey castles: the motte was the mound and its stockade, the bailey an open court lying below and also stockaded. Both were protected, where possible, by yet another ditch filled with water, the moat. In the middle of the motte there was a wooden tower, the keep or *donjon*, which only became a genuine stronghold at a later date and in places where stone was readily available. The stone castles of the French and German nobility usually had only a single communal room in which all activities took place.

In such straitened surroundings, where warmth, light and comfort were lacking, there was no way of creating an air of privacy. It is easy enough to understand why the life of the landed nobility was often so unrestrained, so filled with harshness, cruelty and brutality, even in later, more "chivalrous" periods. The barons' daily life was bare and uneventful, punctuated by war, hunting (a rehearsal for war), and feasting. Boys were trained to fight from the age of seven or eight, and their education in arms continued until they were twenty-one, although in some cases they started to fight as early as fifteen. The peasants of the surrounding countryside, bound to their lords by a great variety of ties, produced the sparse fare which was all that the undeveloped agriculture of the early medieval period could sustain. Hunting was a constant necessity, to make up for the lack of butcher's meat, and in England and Germany in the eleventh and twelfth centuries even the kings had to progress from one crown estate to another, from one bishop's palace to the next, to maintain themselves and their retinue.

From the tenth century armies were no longer composed mainly of foot-soldiers; cavalry were needed to fight the armies of expert horsemen fielded by the Magyars and the Saracens, and soon by the Normans as well. These cavalry battles were innocent of strategy; the horsemen set on each other *en masse*, and the action resolved itself out of the confusion into a number of single combats. Education in courtly manners eventually had its effect and in the twelfth and thirteenth centuries opponents were captured instead of being fought to the death. The captor took valuable prizes, his prisoner's war-horse, his weapons and his armour, to which was soon added the money from his ransom. But prisoners of lower rank, of another people or another faith were still killed outright like the native peasantry unless they were saved to be hanged on the gallows.

Two distinct strata of nobility can be discerned throughout Europe from quite an early date: *Herren* and *Ritter* in Germany, *barons* and *chevaliers* in France, barons and knights in England, *grandes* and *hidalgos* in Spain, *magnates* and *ur* in Hungary. Naturally there were manifold smaller gradations at various times and in various places, and development was by no means uniform. But by about 1100 the French nobility had become a fully developed, closed social class, with a clearly differentiated greater and lesser aristocracy, jealously guarding itself against intruders. At the same date the Anglo-Norman aristocracy of England was largely composed of poor, landless adventurers, living off their lord's table and only very gradually establishing themselves as landowners in the place of the old Anglo-Saxon nobility, who had mostly emigrated or been expelled. In Germany from the eleventh century onwards the unfree *ministeriales* were coming into prominence as servants of the king and the administrators of the Empire, and from the twelfth century an increasing number of free vassals joined the ranks of the *ministeriales*, where there were prospects of rapid promotion, particularly in the Empire's Italian possessions. The higher *ministeriales* then became distinct from the lesser "*Rittern und Knappen, edlen Knechten*".

There was a close connection between the aristocratic government of Europe and the development of feudalism, an institution which varied greatly in its effects from country to country. The catchword "feudalism" is not without its dangers, since it conceals some important differences and contrasts between social and political developments as they occurred in Eastern, Central and Western Europe. Pronouncedly aristocratic states of a "feudal" character, such as Poland and Hungary, were precisely those where feudalism completely failed to establish itself. And England, "the most feudalized country of Europe", was in fact the place where feudalism, once established, made the least headway.

Vassal, a word of Celtic origin, was used in the Frankish period to describe a warrior in the service of a lord. A free man who put himself under the protection of someone more rich and powerful became a vassal or liege-man; he entered his lord's following and became part of his "household", living within his peace and law. The vassal had the obligation of rendering his lord "aid and counsel". By counsel was meant the duty of supporting the lord in all his business and in his numerous lawsuits and disputes with his equals and with other vassals. If the king was his immediate overlord, the vassal was bound to advise him on matters of internal and external policy and medieval kings, even the greatest of them, however impetuous they were by nature, were often scrupulous in taking counsel from their most important vassals. "Aid" meant essentially military service. In France, however, a vassal also owed his overlord or suzerain four financial aids: for the knighting of his suzerain's eldest son, for the marriage of his eldest daughter, for ransoming him from captivity and on his departure for the Crusade. Military service was usually strictly confined to home defence; the Crusade was an exception, and so also, for imperial vassals, was the knight-service required when their lord and king journeyed to Rome for his imperial coronation.

The ceremonial act of homage which confirmed the relationship of lord and man was performed by the vassal kneeling unarmed before his lord, laying his hands in his and promising to become his man. The tie thus created was far from being one-sided and its reciprocity touches on what was a fundamental medieval concept, particularly in Western and Central Europe. The relationship was a contractual one binding both partners equally. Glanville, the earliest of the great medieval English jurists, was clear that a vassal owed his lord no more than a lord owed his vassal, reverence alone excepted. If the lord broke faith, the vassal was released from his obligation to serve. This marked a cardinal point in the political, social and legal development of Europe. The whole idea of a right of resistance is inherent in this notion of a contract between the governor and the governed, between the higher and the lower. The contractual idea also had its part in the innumerable feuds, the civil wars of this medieval aristocratic society, in which one homage was set against another, so that, for example, a vassal holding fiefs of several overlords could be expected to fight on behalf of two lords on opposite sides. The idea of mutual obligation entered even into religious beliefs. The "faithful God" and his saints were bound to keep faith with a believer; the saints, or worse still, God himself, had only to break faith and abandon their "man", their vassal, the believer, in some

ARISTOCRACY AND PEASANTRY 37

conflict or distress of soul, to provoke the gravest spiritual crisis possible in the medieval world, a crisis which could lead to a complete severance, the withdrawal of obedience. This is the theme of Wolfram of Eschenbach's *Parsifal*, the greatest of the medieval German religious epics.

In return for his service, the vassal was granted a *beneficium*, a gift. The greater and more powerful the giver, the greater might be the *beneficium*. God, as Lord and Emperor of Heaven, granted terrestrial and celestial felicity, portions in His kingdom. Christian kings invested their vassals with fiefs, with offices and positions at court. In early medieval France and Germany, where the break-up of Charlemagne's Empire had left an enormous estate in bankruptcy, such fiefs might be so large that they formed the basis of future Kingdoms. On the other hand a fief might be so small that the vassal and his family could not live off its revenues.

The desire for land, for a fief, was freely voiced in the ranks of both greater and lesser aristocracy, particularly by younger sons who could no longer expect any patrimony. War, civil wars, incessant feuds and rebellions, even the Crusades, all must be seen in the context of this land-hunger of the aristocracy, an aristocracy seeking a livelihood. The acquisition of new lands in England, southern Italy, Spain and north-eastern Europe is one of its most obvious effects. The landless son of a king, John Lackland, conjured up one of England's greatest and most pregnant crises. The landless sons of the lesser nobility were a dynamic element of permanent unrest: anyone who could win their support had the means of founding a kingdom, of conquering a new world. After the Battle of Hastings delivered England into his hands in 1066, William the Conqueror set himself up as overlord of all the landed property in the kingdom; he parcelled up the two thousand odd cultivated estates into about two hundred major fiefs, and granted them out to his immediate vassals, his barons or tenants-in-chief. They in turn granted out portions of their fiefs to lower vassals.

Once invested with land, the vassal entered the household of his feudal superior. He became a retainer and looked to the household to give him protection, peace, justice and security. Highest of all was the king's household, and to it were attached the households of tenants-in-chief and subtenants, great and small alike, like the rosette of subsidiary chapels surrounding the great "House of God" in the Romanesque churches of the twelfth century. Every household was thus under the protection of a greater, and expected to live under its shield and peace. Europe, aristocratic Europe, was a community made up of some ten thousand smaller houses and a few hundred greater houses, all of them conscious of the overriding protection of the "House of God", the household of Christ the King, but all seeking to assert themselves, and forming alliances against each other. The great struggle between the house of Austria and the house of France, which determined the destiny of Europe between the sixteenth and the eighteenth centuries (and enabled England to build up her enormous colonial empire), was the last spasm of life from the old Europe of a thousand warring houses, its final epitome.

For it must be accepted that feudalism, and, indeed, the whole aristocratic structure in Europe, was ambiguous in its potentialities: it could lead either to anarchy or to order, to the evolution of modern states or to the break-up of all the existing more comprehensive political systems.

A weak monarchy was quite powerless to prevent the evolution of hereditary tenures (as in France, Germany and Italy from the ninth to the eleventh century); nor could it avoid being outstripped by its powerful feudatories, who often had more land, and therefore larger armies, than their royal suzerains. The situation became even worse when not only landed estates but also governmental rights and royal offices were alienated as fiefs. This happened most conspicuously with the transfer of public jurisdiction in the old local government divisions or counties of the Carolingian Empire. Investiture with public rights played an important role in the Empire, where the chief recipients were the bishops, and, later on, the consuls and *gonfaloniere* of the North Italian cities. From this situation sprang not only the great conflict between the papacy and the German Emperors, but also the rise of the Italian communes to independence as city states.

In England and France the monarchy succeeded in retaining control over public rights and royal offices, though in France this chiefly meant that the monarchy never relinquished its legal rights. William the Conqueror retained the numerous Anglo-Saxon local jurisdictions, the shire, hundred and borough courts; they were still to do justice according to English law, controlled not by the aristocracy but by the king. His most conspicuous success was in imposing a universal oath of fealty which bound all feudatories of whatever degree directly to the king. There was Carolingian precedent for such an oath and it reappeared in the Norman kingdoms of England and Sicily to become the mainstay of a strong royal government. In France there emerged the analogous institution of liege-lordship, which took precedence over all other feudal ties. "Liege" is derived from the Norman *lidugr* (free, unrestricted). Fealty to the king as liege-lord had prior claim over the ordinary fealty due from every vassal to his immediate lord.

But how often it happened that homage clashed with homage! For example, there were those great vassals who held simultaneously of the German and the French or the French and the English kings. On whose side would they stand when two such liege-lords demanded the performance of their feudal duties of military service and counsel at one and the same time? Then there were those lesser lords, particularly in the Empire, who held fiefs at once from the king, from bishops and from monastic houses. Whom should they follow when king, bishop, Pope and abbot were in conflict with each other? Many of the bishops must have found such decisions particularly agonizing. As princes of the Empire they were vassals of their suzerain, the King and Emperor; as princes of the Church, of the household of God, they were bound by oath to their suzerain the Pope. The bishops of the Holy Roman Empire were faced with this conflict between the eleventh and thirteenth centuries; the same situation broke Thomas à Becket.

Feudalism, the overlordship of the aristocracy, gave rise to extremes of mobility and immobility. The feudal nobility were always on the move, continually on the watch for a fief going begging, to be had by marriage or by force. Somewhere there must surely be a young cadet of some royal house, or an enterprising freebooter, anxious to recruit a following by holding out the promise of rich estates. Perhaps in the south of France, where those Albigensian heretics were waiting to be suppressed; or in Spain and Portugal, occupied by the Muslims; or even in the Empire of the Rhomaioi, where the Emperor in Constantinople could no longer hold the reins of government steady in his hands. Above all, there was the Holy Land, the land of the supreme suzerain, Christ the King, who had promised his ancient birthright to his vassals.

But feudalism led also to the opposite extreme, to the domesticated court aristocracies, tricked out in the finery of their court apparel and court manners, which clustered round the thrones of victorious monarchs in Madrid, London and Vienna. And Versailles, with its Hall of Mirrors, the great palace of the Sun King, is still the symbol of a monarchy victorious over its feudal aristocracy after five centuries of conflict waged with the help of loyal and gifted servants.

There was much ground to be covered before this frozen immobility was reached. The baronage who made history in the twelfth century and the later Middle Ages were energetic men, and kings who lived their lives in the saddle, like Henry II of England and the Emperor Frederick II, were themselves supreme examples of the type. Their very physiognomy was watchful and predatory, hawk-like. Their life was one of immense, strenuous activity, passed in conflict, hunting and pilgrimage. Cool-headed, stern to the point of harshness, they had their wits about them and knew how to crack a joke with their subordinates; they were quick on the draw and ready with their tongues, their talk and songs full of the joys of battle. They could be brutal, even in dealings with their women: a man "took" a wife, calculating her value as an object for political and economic ends. Questions of close calculation, indeed, absorbed much of their attention. How many men could such and such a fief support? How strong was this or that rival? What opposition was to be expected from the armies of the king of France or the Pope in Rome in such and such a conflict? Educated in the manners and habits of their own rank and people, they were steeped in a culture which revered the customs sanctified by ancient usage, venerable and sacrosanct law. In fact they were very well versed in law, thoroughly competent in the feudal and territorial laws of their sometimes very mixed bag of subjects, all living under their own laws, territorial, municipal or customary. The more injustice abounded, the more urgent it seemed to keep formally to the proper courses of the law. Litigation was second only to feuding and warfare as a form of conflict favoured by the baronage: indeed, for them trial by battle and trial by law were both forms of single combat. "God and my right": let God determine the issue, in the duel and in the ordeal.

Because of their common beliefs and Christianity, there were very strong bonds between the baronage and the common people. The finer points of book-learning and piety were left to the younger sons, cousins and kinsfolk who were placed as clerks, monks or nuns in monastic establishments of their own foundation and under their own control. Any baron of exalted rank or influence in Church and State could get his relations appointed to bishoprics or abbacies or to a lucrative position in a cathedral chapter.

Restless, delighting in *chevauchée*, impetuous in speech and action, yet tenaciously clinging over several generations to their rights to some great French or English fief, these barons, with all the hardships of their vexatious, combative existence, revelled in the exuberance of feasting and high festivals. The feast-days of Christ the King and His saints, the "tenants-in-chief" of the Kingdom of God, were often made to coincide with the feast-days of the "house". On these great festivals of the Church's year, marked by solemn celebrations in the House of God, perhaps also by the dedication of a new church, the festivities in the household gave opportunity for taking counsel from the vassals: perhaps about a feud, or a campaign, or a marriage, within the house itself or in the house of an enemy or vassal. The festivities, which would continue for several days and nights, wound up with an orgy of drinking: the drinking companions were all trusted advisers, their loyalty beyond any doubt. In Eastern Europe, in the Baltic lands and Tsarist Russia, the provincial nobility continued to observe these old festivals in the old way (they lasted for at least a week) almost to within living memory.

In its twelfth-century heyday, the medieval baronage, still restless and mobile, still ambitious and full of life, was confronted with a great crisis which threatened its existence from within and without. The ascendant monarchies of the West were encroaching on their freedom and their power. And this was not all; urban communities were rising to prosperity through industry and trade, and the early adoption of a money economy, capable of producing goods and luxuries and deploying an economic and financial power beyond the resources of an often impoverished aristocracy. The Mediterranean world and the Near East, increasingly familiar through legend, ballad, and personal campaigning, only bewildered them. For the "Frankish" knights of Western Europe were regarded with deep disdain by the cultured Byzantine court aristocracy and by the highly civilized world of Islam. Irritated and bewildered, the Western baronage was for the most part disturbed by a growing and profound insecurity. Their answer to the challenge was threefold: a vigorous participation in heterodox religious movements; involvement in the intellectual warfare of the thirteenth century; and the formation of closed court aristocracies.

As has been said, the aristocracy lived off, and mostly on, the land; they lived off their peasants, who were bound to them by a great variety of formal ties. In England, at the time of the Norman Conquest, the great majority of peasants were in some degree unfree. This unfreedom should not be confused or identified with slavery, whether ancient or modern—although there were slaves in Europe until the seventeenth and eighteenth centuries, mostly Slavs captured as booty in Eastern Europe (because of their name medieval people thought of them as predestined slaves), or prisoners of war from the Eastern Mediterranean. The English villein, the French *vilain* and the German *Holde* were all bound to their lords by the specific obligation of rendering services and dues. The villein worked his lord's demesne and also had to pay something from the revenues of his own plot; he required to be at his lord's service for manual and team-work, to build castles, roads and bridges. Everyone was under an obligation to take all his grain to the lord's mill to be ground, for which payment was naturally exacted. In addition to windmills (which probably originated in Persia), there were also water-mills; by the end of the eleventh century there were over five thousand of them in England, about as many as there were knights in the army of the English king. The mills, like the castles and the bonds of obligation, demonstrated the hold of the baronage over the countryside and its people. Most oppressive of all was the liability (in France) to pay *taille* or tallage, which was nothing but an arbitrary tax, levied by the seigneur as and when he found it "necessary"; it was taken both from free and from unfree peasants. None of these peasants were slaves, however; the monarchy and the Church offered them protection, chiefly because both institutions were concerned to safeguard the "good old law", which was the peasant's own law, the law he defended in the manorial courts. These, however, came under the lord's control; he appointed, or at any rate confirmed in office, the provost or reeve, who was the judge of the court, and who might be subjected to heavy pressure from the lord, or in his absence, the lord's bailiff or steward. But where a lord was very dependent on the goodwill and labour of his peasants, and was often absent, occupied in warfare or political affairs, the peasants had a chance to improve their position.

The origins of the unfreedom of the medieval peasant were various. In the Mediterranean lands it stemmed from the arrangements of late antiquity, when the peasants were bound to the soil by the state, in order to make sure of its taxes. For people in this situation the invasion of their lands by Germans, Saracens, Normans, Spaniards or Frenchmen meant only a change of masters, not of status: and the position of the Sicilians and south Italians is much the same today. In the Germanic North the pattern of development was different. During the stormy centuries of the early Middle Ages free peasants often "commended" themselves, more or less voluntarily, to a lord. Anyone who commended himself to his lord's protection was in return relieved of all military service, which the lord now performed for him through his knights; the peasant, for his part, became liable to pay rent on behalf of himself, his family and his landed property. As an example of what was happening, there is evidence from a particular district of the Salzburg region in the eighth century of the absorption of 237 small free peasant holdings into 50 greater estates, of which 21 belonged to the Church, 12 to the Dukes of Bavaria and 17 to other great lords. This alienation and amalgamation of free peasant properties was one of the most important and momentous developments in the social history of Europe, perhaps only comparable to the decline of independent small-scale manufacturers, tradesmen and *entrepreneurs* which started in the late nineteenth century and is still proceeding. Like their peasant predecessors, these independent middle-class industrialists and traders have "voluntarily" surrendered their businesses into the ownership or control of some larger industry, bank or combine, or even to the state, in which case the surrender has usually been even less "voluntary".

The unfree peasants of Western Europe, the serfs, were thus the descendants of the dependent peasantry of Carolingian times. Their name was a bequest from the slaves of antiquity (*serf* < *servus*); nevertheless they possessed certain rights in law. In addition to the property they held from their lords they might also have a free property of their own, an allod. Their lord owed them protection and patronage, they owed him obedience and aid, in the form of personal services and payments. An annual payment of a small sum known as "head-money" set a symbolical seal on the bonds of their personal attachment. Tallage, an extraordinary tax, might be demanded from serfs, and also from those who were nominally free whenever a lord was in difficulties. Special payments had to be made by a serf marrying outside his lord's dependents, and by a serf's direct heirs when he died: this "death duty" entailed the surrender of the best head of cattle, or, in some districts, a share of the chattels.

In the twelfth century, apart from some tiny and much debated areas (debated, that is, among scholars), there were no longer any completely free peasants. The peasants described as "free" were nevertheless bound to a lord in a protective relationship of some kind, just like the rest. But the greater the lord (for example if he were the king or a great vassal, with a hundred and more estates), and the more remote his court, the freer was the peasant. Bound to the service of one or more lords, the rural population of Europe lived in varying degrees of dependence, unfreedom or serfdom, and the distinctions of grade were in practice as great as that between highly born vassals of the crown and "knights and noble squires" who had virtually nothing to call their own, or between highly educated wealthy prelates and village priests bound to the soil. Our vocabulary does not even possess the words necessary to distinguish clearly between the different groups, classes, and ranks of "free", "half-free", "unfree" and "dependent" peasants. And the actual situation was more confusing still, for in many places a "free" peasant might be more oppressed and much poorer than an "unfree" peasant living only a few miles away.

But, despite the gravitational downward pull of further oppression and the rapid increase in the numbers of serfs in some areas, some classes of peasants, and some individuals, were working themselves higher up the social scale. By the twelfth and thirteenth centuries the peasantry had become a factor kings and nobles had to reckon with, even to the point of calling on their help, as in France where peasant troops fought victoriously on the king's side against the "robber barons", the great feudatories.

Barons and kings were eager to increase their revenues and took in hand the clearance of forests and the improvement of land which had become marshy or arid through neglect. Peasants were urgently needed for this work of in-

ternal colonization and they were in good supply since the
vicissitudes of medieval life, war, harsh masters, and their
own *Wanderlust* were continually driving them from their
homes. Those peasants who had, as it were, won their freedom by invitation, were known as *hospites;* they received a
charter which promised them protection against unjust oppression, excessive dues, and arbitrary actions on the part
of the landlord. Numerous new settlements (for example the
villes neuves in northern France) originated in this way. To
attract more settlers, the "recruiting officers" read the charters
aloud at markets in other districts, like the North American
railroad companies in the nineteenth century when they
needed pioneers to colonize the empty lands of the West.

In twelfth and thirteenth century Germany one went not
West but East. The kings of Poland, Bohemia and Hungary
and the German princes were colonizing Brandenburg, Prussia, East Prussia and the Baltic lands as far as Riga. They all
needed German peasants, and increasingly tended to look
for them through agents known as *locatores*. The *locator*
recruited the peasants, took care of them on their long
journey, staked out the new territory, and put up an enclosed camp. In return for all this he was recognized as
"provost" of the local court and given the monopoly of
local amenities, such as the ale-house and the mill, and
sometimes also of the sale of bread, meat and fish. His position was then made hereditary.

The medieval world, particularly the "open" world of the
twelfth century, thus offered opportunities to at least a section of the rural population, particularly in the East and in
Germany, the Netherlands, northern France and England.
For example, during the thirteenth and fourteenth centuries
more than 1,200 new villages were founded in Silesia alone
in rather less than 150 years. In Western Europe, however,
the thirteenth century also saw the beginnings of stagnation
in agriculture and of a corresponding deterioration in the
peasants' position. Europe was already starting to turn in on
itself, social and geographical boundaries were becoming
more rigid.

This inevitably affected the peasants. Clearing of the waste
land stopped; in fact some lords, eager for cash, were already converting arable into pasture, buying up and ex-
propriating peasant farmers. In England and France this
development was a cause of conflict between the king and
the barons. During the thirteenth and fourteenth centuries

English villeins were contesting their freedom in the royal courts. Feudal estates changed masters much more frequently than used to be realized—by marriage, death, sale, or confiscation. When property changed hands the peasant stood an equal chance of losing or gaining from the change. The manorial courts, which regulated the affairs of the peasantry, had not always kept a written record of their proceedings, so that it was often very difficult for a peasant whose lord claimed him as a villein to prove his freedom in court. From the thirteenth century onwards the English courts were filled with peasants' pleas about "distraint", that is, enforced services and payments demanded from them by old and new masters. But at the same time, some peasants were able to improve their position and many villeins succeeded in purchasing their freedom from their lords. In this they were sometimes assisted by the Church, or, in France, by the monarchy, since under the strict letter of the law an unfree peasant, who had no possessions of his own, could not buy his own freedom. The lords' growing need of money gave industrious and enterprising peasants an excellent means of bettering themselves. The "free" peasants who were under royal protection later merged with the burgesses to become the "Third Estate", sending their representatives directly to the Estates General, the representative body of the different estates. In southern France, which followed its own path of development and was only very slowly brought into line with the north during the thirteenth century, peasant and urban communities often acted side by side in a successful struggle to make their voices heard on political matters.

There is an interesting contrast in the attitudes towards their land of the French and English baronage, a contrast which had an important effect on political and social development. Anxious to avoid the trouble of farming them for themselves, the French seigneurs fell into the habit of transferring their estates to the peasants to work in return for money rents. In consequence, as the nobility became more and more involved in campaigning, court life, and even in intellectual pursuits, they drew further and further apart from the life of their peasants, until they were nothing but a remote and oppressive burden. In England, however, the baronage were taking an active interest in agriculture from early in the thirteenth century. The period between 1200 and 1340 has been justly described as the "great age of demesne farming", the great age of the development of baronial estates. Walter of Henley's small but very important manual *On Husbandry,* which describes the essentials of this demesne economy, is a characteristic product of it. The lord was keenly interested in improving the yield, made his peasants work harder, grew for the market and not simply for subsistence, and took advantage of the rising prices for agrarian products. With their venture into wool production, it could be said that the English nobility were among the first to turn agriculture into an industry. Peasants were bought out or expropriated to make room for sheep. In striking contrast to their continental counterparts, the English aristocracy carried on and extended this commercial tradition; and later their involvement in trade and industry was to link them with the bourgeoisie and also make them amenable to changing conditions, social, political and intellectual.

Meanwhile, the peasants' activities were becoming more and more restricted. Even the forests belonged to the king or to some noble lord, to hunt there as they would, ruining whatever young crops were left in the neighbouring fields after wild pigs, roebuck and red deer had had their fill. And it must not be forgotten that medieval peasants, like the medieval clergy, had a passion for the chase, although it could only be indulged by poaching. Arable land was also becoming scarcer, since some of it was being turned into pasture for sheep. There was nothing inherently objectionable about sheep. Rightly used, they were hard-working and serviceable animals, providing dung to manure the ground, milk for cheese, skin for parchment and fleece for wool. But side by side with the peasants' sheep there were now the lord's sheep, no longer beasts of all trades but devoted only to the production of wool.

Development elsewhere in Europe was equally diverse during the later Middle Ages. In Italy, where city states were rapidly becoming established, the nobility lived in towns and became assimilated with the town bourgeoisie. Here man was an urban animal, life meant urban life and culture urban civilization. The peasants of the surrounding countryside had no share in all this. They lived on in their shacks or their wretched farmhouses and stables, sinking to the level of the late Roman *colonus:* nothing in their lord's village was theirs except the clothes they stood up in and their own families, and even these might be required by the lord for his own use. Alongside them were tenant-farmers, peasants who paid rent and dues and were free of lordship.

In Spain, the conquerors from the north who took the country from the Arabs managed to attract some "free" peasants as settlers. These Christian peasants found the countryside already populated by a rural proletariat, sunk in the depths of oppression and squalor, which had been there since late Roman times—their counterparts can be seen today all over the Mediterranean Arab world. The pastoral economy practised by the aristocracy, and the disorder arising from the growing weakness of the monarchy in the five Christian kingdoms, all conspired to depress the status of the free peasants to the lowest level.

This levelling down, this paring away of rights to the minimum, was a characteristic feature also of Germany and of Eastern Europe towards the end of the Middle Ages. The German aristocracy, unhindered by the monarchy, which was engaged in critical struggles in Italy and with the Papacy (not to mention the German princes themselves), made every effort to reduce the "free" peasants, who had been subject only to certain exactly stipulated annual obligations, to the lower status of serfs and to the performance of increasingly arbitrary duties. This Germany contained the seeds of the "Land of Serfdom" described by Herder and Lessing in the eighteenth century, *terra oboedientiae*. There was a particularly marked deterioration in the legal and economic position, in fact in the whole standard of living, of the German peasants living in the north-east; here there was a substratum of old Prussian and Slavonic serfs to form the basis of a servile peasant community. This belt of serfdom extended over the lands east of the Elbe, Bohemia, Moravia, Poland and the Baltic region, all of them now largely in the power of the aristocracy. Over this whole region, where there were no royal courts to protect the peasantry, the nobility appropriated all governmental rights for themselves and their estates became large-scale agrarian enterprises. The result for the peasants was that the late medieval and early modern periods saw the creation of a new, hereditary serfdom.

Even so, this European serfdom differed fundamentally from that of the Russian peasant. In Russia it was the state that was largely responsible for the evolution of serfdom; it was by government decree that the peasants were bound to the soil, the soil of the aristocracy and the monarchy.

This state-serfdom (*gosudarstvennye krestjane*) had its roots in earlier forms of enslavement from the period of immigration and conquest by alien peoples. Slavonic tribes thus became subject tribes, owing tribute to their Alan, Gothic or Magyar lords. The Kievan state took over several such dependent groups and made them *smerdy*, that is, tributary serfs of the princes of Kiev. The Mongols, when they came, imposed fresh forms of servile obligation on these peoples, setting local agents over them to keep them to their duties. These agents, members of the Horde, were called *kalannye*, which means people bound to perform a special task or *kalan*. After the break-up of Mongol rule in western Russia (i.e. the Ukraine and White Russia) these serf communities acquired new masters, those in Galicia the King of Poland, those in other parts of the Ukraine the Grand Duke of Lithuania. The Grand Dukes of Moscow obtained from their Mongol overlords power over the servile communities in the rest of Russia. During the Mongol period even free Russian peasants, obliged to pay tribute to the Khan, were reduced to dependence on the nobility, the only class capable of meeting such an obligation, who thus came to regard the peasants as "theirs". It was at this period, when all peasants were obliged to pay tribute, that the Russian word for peasants first appears: *krestjane* (Christians), used originally of peasants on monastic estates in the fourteenth century, when the monastic landlords had assumed the responsibility of collecting the tribute from the rural population.

The later extension of serfdom in Russia and its establishment by law as a universal institution, between 1581 and 1649, falls outside our period. As late as the seventeenth century slavery and serfdom existed side by side; in the eighteenth century, however, the two merged into the new "body-serfdom" in which the peasant himself, instead of his land, was bound to the lord.

From at least the tenth century Slavs and other "heathens" captured in war were sold as slaves by the Christian knights of the West. In the twelfth century Henry the Lion sold Danish (Christian) prisoners as slaves through the agency of his Slav allies and Diepold von Vohburg sold southern Italians through his mercenaries. This was indeed an appropriate meeting of the Mediterranean south, where classical slavery still persisted, and the Slavonic East! In the late thirteenth and fourteenth centuries domestic slaves were imported into Italy via Venice. The Church, in this as in other respects the heir of classical antiquity, was far from condemning slavery. Its leading thirteenth-century theologians such as Thomas Aquinas recognized slavery as morally justifiable and an economic necessity, quoting Aristotle in support. From the fourteenth century the Popes habitually threatened their enemies with enslavement: in 1303 Boniface VIII pronounced this sentence on the companies of the Colonna, in 1309 Clement V put Venice under the ban of slavery, and Bologna, Venice and Florence were all later to suffer the same otiose condemnation. Pope Paul III condemned as slaves all Englishmen who sided with Henry VIII: they were to be free booty for the Crusaders who would come to defeat them.

It is essential to realize that the medieval peasant lived in genuine fear of being reduced to serfdom or even of being virtually enslaved under one of the many possible forms, open or concealed. This is one reason why the countryside was often a focus of unrest and rebellion. From Carolingian times, peasant risings and wars were endemic in rural society; they were often so numerous and so "normal" that the monastic chroniclers did not bother to describe them. But in the late eleventh and early twelfth centuries they became more significant and could no longer be dismissed. Europe's first "Marseillaise" is a battle-song commemorating a great peasants' revolt which took place in Normandy in the eleventh century: the first revolutionary song of antiquity, which comes from Egypt, originated in similar circumstances. Leagues of peasants, *Eidgenossenschaften,* formed a political, and soon also a religious, underground, in which "heretical" sects and other refugees from society sought protection and concealment. And this had been happening long before the emergence in the middle of our period of a peasant league which developed into an autonomous state: Switzerland, *die Eidgenossenschaft* par excellence. Indomitable, greatly feared and greatly respected, Switzerland advanced steadily to freedom. It still retains many of its original characteristics in the independence and self-assurance of its cantons and valleys, and its very names, *die Eidgenossenschaft,* the *Confoederatio Helvetica,* the *Bund* (confederation), are a living memorial to those many leagues which sprang from the peasant world to be crushed by the armies of lay and ecclesiastical princes.

In the early thirteenth century, some fifty years before the first rising of the *Eidgenossenschaft,* there had been a rising among the *Stedinger*, peasants on the colonial lands of the archbishopric of Bremen. It was only crushed after a campaign lasting five years (1229–34) and its defeat was only finally achieved by a crusading army led by the Duke of Brabant and the counts of Holland, Geldern, Lippe and Cleves, the élite of the nobility of north-western Europe. The Church, which had proclaimed a Crusade against these heretics, set the Inquisition in operation against them.

The later part of our period is marked by the outbreak of peasant wars on a serious scale. The Jacquerie broke out in France in 1358, the English Peasants' Revolt, led by the priests John Ball and Jack Straw, with Wat Tyler as its military leader, succeeded for a brief moment in 1380 in capturing both London and the king, Richard II. There were peasant uprisings in Spain between 1395 and 1479, particularly in Catalonia, whilst in Flanders and parts of northern Germany unrest was endemic throughout the later Middle Ages. The medieval peasants were caught between two conflicting forces, whose pull and counter-pull can be seen at work in these uprisings. On the one hand, there was advancement to be gained from a tenacious fight for the "good old law", which at times was in reality very recent law, only needing to be fought for to be won. It is not unusual to find self-assured and prosperous peasants as the leaders of such struggles; in Switzerland they carried the day. But even in the midst of such determined struggles to win for the peasants a status of their own in law, society, politics and religion, the fear of deprivation was never far away. The peasants' constant fear was of yet more oppression, of falling into abject poverty, of hunger, of impotence before the law, of becoming landless, of being torn up for ever from their roots. The peasants of the Middle Ages were often as restless as their ancestors had been during the long centuries of the *Völkerwanderung*, a movement which indeed was not yet over. Russian peasants carried their restlessness very far afield, turning it to fruitful account in the colonization of Siberia, an enterprise of great moment in world history. And we have seen that German peasants in the twelfth and thirteenth centuries went eastwards to colonize. Medieval peasants deserted "their" land when their masters' oppression and exploitation seemed unbearable to them, or when their masters' enemies had so devastated their fields that they could no longer feed themselves. Epidemics, famine, bad harvests and other natural catastrophes were further reasons for leaving the land and to these must be added the primitive nomadic instinct which had remained active among the peasantry from prehistoric times, and which in the Middle Ages found an outlet in pilgrimage. For there was a continuous stream of peasants along the great pilgrim routes of medieval Europe, from England and Scandinavia to the Holy Land, to Rome, to Compostela, just as in later centuries there were always Russian peasants on the road to Kasan, Kiev and Novgorod. A peasant from Upper Bavaria, who died as late as 1866, had gone on pilgrimage three times to Rome, twice to Jerusalem and once to Compostela, a convincing demonstration of the continuity of peasant life in all its mobility and conservatism!

The conservatism of peasant life provides an essential ground bass to the richly orchestrated continuity of European history over the last thousand years. Indeed, archaeological research, chiefly in France, has shown that over wide areas of Europe the civilization of peasant society goes back anywhere between ten thousand and twenty thousand years, in fact to the later Stone Age. This peasant civilization depended on the use of a few particular tools (wheel, plough, harrow) and was regulated by a calendar of feasts which governed the relations between the living and the dead, old and young, men and women, blending "technology", "magic", work, religion, work-days and feast-days into a satisfying whole. This peasant civilization survived in Europe until the advent of machines in the mid-nineteenth century, and lingered on in some backward and remote areas until as late as the first, or even the second, world war. The peasants, conservative in ways of life and thought, their feet planted firmly on the ground, were a stabilizing force. The land was itself something permanent, remaining unchanged throughout the tempests of war, revolution, and intellectual and spiritual upheaval. The peasantry were bound to the soil and throve on it; they belonged to nature, and the natural aspect of the land over wide areas of Europe scarcely altered until the coming of the industrial revolution.

The sustaining virtues of the land, immense calm, immense patience, endurance in the face of suffering, disease, hunger and death, were always present. Study of medieval skeletons has shown that throughout the Middle Ages the peasantry were chronically undernourished, and there was a high mortality among their children. The men who grew the food and tended the beasts had sometimes little enough bread for themselves or milk for their children. The tillers of the soil were accustomed to accepting the land's cycle, which brought hunger and plenty, feasting and festival, birth and death; they lived in permanent communion with its familiar spirits, its deities and its dead. And around them all the time were the beasts and the fields, the harvests of their labour and the instruments of their toil.

The European peasant evolved for himself a specifically peasant culture based on his toil. It was this that enabled him to carry through the great agricultural settlement of Europe which took place between the sixth and the thirteenth centuries, domesticating the European landscape and also producing a slight surplus of population during the twelfth and thirteenth centuries, chiefly among the peasants themselves (urban populations started to increase somewhat in the twelfth century, but not at the expense of the countryside). The outward expansion of Europe and the intensification of its intellectual and spiritual life were both made possible by these achievements. The peasants had their pride too, the pride which grew from wringing the best and most serviceable return from a harsh soil, harsh masters and a harsh God. The note of pride is sounded in William Langland's great poem *Piers Plowman*. The poet, clearly an educated man who owed much to Franciscan inspiration, speaks of his vision of the peasantry, "the poor folk": Peter the Plowman stands for all who sustain the world by their toil on the land, the peasant, the natural man. But Peter is also the Son of Man, Christ, whose blood manures the "field of folk", whose passion ploughs it for the new seed, the new generation of men; and finally he stands also for the Church, pregnant through the Holy Ghost with the united brotherhood of the future. Christ, the true husbandman, gathers the harvest of mankind within this house of unity: "And he called that House Unity—which is Holy Church in English."

In this house all men are brothers, blood-brothers of Christ:

"For we are all Christ's creatures—and of his coffers rich,
And brethren as of one blood—as well beggars as earls,
For on Calvary of Christ's blood—Christendom gan spring,
And blood brethren we became there—one body won,
As *quasimodo geniti*—and gentlemen each one.
No beggar or serving boy among us—save sin made him so."

That House Unity: the poet sees in the Church the House above all other houses, with all men free blood-brothers, ennobled through Christ's sacrifice: "and gentlemen each one".

But could it really be said that the Church, the "House of Unity", stood open to all, offered all men, of whatever rank, protection, shelter, justice, security and peace? The answer must be equivocal. The imposing ceremonies which marked the dedication of the lofty Romanesque and early Gothic cathedrals of the twelfth century were attended by kings, noblemen, a flock of bishops and church dignitaries and a mass of the people. Together they heard the hymns and prayers extolling their new House of God as the image of the Heavenly City, the New Jerusalem. Yet only a few decades later, early in the thirteenth century, Innocent III, the greatest of medieval Popes, had his traumatic vision of the whole House of the Church in ruins. The watchmen of the Church looked with alarm on the apostasy so widespread among both nobles and peasants in large parts of south-western and central Europe, men who refused to accept the shelter of the Church or to recognize in it the terrestrial image of the House of God.

The triumphant cry of Luther's great Protestant hymn *Ein' feste Burg ist unser Gott* ("A safe stronghold our God is still") expresses the resolution of a drama played out in the later Middle Ages. For the House of the Church was now a ruin, hemmed in by other citadels, the castles of the nobility, the hutments of the peasantry, the city walls of the medieval town, and, not least, the palaces and schools of a secular, courtly, intellectualized culture, continually growing richer and more diverse.

In our modern cities the churches are swallowed up by the great mass of houses, or stand forlorn among them in unique isolation, like museums. This is the final result of the Church's great struggles and crises in the later Middle Ages when it strove in vain to exalt itself above the nobles and the masses, asserting its sway over a power-hungry nobility and a suffering people, claiming to control the passions of philosophers and lovers alike. Thirteenth-century churches reached in aspiration to the sky—indeed overreached themselves: many collapsed soon after they were finished. The Popes who aspired to spiritual, political and legal supremacy over the kings and states of Christendom also overreached themselves. During the thirteenth and fourteenth centuries the theologians and canon lawyers constructed higher and higher edifices, reaching to the skies and beyond, to house the Church's intellectual, spiritual and jurisdictional claims. The Pope was made to appear a supernatural being, "no longer man, not yet wholly God", an angelic governor, *kosmokrator*, clothed in the symbols of divine omnipotence.

This exaggeration and excess can only be interpreted as a flight into the beyond, to a region outside earth and time. From the early thirteenth century the Church lost its taste for thinking and writing about history, whether considered as theology, philosophy, or chronological narrative; where once history had flourished, the field was now given over to rhetoric, to set-pieces of historical description, usually describing episodes from ancient history, chosen merely as examples of good and bad conduct. Beyond the earth we cannot go; but we can turn our attention back to the medieval people who inhabited this terrestrial world, and to their religious beliefs and practices, which concealed as many complex and contrasting elements as any of the other phenomena of medieval life and reality.

CHAPTER 3

THE FAITH OF CHURCH AND PEOPLE

MEDIEVAL popular religion was a lively mixture of many different elements, heathen, antique, "folk" and Christian. It was the religion of the peasants, of a wide section of the nobility, of the urban bourgeoisie, of the humbler clergy and of the monks of the older monasteries. On the face of it, it seems that these various elements must often have been in conflict, yet in everyday life a comfortable co-existence was apparently achieved. The case of Brittany illustrates the point. To this day it is regarded as the traditional bulwark of French Catholicism, the most purely Catholic of all the regions and peoples of France. Yet Catholic sociologists have shown that its religious vitality has been based on a potent admixture of four religious cultures: primitive folk religion, Gallo-Roman polytheism, and two kinds of Christianity, the late Roman and Celtic varieties. The balance between the various elements was always shifting, which makes it very difficult to decide, for example, exactly when magical spells gave way to prayer in the Christian sense, and *vice versa,* to say when prayer was imperceptibly translated into the practices of magic. God's house, the church, stood on the site of the pagan sanctuary and assumed its functions. The Church calendar followed the pagan calendar, whose feasts and ceremonies dominated the whole of living from the cradle to the grave. Pagan deities and good spirits were transformed into saints, whose presence was closely felt; they could be bargained with, and men liked to be buried within reach of their saving powers.

Christianity and the Church descended on such peoples clothed in the prestige of supernatural power. The Christian God was a God of power (there was often no distinction in popular piety between Christ and God the Father), at once the Lord of terror and the Lord of joy. Man was enslaved to the devil by reason of his sin, but owed his obedience to God. *Fides*, faith, meant obedience, religious and political; it was a powerful law binding man in fear and love (*timor et amor*) to the Lord God and the blessed saints, God's allies in the war against the devil.

The whole of life was a battle, a battle between God-the-king and Satan-the-king, between evil spirits and the doughty retinue of Christ, the warrior king, whose standard-bearer was St Michael. The Mass and the sacraments, as aids to salvation, made an inestimable contribution to the war. Honorius of Autun, whose commentaries and Biblical expositions are typical of the early twelfth century and are still largely relevant for later periods as well, looked on the Mass as a battle with the devil. The priest's vestments represented the armour of salvation, he himself as Christ's deputy led the people into the eternal Fatherland, after a bitter struggle with the ancient Enemy. This folk interpretation of the Mass was retained by two other influential commentators, John Beleth and Sicard of Cremona. It was rejected by the schoolmen of the thirteenth century, but they failed to eradicate it from popular piety. Another equally popular folk interpretation, also mentioned by Honorius, saw the Mass as a judicial tribunal where God judged the sinning people, with the devil as prosecutor and the priest as defending counsel.

One can get a very good idea of what this folk religion meant merely by studying the Romanesque churches of pre-Gothic Europe. Churches were being built in this style, principally in France, Germany and central Europe, from the time of Charlemagne, and by the twelfth century the Romanesque church had become the ordinary church of the people, and as such survived throughout the medieval period despite the invasion of Gothic and other new styles propagated by the reforming Orders. It was a potent influence in moulding men's lives.

The Romanesque church, with its strong stone walls (the houses of the people, even the "castles" of the nobility, for a long time continued to be built of wood, so that stone was itself something sacred), and its squat but massive tower, was God's stronghold on earth. Here God alone was lord of all. Here He provided peace, security and joy for true believers. Here were exorcized all those wicked spirits, monsters of Hell, who tempted men to sin, dragging them to death in their nether kingdom. The banishment and binding of these demons would very likely be depicted in sculpture on the exterior stonework or even on the capitals of the columns inside. The house of God, the church, offered shelter, protection and justice to man, perpetually persecuted for his sins. Negative energies were transformed into positive power by penance, confession and the sacraments, and men were led towards healing and salvation. Evil was banished beyond earshot of the church's bell. For here in the consecrated church was a source of divine energy, stored up in the sacramental presence of Christ the King, and in the power radiating from the tombs of the Church's particular saints and from any other holy relics it might possess, however infinitesimal. These relics were eagerly collected from all over the world by the patrons of churches, bishops, abbots, lay lords and priests, to enhance the wonder-working power of their sanctuary and attract pilgrims and money into the land.

Men liked to be buried in the protective shadow of their church and its saints, in this holy company to await with fear and joy the final resurrection and the Last Judgment. Much importance was attached to the commemoration of the dead. The nobility, the clergy, and above all the monks saw it as a means of drawing the living *familia* into the greater brotherhood of the dead. It was because their liturgical ceremonies in honour of the dead were so impressive that the Cluniacs, the vanguard of the great monastic reformers, won over the aristocracies of France, Spain, Hungary and the Empire to their cause. From very primitive times honouring the dead has taken the form of ceremonious eating and drinking, as a means of uniting the participants with the saints and departed spirits. In the Middle Ages monasteries and churches received rich endowments which obliged them to hold a feast and pass the loving cup on the obit day of the individual commemorated and on the feast-day of the patron saint of the house. In old Norman and Breton houses an empty place is still left for the dead on the appropriate days. At the monastery of Kremsmünster in Upper Austria, a boar is consumed each year in honour of the founder's son on the anniversary of the foundation of the house, a ceremony which has continued without interruption from 777 up to the present.

The complaints about intemperate eating and drinking among monks and collegiate clergy, which in the twelfth century became increasingly strident (England produced a conspicuous example in the *Apocalypse of Golias*, a sharp satire which expatiates with relish on these and other vices), must be seen in this context. The idea of a love-feast between Christ and His household, that is the company of the Apostles and all believers, was central to the Gospel's account of human redemption; eating and drinking at commemoration feasts held on holy days was a means of furthering that redemption. Since this was their view of the matter, it was with a good conscience, indeed with the best conscience in the world, that people and clergy, nobles, bishops and monks celebrated in this fashion their union with the dear departed. Before the Church was invaded by heresy and reform, the clergy were in close sympathy with the beliefs and feelings of their people, and this was what gave the Church of this period so open and tolerant an aspect.

The clergy were also at this date still firmly embedded in their own social class. The higher clergy, the bishops, the abbots and the cathedral dignitaries, shared to the full the lives of their secular cousins, in hunting, jousting, feasting and feuding. Church councils (e.g. the Second Lateran Council of 1139) tried in vain to break them of these habits. As in Russia before 1917, the parish priests were men of the people and shared their rural pursuits. A parish priest who had no other opportunity of indulging his love of hunting went poaching; and he had sons to succeed him. Clerical celibacy was imposed on country districts only with difficulty; it was as hard to introduce into Europe in the twelfth and thirteenth centuries as into South America in the twentieth. Popular religion gave great prominence to the battle between Heaven and Hell, between flesh and spirit, yet the two were intimately linked, two faces of one reality. The battles of a parish priest or a monk with the devil were no different from his battles with an enemy in the next village or monastery. God and the Evil One, the blessed saints and the wicked demons, were just as close and familiar as the animals and implements which made up the routine of daily life. There were laws for dealing with them, as with any other matter; only so could man do what was "right".

Every object had its *ordo*, its own legal status, defended its own honour and was answerable for its own actions. Thus a sword which fell from the wall could be brought to account in court, so could cockchafer grubs which ravaged the fields (as in a trial at Basel as late as 1478), so could rats (there was a great rat trial at Autun around the middle of the sixteenth century), so could toads, witches and bad neighbours. *Dieu et mon droit* was the permanent watchword; and in the quest for right, faith was a most powerful weapon. From early in the Middle Ages the Church was gradually forced to extend its blessing to the very ancient customs of duel and ordeal, so deeply rooted in popular beliefs. The priests found themselves blessing not only such customary objects as houses, animals, and the harvest, but also the things used in the various ordeals: water and fire, iron, plough-share and cauldron (for the ordeal by boiling water), bread and cheese (for the ordeal of the blessed morsel), and the shield and stock of duellers. There was a preference for holding the ordeal either in the church or just outside it; for this was the supreme seat of justice, and here God, the Lord of all justice, would surely help a man to find his right. The great portals of the Gothic cathedrals with their portrayal of the Last Judgment still testify to this office of the house of God.

Medieval piety has often been reproached for its materialism, its reversion to magic and sorcery, its lack of genuine spirituality, its vulnerability to superstition. Such charges are understandable, coming as they do from people whose experience of life has been quite different, but they do not do justice to the realism and vitality of the faith this piety supported. It was a sober, hard-headed, serious faith, devoid of sentimentality (romanticism of any kind was alien to the medieval temper) but not without joy. Medieval popular religion was militant and it was concerned with justice: these were its two fundamental characteristics, and they enabled it to fulfil an important function in a society dominated by war, when everyone had to fight for his right, and when lawlessness was a daily occurrence. This faith fulfilled another and particularly important function. The whole natural world lay "in jeopardy", threatened by unknown mysterious powers, full of perils and terrors; in times of famine, pestilence and flood, and in the daily "accidents" which cost a man his life, such powers came out into the open, revealing that the beauty of outward appearances was only skin deep and that underneath lurked explosive forces always ready to erupt. Experience of this kind could only be matched by a faith imaginative enough to comprehend all terrors and horrors in its image of God. God, the Lord of life and death, was the Lord of dread and equally the Lord of joy: the terrors of the Lord of

Sinai, a volcano spitting fire, are felt in the midst of the solemn joy of the Church's celebration of the Mass.

Injustice, war, feuds, the general horror of life—all could be overcome by fighting for justice, by righteous warfare (above all between sinners and the devil), and by observing the solemn ceremonies of God's house and one's own. Call this common medieval piety naïve and primitive if you will: in its day it fulfilled vital functions in the life of man and society. To evaluate what was achieved by medieval popular religion, with its mixture of archaic, "heathen", folk and Christian elements, it is pertinent to ask what functions religion fulfils in the life of a Christian in the industrial society of the twentieth century. Medieval man had a single faith: God, the saints and the priesthood all worked together towards his protection, healing and redemption. These functions have now been assumed by other "callings": by doctors and psychoanalysts; by technicians and agronomists; and by industry, with its large-scale undertakings, devoted to economic activity of all kinds, to entertainment and to war. The atomic pile has replaced the sturdy little village churches, whose task was to convert men and so transform them that, redeemed, liberated and sanctified, their transmuted bodies might rise to a higher state. Their successors are at work on the transmutation of the material elements. Man is left at the door, more than a little apprehensive of what may happen if the explosion of the nuclear energies collides head on with the explosion of his own ego, his untutored, immature, untransmuted inner self.

To return to the people's faith in the Middle Ages. If we look for the heart of the Church, in the days before it was transformed by the impact of heresy, Islam, and its own reforming movements, we shall find it in the cloister. This is a fact of quite exceptional importance: up to the middle of the twelfth century the leadership of Christendom was largely in the hands not of Popes, canon lawyers and university trained theologians, but of monks. The half-century before 1122 was dominated by a series of monastic Popes; and Bernard of Clairvaux was the uncrowned Pope of his time. The great theological teachers were monks, for example Hugh of St Victor; so were the first great philosophers of history, such as Otto of Freising and Joachim of Flora. Monastic preachers taught the people and were the custodians of their culture. It was in the shelter of the monasteries that folk art was preserved and cherished, in the Romanesque animal symbolism which harks back to the period of the migrations and older centuries still, or in the recording of folk ballads and poetry. The monks lived in the midst of the people and shared their joys and sorrows; it was to the monasteries that peasants fled for refuge, to escape the pangs of hunger and the feuds of their aristocratic overlords.

This deep involvement of the monks with the people at all levels of society meant that the people on their side expected, or rather demanded, a very high standard of conduct from them. They were to be perfect, as Christ Himself was perfect. This is something of far-reaching political and social importance, which must be appreciated, and without it even the Reformation cannot be properly understood. People outside the monasteries, noblemen, peasants, bishops, church dignitaries, village priests, caught in the toils of secular conflicts and passions, were only too well aware that their lives fell far short of the highest Christian standards. They were convinced—it was the most deeply held conviction of medieval Christianity—that it was impossible to live in the world and be wholly and entirely a Christian. Yet there must be people capable of leading a perfect Christian life, in some place apart, and the monks in their cloister were called on to do this. It is surely significant that the cloister was called the "gate of Paradise", or simply Paradise itself. All the hopes, prayers and demands the medieval Christian set on the monks and the monasteries were centered on one expectation: that they would achieve the complete sanctity of a perfect Christian life. It was well known that a Christian's highest duty was to become holy, to become a saint. But for most men this could only be achieved vicariously. The world was full of violence, steeped in mortal sin and depravity; amid such confusion only a monk could achieve personal perfection.

This conviction was at the root of all reforms and reformations: for once the monks failed, the whole world order and the Church itself was at stake, exposed as an illusion, a fiction, a lie, since there could no longer be any hope of Christian perfection here on earth. Everything therefore depended on preserving the purity of monasticism, which meant reforming it when it became decadent and corrupt. Anyone seeking Christian perfection could renounce the world in favour of the cloister. But what could he do if the monasteries themselves had become sinks of iniquity, no better than brothels, "snares baited with whores" (to quote some of the charges levelled by the chroniclers)? When monasticism became corrupt, the nobly-born virgins who entered nunneries were exposed to the risk of defilement, and their brothers in monasteries to a lifetime of vainglorious brawling and drunkenness. All Christians, of whatever rank, had thus a vested interest in monastic reform. From early in the Middle Ages, and particularly from the ninth century, a series of reforming movements runs like a bright thread through the history of the Church. During the tenth and eleventh centuries such movements became more concentrated and took on a wider social and political significance; by the twelfth century, further strengthened by the new orders created specifically for reform, the monastic orders had prepared the way for a new epoch dominated by a papally-controlled Church whose chief agents were the new teaching and mendicant orders.

It must be emphasized that many of the reforms prior to the twelfth century, and even the majority of the new orders founded during that century, were essentially conservative, dealing only with the reform of existing institutions. The pattern was as follows. A nobleman, or it might be a bishop, or even a king or Emperor, would collect together a dozen monks (the abbot with his twelve monks represented Christ and His twelve apostles), and settle them on his land and under his jurisdiction to be a little oasis of sanctity: there they were to pray for their lord and his family, offer the Mass and say the Divine Office, bury and commemorate the dead. With monotonous regularity after two or three generations monastic discipline would start to decline. This decline had various causes: increased wealth, from fresh endowments and bequests; idleness, since only the first part of the old Benedictine rule *ora et labora*, "pray and work", was still observed and there were lay brothers and villeins to work the monastic estates; and, not least, contact with the "world". The monastery had become "corrupt". To postpone reform was dangerous for the countryside at large and for the health and salvation of the founder's family. The founders or their descendants therefore set about reforming "their" monastery, with the assistance of bishops, other abbots and maybe even the Pope. The monastery had to be restored to the pure observance of its rule, which might be either the reformed rule of St Benedict, the patriarch of Western monasticism, or the rule erroneously ascribed to St Augustine, which was in fact a new departure. There were thus any number of monastic reforms, all with the same object, to restore the monasteries to their proper functions, the performance of their specific duties. There was no thought of reforming the world at large, or even the Church and secular Christendom: this would come about indirectly, once the monasteries had regained their spiritual health and could irradiate the surrounding world with their health-giving influence.

The reform movements and the reforming orders of the eleventh and twelfth centuries worked indirectly towards the reform of the Church as a whole, and of secular Christianity, by creating little enclaves of sanctity. Wherever a new monastery was founded or an old one reformed, the bloodstream of Christendom was purified: these life-giving cells were heaven on earth, places of refuge for Christians fleeing from the world in search of Christian perfection. But the older monasticism, based on the Benedictine system, reflected the self-sufficiency of an earlier age. Monasteries on this pattern were in practice completely independent, little empires in themselves. During the twelfth century it is not uncommon to find them proudly and successfully resisting the forcible entry of outside reformers who sometimes, indeed, found that the boot was on the other foot. For example, German chroniclers describing the ejection of such intruders triumphantly record the victory of the "good old use" over all foreign invaders (French reformers, perhaps) and the preservation of the custom of the founding fathers.

The trend of the times was towards the foundation of new orders. They were needed partly to meet the general call for reform and partly because the Papacy, oppressed by the Church's increasing necessities and the weight of its own pretensions, was in search of allies. An "order" now came to mean a monastic congregation in which individual monasteries came directly under a higher jurisdiction, responsible for their spiritual discipline and, where necessary, for their reform; such orders sought and obtained papal approval. Monastic reform was no longer left to chance, or to the whim of an ecclesiastical or secular lord, but was the concern of an increasingly regimented order, meeting regularly in chapter, its governing body. In the twelfth century, therefore, we find a closely-woven network of systematically planned new foundations and monasteries side by side with the loose-knit, less rigid monasticism of the early Middle Ages. In Germany there was the Congregation of Hirsau, set up in the late-eleventh century, which was a group of reformed Benedictine monasteries on the Cluniac model. They were the first monasteries in Germany to break with the aristocratic tradition, to set up an institute of lay brothers, to train itinerant preachers, and to form companies of laymen living under monastic spiritual direction, all in the interests of increased asceticism.

Asceticism was the positive response of monasticism to the world outside; its rigours were intensified to match the increasing violence and affluence of secular life. The Order of Grandmont, the Carthusian Order (founded by Bruno of Cologne in 1084), the Order of Fontévrault, founded by Robert of Arbrissel about 1100, and numerous smaller cells and groups all testify to the vitality of the growing ascetic movement. The features common to them all, flight from the world, exaltation of poverty and the imitation of Christ, can only be understood in the light of the extreme "worldliness" of the medieval Church and of Christendom at large. Such "worldly" Christians were now aroused, often for the first time, to a genuinely Christian recognition of the wickedness of the world; this could not have happened without the heightened awareness, the deep penetration of the individual conscience by the fundamentals of Christianity, which were the achievements of asceticism.

The twelfth century also saw the birth of two orders which in many ways pointed to the future: the Cistercian and the Premonstratensian. In their earliest period the influence of the Cistercians was as invigorating as a draught of spring water. One feels this pristine quality in their buildings, many of them still standing, set in quiet wooded valleys, unforgettable in their sober simplicity and the beauty of their unmortared, closely fitting stonework. Bernard of Clairvaux, the most powerful and influential ecclesiastical figure of his age, entered the order in 1112, during the reign of the third abbot of Cîteaux, the Englishman Stephen Harding. Bernard founded 65 daughter houses from his own house of Clairvaux and by 1270 the Cistercians had 671 abbeys in Western Europe. The organization of the order was like that of a great aristocratic connection: at the head stood the abbot of Cîteaux, next to him the abbots of the first four daughter houses. Every monastery had the right of supervising its own new foundations. The field and manual work was done by lay brothers, and the "grey monks" (as they were called from the colour of their wool habits) were profitably active in the colonization of the Slavonic lands of the East. The Cistercians were purists, but purists with discretion: they came halfway towards the mood of Gothic, for which the style of their building had already prepared the way. In their sense of measure and proportion, in their feeling for clarity and classical beauty, not least in their gift for spiritual friendship, they came close to the twelfth-century humanists. Where the humanists are most tender in their praise of divine and earthly love, they often owe their exquisite delicacy of expression to Cistercian inspiration. It was a later generation, made prudish and censorious with the anxious times, that banned the Cistercian commentary on the Song of Songs.

The Premonstratensians, or "white canons", founded by Norbert of Xanten (✝1134), devoted themselves to the performance of the liturgy, to preaching, to the care of souls and to theology. They also played an important part, particularly after Norbert became Archbishop of Magdeburg in 1126, in the conversion and colonization of the lands east of the Elbe. Although its organization was aristocratic and to some extent centralized (there was an Abbot-General at the head), the order developed on a federal and regional basis, more in keeping with medieval circumstances. The individual houses were grouped into geographical and national units called *circaria* (in the thirteenth century, the heyday of the order, there were 31), which together made up the General Congregation: and there is evidence from an early date of certain national antagonisms, for example between Frenchmen and Germans of noble birth. In their earliest period, the "white canons", like the order of Fontévrault, established some "double monasteries", that is, communities of both men and women. This form of monastic life had once been characteristic of Irish monasticism and had enjoyed a partial revival in England during the twelfth century under Gilbert of Sempringham (✝1189). But it did not survive on the Continent and was discontinued on the order's own initiative.

Contemporaries regarded the new monastic groups and orders with a mixture of wonderment, hope and fear. Would these new monks really rejuvenate Christendom? Or were they the harbingers of the end of the world, the Last Judgment and the reign of God on earth? How could this new diversity (the orders differed from each other in customs, dress, modes of piety and liturgical observance) be reconciled with the unity of the Church? Hatred, mistrust and jealous rivalries soon came to the surface between the "grey monks" and the "white canons", between both and the older Cluniacs, between new foundations and old-established monasteries and cathedral chapters; the conflict between the Franciscans and Dominicans was yet to come. But what contemporaries found even more alarming was that even these new foundations were clearly not equal to meeting the urgent religious aspirations and expectations boiling up among the people; nor could they counter the inrush of new intellectual and spiritual movements from the Mediterranean lands. At the outset of his mission, Peter Waldes, the founder of the Waldensians, entrusted his two daughters to Fontévrault. But this was only one small, almost casual link between the older reform movement and the new; it built no bridges.

Monasticism, whether of the older type or in its newer twelfth-century dress, remained an aristocratic institution, committed to the land and to an agricultural economy, remote from the towns and set apart from the "masses", though there would always be exceptions to this rule, areas where the dividing lines became blurred. The monks had little sympathy with the fresh intellectual life bursting out to its stormy springtime in the cathedral schools and universities. None of this belonged to their office: it was not included in their mandate. They had, indeed, already shut themselves off from those places where the current of life in the twelfth and thirteenth centuries was at its most powerful and electric: the new towns and the schools of higher learning. The religious flux and unrest now taking hold of the towns, the countryside and the intelligentsia, passed them by.

Stabilitas loci: the churches and monasteries of the older dispensation stayed within the narrowly circumscribed landscape in which they had their roots. There were always individual exceptions, and admittedly both the Church and the monastic orders were international institutions, but although monks might be sent on commissions which would take them away from the mother house for a long or short period, they were bound to their monasteries for life. The thousand-odd Benedictine monasteries, priories, abbeys and cells, and the hundred-odd new orders modelled on the same pattern, were oases, geographically remote in forest valleys, on the banks of small streams, on the mountain heights of Italy and Germany, in the wide plains of the East, in the torrid wastes of the Provençal South and in the green fields of the British Isles. These older monastic houses were tranquil poles of undisturbed quiet, fixed in immobility (in the best sense of the word, though at times it might be less favourably interpreted). The monasteries could welcome and find a home for refugees from the great unrest of the times, but they could neither remove nor conceal its causes. Large areas of mind and spirit were left vacant for future religious and intellectual development. It was in these virgin territories that the forces were set in motion whose forward thrust would lead to the creation of a "new" Europe.

CHAPTER 4

URBAN LIFE AND ECONOMY

THE towns of medieval Europe, steadily increasing in numbers throughout the twelfth century, were diverse in origin and varied greatly in legal status, size and importance; each was different from the next, yet all shared a family resemblance. They were one embodiment of the driving forces which were creating a new Europe and in the later Middle Ages a few were to become really great powers, with a hold even over kings and Popes. Their political and economic influence reached deep into Russia and extended widely over the Near East, where proud Italian city-states flaunted themselves as the heirs of the oldest kingdom of Christendom, the Empire of East Rome. Towns were springing up all over western and central Europe. In some areas they crowded closely—too closely—together; elsewhere, as in the eastern plains, their church towers could be seen from miles away, dominating the thinly settled countryside.

Inside the towns everything was crammed into the narrow space fenced in by the walls and closely guarded gates: churches, chapels, monasteries, counting-houses, the town hall, guild and fraternity houses, the dwellings of the town's leading citizens, the schools and college halls of the university. Life inside the walls was ebullient, raucous and quarrelsome. The restoration of order by ringing the church bells or through the intervention of the town watch or the town government (often very strict) was an everyday affair. As more and more people crowded into the towns, their numbers swollen by foreign visitors, more and more houses, churches and markets were built to accommodate them. The grand houses of the richest and most influential families became more ornate and gaudy, the civic buildings, proclaiming the town's power and self-confidence to friends and enemies alike, grew ever more magnificent. And townsmen built their own churches in opposition to those belonging to the town's former masters, the bishops, counts and territorial princes from whose power they had escaped after a struggle often lasting for generations.

In the twelfth and thirteenth centuries Europe blossomed with prosperous towns; but decay then quickly set in. The wasting away of towns in the later Middle Ages was the most obvious symptom of the stagnation which afflicted those centuries, of the decline in population and the tendency of people to stay at home, cooped up within the enclosed Europe of the early modern period, and this in turn produced the mistrustful, defensive ghetto mentality which set nation against nation, creed against creed, town against town.

The rise of the towns, which had started in the tenth and eleventh centuries, had in many places been a very slow process. The fall, however, came suddenly. Many towns were set on the downward path long before the depopulation brought by the great pestilence of 1347–1350, before the crippling of trade by the wars of the later Middle Ages, and before financial catastrophe had come to overwhelm the great banking and merchant houses of Italy and Germany. Cities which had been wealthy and flourishing were laid low by more successful rivals, as for instance in Italy: Amalfi, Siena, and dozens of smaller towns failed to hold their own against Venice, Milan, Florence and Genoa. New foundations often turned out to be unsuccessful speculations. They attracted insufficient trade and traffic, and after a few generations, as the grass grew again, the town reverted to its former agricultural status, or the port silted up, as at St Louis' grandiose new settlement in Provence, Aigues-Mortes. Even the towns of Champagne sank into insignificance, though they had been among the proudest in Europe, and during the twelfth century highly important centres of trade and finance on account of their great fairs, held under the protection of the counts of Champagne. Between the fifteenth and the nineteenth centuries Bruges was a dead city, a "ghost town", evoking only memories of its thirteenth and fourteenth century glories. The rise and fall of different towns owed much to the vagaries of royal favour and disfavour.

Early nineteenth-century travellers experienced a romantic melancholy in contemplating the decaying medieval towns of Italy, France, and south-western Germany; indeed there are still such places today. They call to mind a man dressed in finery now too large for him. The petty bourgeois towns-folk huddle among the long-deserted palaces and the enormous churches there are no longer crowds to fill. The great market halls are tenanted by junk dealers, there is a garage or small mechanic's shop in the abandoned mon-astery. Time, and the highroads of the new age, pass them by. But what is not always realized is that even in the later Middle Ages they presented a similarly forsaken picture.

It will be useful to keep this picture in mind in order to appreciate how much energy was expended in creating urban life in Europe. Hundreds, even thousands, of towns never grew to have more than a few hundred inhabitants. Many others never exceeded a few thousand. As in the processes of natural evolution, the evolution of urban life was achieved only at enormous cost; many attempts foun-dered and sank, unable to withstand the inclemencies of time. Some succumbed to accidents, to a sudden emergency, to one of the many disasters which might doom a town to extinction: the death of its patron, a battle, the accession of an alien ruler or an unfortunate domestic policy on the part of the governing oligarchy. We should remember this grim background of medieval town life, often gloomy and al-ways harsh, whilst we admire the luminous beauty of its art and culture, its intellectual and spiritual power. Medieval urban civilization has three great glories to its credit, which rank among the highest of the permanent achievements of the Middle Ages. Dante's *Divine Comedy* is a unique hymn of hate and love to his city of Florence, from which he was expelled. Thomas Aquinas, the son of a country nobleman, who, like his master, the Emperor Frederick II, had an inveterate mistrust of towns, nevertheless introduced the image of the city into his theology as an analogy of the Church and the cosmos. For Aquinas, the city was the ideal type of human settlement, offering the greatest possible economic security based on self-government and self-suffi-ciency. The third great legacy of the medieval town was the university, which betrays its urban origin in numerous ways. For example, the art of *disputatio* or learned debate was a heightened and intellectualized form of the many verbal contests which were a daily occurrence in medieval towns, in the market-places, in the town courts and in the delibera-tions of the council chamber, as the citizens hammered out their differences, secure in the protection of the town's freedom.

The towns of medieval Europe differed radically from those of the great non-European urban civilizations of the Near East and the Mediterranean, from the towns of the Arab world and also of Russia. These non-European cities were often far more advanced than the European in technology, hygiene, industrialization and general level of civilization. Between the ninth and the twelfth centuries, the towns of the Russian interior were in many ways superior at least to those of northern Europe. Early medieval trade routes ran from the east along the Russian rivers and into the Baltic regions. Recent excavations at the capital city of the Bulgars, between Kazan and Kuybyshev, have shown that here at least, deep inside Russia, oriental and late classical influences were still quite marked until the sack of the city by the Tartars in the middle of the fourteenth century. Built on a site covering four square kilometres, its plan was identical with that of the great Hellenistic and Islamic cities. There were large public baths, a municipal water supply, a royal palace complete with central heating. The city's trade extended to China (porcelain and glass), Japan (ceramics), Kiev and Novgorod (weapons) and Byzantium (jewellery and pottery). The primitiveness of early medieval towns in Europe can only be appreciated if they are compared with the much more civilized Hellenistic and Arab cities of the Mediterranean and the Near East. Such cities had existed since the time of Nineveh and Babylon, all built to the same basic pattern. But the small towns of Europe had the advantage of them in two respects, their freedom and their individuality; both these characteristics had their roots in the diverse historical situations in which Europe's towns had their origins.

The towns of southern Europe grew up in a climate which had favoured urban life since early antiquity and where even farmers took kindly to close settlement. In the Germanic, northerly parts of Europe barons, knights and peasants for a long time preferred to keep to their fortified homesteads. In the twelfth century the two streams of urban development, the classical and the Germanic, converged. The towns of southern Europe, of Italy, Provence and Spain, were becoming more conscious of their classical roots and were also starting to develop along new lines; in the north there was a growing recognition of the commercial, legal and defensive advantages offered by urban settlement. At the point of convergence of Romanic and Germanic languages and institutions lay the regions which were to be the first centres of urban culture north of the Alps—Flanders, Burgundy, and the valleys of the Meuse and the Rhine.

Let us look first at the south, where men took pleasure in urban life. Homer's world was already a world of cities; the city was the seat of the gods and of the city's ruler, the king. This idea of the city as the common habitation of gods and men was carried over into the Middle Ages, when each city had its own patron saints. "Holy Cologne" was protected by the Three Kings, the eleven thousand virgins, St Martin, St Patroclus, and many others. The Greek cities, originally the residences of landed proprietors, were religious and political centres. Here lived the rulers and their slaves; in its heyday Athens had a population of 130,000–150,000 free men, and 100,000 slaves. From the thirteenth century onwards, particularly in Flanders and Italy, and later on in the larger cities, Paris, London and Cologne, medieval towns also had their substratum of an unfree proletariat, numerically very strong but impoverished both in means and rights, which soon became a political and religious "underground", thus creating the explosive situation of the later Middle Ages, when towns were hotbeds of permanent unrest.

Roman urban civilization, under Etruscan influence, developed in close dependence on Asiatic models. The rituals attending a town's foundation, its square layout with four principal streets (carried later by the Spaniards to America), the location of the military and priestly magistracies in the centre of the square formed by the city, all recall the cities of Asia Minor. Sumerian decorations and motifs even crop up in medieval churches.

In the oldest towns north of the Alps, the Celtic *oppida*, there were not only quarters reserved for the nobility and for religious cults, but also a quarter for commerce. The Germanic *oppida* were places of refuge, fortified defensive positions (*burgs*); and they, too, were at the same time religious and political centres, and markets. In the north a town started with the building of a stockade round the wick, the merchant colony where long-distance traders had their depots; thereafter, wick and burg grew up together. The tendency of these traders to settle in one place was a powerful influence in the growth of early medieval towns. These early Germanic traders and their successors the Vikings (even in the grave the Vikings kept both their swords and their merchants' scales) were itinerant traders. In the fluid conditions of the age it was possible for peasants to change their occupation as occasion offered, so that the same individual might in turn be hunter (catching fish or seals, or going after eggs in bird colonies), merchant or soldier. In Norway the arrangements of the Viking age lasted into the thirteenth century and kings, peasants, noblemen, clerics and burghers were all traders.

It was in communities of this type, where all shared in the great risks of long-distance trade, that a guild system developed, a Germanic institution which was to be one of the bases of the later medieval system of guilds, corporations and fraternities, which also owed something to the classical *collegia* and to the compulsory organizations set up by early medieval town governments for the control of certain trades. In its primitive form, the Germanic guild was a military and religious brotherhood, in which the dead entered into the living by a kind of demonic possession, and the living gained strength from the dead by participation in the sacramental banquet. It was the guilds which gave medieval towns their political and economic vitality, often enough as a result of their prolonged and bitter rivalries. Colourful reflections of their rich and exuberant life are still to be seen in the ceremonial processions of the *arte* which mark the annual festival of the patron saint in Florence, Siena and some of the small Italian towns. There are late medieval paintings which show the guildsmen bearing arms and wearing the ceremonial dress of their fraternities, leading the colourful procession of banners, saints and relics proudly through the streets of their town with an obviously proprietary air.

Towns grew up in the north once itinerant traders had settled down in one place and become merchants. At Cologne, Regensburg, Verdun and Namur the wick had been enclosed by a wall before the eleventh century, and in other places, including Mainz, Cambrai, Rheims, Beauvais, Noyon and Tournai, the old Roman walls had been repaired as a defence against the Northmen at an even earlier date. Verdun in the tenth century was the centre of a considerable traffic in slaves, which were imported from the Slavonic east and sold off to the south, particularly in Spain, where eunuchs were in demand for the courts of the Caliphs. The eleventh century saw the emergence of another group of towns, episcopal cities (*civitates*), with a surrounding wall which now included the merchants' settlements, as for example Liège, Würzburg and Magdeburg.

As the towns developed, they produced their own governing class, who modelled themselves on the landed nobility and attempted to get on equal terms with them through intermarriage. In north-western Europe, however, the gulf between the hereditary landed nobility and the urban patriciate was never really bridged and remained as a serious rent running through medieval society.

In the twelfth and thirteenth centuries the principle "town air makes free" slowly established itself, though it by no means became general; towns acquired the right of asylum and took pains to secure from their overlords charters confirming their municipal law. The idea of freedom was at the heart of all such codes of law: the town was thought of as a *libertas*, a liberty, an oasis of freedom protected by law. Men flocked there in increasing numbers in search of work, bread, justice and a roof over their heads; they had had their fill of wandering.

In Italy, the legal concept of "town peace", inherited from the Lombards, was already well established by the twelfth century, and there was no need for the roundabout method of arriving at it gradually, as an extension of "castle peace". The town constitution of Genoa of 958, which is really a charter of liberties in favour of the inhabitants, confirmed by the kings Berengar and Adalbert, is the earliest surviving example of its kind, although it is paralleled by Spanish documents of the same period. In both Italy and Spain the privilege of urban status was conferred by a grant of "immunity", a special royal protection valid for one particular place. In Northern Europe, the itinerant merchants placed themselves directly under the king's protection and thus won royal recognition for their customary merchant law, the basis of municipal law north of the Alps. In many cases the principle "town air makes free" was made to serve government policy, as in Spain, where men were needed to rebuild towns after the reconquest of the country from the Moors.

The townsmen of north-western Europe, and of the eastern towns they helped to found, were hostile to the aristocracy and the feudal system, and turned naturally to the monarchy as their protector and ally. But in Southern

Europe, particularly in Italy, the towns were the centres of aristocratic landed properties, and the nobility were drawn into the life of the city and took to trade, particularly overseas trade, at an early date. The *habitaculum* treaty of Genoa actually forced the defeated nobility to spend part of each year in the city. In the twelfth century the larger towns gained complete ascendancy over the *contado* and the neighbouring aristocracy. The "patrician treaties" made in the thirteenth century between the Rhenish towns, particularly Cologne, and neighbouring lords illustrate yet another type of relationship: the parties retained their separate identities as burghers and noblemen and concluded mutual non-aggression treaties as equal partners.

A brief tour through the urban world of the high Middle Ages may very well start in Italy, whose towns were among the most lively and colourful phenomena of medieval civilization: what we call the Renaissance was in many ways wholly their achievement. Towards the end of the eleventh century there emerged, with royal (or imperial) sanction, the institution known as the consulate, at Lucca and Pisa in 1081, at Milan in 1094, at Genoa in 1099; during the first thirty years of the twelfth century it appeared at Bergamo, Bologna, Brescia, Modena and Verona, and in 1138 at Florence. This was a specific indication of the growing political maturity of the communes, whose municipal government was becoming all the time richer, more varied and more independent. The consuls themselves came from noble or wealthy bourgeois families, and brought the confident awareness of their own high social rank to reinforce the self-assurance of the towns they represented. Closely linked with the consulate was the system of sworn brotherhoods (*societas, communitas, compagnia, coniuratio*), the companies of guilds, corporations and old patrician families whose original purpose was to diminish internal dissension and prevent the formation of parties: but in true medieval fashion, the towns, supposed to be oases of peace, were the scene of perpetual quarrelling.

The city above all others, the *urbs* par excellence of both the ancient and the medieval world, was Rome. In the tenth century the Holy City was guarded by 181 towers and 46 fortresses. By the thirteenth century these had been increased by more than 500 bell-towers and turrets, most of them belonging to the nobility; and if an enemy destroyed one in the evening it could be restored by morning. The bitter feuds of the great noble dynasties kept the blood flowing through the streets: Frangipani and Pierloni, Anibaldi and Savelli, Conti, Orsini, Capocci and Colonna all fought and intrigued against each other. The history of the Church and the Papacy can only be understood against this background of aristocratic strife; the birds of prey, the eagles and the vultures, were lodged in the Holy City itself, always prepared to swoop on their enemies. Their heavily armed partisans were everywhere, perched on the temple fortresses, below the aqueducts, in the Colosseum. The Colonna lived on Monte Citorio, where the modern Italian parliament has its seat; their feud with Boniface VIII, the Pope of the Gaetani dynasty, was to hasten the end of papal rule, and with it shatter the ambition of the ruler of the Holy City to become the Mayor of Christendom at large, the ruler of all the peoples of a united Europe.

Even in the thirteenth century foreigners had begun to protest at the state of the city: it was a filthy, disease-ridden place, a nest of robbers, where a visitor was bled white by the rascally natives and had his health ruined by the shocking food and the attentions of scorpions and mosquitoes. The chorus of invective against the "wicked city of Rome" rose up from all over Europe, and contained a large element of the general distaste and unease felt by rural populations for the "city", a resistance particularly strong in the Germanic north, where it survived until well after the time of Luther. Later on other cities were to usurp the place of Rome as the "Babylon of wickedness", first Paris (cf. the preaching of Jacques de Vitry), and afterwards London (cf. Bunyan and Blake).

There was almost incessant warfare between the Italian cities: wars between Venice, Genoa and Pisa, between Florence and Siena, between Florence and Pisa, Pistoia and Arezzo. The catalogue could be continued: Milan against Cremona, Bologna against Modena, Verona against Padua and Cremona against Mantua. The tocsin was always being sounded to signal a surprise attack, as was the bell which summoned the pugnacious citizens to arms when an offensive was in the offing. When a town was at war, particularly if it was a small town, all men between the ages of 14 and 70 might be liable for military service. The troops might be led into battle by a sacred war-chariot, the precious palladium of their city: at Florence there was the famous Carroccio, drawn by two steers decked out with red hangings,

Cremona had its Berta, Parma its Blancardo decorated with pictures of the Madonna and the town's saints on a white ground. The chronicle of Parma vividly describes the temper of the embattled townsmen:

> Then the Milanese besieged the Cremonese, they blew upon their trumpets before the walls and called: "Come out then, you miserable rabbits, and stand battle." But the Cremonese dared not come out.

Even in the midst of all this fighting, a few cities grew astonishingly in size between the twelfth and the fourteenth centuries: Siena and Pisa increased their populations to over 30,000, Florence grew from 6,000 to almost 74,000 in the fourteenth century, Venice and Milan came close to 100,000. A description of Milan written in 1287 by a native, Bonvesin da Riva, is clearly somewhat boastful, but its exaggerations are characteristic of Italian civic patriotism. There were, he says, 3,000 mills, 1,000 taverns, 400 notaries, 200 judges, 200 doctors, 150 hospitals, 80 schoolmasters, 50 letter-writers, 3,000 altars, 1,345 churches, 120 clock-towers and 10,000 religions. Such were the embellishments of the great and affluent city which the Emperors from Frederick I to Frederick II detested and feared but could not overcome.

The economic power of the Italian towns had a threefold basis: a variety of flourishing industries, overseas trade and banking transactions. And the distribution of political power within the Italian towns was largely determined by the economic power of the various groups within it.

It will be helpful to look for a minute at the internal structure of a rich Italian "metropolis" as it was at Florence in the thirteenth century. The stratum of the city, the *primo popolo*, was made up of the members of the seven foremost guilds, or *arti maggiori*. The premier guild was that of the judges and notaries. Then followed in order: the important merchants from the Callemala, the street leading from the market hall to the cathedral; the money-changers; the linen-weavers; the middle-class traders from the quarter of Por' Santa Maria; the small shop-keepers, apothecaries and physicians; and the fletchers. Sharply distinct from the *primo popolo* were the fifteen to twenty smaller guilds and corporations of the *arti minori*, the lesser folk or *popolo minuto*; among these a few guilds stood out as leaders, the smiths, the carpenters and the wine-dealers. The proletariat, strong in numbers from an early date, and the party of the extreme left, could make themselves felt during a riot: they found their leaders in men of the butchers' guild, who were used to handling sharp knives and bleeding carcasses.

By the twelfth century the Italians had already developed many flourishing industries, based on their patience and skill in processing wool, cloth, leather, iron and wood, and their talents as craftsmen and artists. The capital produced by these industries was used by leading Italian citizens to create more wealth. It was they who instructed Europe in matters of financial theory and practice, in banking and in the productive use of capital.

Banking transactions presupposed a stable currency, secure from the danger of frequent and arbitrary debasement of the coinage, which was a popular method of "making" money among medieval princes. In 1192 Venice struck a silver grosso to the value of twelve pennies, in 1252 Florence struck a gold florin to the value of a pound (the old Austrian and the modern Dutch gulden recall their Florentine ancestry in the *fl.* which is their abbreviated symbol); in 1284 Venice struck a gold ducat, later called zecchino, of the same weight and fineness as the Florentine florin. These gold coins, together with the later French écu and the silver *gros tournois,* which was created in 1266, formed an internationally accepted standard of value comparable to the dollar of our own time. Lombard Street in the City of London and the use of the word *Lombard* in modern German for a deposit bank are reminders of the time when the "Lombards", i.e. Italian financiers, covered the whole of Europe with the banking operations which made Florence, Siena and Genoa the leading financial powers of the day.

The great economic and political power of Italian finance would have been impossible without overseas trade. From the mid-eleventh century the Italian maritime cities had taken over the carrying trade from the Byzantine Empire, whose commercial fleet had fallen into decline, and this gave them control of the commerce of the eastern Mediterranean and of the Near and Far Eastern trade. The trade-routes leading north over the Savoy passes became the special preserve of the traders and financiers of Lombardy and the inland Italian cities. This gave them access to the trade fairs of Champagne and to the urbanized regions of northern France, Flanders and north-western Germany, the most important centres of trade and industry north of the Alps. Here the Italians linked up with German merchants, whose trading connections extended as far as Novgorod, and with Englishmen and Scandinavians.

Venice, Genoa and Pisa profited enormously from the Crusades of the twelfth and early thirteenth centuries, when they had the monopoly of transporting and supplying the Western armies. They also succeeded in establishing their right to a third of each of the conquered Syrian towns. Here they built up the "earliest European colonial capitalism", putting their subjects, the majority of them non-Christian, to forced labour in their industrial enterprises. By this means they acquired the monopoly of silk and glass manufacture. The names of fabrics such as damask (from Damascus), muslin (from Mossul), and gauze (from Gaza) recall this golden age of Italian Levantine trade. By the mid-thirteenth century the two great rivals, Genoa and Venice, had complete control over their respective spheres of influence, for Genoa the Black Sea ports, for Venice the Greek islands. Slaves were also an important and constant item of merchandise and slave markets were set up at Venice, Florence and Rome; eminent citizens kept slaves as a matter of course. A lurid light is thrown on the unscrupulous mentality of the Italian traders by the sale into slavery of French and German children, followers of the Children's Crusades, who landed at Italian ports and were sold off by the shippers to their Muslim business associates. Slavery came to an end largely for economic reasons—where industry was highly developed it became unprofitable. It was abolished first in the smaller towns, at Pistoia in 1205 and at Assisi in 1210, but in Bologna only in 1256 and in Florence in 1299. Official prohibition, however, at first only brought about a very gradual alteration.

Italian merchants were on remarkably cordial terms with the infidels, the Muslim princes of the Near East, and the Almohades, Berbers from the High Atlas who ruled Muslim Spain from the mid-twelfth century. Both Italian and Provençal merchants were given permission to settle at Tunis, Bougie and other trading stations on the Mediterranean.

The Italians left one dangerous legacy to Western Europe as a whole. The incessant extortions and plundering raids of the maritime cities, with Venice and Genoa at their head, which culminated in the conquest of the Byzantine Empire during the Fourth Crusade, aroused the undying hatred of the Eastern Church and its Muscovite successors. The Italians, with their naval and commercial fleets, their "nationalized" economy, and their system of taxation, which they introduced into their Byzantine possessions, represented the "avaricious", "war-mongering", "unscrupulous" West. After 1205 the Doges of Venice proudly styled themselves "Lord of one-fourth and one-eighth of the Empire of Romania".

Struggles for power within the Italian cities were just as bitter as the struggles between the cities themselves; here the contenders were political factions, patrician families, each with their clientèle, and the "greater" and "lesser" guilds. There were heated battles between "Guelphs" and "Ghibellines" (these labels originally designated supporters of the Hohenstaufen Emperors and the Popes respectively), who succeeded in driving each other out of the city by turns, so that by the mid-thirteenth century the situation was ripe for dictatorship, though at first this often took a disguised form. There were many potential candidates for the role of dictator: *candottiere* (noblemen who had turned mercenaries), imperial vicars, who had been appointed by Frederick II and retained control over the town government after his death on their own responsibility and, by no means least, representatives of aristocratic and patrician families, fighting to control their own towns. In the mid-twelfth and thirteenth centuries an attempt was made to check this development by the introduction of the official known as the *podestà*. A *podestà* was called in, sometimes for only a year, to ensure a measure of internal peace, to restrain the deadly enmity of the political factions and to help withstand the pressure of the lower classes of citizens, who were clamouring for a share in the government. The *podestà*, who assumed all the administrative and judicial functions of the town government, was an outsider, an administrator with a legal training. He was assisted by his staff, the *stato* (hence state), most of whom were graduates of Bologna; after his year (or years) of office had expired, the *podestà* became accountable for his conduct of the government.

The "state" thus makes its first appearance as the artefact of an impersonal kind of lordship offering technical competence in the law as its credentials. It is quite clear why a police force also came into existence alongside the judicial and administrative bureaucracy, which served the people by ruling them. The *podestà* had his own posse of police, to act as his bodyguard and to carry out his policing measures. This type of constitution admirably suited a juristicallyminded, mature, literate, urban bourgeoisie, and was a tribute to their political skill and judgment, but only so long as they were prepared to put into practice their idea of the city as a work of art, the creation of divine and human reason. For this very reason it was ill-adapted to the rigours of political combat, both internal and external. When such conflicts occurred, the *podestà* was either pushed aside or became the ruler of the city in his own right.

Florence and Venice developed interesting forms of government peculiar to themselves. The free republic of Florence was for a time an aristocratic "democracy"; the rule of a patrician élite, drawn from the seven leading guilds, was embodied in the *signoria* with its twelve commissions, committee of town management and complex electoral procedures. The fate of Dante, one of the city's many political *fuorusciti* or exiles, shows to what depths of slippery injustice and spitefulness the internal struggle for power could descend. The rule of the *signoria* lasted from the death of Frederick II in 1250 until the establishment of Medici rule by Cosimo de Medici (1389–1464), who succeeded in subduing all his internal enemies.

The Venetian constitution, a work of art much abused, much envied and much admired, remained intact from the twelfth century until the end of Venetian independence in 1797. Venice is an example of an aristocratic government which succeeded in stifling all attempts at dictatorship. From 1192 onwards the Doge was bound by his electoral promises to submit to the Greater Council of the 180 and the Smaller Council of the 60. The ruling aristocracy made itself a closed caste, secured from internal and external aggressors by a government police force controlled by the "Ten", a standing commission responsible for the security of the Republic. Western political thinkers of more modern times, including the men of the French Revolution, have been fascinated by the details of the political, judicial and administrative structures of the Venetian state. James Harrington used many features of its constitution in his *Oceana,* a political Utopia which was highly influential as a model of the constitutional state of the future, and through this medium some details of the Venetian constitutional practice were absorbed into the constitutions of the North American states where, in an altered form, they still survive.

From the twelfth century, the driving prosperity of the Italian cities was a force in European affairs at large. The financial and commercial activity of Italian merchants took many forms. They made loans at high rates of interest to the crowns of Naples, France and England; in return they were given licences for the purchase and export of grain and wool, rights over mints, salt-works, and the collection of taxes or other imposts. The Francesi of Florence were the treasurers of Philip the Fair of France, the Frescobaldi administered Gascony under Edward II, the Bardi collected the taxes for the Angevins in the Abruzzi, the Peruzzi controlled English finances in the time of Edward III. In the thirteenth century the import and export trade of France was in Italian hands. Their privileges, their bearing, and their wealth all aroused the jealousy of the masses and of indigenous small traders, with the result that risings against Italians were not infrequent. They were persecuted, like the Jews, as unwanted foreigners, and in 1311 Philip the Fair ordered their expulsion from his kingdom.

Southern France, especially Provence, had many economic, cultural and religious ties with the urban civilization of Italy so that in some respects the whole area formed a unit. Italian merchants established considerable colonies in southern France, settling there with their wives (like Messer Bernardone, the father of St Francis): working in close co-operation with their Provençal business associates, they extended their activities into Spain and the Islamic Mediterranean. Spanish chronicles relate how at the instigation of Italian and French merchants the people of Compostela, Oviedo and Sahagun revolted against the ecclesiastical authorities; this can have been no chance occurrence. These merchants were intellectually alert and spiritually restless; they spread Waldensian and Cathar teachings, together with the soft, melodious speech of Languedoc, throughout Italy.

Southern France in fact belonged to the South, and looked much more to its Italian and Spanish neighbours than to the alien North, where even the language was different. Southern France, only slowly and after a bitter struggle brought into subjection by the North, began south of the Loire; it included Aquitaine, the English Angevin Empire, and Languedoc from the Rhône to the Pyrenees, an area very loosely under the jurisdiction of the counts of Toulouse. This was a region rich in towns, small towns of very independent temper, whose wealthy citizens made treaties both with each other and with Italian towns. Peoples from all over the Mediterranean mingled with each other in the ports of Narbonne and Montpellier. There were prosperous Jewish, as well as Italian, colonies, and the Jewish merchants left their distinctive mark on the towns of southern France. Here in the South the Jews were merchants on a grand scale, bankers, consuls (i.e. high-ranking town officials), and financial advisers to bishops, abbots and aristocratic landowners. Large marts at Béziers, Nîmes, Toulouse and Carcassonne created close contacts with the fertile countryside, where even the peasants lived readily in small towns. The French kings included these southern towns in their patronage, which was extended both to the numerous small older towns and to the new foundations of the twelfth and thirteenth centuries, which were attached to the monarchy through the institution known as the Consulate and placed under royal protection. These Consulate towns indeed were the southern equivalent of those two hundred northern French towns, the "communes", which had achieved a superior legal status under royal patronage.

From the twelfth century the whole area under the jurisdiction of the French monarchy had become covered with hundreds of small enclosed towns (villes closes), whose burghers were struggling, tenaciously and with very varying success, to enlarge their rights. Here and there were some larger towns, with from five to six thousand inhabitants, and perhaps ten with over ten thousand, but only Paris was a really large city. The French bourgeoisie was of humble, usually servile origin. Fugitive craftsmen, peasants and tenant-farmers escaping from their lords took refuge in towns where only lords "with a long arm", the king and the more important counts, could reach them, but their uncertain legal status prevented them as they prospered from becoming a genuine patrician class. The burgesses (citizens) purchased privileges and rights from the existing lord of the town, and entered into sworn confederations (conjurationes) against him: at Vézélay against the abbot, as lord of the town, at Cambrai, Chartres, Beauvais and Laon against the bishop, at Amiens against the barons.

Great lords, however, were quick to see the economic and financial advantages which might accrue to themselves and their territories from the advancement of "their" towns, and consciously set about their promotion. Pioneers of this policy were the counts of Flanders and the Capetian kings, who took care both to keep for themselves the two most important cities of their kingdom, Paris and Orleans, and to strengthen their power by taking towns in the lands of the great feudatories under their special protection. In the Angevin Empire, the English kings, as Dukes of Normandy and vassals of the French crown, promoted the towns of Rouen, La Rochelle, Bayonne and Bordeaux, in keen competition with their suzerain in Paris.

The binding links between South and North, the points where the two trading areas interlaced, were the twelfth-century French fairs at Saint-Denis, at Beaucaire on the Rhône, at Chalons-sur-Sâone, and above all in the four Champagne fair towns. A few of the places where fairs were held achieved European stature: Bruges and Geneva in the thirteenth century, in the fourteenth century Frankfurt-am-Main. The prototypes, however, were the Champagne fairs. Deliberately fostered by the protective policy of the counts of Champagne, these became in the twelfth century the chief emporium of Western Europe. The counts of Champagne guaranteed safe conduct to and from the fairs for all merchants travelling through their territories and a special jurisdiction, with stringent penalties for breaches of the peace, turned the whole area of the four fair towns, Provins, Troyes, Lagny-sur-Marne and Bar-sur-Aube, into an economic sanctuary. There were six markets all told, so that fairs lasted practically the whole year through. At the fairs were handled the transactions of the textile industry, the first important industry to be developed in Western Europe. England supplied wool to be woven in Flanders and in Artois, in Brabant, in Hainault, in the towns of the Meuse valley and in Champagne itself. A great deal of weaving was also carried on in Paris. Sixty cloth towns of north-western Europe looked to the fairs of Champagne to provide a market for the finished goods. The export trade went principally to the south. Italians from Genoa, Asti, Milan, Piacenza, Bologna, Venice, Florence, Lucca, Siena and Rome were the financiers behind this business here as elsewhere. The prosperity of the Champagne fairs attracted a stream of German visitors and immigrants into France. They came as merchants, craftsmen, students and soldiers, and proceeded to establish German colonies in Paris, Orleans, Montpellier and Avignon. But when Philip IV acquired Champagne in 1284 his fiscal exactions sent the fairs rapidly into a decline. Under the leadership of Venice and Genoa, the Italians now took the sea-route to Flanders in order to reach the centres of the cloth industry; there they met merchants from Germany, the North and England. Bruges inherited the position of the Champagne fairs, whose towns now sank into the slumber which engulfed so many medieval towns.

In England boroughs went back to the time of the Anglo-Saxon kings, when they served as safe places to hold a market, to transact business before witnesses and for the minting of money. As fortified positions, they could also offer shelter and protection. All modern English county towns have some link with the Anglo-Saxon past. London's development was unique. Its leading citizens were recognized as *barones*, and addressed as such by William Rufus and Henry I. They claimed for themselves the right to play a particular role in the making of the king. The leading burgesses of the Cinque Ports, responsible for supplying the king with sea transport, also succeeded in obtaining recognition as *barones*. But against these proud pretensions must be set the hard fact that after the Conquest and throughout the twelfth century many towns went into a decline from which they recovered only with difficulty. Even when they successfully freed themselves from the control of the sheriff royal opposition thwarted their attempts at turning themselves into "independent" towns, on the model, for example, of the French communes.

Medieval English towns were small, like most of their continental sisters, with between one and six thousand inhabitants. In the late eleventh century only York had probably already more than eight thousand.

London's great importance, soon to become overwhelming, is noticeable even in the Anglo-Saxon period. As evidence of its special position, it had its own highly developed system of courts. From the twelfth century London was so rich and powerful that the kings had to use great circumspection in dealing with "their" city. An instructive illustration of specific London patriotism and political self-awareness is provided by the London Glosses on the Laws of the Anglo-Saxon kings, composed about 1205 or 1215. From this one discovers that at least a few of London's citizens during the years of intellectual and political ferment between 1189 and 1215 were thinking in terms of "democracy" and finding the realization of their ideas in an idealized Anglo-Saxon past. It was about this time too that the first school of Anglo-Saxon law was established in London. The London Commentaries on the laws of the ancient kings rest their case on the reciprocal tie uniting king and people. They lay stress on the community, the *communa*, offering the sworn brotherhoods of London as the model for the whole kingdom. The alliance between the people of London and the king is presented as the foundation of the English state, and the subjects' oath is transformed into an oath of brotherhood, such as bound the members of the guilds. All Englishmen are called, as sworn brothers (*fratres conjurati*), to the defence of the monarchy and the kingdom against their enemies and to protect the peace and "dignity" of "our Crown" (in France, too, the royalist patriotism of the burgesses of Paris supported the king in times of crisis).

The London Glosses, a typically medieval amalgam of fiction, political day-dreaming and sober realism (they are meticulously considerate of feudal interests in the shires) cloak their most formidable and prophetic ideas under an appeal to the law, to the healthy legal sense of the English people: the king, assisted by his counsellors, should exercise his jurisdiction within the limits of the good old laws, setting aside any thoughts of arbitrariness, force, or bending the law to suit his will.

In provincial English towns life was usually quiet and uneventful. In the twelfth century the majority of the houses, and even the churches, were still built of wood; the stone houses of the wealthy burgesses are mentioned as rarities. Their streets were narrow, as Steep Hill in Lincoln still is today. Industry was on a modest scale; the guilds and corporations which emerge in the twelfth century all had some connection with wool (weavers, fullers, etc.). The bulk of the overseas trade was in the hands of foreigners, often Italians. As in Eastern Europe in the nineteenth and early twentieth centuries the leading merchants and money-lenders were often Jews, who were among the first to build houses in stone, partly in self-defence. In the twelfth and thirteenth centuries there were frequent anti-Jewish risings, at times instigated by popular preachers. Henry II tried to protect the Jews, but at the coronation in London of his successor, Richard Coeur de Lion, the London mob rose against the Jews and many other towns closed their gates to them. They were finally expelled from the Kingdom by Edward I in 1290. His predecessors had seized every possible opportunity of robbing and exploiting the Jews, who were under the special "protection" of the monarchy. Their expulsion could now be justified on the grounds that the kings also had the duty of protecting "their" towns, whose native citizens were now capable of assuming the economic role hitherto filled by Jews and aliens. In both France and England the monarchy built the towns into the fabric of the state; the crown relied on the trained legal and political talents of the townsfolk, regulated the price of food and raw materials, and, through taxation, reaped as much profit as possible from the towns' powerful economic resources.

The wealthy Flemish towns, the meeting-place of English, French, German and Italian traders, were more turbulent and less restricted than their English neighbours. Here the organization of the cloth industry, controlled by three towns, Bruges, Ypres, and Ghent, followed the "putting-out" system. Work was given out to be done at home by people living in the country or in the smaller towns, which were economically and politically subordinate to the three larger ones, whose rule was harsh, arrogant and cruel. It was in Flanders early in the thirteenth century that an advanced form of capitalism first made its appearance in Western Europe; capital, economic power and political authority were concentrated in the hands of a tiny minority, a wealthy patriciate, who became the masters of a proletariat endowed with nothing but their ability to work. The trader supplied the raw material and supervised every stage of its processing, i.e. the weaving, fulling, dyeing and cutting, and undertook to sell the finished product. Often he paid not with money but in kind (as under the Manchester capitalism of the late eighteenth century), and in this way his workmen were in his power for better or for worse. Since more and more people were flocking into the towns from the countryside—a landless proletariat, driven out by hunger and their lords' oppression—the *enterpreneurs* could always be sure of a rich supply of human material.

Within the larger towns there developed a struggle for power between the patricians (the *poorters*), middlemen protected by law (direct dealings between clients were forbidden), and the guilds, particularly the weavers' guilds; and both were threatened from below by the lesser guilds and the exploited proletariat. There was also rivalry between the three large towns, particularly Ghent and Bruges, who were jealous of their privileged position. The French kings, who were eager to gain a hold on the wealth of the Flemish towns, were ready to intervene on behalf of the *poorters* when their position was threatened, and the Dukes of Burgundy were later to play a similar role.

The landscape of Flanders was already urbanized, with one town merging into another, linked by villages and markets. It is not surprising that Flanders was also a centre of social unrest, the battlefield of an interminable social struggle soon to spill over into France and Germany. The struggle was no longer the old one of towns against episcopal or feudal overlords, but of lesser guilds against greater, urban masses against patricians and powerful guilds. Between 1297 and 1328 a civil war raged in Flanders between the great burgesses (the *majores, goden*) and the small craftsmen (*minores, gewaden*). This had been preceded by anti-patrician risings in parts of France, for example in Beauvais, Provins, Rouen and Paris, and as the civil wars in Flanders ended, struggles between guilds and patricians over the control of town government broke out in Germany, at Ulm, Frankfurt, Nuremberg, Mainz, Strasbourg, Basel and Cologne. An event which occurred in the middle of the Flemish wars signalled the approaching end of feudal Europe. In 1302, in the Battle of the Spurs at Courtrai, the Flemish "democratic" army, under a weaver named Conink, inflicted a crushing defeat on the most dazzling array of chivalry put into the field in the later Middle Ages, the army of Philip the Fair of France, the most formidable prince in Christendom. The golden spurs of the slaughtered knights were gathered up in triumph by the victorious townsmen.

The winds of change blew almost incessantly through these "Nether Lands". The great sixteenth-century rising known as the Revolt of the Netherlands, the war of Dutch independence against Spanish rule, grew from internal struggles which had already lasted more than two centuries and in which social unrest was frequently bound up with religious mysticism. "War against the rich and the priests" was the watchword of Ypres in 1323 and of Bruges in 1328. The lower classes saw themselves as a people apart, the "people of God". Starting in Ghent under James van Artevalde (the leadership later passed to his son Philip), there grew up between 1338 and 1382 a "democratic" movement which rapidly spread to France and Germany. By the fourteenth century many lives had already been lost in such revolts, particularly in French towns. In Flanders, the centre from which these movements spread, the situation was radically altered after the slaughter of twenty thousand artisans at the Battle of Rooseborke, November 1382, when Philip the Bold of Burgundy established his rule over the Flemish towns. His successors suppressed subsequent revolts at Bruges (1436–38), Ghent (1431–1436–1448), Liège and Dinant (1408–1466–1468). The will to freedom, however, they could not suppress, and it was kept alive among the small craftsmen, artisans and peasants although the more substantial burgesses and patricians preferred to look to the prince as their safeguard against unrest and disorder.

London's Cannon Street Station was formerly the site of the Hanseatic steel-yard, and remained Hanseatic property until 1853. From the thirteenth to the sixteenth centuries it was the western terminal of the vast Hanseatic trading system which linked England with Germany, Scandinavia and Russia, and connected up in Bruges with the south-west axis of European trade, which ran through France to Venice and thence into the Mediterranean and the Black Sea. The league of cities known as the Hanse was a highly-developed and unique organization, of European stature. At its height it comprised 160 towns from Dinant to Reval, including Breslau, Erfurt, Cracow and Stockholm, with counting-houses or factories as its outposts in Novgorod, Bruges, Bergen and London. The peak moment of its power came in 1370 when by the Peace of Stralsund the Hanse could dictate that the Danish council of estates should elect no new king without its consent. Under this treaty, concluded with the strongest power in the Baltic, twenty-three Hanseatic towns were made free of Denmark's herring trade. Fish was much in demand as lenten fare and the Hanse carried this trade as far as the Alps and into France.

It was actually in London that this large-scale trading organization, which turned the whole of Northern Europe into a single trading area, was first given the name Hanse, meaning group, company. By the year 1000 German merchants from Cologne and Westphalia had already been accepted in London on the same legal footing as its indigenous citizens. From that time English trade long remained largely a preserve of the Cologne merchants, who had their guildhall in London during the reign of Henry II. In the thirteenth century there emerged, not without numerous internal struggles, the London Hanse of the Germans, which was a union of the merchants of Cologne with those of Lübeck and Hamburg. They exported English wool to Flanders, to become the foundation of the Flemish cloth industry. The centre of this trade was at Bruges, in 1313 designated by royal authority the official staple town for English wool and hides. German merchants in England were under royal protection and in 1303 Edward I drew up an important schedule of protective measures for all foreign traders, the *carta mercatoria*. When this had to be revoked to meet the protests of English merchants, a special privilege was issued for the Germans alone, in 1334. London's great Hanseatic factory or steel-yard was put under the direction of two aldermen, one English and the other German.

In the Baltic lands the Hanseatic merchants followed in the steps of the Northern Vikings, who had used this route to reach Russia and Byzantium. Between 900 and 1200 the number of German towns in this area increased from 40 to 250. Lübeck, probably first founded by the Wends about 1050, was refounded in 1143, this time as a German town, and greatly advanced by Henry the Lion; with his fall, the way was left clear for the city to govern itself and the councillors of Lübeck, the "consuls", were confirmed by a privilege of Frederick II in 1225. The rights of the Duke's representative in the city were transferred to the self-governing burgesses. Lübeck became the leading member of the group of "Wendish" towns forming the core of the Hanse. Within a century of the foundation of Lübeck, the Baltic Coast from Lübeck to Reval and Nerva had become German and Lübeck itself was the model for town settlements throughout the region.

Representation of the Germans, above all German merchants and shippers, in foreign parts was in principle the task and aim of the Hanse's predecessors, known as the "United Gotland Travellers of the Holy Roman Empire". This was a league of German merchants based on Gotland, the earliest centre of the Baltic trade. The church of "St Mary of the Germans" was dedicated at Whisby in Gotland in 1190; today Whisby is a ghost town, its old churches and ruins a reminder that medieval north-eastern Europe had its period of splendour. From here trade-routes ran to Finland and to Smolensk, and to the Gotlander factory at Novgorod. Gotland was a clearing-house in artistic matters as well, importing Westphalian architectural styles by way of Corvey, and passing on Islamic-Byzantine styles in exchange. By the second half of the twelfth century these German traders had already appeared at Novgorod, one of the largest, most powerful and most populous cities of Europe. Novgorod commanded a vast territory, reaching to Siberia, and had the monopoly of the highly coveted fur industry. Russian furs made the Germans masters of the Baltic. Adam of Bremen observes that men strove for the fur trade as for their eternal salvation. Fur apparently possessed magical powers, and in the Middle Ages a luxury fur was the supreme mark of prestige in the matter of dress (as it is today), aspired to by Emperors, princes, prelates, patricians and people alike. Anyone unable to afford the expensive skins (ermine, sable, weasel, squirrel, bear, beaver, musk, lynx, otter, polecat, marten or fox), nevertheless aimed at one of the cheaper varieties, hare, rabbit, lamb or wolf. In addition to furs and skins, Novgorod also dealt in honey (the substitute for sugar), wax, mead, hemp and flax. The Germans brought in exchange salt, a highly prized commodity, Flemish cloth, and sometimes provisions as well (for example at the time of the Novgorod famine in 1230). The eastern lands could also supply pitch, tar, charcoal and potash.

Between Lübeck and Novgorod, however, lay vast stretches of land occupied by heathens—Lithuanians, Prussians, and other lesser Baltic peoples of Latvian, Estonian, Slavonic and Finno-Hungarian descent. From the twelfth century a steady stream of Westerners flowed into these fertile lands ripe for development. The rise of the Hanse was inseparably linked with German infiltration into these regions. In the second half of the all-important twelfth century there was a radical alteration in the motives behind this eastward expansion, which until as late as 1147 had been thought of in terms of a crusade against the pagan Wends. Now, however, peaceful settlement became the primary aim. Slavonic personal and place names were retained, the Wendish aristocracy was assimilated into the German, and a long process of amalgamation of the races began. Settlement was organized by the princes, whose appointed agents, the *locatores*, acted as recruiting officers. The towns they founded were small and designed primarily as markets, having a central market-square and a regular, cruciform street plan. These German settlements provided the model for the "counter-colonization" of the Slavonic princes, who now embarked on the systematic settlement of the broad forest lands of the fringe areas.

"Nach Ostland wollen wir reiten," *"nach Ostland wollen*

wir mit . . . dort ist eine bessere Statt." ("We want to go to the Eastern lands," "to the Eastlands we will go . . . to find a better place.") This was the song of the German youth movements between the two world wars, but it by no means originated with them, and is in fact a Flemish folk song. In the Middle Ages Flanders was one of the centres of over-population to provide settlers for Eastern Europe, oppressed townsmen in search of land, food, and greater freedom before the law ("liberties"). In fact the whole of Western Germany was gripped by this migratory urge, which had three successive peaks, about 1150, about 1210 and about 1250. People from the middle and lower Rhineland went to settle in Hungary and the Siebenburgen, from Flanders and Lübeck to the Baltic Lands; Hollanders, Zeelanders and "Flandrers" (Flemings) had already pushed out into Brandenburg and the thinly settled Slavonic and East German lands of Central Europe, to Halle and Wittenberg, Dessau and Zerbst, Saxony and Thuringia. The inundation of valuable food-growing districts on the coasts of Friesland, Zeeland and Holland was another powerful incentive to migration.

Medieval Europe, like large parts of Asia and Africa to-day, was a hunger zone, and with hunger for bread went a hunger for land. A contemporary proclamation promised trekkers to the East a land rich in meat, honey, poultry and corn: "Come then, you Saxons and you Franks, you Lotharingians and you Flemings, and do deeds to win salvation for your souls and a portion of the best land in the world." The main burden of clearing and settling the land in the German East was borne by the territorial princes, together with bishops, monastic houses, the nobility and the military orders. The monasteries were allowed to grant out their land in return for rent. Templars, the Knights of St John, and the Teutonic Knights (called in Livonia "the sword-bearing brothers of Christ's chivalry", sword brethren for short) fought their way eastward by the sword, the cross and the plough. The men of the twelfth and thirteenth centuries were quite untroubled by the serious moral problem posed by this linking together of conquest, Christian missions, land settlement and rule over alien peoples.

Slavonic princes also made an important contribution to the German settlement of the East in Mecklenburg, Pomerania and Pomerellen and it was the Polish Duke Conrad of Masowia who called the Teutonic knights into Prussia, an action decisive in the history of Eastern Europe; its effects can still be felt today.

The Teutonic knights and the Hanse worked closely together. Even before the days of its great eastward expansion, Lübeck had already shipped large numbers of settlers overseas (as it did to America in the eighteenth and nineteenth centuries). Riga was captured in 1201, and in less than two generations the southern coast of the Baltic was overrun with German corporate towns. Rostock was founded in 1218, Wismar in 1224–49, Reval in 1219, Narva in 1223, Danzig in 1224. In the spring of 1231 the army of the Teutonic Knights crossed the Vistula. In 1309 the High Master of the Order (founded originally for service in the Holy Land, an association recalled by the name of Thorn, the Order's first foundation in Prussia) moved his seat from Venice to Marienburg; the balance of Europe was shifting from the Mediterranean to the East. A century and a half later the territory of the Order had 93 towns and 1,400 villages, with 60,000 peasant holdings. The towns were given the Law of Kulm, a daughter code of the Magdeburg municipal law (written down in 1188), which was itself adopted by many towns in Brandenburg, Silesia, Prussia, Bohemia, Hungary, Poland and Wallachia. The law of Lübeck had a similar prestige. This pattern of mother towns conferring their laws on a number of daughters is repeated all over Europe: Rouen in France, Arras in Flanders. In England towns at first followed the example of Rouen, and later looked to native models, London, Oxford and York. In Germany, apart from Magdeburg and Lübeck in the East, the "mother" towns were Cologne in the lower Rhineland, Frankfurt-am-Main in central Germany, Freiburg in south-west Germany and Vienna in the south-east.

From the Hanse of the German traders there grew the Hanse of the German towns, a league of towns protecting their traders, winning privileges for them in foreign lands, guarding their trading routes by land and water, and driving away from their preserves alien traders who were not members of the Hanse, whether Russians, South Germans or Lombards. The nucleus of this Hanse of towns was the League of Lübeck, Wismar and Rostock, later enlarged to include Stralsund, Greifswald and Stettin and other newly-founded towns of the eastward expansion; Kiel, Hamburg and Lüneburg came in later. The leading member of the Western group of the Hanse was Cologne. This league, or rather leagues, of Hanseatic towns, was very loosely organized, in contrast with the urban alliances of southern and south-west Germany, which were on a political and military basis. "Diets", when some of the Hanseatic towns met to confer together, were held only at very irregular intervals and their resources were pooled only in the face of a particularly grave threat, for example the struggle with the king of Denmark. The German Hanse never took the field as a body, never waged an offensive war, and had no navy of its own. (England was the only country at that time to possess its own navy: in 1215 King John had fifty-two galleys.) Merchant ships had to be laboriously converted into warships for every campaign; once armed, they were known as "peace-ships", since their task was to restore peace, and they were chiefly used against pirates. These wealthy, enterprising and far-sighted north German towns preferred trading to warfare. Satisfied with the reality of power, the Hanse was content to forgo its ostentatious exercise. England, which inherited the Hanseatic ascendancy in the oceans of the world, largely adopted this policy as a basic maxim of maritime power.

The sharpest weapon in the Hanseatic armoury was the trade embargo, by which towns and nations could be forced to adapt their trading policies to suit the Hanse. The Scandinavian kings were particularly vulnerable to it. The Hanse had outposts in all the countries they traded with; these were the "factories" which protected the interests of Hanseatic traders and served as living quarters for permanent representations of each of the Hanseatic towns. They were privileged areas (in the case of Novgorod an entire township), containing offices and law-courts. The most important of these outposts were the London steel-yard, the Peterhof at Novgorod, Bruges, which was the Hanseatic staple for Western Europe, and Bergen, the centre of the stockfish trade. To these must be added a number of smaller factories in England, Sweden, Denmark and the eastern coastal districts of the Baltic. Such counting-houses and factories had a markedly stimulating effect on the productivity of the host countries. For example, the exploitation of Sweden's mineral resources was greatly intensified, but still more striking was the effect on the agricultural yield of the entire Baltic region. By means of the Hanse, food and raw materials from eastern Europe were made available to the west. The big-bellied holds of the Hanseatic cogs carried to the west butter, cheese, bacon and lard from Denmark and Sweden and grain from Prussia.

An old Hanseatic saying characterizes the chief centres of their trade: "Cracow is built of copper, Whisby of pitch and tar, Reval of wax and flax, Riga of hemp and butter, Rostock of malt, Danzig of corn, Hamburg is a brewery and Lübeck a warehouse." Hamburg was the foremost beer-brewing town of the north, supplying beer for export north, south, east and west (as far as Amsterdam).

The Hanse imported manufactured goods from western Europe, particularly from the inland regions of Germany, and also luxury articles from the east, above all the spices which were so important to the medieval table. Pepper, in fact, became the collective name for all exotic spices. From Hungary they took back lead, quicksilver and copper.

On the eve of the second world war anyone travelling say from Bremen and Hamburg to Riga and Reval gained a very clear impression of the homogeneity of these Hanseatic towns, still unscathed despite the troubled centuries which had intervened. There were still churches dedicated to the patron saints of merchants, mariners and fishermen, St Mary, St Peter, St Nicholas and St James. Other favourite patrons were St John, St Clement and St Katherine. Many of these churches were modelled on St Mary's, Lübeck. Huge, lofty red-brick edifices (which usually took fifty years and more to build), they testify to the passion for building among the wealthy, self-confident burgesses. Their churches were the place where civic, dynastic and guild representatives came together, a communion of the living and the dead, just as the citizens took counsel and feasted together in the houses of the guilds and patrician families. Some of the more important merchant families had seats in half-a-dozen and more of the towns between Lübeck and Dorpat. Everything was dictated by family relationships. Marriage was a matter of high policy, an instrument to be used in extending the bounds of economic empires. The second world war took its toll of many proud patrician houses, churches and monasteries in the Baltic region, including the Schwarz-haupterhaus at Riga. The Hanseatic qualities of self-confidence and pride in the achievement of a class of free traders, well versed in the ways of the world which lay open at their feet, have survived in Bremen and Hamburg; and this is yet another legacy of the European Middle Ages.

Side by side with European urban civilization was the

quite different type to be found in Russia, in which older elements, common to Europe as a whole, were combined with features which were Asiatic and Islamic—or which at least bore a strong resemblance to Asiatic and Islamic models. In the course of the thirteenth and fourteenth centuries German traders brought the specifically European type of town to Poland, Bohemia and Moravia; however, the true dividing line separating western from "Asiatic" urban civilization runs straight through the middle of Hungary, and this was equally true in the Middle Ages. The towns of southern Hungary, Transdanubia and Siebenburgen (e.g. Fünfkirchen and Grosswardein) were part of the western family circle; the towns of the Hungarian lowlands, such as Szeged and Nagykoras, which originated as pastoral settlements, belonged to that other, eastern, world, whose most important distinguishing feature was the absence of a town bourgeoisie. This was a factor of the highest significance politically, socially, intellectually and psychologically.

On the frontier between the two urban types stood Novgorod, the most easterly foothold of the Hanse. Novgorod was a world in itself. Its name means "new town", and it achieved autonomy in the twelfth century, thanks to the drive and vigour of its popular assembly, the *Vječe* (made up of country people, not burghers), which succeeded in capturing the privileges of the Prince. From 1126 it was this assembly that elected the governor, the *posadnik* or *borckgrave*, the Prince's representative. Between 1136 and 1238 thirty-eight princes ruled in Novgorod; with an average reign of two to three years each, they were clearly puppets. From 1156 the people even elected the bishop (after 1165 it was an archbishop), which was without precedent in Europe, and in 1211 an unpopular archbishop was expelled. Novgorod reached a population of twenty thousand as early as the twelfth century. There were three classes in the city: the "black masses", *černj*, that is, labourers and artisans; *kupcy*, the prosperous merchants; and the *Bojars*, comprising about forty families, an élite of ruling dynasties. The *Bojars*, who had vast estates, lived on the left bank of the Volkov, protected by the bishop's fortified palace. They owned numerous slaves (*cholopy*). The popular assembly, the *Vječe*, in practice had only the right of saying yes or no and the actual government was carried on by a secret council of fifty. Pitched battles sometimes developed between the two leading sectors of the city and the wealthy *Bojars* paid cheer-leaders to shout down dissenting voices in the *Vječe*. The Novgorod army was very strictly organized, and there were permanent commissions charged with keeping the roads serviceable and with construction work. The surrounding country was divided into five equal *pjatiny*, which came to a point at Novgorod, fanning out into the country to a depth, in some cases, of 400 miles. The fourth *pjatina* extended from the Volkov to the White Sea, taking in Lake Onega on the way. This division of land had the advantage of protecting Novgorod's trade-routes by land and water. A *pjatina* was always put under the control of a *Bojar*. In addition there were large territories obliged to pay tribute to the city, and several allied towns.

By the twelfth century there were already thirty-seven monasteries in and around the city of Novgorod and innumerable churches and chapels; there were eight churches in the market-place alone. The turrets of the town's fortifications, which were numerous, also served as churches. The archbishop had his seat in the *kremlj*, the castle-palace. Novgorod's magnificent cathedral of Santa Sophia, recalling its name-sake at Constantinople, was the political, ecclesiastical and spiritual centre of this proud city-state, an East Rome in itself. The supremacy of Santa Sophia was challenged by the German cult of the Virgin, introduced by the Teutonic Knights into their territories. The conflict was not merely figurative, both sides carried their church banners with them into battle. Traces of this conflict between East and West Rome survived into the twentieth century. The name of Alexander Nevsky, Grand Duke of Novgorod, who defeated an army of Teutonic Knights on the frozen surface of Lake Peipus in 1242 and is venerated by the Russian Church as a saint, was given to the panzer brigade fitted out from ecclesiastical funds and donated to the Red Army as the Church's contribution to the defence of Russia against the Germans during the second world war.

From Novgorod the "Prussian road" (so described from about 1250) led along the left bank of the Volkov towards Riga. The right-hand bank was the business quarter, where the *Lodjin*, the large flat-bottomed Russian river-boats, tied up. The two Hanseatic buildings, the Peterhof and the Gotenhof, occupied a uniquely commanding position. There were still Russian traders in Denmark, Sweden and Gotland in the twelfth century, but they were being driven out of business by the Germans, whose wares were "brought to the door", were cheaper, of better quality, and more certain to arrive. The Germans, moreover, had the backing of their trading network with its nodal points in the numerous towns founded in the Eastland between 1158 and 1250. From early in the thirteenth century they started to press forward deep into Russia and to join up with the Bulgars on the Volga, whose huge capital city was briefly described at the beginning of this chapter. The Volga route opened up vistas of trade to Persia and to China. Spices, "pepper", and silk were imported along it from the Far East, until the Mongol onslaught brought everything to an end.

Within the unique "empire" of this great and impressive city the Germans had their own well-defined domain, the factory of Novgorod. The Peterhof was separated from the surrounding Russian world by wooden stockades and stone walls; bloodhounds guarded it by night. As a last defence against sudden uprisings of the city mob (a peril also recognized by foreign merchants in London, Paris and in Spanish towns), there was the stone-built church of St Peter, and it was here that the balances and the stocks of goods and provisions were kept. The priest in charge acted as scribe for the merchants. This small, autonomous, all-male German community (no women were admitted to the Peterhof), kept strictly apart from all contact with the Russians, was ruled by an alderman. Russians were not allowed into the German warehouses to inspect and sample the wares, although Russian goods were submitted to searching scrutiny and were carefully gone over before any purchase was made. The Germans refused the Russians any form of trading credit.

Two worlds confronted each other, mutually hostile, yet for centuries bound by close commercial ties. Germans might learn Russian, but Russians did not learn German; the Orthodox clergy thought that learning foreign languages, like foreign travel, would only tempt Russians into heresy. Despite this xenophobia on the part of the Church, more and more Germans braved the perils of the journey to the Russian interior. In 1210 and 1229 Germans were appointed counsellors of the Russian princes of Smolensk.

To conclude this tour of European towns from the twelfth to the fourteenth centuries we will glance briefly at the towns of the Russian type, towns without burgesses. At this period of the Middle Ages between ten and fifteen per cent of Europe's total population lived in towns; in certain districts the percentage was already as high as twenty-five. In Russia, the proportion of the whole population living in towns was only 2.5 per cent as late as 1630, and in 1796 was still only 4.1 per cent. Russian towns, most of them very small, were built of wood, and this remained the case until the nineteenth century. Their nucleus was a fortress (the original meaning of *gorod*, the Russian word for town, was "tribal refuge"); traders and artisans settled nearby in the suburb or *posad*. The highest ranks of society, the princes and their armed followers, engaged in trade. Later on came "clients", privileged merchants who carried on their business under the orders of the Tsar, and were in a sense his employees. The Tsar of Moscow was the biggest merchant of his region. As in the early medieval towns of Western Europe the town's seat of government, the *kreml*, was firmly separated from the suburb by walls and a fortress. The merchants and artisans of the *posad* never became a unit recognized by law, a corporation, and Russia had no corporate towns on the western pattern, no municipal law, no legal maxims such as "town air makes free". Free and unfree lived side by side in the *posad*. The peasants who were later attracted to the towns remained serfs, and could be hauled back to the land by their lords at any moment. The standard of craftsmanship in these Russian towns was low, the techniques clumsy and primitive. Industry was largely a peasant activity, and in consequence the towns produced no guilds or fraternities. The same individual might be at once tailor, cobbler, farmer and woodworker. Town and country merged into each other, in contrast with Western Europe, where the rights and privileges of the towns, the basis of their rise to freedom, created an essential distinction between town and country. In Russia the aristocracy ruled their people in town and country alike.

It was the lack of a town bourgeoisie (together with the subordinate status of peasantry) which gave Russian society its oriental character, quite distinct from the society of Western Europe, both in the Middle Ages and later. The "several hundred cities" ascribed to Russia in the thirteenth century sank back into the countryside and were ruled by the land's masters. The towns of Western Europe, pushing out in the thirteenth century to Revel and Dorpat, raised themselves above the countryside, masters of their laws and liberties: in them the free speech of Europe was born.

CHAPTER 5

THE TWELFTH CENTURY
AWAKENING

EVERYWHERE in Western Europe during the twelfth century, in France, Germany, England, Italy and Spain, men's hearts and minds were waking to a new appreciation of the world, its colour, its vastness, its perils and its beauty. There was curiosity about the world in all its aspects, the world of men, the world of the spirit, the world of the cosmos and the world of nature. This was a germinal time, pregnant with a thousand possibilities, and the material and themes treated by the men and women of this age retained a compelling attraction for poets and speculative thinkers right through the Renaissance and Baroque periods and down into the eighteenth century. The twelfth century broke the ground, but the harvest would be reaped by posterity and by men of quite a different temper. There were immeasurable potentialities in the permeation of philosophical, scientific and mystical thought by ideas of alien origin, classical, Arab, Jewish and Oriental (some chronicles actually describe twelfth century Pisa as an "Oriental" city). The first task, and it was undertaken with feverish intensity, was one of translation. The chief centres of this activity were Toledo, Montpellier and a number of Italian towns, from Cremona in the north to Naples and Sicily. Although the bulk of the new material was alien, some of it was in fact long familiar from excerpts in the writings of the Fathers. But this was merely the first breath of fresh air, a pleasurable titillation, some might say a temptation. Only the high scholasticism of the thirteenth century could make a system out of this alien material.

This readiness to welcome new material was matched by a liberal atmosphere in the schools, where a youthful and enquiring intelligentsia was arming itself mentally and emotionally for the encounter with the hallowed philosophical and poetic giants of the past. Young men of this calibre were to be found in the cathedral schools, particularly those of France (Chartres, Rheims, Laon, Orleans and Paris), and in the earliest universities, at that time still very open and flexible, not to be compared with the rigid, exclusive schools of the later Middle Ages. There were also the "wandering scholars", who were a typical phenomenon of the twelfth century, in which there was so much literary and intellectual movement. These *vagantes*, who were unbeneficed clerks, were acute observers of their times, specialists in satire and irony, and, a few of them, highly gifted poets. Simultaneously, at the first really "courtly" courts known in Europe, great poets were spinning that golden yarn which, although made thin and colourless by incessant handling, has provided material for the novel up to and including our own time.

The twelfth century used Latin both as the instrument of thought and speculation and as the medium of creative imagination. Latin was the speech of the intellectual world throughout Europe, a world at first inhabited exclusively by clerks; and when laymen came to join them they went through the same preliminary education. The Latin of the uncommitted twelfth century was far from being the precise scholars' tongue it was to become when Thomas Aquinas and the thirteenth century schoolmen were wielding it as the chosen instrument of logical, "purely scientific" and juridical thought, when each word was restricted to a single meaning and ever more rigorously and narrowly defined, until it was reduced to a single dimension. The Latin of the twelfth century, and especially the Latin of theologians and philosophers, was a living, flexible language. Each word easily accommodated several layers of meaning, often of great ambivalence. An individual found in this "open" language room to express the religious experience of his childhood, of his people, and of a thousand years of history. Words were still ciphers, symbols, sacraments, a bundling together of different meanings, signposts directing attention to something beyond. The schoolmen of the thirteenth century (and to some extent also of the later twelfth century) had no use for this sort of language: they tore it to pieces and condemned it as "imprecise", "illogical", "unscientific". Yet it was just this kind of language that was eminently suitable for speculative writing and for expressing in all its nuances that spirituality, so instinct with intimations of God and the natural world, which distinguishes some of the most interesting thinkers of the twelfth century.

A preliminary word may be said here about the vernacular literature which was growing up side by side with this "open" Latin. There is magic, in every sense, in the folk poetry of the twelfth century. But the charm of the early vernacular poetry of Spain, Provence, northern France, Germany and the Netherlands soon started to freeze into a polite upper-class diction, strictly limited to a fashionable repertoire in which the language was purged of its "provincial" elements. The vernacular was transformed into the metallic, lucid, somewhat precious language of a social élite of cultivated people, and this was to set the stage for five centuries of courtly versifying, which all too easily became mannered and pedantic. By the thirteenth century the victory of this self-imprisoned poetic style and of the theological, philosophical and poetic systems which went with it was already assured.

The twelfth century was an open age. In intellectual matters this meant that its touch was sometimes fumbling and uncertain, that problems were attacked hastily before the necessary preliminary work had been done, and that men had an unwarranted confidence in the power of reason, and of numbers, mathematics and geometry, to give decisive answers to the puzzles of the universe. In men of another temperament there was excessive reliance on eloquence, on the virtues of long words and beautifully-turned sentences.

Intellectuals of conservative cast, and they were in the majority, resisted such impetuosity. They included masters of cathedral schools, members of secular orders who were teachers in the new universities, episcopally appointed university chancellors, bishops, and leading theologians and spokesmen of the religious orders. As each new twelfth century thinker appeared, it was very likely that he would soon be surrounded by a crowd of hangers-on, rivals or overt enemies, all concerned, from a variety of motives, to expose him as an "innovator". In narrowly orthodox circles, the main accusation levelled against heretics was that they were innovators, men of the "new truth"; the same charge was to be made five centuries later, at the time of the Counter-Reformation. The German word for heretic, *Ketzer,* is derived from Cathari, meaning "the pure"; and in the twelfth century the whole of south-western Europe had already been penetrated by the teachings of the Cathars, the Waldensians, and a dozen smaller heresies. Thus any twelfth century intellectual, theologian, philosopher or natural philosopher with a taste for speculation found himself engaged simultaneously on three fronts. He had to defend himself from the attacks of his more conservative colleagues, he was expected to resist "heretical" innovators with whom he may well have found himself in some sympathy, and he was likely to be in conflict with colleagues who were "progressives" like himself, but belonged to a different school of thought. Such a situation produced some very complicated relationships and highly dramatic, even tragic, controversies. The lines of the three battlefronts not infrequently became hopelessly entangled: "conservatives" and "innovators" found themselves now allies, now adversaries, without understanding each other's positions. Two characteristics of intellectual controversy now reappeared for the first time since the great Christological debates of the second to fifth centuries: first, the atmosphere of heightened temper and sensibility in which such disputes were conducted, and second, the suspicion and jealousy felt by the participants for each other. This spirit of contention was to stay. The jealousy was all the more bitter in its effects when it was suppressed at the austere dictates of a rigidly disciplined conscience, the natural result of an incomplete awareness of the depths of personality. The twelfth century has its conspicuous examples of *rabies theologica,* of the rancour which so often accompanies theological debate, and of the group egoism and vanity found sometimes in religious orders and universities.

The intellectual world of the twelfth century looked both to the past and the future. Looking to the past meant allegiance to the thousand-years-long tradition of a circuitous approach to the mysteries of the triune God, in a spirit of awe and love. Such divine mysteries were "comprehensible" only through symbolism and the reverent interpretation of symbols; they could be revealed to human experience in images and allegory, but might never be completely exposed to view. Looking to the future meant embracing boldly and without prejudice a philosophy which included in one system God, nature, the world and man. Anselm of Canterbury (1033–1109), standing on the threshold of the twelfth century, had one foot in the great tradition of the past and one in the somewhat perilous future.

The external course of Anselm's life reflects the academic changes of his time: from Italy, the land where the study of grammar and logic had continued without interruption, he went first to France and then to England, two countries which formed a cultural unit. Born at Aosta, of noble parentage, he went to school at Bec, and so shared in the vigorous cultural life of the Norman monasteries of the day; here he was a pupil of Lanfranc, jurist and dialectician, himself a native of Pavia, and rose to become prior and abbot. Anselm has been called the father of scholasticism. This can be accepted only in a very limited sense, and only if it is applied to his unbounded curiosity and his explicit intention of thinking "rationally"; for these traits could well be taken as corresponding to the later rationalism of the schoolmen. The nerve-centre of the thought of this great but avowedly conservative philosopher becomes visible elsewhere in his work: in his ontological proof of God, which remained a subject of dispute among European philosophers, who misunderstood it, until after the time of Kant; and also in his *Cur Deus Homo?* ("Why did God become man?") The ontological proof of God runs as follows: the existence of God is proved by the very idea of God; even an atheist understands the concept "God" as meaning simply "greatness than which nothing greater can be thought." But this "God" cannot exist in the understanding alone, for something still greater can be thought of as existing in the reality outside. "Therefore there exists both in the understanding and in reality something than which a greater cannot be thought."

Even during Anselm's lifetime there were clever logicians, such as Gaunilo, a monk of Marmoutiers, who could show that according to formal logic this "proof" miscarried. But in saying this the logician was wide of the mark (though this was clear neither to Anselm nor to his opponent). Anselm's "concept" "God" was much more than a verbal concept; it embraced all human experience of God, God's impact on man's whole being, his understanding, his emotions and his conduct. This is just as much a manifestation of Anselm's much-cited rationalism, his belief in reason, as is his justly famous apothegm, *"credo ut intelligam"* ("I believe that I may understand"). Faith expands the heart and mind, creating that inward spaciousness in which alone reason can work: *"fides quarerens intellectum"* ("faith seeking understanding"). Such faith was no fly-by-night, which spread its wings only while thought was nodding, but a joyous, serene trust in the Godhead as the creator of man as a rational being. Belief of this kind sought illumination for the mind, was ready to understand and be understood. Anselm expressly lays it down that men whose belief was unthinking, false, or even dead, should be convinced by the light of truth, by rational exposition.

Anselm wrote his dialogue *Cur Deus Homo?* for his uneducated rustic monks at Bec, though he also had other readers of a quite different background in mind. There are three important points to notice about it. First, the dialogue form, of which Anselm made great use; he loved a debate. At this period theology, philosophy and the subjects of the seven liberal arts (grammar, rhetoric, dialectic, arithmetic, geometry, music and astronomy) were all made occasions for debate: with a pupil, with the great teachers of the past, or with some contemporary academic opponent. Such disputes were informed by the *eros* of the educator, who was moulding the pupil's mind, and the *eros* of the *agon*, the contest. Nor can we consider this preoccupation with combat fortuitous, when we realize the social origin of those who took part; these monastic and university teachers were noblemen, not infrequently of the highest rank, seeking new forms of conflict commensurate with the enormous burden imposed on their class in an open, undefended Europe, physically and spiritually assailed by the storms blowing in from the East.

Secondly, this dialogue once again underlines, and in striking fashion, how much in medieval times the common conception of the world was coloured by the religious-political assumptions of the masses during the Middle Ages: God was fighting to redeem man who, because of his sin, had become the booty of another king, the devil. Christ, God's son, paid the penalty owed by man for his grave offences, by which he broke faith with God. "Felony", breaking faith, was the gravest crime known to this society. God the Son restored the damaged honour of the Lord of Heaven, his incarnation and crucifixion re-established "friendship" between God and man, and brought the kingdom of Heaven back to its just order. John of Salisbury, the great English humanist of the twelfth century, passes over this thoroughly folk theology, as expounded by the Primate of England, in icy silence; the fact that he does not mention it at all in his biography of Anselm is an indication of how greatly the intellectual climate altered in the space of only a few decades. Thirdly, our interest is seized by Anselm's posing of the question central to his dialogue, *Cur Deus Homo?*, which leads us directly into the humanism of the twelfth century.

Twelfth century humanism, delighting in the world, in books, and in argument, revolved all the while round man

himself; it was anthropocentric, seeing no sense in philosophizing over God and nature unless man himself was also
in the picture. This was something the "strictly scientific"
theological systems of a slightly later date, with their hard
and fast categories, were apt to overlook. Theology postulates,
and must include, anthropology, the study of man.

Even in the early twelfth century there were some sensitive monastic thinkers who did not cease to contemplate and
celebrate the mystery of man. Hugh (1096–1141), master
of the monastic school of St Victor's in Paris, the son of a
Saxon count, and one of the most influential theologians of
his century, taught that God created for the sake of mankind: "mankind is set in the midst of creation". Man, that is,
stood between God and the visible world, and had a portion
in each. The world served mankind, mankind should serve
God. Man had been given a great freedom, *magna libertas*:
he could not be forced to turn his heart to God, the highest
good. To serve God in freedom meant using the highest gifts
of head and heart mankind had received from God: reason
and understanding on the one hand, faith and the strength of
a loving heart on the other.

But here was the parting of the ways. Bernard of Clairvaux (1091–1153) fought for the primacy of the heart; he
was himself in his own day the most powerful and passionate
representative of its virtues. Peter Abelard (1079–1142), the
toughest intellect of his time, fought for the primacy of
reason, of the head. The controversy between these two men
revealed an abyss; and for centuries afterwards theologians
and philosophers were to occupy themselves just as much
with widening it as with attempts at bridging, or, indeed,
concealing its existence. European thought from this time
onwards cannot be understood without taking note of these
dialectical efforts to reconcile or separate faith and knowledge, reasons of the heart and rational understanding; the
two have finally become so diametrically opposed that Christian believers regard scientists as professional unbelievers.

Bernard of Clairvaux, the son of a Burgundian nobleman,
was twenty-one when he entered the Cistercian Order; three
years later he became abbot of Clairvaux, an office from
which he "ruled" popes, kings, bishops, prelates, nobles and
common folk. The Crusade of 1147 was as much his achievement as was the foundation and reformation of numerous
monastic houses, from Sicily deep into Eastern Europe. It
is pertinent to ask what was the source of this extraordinary

authority, which is the key to Bernard's religious thought; it is as if his thinking rebelled against the daemon of his own nature, pressing him all the time to invoke against his natural pride, hot temper and spleen the powers of humility and love. Bernard's Cistercian brand of humanism acted out the drama of his own personality under the image of mankind: man was made in the image of God, and had a "great soul", *anima magna*. A good man could stand upright and erect before God. But man was bowed low by sin: the bent soul, *anima curva*, turned away from God in rebellion. The source of all sin was wilfulness, *proprium consilium*: man thought he knew better than God. Bernard was here describing his most intimate temptations: was it an accident that his formidable anger was kindled to its depths when he thought he could see, indeed was forced to see, this "wilfulness" at work in a man of different philosophy and beliefs?

Faith set a man on his feet again, restored his soul to its native nobility. Faith meant humble submission, the illumination of reason and the banishment of self-will, so that the will was again opened up to love. Loving now without reserve, man yearned only for union with God. Man's aim, fulfilment and highest dignity lay in becoming absorbed into the Deity, being caught up wholly into the process of love in which God the Father embraced God the Son, encircled by a blazing nimbus lit by the flames of the Holy Ghost. "Heart speaks to heart": the heart of man called to the heart of God, and God's heart called to the heart of man. Bernard's mysticism, inspired by St Augustine and the Song of Songs (on which he wrote a Commentary, incandescent in its fervour), set up currents of great spiritual power which remained a force for several centuries; German mystics of the fourteenth century, Spanish mystics of the sixteenth century, French mystics of the seventeenth and eighteenth centuries all found inspiration in him. So too did Martin Luther and the Pietists, the Deists and the Quietists. Bernard's exposition of the "beautiful soul" and the "noble heart", his sense of having mastered the world, recurs, deformed and secularized, in the English Romantics and in Rousseau; the young Goethe was still under his spell.

Bernard, the first exponent in Europe of sensibility and "love" (that is, the inmost and most personal affections of the heart, of the inner core of the individual), was among the first Western Europeans to create that interior life which would henceforth so markedly distinguish Europeans from people of other cultures. This interior life was spacious enough to accommodate a full range of emotions, intellectual energies, spiritual experiments, trials and temptations; in such a richly mounted orchestra there were many voices to contest the theme. How simple, how uncomplicated seems at times what we know of the inner world of other civilizations compared with this sensitivity and clear differentiation of the various roles, this broad tonic scale, this bold spectrum. The ascents into Heaven and the descents into Hell of the European soul—journeys into its own inner depths—undertaken originally as part of the hard task of disciplining the "whole man", were later to become favourite material for the "confessions" of poets and novelists.

Bernard of Clairvaux, however, was not interested in creating literature; like St Augustine, his great predecessor and master, he knew the temptation only too well from his own experience: the "honey-tongued teacher of the Church", the *doctor mellifluous*, could very easily have allowed himself to be carried away on a stream of beautifully-turned eloquence. In order to subdue his own inclinations, Bernard fought against the seductive beauty of form, against sensuality and luxury wherever he found it: in the art of the Church and among the other Orders, in the lives of bishops and popes. Bernard of Clairvaux sought neither formal beauty nor power; but he used both, with that candid indulgence of his own inconsistencies that a genius always allows himself in order to carry out his proper work—in this case the formation and education of men.

Bernard had a passion for educating. He saw himself as the preceptor of popes and kings, of his own Order and of the other monastic congregations of his time, especially the newly-established Order of Templars, to whom he showed particular favour, and the young noblemen of Europe, whom he would have liked to sweep wholesale into his monasteries.

It was, indeed, during the twelfth century that youth made its first real appearance on the European stage, full of physical and mental curiosity, hungry to taste reality. Especially remarkable is the preponderance of youthful clerks, ready to work and learn, to explore the cosmos of mind and spirit: a *Sturm und Drang* of young men—very soon to be joined by young women—always eager to know more, to find out more, experience more, to love and even suffer more. For the first time large numbers of these "young people" (who might be any age, 12, 17 or even 40) were aroused to the depths of their being, depths as yet unclaimed either by conversion to Christianity or by folk culture; this stirring also made itself felt among the people at large.

Europe was awakening; and its intelligent young manhood roused itself to go in search of teachers, spiritual leaders, masters of the inner life, masters of the intellect, philosophers. The grim battle in which Bernard of Clairvaux overthrew Abelard can perhaps only be understood as the confrontation of one *eros* with another. The ultimate question for Bernard was who should command the allegiance of Europe's young manhood. Were they to fall victim to intellectualism, to the "shameless curiosity" (as he called it) of the man Abelard, who so boldly poked the defiling fingers of his intellect into everything tearing everything apart? Were they to belong to this man who did not shrink from reaching into the Holy of Holies, the untouchable heart of God, the Holy Trinity? To a man who stripped down the Trinity by logical analysis, like a shopkeeper peeling an onion?

"The son of a Jewish father and an Egyptian mother"; such was Hugh of St Victor's description of Abelard. Hugh, in general a level-headed and reputable thinker, had clearly sensed the racial difference between Abelard and himself, the son of a German nobleman. So long as the expression "racial difference" is taken in its natural meaning, undistorted by the prejudices of a diseased ideology, there is no harm in pointing out the two racial extremes represented by the two great adversaries, Bernard and Abelard. The Burgundian Bernard, tall and lean, blue-eyed and red-headed, proud, hot-tempered and magnanimous, corresponds very closely to a certain "Germanic" ruling type. Abelard, the small, dark-haired, sensitive Breton, himself acknowledged that he owed something of his personality to the nature of his country and his people. The Bretons were men of the sea, like the Greeks, who fondly gave it eighty different names. For such men mind and spirit were by nature volatile, agile, wayward and rebellious, blown like the sea a thousand different ways at the breath of *pneuma*, the wind of God. Abelard was to found for his Heloise a nunnery dedicated to the Holy Ghost under its Greek name, the Paraclete.

Peter Abelard began to teach on the Mont Saint Geneviève near Paris in 1113; a free-lance teacher, he drew an unprecedented crowd of students. They were soon to flock to him from all over Europe. Two generations later, when the universities had become further developed, such informality would have been impossible. Abelard was the successor of the itinerant teachers, "grammarians" and "dialecticians", who during the late eleventh and early twelfth centuries wandered from town to town and from country to country, setting up a "school" wherever it seemed propitious. They taught grammar, rhetoric and dialectics, subjects which formed an introduction to philosophical and logical thought, the required preliminaries for the study of theology. What was the attraction of this particular teacher, who made the student body of Europe hasten to his feet?

Many were drawn primarily by his professional skill, the audacity and elegance with which he handled logic and dialectics, using them with the delicacy of a scalpel to probe the confusions, obscurities and contradictions of the accepted and venerated "authorities", the Fathers of the Church, the Bible and the collections of Canon Law judgments. Others were fascinated by a mind critical of the contemporary intellectual and political scene. University teachers of the twelfth and thirteenth century, like their successors, very often remained aloof from the modern world: in all their weighty works there is practically no reference to the concrete problems troubling the men of their time. Abelard was different: he was planted firmly in the life of his age. His love-songs were sung in the streets of Paris, his sermons are full of direct references to the corruption of the Church, to the primitive superstition of the monasteries (Abelard was for a time abbot of an old Breton monastery), to the political gambles of ambitious prelates playing at power politics, and to the barely Christian conduct of the older aristocracy. Arnold of Brescia, the unfortunate revolutionary who attempted to "reform" and "democratize" Rome and the Church, anticipating Cola di Rienzo, was Abelard's direct disciple.

Such very unacademic conduct on the part of Abelard attracted the young intellectuals, always ready to listen to plain speaking, as much as it alarmed his colleagues at Paris and in cathedral schools elsewhere in northern France. In all seriousness, his critics asked whether Abelard could really be in earnest with his dialectical prevarications. They described his theology as "stultology" (a reproach thrown at him by Bernard), mere idle chatter puffed out with learning, but at bottom quite irresponsible, a talking to pieces of the mysteries of faith. The only conclusion to be drawn was that Abelard was at once the most adroit and the most dangerous corrupter of European youth.

This fear of corruption was the most serious motive uniting simple monks, reputable conservative theologians and men such as Bernard in their opposition to Abelard. We may well remind ourselves that Socrates was also accused of seducing the young to godlessness. This little man, Abelard, already compromised by his scandalous affair with the niece of an influential member of the Paris cathedral chapter, appeared to his adversaries an unmitigated scoundrel; he was a destructive intellectual, a wicked "progressive", who took pleasure in fuddling the wits of the students and destroying their faith; with his sophistries and conceit he gambled away the certainties of faith, which had seemed fixed for all time.

Abelard was not, of course, the ogre his detractors made him out to be. His irony and astringency concealed a delicate and sensitive spirit, wanting only to see things clearly. He aimed at pure knowledge and a purified faith. He could not see God as the Lord of Dread, *Rex Tremendae Majestatis*, menacing mankind with slavery; for him God was pure spirit, burning with the refining fire of the Holy Ghost. God as spirit gave himself to mankind in two precious gifts, reason and love. Abelard's importance for the history of his own and later centuries lies in three fields: philosophy and theology, ethics, and the education of a new type of man.

The much-persecuted Abelard, condemned by the Councils of Sens and Soissons, forbidden by the Pope (at the instigation of Bernard of Clairvaux) both to teach and to write, was one of the fathers of scholasticism, of the systematic use of reason in the discovery of truth. With the help of this method theology became a science; Thomas Aquinas and the academic philosophers of the later Middle Ages all rest on Abelard's shoulders. Abelard created his system as a development of the methods of Aristotle and of a few canonists of the period shortly before his own. Truth was to be sought and found by posing a rational question, answered by a much qualified yes and no, *sic et non*, and so, with the help of methodical doubt, the problem could be solved. A dispassionate, honest approach to a question was only possible if faith and knowledge were first (at least for the time being) kept clearly distinct. Faith, so easily confused by emotional excitement, should not be allowed to stand permanently in the path of reason; and reason for its part should not use the intellect as the means of solving the final mysteries of faith, which were inaccessible to reason. Bernard's attack on Abelard was by and large misdirected; it found its mark only in so far as Abelard did in fact try to show that a much wider and larger field was accessible to knowledge and man's rational capacities than the older theologians had dared admit. As for his attempt to prove the rationality of the Trinity, which aroused Bernard's special condemnation, Abelard was in line with a great tradition stretching from Anselm of Canterbury to the bold thinkers of the school of Chartres and to Richard of St Victor; it was, in fact, one of the main themes of the century.

Abelard's intentions were creative: he was a master builder of man's inner kingdom, for him primarily a kingdom of the mind. Access to this inner kingdom was greatly hindered by the impassive, "materialistic" bulk of medieval ethics and its system of penance, which saw guilt, sin and expiation as a legal transaction made with God: the sinner had to pay God the King a definite graduated fine for each sin, each breach of faith, just as a murderer had to pay a definite graduated fine for killing a nobleman, a clerk or an unfree peasant. The inner core of personality was barely touched by such rough and ready ethics. Abelard taught that everything depended on conscience and on the education of the conscience, or inner conversion: intention and not deeds was what mattered. Wealthy monasteries, attacked by Abelard on other grounds as well, were particularly sensitive on this point, since they received numerous rich benefactions from wealthy sinners of high rank, who made monastic endowments in expiation of their sins. If everything depended solely on an inward change of heart, where would be the point of these "good works"? Abelard had here stumbled on a wasp's nest, and he knew it. The need to follow up his critical work by practical action, through education, must have appeared all the more urgent.

This is the subject of his famous "correspondence" with Heloise, now abbess of the Paraclete. It is not certain whether this is a genuine correspondence between the woman he so deeply inspired and moulded and himself, her friend, lover and teacher; the whole "correspondence" may in fact have been written by Abelard. More important than this dispute over the roles of the correspondents is the content of the letters, whose magical influence was felt by Petrarch and by humanists and pious people during the fifteenth, sixteenth and seventeenth centuries, and is still alive today.

In these letters Abelard presented his monastic and masculine contemporaries, whose minds were obsessed with power, honour (in Heaven as well as on earth), war, violence, and "their right", with the idea that the type of the new Man was to be found in Woman: hers was a higher form of manhood, refined in soul and spirit, capable of conversing with God the Spirit in the inner kingdom of the soul on terms of intimate friendship. Abelard stressed the point that Christ's women disciples, his dear friends, his "apostlesses", stood closer to him than any of the men; it was to them that his resurrected body appeared in the joy of Easter Day. Abelard elevated Mary Magdalen, the patron saint of women sinners, above the militant saints of the feudal Middle Ages, and so initiated a Magdalen cult; this peculiarly feminine form of spiritual eroticism can be seen depicted in the full flower of early Italian Renaissance art in the Bargello at Florence.

Such ideas could not fail to startle and enrage the "monkish schoolmasters" for whom God was above all Man Incarnate, and to whom mind and thought were things not to be tampered with by impure womankind. The Penitentials and treatises on marriage of the twelfth and even the thirteenth centuries betray a deep-rooted hostility towards women. Abelard sought out the youth and the women of Europe, calling on them to think boldly and to dare to love with passion, as befitted new men.

All this certainly seemed to stamp him as a seducer of youth. Bernard of Clairvaux obtained permission from Bishop Stephen of Paris to preach against Abelard before the students of Paris, perhaps in Notre Dame itself. Abelard was not mentioned by name in this sermon, but everyone knew he was the target of the great preacher's attack on professors and their vainglorious arrogance: he does, indeed, single out one man as a "hydra of wickedness" under a semblance of piety, the impure seducer of an unsullied dove. Bernard had already been busy with letters addressed to bishops, cardinals, and to the Pope himself, in an attempt to have Abelard unmasked as the arch-heretic of the day. He castigated him as a monk without vocation, an abbot without office, who indulged in illicit relations with women. All this was a wicked calumny, but to Bernard it seemed self-evident truth: since only an evil-liver could teach falsehood, and Abelard was a false teacher. This is worth pausing over for a moment, for it is a perfect example, from the internal politics of the Church where the practice originated, of the way a denunciation builds up. A nonconformist in thought or belief is accused of "immoral living"; he is incapable of "pure", "sound" thought, because his habits are depraved, and therefore he must actually be immoral. And he must be immoral because his thoughts do not conform, which completes the vicious circle.

There can be no excuse for Bernard; what is more important and more just is to try to understand him. The Abbot of Clairvaux was convinced that Abelard was destroying his own lifework, the education of a new man inside his monasteries. The object in dispute was the youth of Europe. Bernard was filled with alarm at the thought of young intellectuals all the way from Paris to Rome, even the Pope himself, surrendering to the play of intellect, to mental "curiosity". His concern was serious, and not unjustified. Once the triumph of scholasticism, the theology of the universities, was assured, an abyss did in fact open up; on one side of it was Christian ethics, the nurture of the soul, on the other the study of theology. The theologians were cut off from the pastoral priests, and remained so for centuries. The theologian thinks about God and a thousand other things besides; as he thinks, spirit and life, God and man, draw further and further apart. Bernard saw in Abelard the victor of the future, the great traitor, responsible for intellectualizing and dechristianizing theology, the champion of the learning which would take the place of wisdom and piety. What he completely overlooked was that Abelard, although admittedly a pioneer, nevertheless stood at the centre of a great movement which even without him would have seized Europe's young manhood in its grip.

From the time Bernard preached against him in Paris, Abelard realized that this powerful churchman was determined to destroy him. He also knew that there was one battlefield on which he could expect to meet Bernard as an equal, indeed as a superior. This was a public disputation, in which the two parties met as antagonists, with an impartial judge to weigh and adjudicate on the value of their arguments. Disputations between theologians of different persuasions were quite commonly held at the courts of Arab princes and later at the Mongol court. They first became common in Western Europe in the twelfth century.

Abelard's friends persuaded the Archbishop of Sens to invite Bernard and Abelard to such a contest. Abelard accepted gladly; Bernard knew himself unequal to the challenge, and unknown to Abelard and the public he secured episcopal condemnation of his opponent in advance. On the Sunday after Whitsun in 1140 Abelard presented himself in the cathedral of St Stephen of Sens, before a congregation including the King of France and his retinue, professors, students, counts and high church dignitaries; when he sensed that he was facing a court, and a court that would pronounce against him, he appealed to the Pope and left the cathedral. It did not take long now for Bernard to achieve his aims, the condemnation of Abelard as a heretic, the excommunication of his adherents, Abelard's banishment to a monastery and the burning of his books. Pope Innocent II himself prepared the bonfire at St Peter's.

An earlier letter of Bernard's charged the Pope with the task of "eradicating" Abelard's heresy, and thus set on record his fateful belief that intellectual movements could be "liquidated". But Bernard's triumph was followed by Abelard's victory. Accepting his sentence in humility and silence, Abelard died in 1142 at a daughter house of Cluny, then under the rule of Peter the Venerable, an abbot of great magnanimity who treated Abelard with the highest respect and honour. Bernard could not shake off his guilt; in 1184 he was reprimanded by cardinals of the Roman Curia when he wanted to employ the same tactics against another courageous spirit, Gilbert de la Porrée, a friend of Abelard's. Many of the leading thinkers of the day were strongly influenced by Abelard; John of Salisbury, Otto of Freising, Pope Alexander III, Gratian, the founder of the new Canon Law, and Peter Lombard, Bishop of Paris and schoolman.

In a letter to Bernard written before the last act of the tragedy, Abelard suggests the great theme which was to dominate the intellectual summer of Western Europe once the storms of its present springtime were past: *diversa non adversa*. Minds are diverse and heterogeneous, each is of its own kind; but from this very diversity should rise a harmony in praise of God, and diversity should no longer imply enmity. It was in this spirit that the young intellects of the twelfth century sucked like bees (the comparison is a contemporary one) at the honey of antiquity, transmitted to them by the culture of Islamic Spain.

Chartres, and the intellectual activity of the great teachers, friends and scholars associated with its cathedral school, is perhaps the most luminous symbol of the intellectual movement of the twelfth century in all its pristine youthfulness and egregious audacity. Abelard himself may have studied mathematics there under Thierry.

The cathedral school was presided over by two of Abelard's Breton compatriots, the brothers Bernard and Thierry, and by Gilbert de la Porrée. The patron of the school was Godfrey, Bishop of Chartres, an aristocrat from an old Beauce family, a great statesman, a friend of Bernard of Clairvaux, and perhaps a pupil of Abelard. It was he who appointed the three great chancellors of the cathedral school, Bernard, Gilbert and Thierry. The tremendous intellectual influence of the school, which would long outlive the twelfth century, had already spread as far as Sicily and perhaps even into the Islamic world; Chartres itself was very much influenced by Islam. The radiant grandeur of the humanism of the school of Chartres is still there for all to see in the western façade of the cathedral, built during the time of Bishop Godfrey and perhaps the most beautiful of all medieval façades.

In a contemporary letter Thierry of Chartres is described as "probably the most important philosopher in the whole of Europe". The expression "Europe" is arresting; it is a long time since it was last heard. The concept of Europe as it was understood by the theorists of the Carolingian Empire had died out long before. The Popes started to talk of Europe again in connection with the Crusade. But this quotation introduces us to a new "Europe", the open Europe of the young intelligentsia, eager to take to themselves everything anyone had ever thought at any time concerning God, nature, the cosmos and mankind.

Intellectibilitas, a new word coined at Chartres by Clarenbald, reveals a guiding principle of the school: God, the cosmos, nature and mankind can be examined, reasoned about, comprehended and measured, in their proportions, number, weight and harmony. Clarenbald had another saying: "to theologize is to philosophize". Chartres' essentially Platonic philosophy turned theology into mathematics, geometry. Natural philosophers of the sixteenth to eighteenth centuries, until after the time of Leibnitz, continued to be fascinated by these twelfth century thinkers who found the fundamental principles of reality in the mystery of numbers, the mathematical structure of the cosmos. Thierry explained the Trinity by geometrical symbols, and expounded the nature of God's Son as a rectangle. These preoccupations seem somewhat trivial. They may have stemmed from an atavistic belief in the magical significance of numbers and geometrical figures, or perhaps have been influenced by the Cabala and by Neo-Platonist and Islamic speculation. The element of play cannot be doubted, but with it was combined, and this is more important, a sustained effort at understanding the cosmos in its mathematical structure and at establishing theology as the mother of all the sciences, as something to be established rationally, an art governed by strict logic.

Alain de Lille, a student of Chartres, introduced the logical concept of the axiom into theology, and tried to rethink theology as a logical system. Another student of Chartres, Nicholas of Amiens, dedicated his *Ars Fidei Catholicae* to Pope Clement III; "the catholic faith" (so-called for the first time, since it now had to be distinguished from so many other faiths) was a discipline which could be both taught and learned. Theology was the highest form of arithmetic; in Nicholas' hands it was also fitted into the pattern of Euclidean geometry. The aim was to construct a pellucid, rational theology, light and clear like the Gothic cathedrals, in which the number, light, music and architecture of the cosmos—all based on numerical relationships—showed forth the nature of the Godhead itself. We shall see later how close the relation was between the Gothic cathedrals and the conception of the world held by the philosophers of Chartres. Here it can only be briefly glanced at: and a brief mention must also suffice for some of the other, no less daring perspectives opened up by the men of Chartres.

For the first time in the history of Western European philosophy and poetry we find here the idea of "nature" as cosmic power, the goddess *Natura* (in Goethe's sense), radiant and beguiling, the demonic-divine mother of all things. The small band of scholars of the Chartres school who held this view illustrate the ambivalence of the twelfth century intellectual. Poets, natural philosophers, boldly speculative thinkers, they died as bishops and orthodox churchmen. Their thought, their work, the whole course of their lives would have been impossible even one or two generations later. In Italy and southern France in the sixteenth century men were burned for thinking much less dangerous thoughts than a Bernard Sylvestris or a William of Conches or an Alain de Lille, all members of the twelfth century circle at Chartres.

All the same, it should not be forgotten that the members of this small group, as bold as they were learned, were already past masters in the art of Nicodemism: that is to say, dangerous thoughts, dangerous allusions to topical ecclesiastical and political affairs, and above all to ideas hard or impossible to reconcile with the dogma of the Church or the maxims of the prevailing theology, were clothed in symbolical and allegorical forms and put into the mouths of classical poets.

Bernard Sylvestris, poet, philosopher, and author of a commentary on the Aeneid, composed his *De Mundi Universitate* ("Of the Universal Nature of the World") between 1145 and 1153. Ernst Robert Curtius, who knew the intellectual world of the Middle Ages better than most moderns, remarked with justice that in this work Christian ideas have been reduced to "a few ultimate essentials". Here we meet the goddess Natura as the eternally fruitful mother of all (as in the second part of Goethe's *Faust*). The *eros* of the cosmogony, the procreative power of the cosmos, is here celebrated under aspects and forms borrowed with little attempt at concealment from late antiquity. During the later Middle Ages, when his writings were incorporated into Vincent de Beauvais' encyclopedia *Speculum Majus*, Bernard's work achieved a wide circulation in circles keenly interested in intellectual speculation, for example at Avignon, Paris and Pavia and in England and Germany.

The *Anticlaudianus* of Alain de Lille (born *circa* 1128, died at Cîteaux in 1202) aroused and stimulated the imaginations of Renaissance and Baroque writers; Milton borrowed from it for his description of the Palace of Nature. Alain was a pupil of Bernard Sylvestris. In medieval times he was honoured with the title *doctor universalis*, after him bestowed only on Albertus Magnus. Alain de Lille, the author of polemics against Cathars, Albigensians, Waldensians, Jews and Muslims, was clearly aiming at domesticating the wayward intelligentsia of Western Europe within the bosom of the Church. It was just for this reason that he took pains to show that the vital forces animating mankind were lent to nature by God and that they remained his property. There is no denying that the education of the clerical intelligentsia was somewhat puritanical in tone, hostile to nature and took little heed of natural forces; this, together with the contemporary distaste for "filthy womanhood" and "filthy matter", had substantially contributed to making the burden of "sodomy" an occupational disease of the European intellectual. Alain devoted one of his principal works, *De Planctu Naturae* ("Complaint of Nature"), to this theme (sodomy at this period included all sexual abnormalities, but above all homosexuality). Alain enthroned *natura* in opposition to this pseudo-spirituality: let *natura* create a perfect man, "the youth", the new man, who shall live in harmony with the cosmos, and the Golden Age will return. Alain conceived his work as an "encyclopedia", a formative doctrine of "catholic" application for the instruction of all mankind. Christ played no part in the process he described. Alain held that *natura* was not concerned with theology, but that this was of no consequence; the teachings of *natura* and theology were not contrary but diverse, *non-adversa sed diversa*. We meet once again, in a remarkable application, the magic formula of the twelfth century.

At least a few candid admirers of the school of Chartres found on reflection that there was something disturbing about its cosmological, mathematical and "scientific" speculations. Alain de Lille himself, Peter of Celle, Peter of Blois and, not least, John of Salisbury, were all critical of the "excessive" study of mathematics and the "liberal arts" at Chartres. They saw there was a danger that such reckless intellectual experimenting with God, nature and the world would gradually swamp the essential heritage of the Christian faith.

Such criticism is most impressive when it comes from one who was himself educated at Chartres, whose writings contain affectionate sketches of some of its great teachers, and who died as its bishop: John of Salisbury, born about 1115 at Old Sarum, died at Chartres about 1180. In this man, probably of non-noble birth, "whose very smile was serious", twelfth century humanism found its most outstanding personification. In many ways he reminds us of Erasmus of Rotterdam, that great friend and mentor of later English humanism: an "Erasmian" born three and a half centuries too soon. John's striving for moderation, his dislike of tyranny and violence of any kind, his deep mistrust of big words and strong men, his sense of detachment and irony (*forte*, "perhaps", is one of his favourite words), and his passion for frank speaking, all link the great humanist of the twelfth century with Erasmus, the "prince of humanists".

John never became embittered, though there was much that was harsh and bitter in his life. After studying in France, he became the secretary and collaborator of Archbishop Theobald of Canterbury (✠1161) and his chief assistant in his relations with the Holy See. This was during the last difficult years of the reign of Stephen, a king who had little use for ecclesiastics and scholars. Between 1163 and 1170 John lived in exile in France, having taken the side of Thomas Becket. From France he watched with growing concern the conflicts between Alexander III and Frederick Barbarossa. John of Salisbury was a political humanist, anxious to bring about an *entente cordiale* between France, England and the papacy as a counter-measure to the *furor* of the Germans.

"Who made the Germans judges over the people of Christ?" It seemed to John that Reinald of Dassel, the ambitious chancellor of Frederick I, was aiming at world dominance and at making the Roman See an *Eigenkirche,* the proprietary church of his imperial master. John was the first political writer in the West to comment on the different level of culture already noticeable between the "civilized" urban humanism achieved in certain Anglo-French circles and the situation in Germany, where everything was much more archaic, "medieval" and primitive. In Germany the piety of the imperial bishops and people was politically directed. The imperial church was enormously rich, militant and powerful; in alliance with its imperial master, it served the Divine Majesty very much after its own fashion.

In numerous letters to his French and English friends John contrasts his own world with the "barbarism" of the German Empire; his world is one of inner freedom, the urbanity of the city (he is high in his praises of Paris), and of friendship so candid that one's dearest friend could be criticized in the service of truth (for example Alexander III). ". . . Every land is a fatherland for the strong in spirit. Where the spirit of God is, there is freedom." With a complete absence of self-pity, John declares his attachment to the wisdom of Socrates and the Gospels: a man free in spirit must pay for his freedom, with poverty, persecution, and sometimes, as in his own case, with a lifetime spent in exile.

John, the student of Abelard and of the school of Chartres, is the first great thinker to stand for a specifically Western brand of humanism. A modern English edition of the parts of *Polycraticus* in which he sets out his political ideas is entitled simply *The Statesman's Book,* and with good reason. Completed in 1159, the book is dedicated to Thomas Becket, at that time still Chancellor to Henry II. As in his other writings which criticize and chronicle contemporary events,

John is here conducting a war on two fronts. First, there was the "Eastern front" against the presumptuousness and violence of aristocratic rule, intent on maintaining its own "law" by force. This was the reason why he feared the Germans so much, since he saw how their methods were also becoming adopted in the West, each success of Hohenstaufen policy having a magnetic attraction as something to be imitated. But he also saw a way of life developing at the Angevin court of Henry II which he found just as disquieting: a court society of excessive refinement, strangling itself in luxury, subtle scheming, cruelty and arrogance, where character was debased and even an honest man turned into a prattling coxcomb and a hypocrite. In place of all this John pleads for a kingdom founded on justice, a kingdom where free speech and a free Church would be protected by a prince who recognized himself as the servant of the common good. "He is himself in his fullness bound to God, in a large part to his country, in a considerable part to his kindred and closest servants, very little, yet somewhat, to foreigners". John is here anticipating an "enlightened" national monarchy of the kind conceived by Sir Thomas More, having as its last resort against tyranny the permitted sanction of tyrannicide. The name of this quiet, personally reticent man was in later generations frequently invoked as an early champion of the right of rebellion.

John, fully confident that intellect was a tool given to man by God as an instrument of enquiry, recognized Aristotle as the chief of philosophers, though this did not prevent him on occasion from criticizing even "the master of those who know", as Dante was to call him. This free, unprejudiced attitude towards even the greatest authorities of the past is typical of the "open" century. John has preserved for us the famous saying of Bernard of Chartres: "We are like dwarfs set on the shoulders of giants, from which we can see more and further things than they, not so much because of the keenness of our own sight or the magnitude of our own stature, but because we are sustained and raised up by their gigantic greatness."

The "dwarfs" of the twelfth century certainly did all they could to "see more and further things": at Chartres and at Cluny, where Abbot Peter took in Abelard, men were interested in the Koran and in Islam generally. Throughout Western Europe people's attention was turning towards the East. The immense energy put into translation in the twelfth century, and the Aristotelian renaissance, will be discussed in connection with scholasticism and university life in the thirteenth and fourteenth centuries. The same applies to the rise of Canon Law studies and to historical writing and the theology of history, all of which were already beginning to be important in the twelfth century. In passing it may be said that there was a contrast between the "scientific" history, based on documents, typical of the Norman and Anglo-French regions, and the idea of history as a theological and philosophical subject, found in Germany and Italy. Otto of Freising, uncle of the Emperor Frederick I, Cistercian monk and imperial bishop, who was the most important historical thinker of the twelfth century, had a foot in both the "scientific" and the "philosophical" camps.

Rupert of Deutz gives us a first taste of the historical philosophy of German writers at this period; with Anselm of Havelberg it has become much further developed, and with Hildegard of Bingen, who is mentioned briefly by John of Salisbury, it has blossomed into a cosmology. It is evident that intellectual life in the Empire proper long remained apart from that of the West, and was slow to accept the new ideas developing there. In the lands between Cologne, the Rhine and the Danube, between Hamburg, Bremen and Vienna, old traditions for the most part still endured; here was retained the traditional picture of the world and the traditional piety inherited from the Carolingian era. Here there was still unity, indivisibility, while in the West the early schoolmen were already drawing sharp lines of distinction between God, nature and man, between the Church as a clerical institution and secular government. In these specifically German regions, a strong feeling for archaic ways and a correspondingly passionate attachment to the idea that God, man, nature, beasts and things all worked together within a strong framework of law, fought a rearguard action prolonged over several centuries. Here, at the height of the twelfth century, the Germanic epic poetry of the migration period was immortalized in the full momentum of its pre-Christian grandeur. Here Gothic, the latest innovation in art of the new Western world, was known as the "French style" and adopted only in the mid-thirteenth century, or in some places as late as the fourteenth and fifteenth centuries.

In the relaxed, liberal atmosphere characteristic of the West in the twelfth century the important writers could mingle their philosophical interests and theological speculations with the making of Latin verse in conformity with classical rules (the *ars poetica*), and with satirical comment on the contemporary scene. The wandering scholars, the *vagantes*, dared to touch themes and talk openly of subjects which only a little later would be forbidden topics for professors and theologians, even for poets. In such a world Marbod of Rennes (1035–1123) found himself at home. Saluted as the new Ovid, Marbod was the author both of love lyrics addressed to highly-born ladies and of sacred and didactic poetry; he died bishop of Rennes. The schoolmaster Hildebert of Lavardin (1056–1133), who died archbishop of Tours, was perhaps the purest exponent of classical Latin poetry of his time, and as such left his imprint on the whole century. His verses were on everyone's lips; he was the author of satires, very worldly in tone, and of liturgical sequences and elegies. Especially poignant and exquisite are his laments over the ruins of the *urbs beata*, the heavenly and earthly Rome. Hildebert was himself overwhelmed with love-songs addressed to him by ardent admirers, who included the Empress Matilda and Adela of Blois, precursors of the cultivated women who would dominate the courtly society of the new age.

As a standard example of the "vagabond" intellectual we may take Hugo Primas (*circa* 1095–1160), "Hugh of Orleans", who was teaching grammar in Paris about 1142, a kind of *poète maudit*, a poet of the taverns, singing away his love and life and sorrow in wine, woman and song. When he speaks of the world and its rulers and potentates his tone becomes bitter and caustic. Scholars have long tried to identify Hugo Primas with the "Archpoet", the protégé of the imperial chancellor Rainald of Dassel, a down-at-heel devil, like so many of the long line of European writers who shared his situation. In his famous *confessio* the Archpoet sounds a theme to be taken up again and again, and sung to death, by Villon, Bellman, Christian Günther, Rimbaud, Mallarmé and the rest: drink the heady draught of life to the full, down to the bitterest dregs.

Today we would find the satire of this twelfth century "journalism" distinctly bitter on the tongue. It flourished in England, in the Low Countries, in France, and above all in western Germany. The *Carmina Burana* and other contemporary collections of songs, the writings of Walter Mapes and Walter Chatillon and of quite a few more kindred spirits, revolve incessantly in a familiar treadmill of complaints against feudal bishops and church dignitaries, against gluttonous monks and uneducated clergy, against cruel barons. Much of this was admittedly the expression of a momentary mood of personal resentment; but it was also the far from negligible reflection of widespread responsible opinion, which found its spokesmen in a class of people who were not an "estate" and had no chance of becoming one. These *vagantes*, goliards, wandering poets, were all to disappear, condemned by the Church at several councils between 1127 and 1239. Their place was taken by the minstrels, the *jongleurs,* and by the troubadours and *trouvères* of the thirteenth century, who often surpassed them in acerbity and in the deadly precision of their aim.

In twelfth century England, where the vein of contemporary satire was particularly rich—it runs deep even in the work of John of Salisbury—Nigellus Wireker, the great satirist from Canterbury (1130–1207?) produced his *Mirror of Dwarfs*, written between 1170 and 1187, an attack on monastic decadence and clerical and episcopal abuse. At Ghent, the wealthy city rising to become a centre of urban and economic development in north-western Europe, the German schoolmaster Nivard produced his *Ysengrimus*, a satirical poem in seven books, written some time in the middle of the century. This serious, independent-minded man from the Rhineland had felt the magic of France and its civilization without being seduced by it. Isegrimm (Ysengrimus), the wolf, stands for a greedy and uncouth type of monk. This work is unique as a great satire on the monasticism of the age; as the highest example of medieval animal allegory its influence continued to be felt for centuries, and can be traced in the vehement and melodramatic tone of the invectives employed by the humanists and reformers of the sixteenth century. As satire, it is remarkable for the seriousness and objectivity of the picture it presents of the sensuality, secularization and abuses which afflicted the church of the time.

CHAPTER 6

THE CRUSADES AND THE CONFLICT OF EAST AND WEST

THE friction between the West and Byzantium, in which the Crusades played their specific part, was the medieval equivalent of the modern conflict between East and West. The Byzantines thought that the Crusades were purely aggressive in intention, their sole purpose the plunder and conquest of Constantinople and the rich lands of the Byzantine Empire.

During the late eleventh century the Eastern Empire was being raided by new enemies, Turkish tribesmen from central Asia, and in 1091 the Emperor Alexius I requested the help of Pope Urban II. Alexius probably anticipated nothing more than the despatch of a few contingents of mercenaries; what he got, in 1096, was the First Crusade. From that time onward, throughout the whole of the twelfth and until well into the thirteenth century, successive waves of crusading armies continued to arrive from the West. We usually speak of five "official" Crusades: the First, starting in 1096, the Second in 1146, the Third in 1189, the Fourth in 1204 and the Fifth in 1217. But in between there was a continuous trickle into the Holy Land of smaller armies and other groups; some were led by magnates, lay or clerical, others by hermits or even, in two instances, by children. The Byzantines gave full rein to their resentment of the Crusaders, and their attitude of uncompromising hostility has left its mark to this day on their successors in the Balkans and Russia and on the Eastern Church.

The position of the peoples of Eastern Europe was one of especial delicacy, since they were continually being pulled from one side to the other in the tug of war between Byzantium and the West; in consequence they developed an ambivalent culture, perilously poised between the two. Those most affected were the Western Slavs, the Poles, the Czechs, the Slovaks, the Croats and the Slovenes. Even during its years of political decline, when it was menaced both from the West and by the Turks, Byzantium could still fertilize the culture developing so richly among the Balkan peoples.

An important source of the singular lack of sympathy between the Crusaders and the Byzantines is to be found in their divergent views of war. True to the Greek genius of its Fathers, the Eastern Church did not recognize any war as "holy"; a Christian should fight with the "weapons of Christ", his only battles should be spiritual. The various underground nonconformist sects which were active throughout the Byzantine Empire, reaching the Balkans and Western Europe in the twelfth century, took much the same view. The West was following another path. The first Pope to wage war in person in the name of the Church was the German Leo IX (who reigned between 1049 and 1054), son of a Count of Egisheim. His adversaries were the Normans, shortly to become the spearhead of the Crusaders' attack on the East. They captured Leo in 1053, so the "first crusade" had an unhappy ending. By 1096, the habit, now several centuries old, of using political means to further religious ends had become so well-established in the West that the Pauline metaphor of "fighting for Christ" could be interpreted as militant knight-service. In the eleventh century we find a great increase in liturgical prayers for victory, and the earliest records of sword-blessing, which was the first step towards the knight's solemn dedication. This did for the knight what coronation by the Church did for the monarch; the knight was now expected to live by the ethical and religious standards formerly required only from the ruler, and to assume the ancient and royal obligations of protecting the poor and weak, including women. The knight set forth under the banner of Christ, war-leader and king, to wrest the "land of His birthright" from the infidels; if he fell, he had his reward in Heaven; if he conquered he won renown, an estate on earth and the Kingdom of Heaven besides.

This was the time when the reformed papacy, strengthened from within by the Cluniac movement, was seeking to unite Europe under its own leadership. The idea was that instead of rending themselves and each other in their perpetual feuds, the nobility of Western Europe should join forces in pursuit of a common aim, the conquest of the Holy Land. It was of great assistance to the papal plan that the Normans, from their centuries of raiding and brigandage, were already well acquainted with the wealth of Constantinople, and hankering after the capture of the "richest city of the world". Henry VI (1190–1197), Barbarossa's son, and from 1184 heir apparent of the Normans in Sicily, actually laid plans for the systematic conquest of Byzantium. A contemporary, Archbishop Eustathios, has left us a thoroughly jaundiced account of the conquest of Salonika (Thessalonika) by the Sicilians in 1185. There is no point in detailing the incessant demands made by "Crusaders" on the Byzantine Emperors: Alexius III (1195–1203), for example, was forced to levy a "German tax" (the *Alamanikon*) on all the provinces to meet their heavy demands for tribute. But what cannot be passed over are the shrill protests of Anna Comnena, imperial princess and chronicler, who in the early twelfth century voiced virtually all the reproaches to be levelled against the West in the future: the Franks (the collective name given to all Western Christians) were primitive, uncultured, bellicose and predatory, in fact barbarians, beneath comparison with the intelligence and refinement of the Byzantine and Islamic worlds. Their Christianity was superstitious and wrong-headed, riddled with heresies. The whole West was one gigantic apostasy from Christ and genuine culture. In Byzantium, as a reaction against the military superiority of the Western enemy, there evolved the myth of the "corrupt West" and the whole aura and actuality of the cold war. Missionary and propaganda teams were systematically despatched by the Eastern Church to the Balkans, Egypt and the Near East, who united with Byzantine diplomats in preaching the iniquity of the West: "the West stands for war and exploitation, it is incurably tainted by its Roman roots; Rome—West Rome—is Babylon, the mother of all wickedness".

With the capture of Constantinople in 1204, during the Fourth Crusade, a turning-point was reached. On the level of ecclesiastical politics the separation of the Eastern and Western Churches had become complete in 1054; but it was only now that it became an established fact for the ordinary people in the Eastern Church. It created an unbridgeable chasm, which the negotiations for reunion with Rome initiated by several Byzantine Emperors only made steadily wider. The history of this separation is worth describing briefly, since it has a bearing on the division of Europe up to the present time.

The twenty-eighth Canon of the Council of Chalcedon

1

Medieval Europe abounded in castles; Germany alone had over 10,000, most of them now vanished. A thirteenth-century defence tower at Bingen on the Rhine

2 and 3

The lord's fortified dwelling was protection and security to all whom it sheltered against Vikings, Saracens and other enemies: *(above)* the castle of Münzenberg and *(below)* Marienwerder, Germany

4

In Italy the aristocracy tended to live an urban life, erecting their dwellings in towns such as San Gimignano, Tuscany

5

As life became more settled the nobility concentrated on the splendours and comforts of their houses: the banqueting hall at Penshurst Place, Kent

6

A mounted knight on a capital at Gropina, Tuscany: originally the horse was a sign of aristocratic dominance on account of the greater mobility and power which it conferred

7

A life of constant activity, in the saddle, in conflict, in feuding, in hunting, developed forceful personalities such as Ekkehard and his wife Uta, from the choir, Naumburg Cathedral, Germany

8 and 9

In fourteenth-century England the memorial brass of Sir John and
Lady de Creke shows a more stylish, sophisticated physiognomy
(above left). Armorial bearings and heraldic emblems first came
into use in the twelfth century: *(above right)* a German nobleman's
pendant *c.* 1240

10

Though primitive and uncom-
fortable, castles were often
richly decorated with the proud
emblems of nobles and barons:
the lions of the Hohenstaufen at
Hohkönigsburg, Alsace

FVGA VER

11 and 12

War was the chief preoccupation, whether for knights in the saddle,
armed with long shields, spears and coats of chain mail *(above)* or
for foot soldiers assaulting a castle with axes, bows and catapults
(right)

HIC MILITES WILLELMI

ED NES

nouaf nouenunf capta est danuera sine defrasi-
one absq; numulus. Violenta expilatione. ut soli
silio tex uictoria attribuatur. Et aun capetens atu
enis inaulis regis hibilems. n stur aulus mote solu. Tpl
anoz aggredi. si confulus antugens ipsa astria cenebat
sic. Epo icaq; dux milites iph danueram ingressi: pla

Turrf danude

apta igitur aunneta. missaone castri duprox-
sunt explozandaret ab uiri ualle in sieto sic ele
 menu in naulis p paruum slumen quod tap
uns apellatur. ut de castellulis: t uisso uicinali
a querctur. t sic jacouum diligenti explozauem
sum ali appropinquasset ab castrum queslam de

Cu
Dan

Burdens of the Common People

There were degrees of independence and serfdom among European peasantry, but for all it was a hard way of life: a German serf from Mainz Cathedral

14 and 15

Trials of the people in wartime: Normans set fire to a house from which a mother and her child are trying to escape *(right)*. Even in peacetime justice was rough: *(below)* the suffering subjects of King John, sketched by the historian Matthew Paris

16

The cruel face of a medieval executioner, from a stained-glass window at Esslingen, Germany

17

Tillers of the soil such as this Tuscany ploughman at Spoleto, *c.* 1240, were accustomed to accept the land's cycles of hunger and plenty

18

The Bayeux Tapestry shows the first known example of a horse used for harrowing, while a labourer broadcasts seeds by hand

19 and 20

Life on the land had a regular repetitive pattern: *(right)* in autumn pigs were killed; in spring the oxen were led out to plough. *(Below)* French peasants harvesting grapes

21

The battle of life reflected in the battle between God-the-King and Satan-the-King: in a twelfth-century English miniature Christ the mighty Warrior defends the City of God with his spear, aided by the Holy Trinity

22

In the twelfth century Christ was portrayed as the supreme king, with crown and majesty: a Danish crucifix, *c.* 1140

23

Medieval popular religion was concerned with justice; the portals of the great Gothic cathedrals, with their portrayals of the Last Judgment, still testify to this function of the House of God: Notre Dame Cathedral, Paris

(451) had declared that there was complete equality between the bishops of Rome and Constantinople, conceding the Pope a merely nominal and honorary precedence. The "oecumenical patriarch" in Constantinople (the name is used in letters from the sixth century, on seals after 1054 and regularly as a title in subscriptions to documents from the second half of the twelfth century) saw himself as representing the Greek genius of Christianity, the elder brother to his junior, the Pope in Rome. Under increasing pressure from the Turks, the Comneni and Palaeologi Emperors who ruled in the East between the thirteenth and fifteenth centuries tried hard to bring about a union with the Roman Church, as the price of armed assistance from the West; a few Emperors actually went over to Roman Catholicism, but their plans foundered when Rome proved deficient in the necessary aid and the Eastern people obdurate in their resistance to the change. Thus, about 1246, the Emperor John III Ducas Vatatzes minted a bronze coin showing on the reverse St Peter and the keys, and the papal and western dream of achieving supremacy over the East seemed on the verge of fulfilment. Lengthy and inconclusive negotiations were set in train between John and Pope Innocent IV. At the Council of Lyons in 1274—a high-water mark of papal supremacy in the Middle Ages—Byzantine envoys swore assent to the doctrines of Rome and to the papal supremacy in the name of their Emperor, Michael VIII, who hoped for Roman help in freeing himself from the encircling tactics of Charles of Anjou, the heir of the Normans in this and other respects. There was intense opposition in Constantinople to union on these terms. The whole idea reached its final absurdity when a new Pope, Martin IV, a puppet of the powerful Angevin, excommunicated the Byzantine Emperor. Michael retaliated by engineering the "Silican Vespers" of 1282 (when the entire French population of Sicily was massacred) and this struck his enemy's means of attack from his hand.

Nearly a century later, in 1369, the Emperor John V and his immediate followers became converts to Roman Catholicism; the masses and the clergy, however, still persisted in their implacable hatred of the Latins. Despite his conversion, John V did not receive the hoped-for military aid from the West; instead, on his return journey from Rome, he was ignominiously imprisoned for ten months in Venice as a debtor, reaching home disillusioned and empty-handed. This was the fate of all "traitors" who trusted the "corrupt West".

There is, of course, another side to this medal. Maria Theresa, the great eighteenth century Hapsburg Empress, speaks with revulsion of "*graeca fides*", an allusion to the notorious diplomatic duplicity of the Greeks (i.e. the Byzantines) which she recognized in their Russian heirs. In the fifteenth century, pressure from the Turks induced still further negotiations for a union. At the Council of Ferrara and Florence (1438), the Roman dream again seemed in sight of fulfilment. But in 1453 Constantinople fell, and with it the East Roman Empire, which had survived for a thousand years as the most prodigious example of the staying-power of classical institutions and culture. No crusade could save it. In the last years before the fall of the holy city of Constantine, the Emperor-Apostle, Byzantine leaders hardened in their conviction that even the Turkish turban was preferable to the Latin mitre.

All the Crusades have to be considered in the context of Rome's catholic but fruitless ambition to subjugate East Rome and the Eastern Church to the Papacy, which would have led to spiritual supremacy over Eastern Europe and Russia. The only means of bringing Eastern Europe, Russia and the Near East into Western Europe was by way of Constantinople, a fact as obvious to the diplomats of the Curia in the twelfth century as it was in the nineteenth.

But relations between Eastern and Western Christendom were not exclusively conducted on the tragically harsh and always fruitless footing of war and power politics. From quite early in the Middle Ages there was a wide field open to peaceable and friendly contacts; they achieved their benign effects in various ways, cultural, spiritual, religious, in fact through whatever civilizing agencies were at hand. First and foremost there was the great city of Constantinople, a most potent magnet in its attraction for large numbers of pilgrims from the West. The ornate magnificence of the superior and ancient culture they witnessed there deeply impressed the Latins. Equally impressive was the level of hospital organization. The Pantokrator monastery, which was the mausoleum of the imperial dynasty, was also a large hospital staffed by highly-trained physicians. Such organization far exceeded anything in the West.

In the wealthy and hospitable city of Constantinople official disputations like those held at Muslim courts were staged between Eastern and Western clerics. A debate of particular importance for the West was held at St Sophia and St Eirene in 1136 between Archbishop Nicetas and the historian-philosopher Anselm of Havelberg, a German imperial bishop and envoy. On his return journey from East to West Anselm formulated his new theory of world history, which he saw as continual progress under the inspiration of the Holy Spirit. Nicholas of Cues was to make the same journey three hundred years later, and, deeply moved at having felt the impact of two worlds, he prophesied the future unity of all peoples and religions, the dawning of a new age of world peace.

Constantinople was a city with many faces, particularly to Westerners. This was the Virgin's city *par excellence*, and as such was of peculiar significance to the West, where, stimulated by the Crusades and the development of Gothic, the cult of the Virgin was steadily growing. Constantinople has also justly been described as the "medieval Versailles", providing the model for all other emperors, kings and princes, the pattern for the conduct of court life and politics throughout the West. The Byzantine imperial crown was the model not only for that of the German Empire but also the Norman monarchy even while the Norman kings were plotting to attack Byzantium itself. Mention may here be made of one of the features of the subtle political and cultural propaganda used by Byzantine diplomacy throughout Eastern Europe, and as far as Mongolia: crowns and imperial ladies were despatched as "honoraria", gratifying tokens of esteem and useful in the cementing of political alliances. The lower hoop of the existing sacred crown of Hungary, St Stephen's crown, is in fact the famous Ducas crown presented to the wife of King Geza I, a niece of the Emperor Nicephorus III Botaneiates. Piroska, a daughter of St Ladislaus of Hungary, who came to Constantinople as the bride of the Emperor John II Comnenus, taking the name Irene, founded the famous Pantokrator monastery; a mosaic portrait of her with her husband can still be seen in the gallery of St Sophia, where the Crusaders must also have seen it.

During the tenth century the steady flow of cultural influence spreading westward from Constantinople increased. It can be seen most clearly—indeed it is literally visible, even tangible—in the arts: in illuminated manuscripts, in miniatures, on a larger scale in murals and even in architecture. Moreover, Byzantium retained a few bulwarks in the West, strong sources of spiritual and intellectual influence, and of some importance in ecclesiastical politics:

southern Italy, Naples and Sicily were still within the cultural jurisdiction of the East, and the Greek monasteries there were solid bridgeheads of Eastern influence. Monte Cassino and Grottaferrate (where the liturgy is still sung in Greek, following the Byzantine rite) also belonged to the Byzantine monastic world of the Apulian and Calabrian houses. From the eleventh century, Greek southern Italy was in rebellion against Rome, an attitude which at Naples became traditional; it characterized the university in the thirteenth century and the Panormite Academy in the sixteenth, and survived in the "emancipated" libertarian Naples which gave refuge to Benedetto Croce in the twentieth. The winds of the Holy Spirit blew constantly through these southern Greek monasteries, and produced a superabundant crop of religious and religious-political prophecies: the collapse of the West, the destruction of West Rome and the coming reign of the Holy Spirit (the third millennium) were all being predicted from the early thirteenth century onwards.

The closer contacts established in the Crusading era made a broad channel for the westward flow of the rich wares of Byzantine fable and romance: the flood-gates of oriental fantasy were now opened to pour out over Western Europe. The Buddha made his first appearance in the West in Byzantine dress, alongside the heroes of classical and oriental romances. The Bodhisattva Sakyamuni, an incarnation of the Buddha, appears in the Byzantine romance-legend *Barlaam and Josaphat* under the name Joasaph, having previously figured first as Budasef and then as Judasef in the course of the legend's journey from India through Arabia, Georgia and Greece; a final metamorphosis in the West produced the heroic St Josafat of our period, who has a church dedicated to him in Palermo (a city with a Greek tradition!) and attracted veneration in Spain, Portugal and Provence, and later also in Poland, Rumania, England and Scandinavia. The hunger for truth and substance, for holy things, made the West a ready market for the treasures of Indian, Arab and classical romance; Byzantium acted as the broker.

It is now time to consider in more detail what effect this wider range of vision had on the formation of Western Europe. How were Western attitudes altered by the new perspectives opened up by the Crusades?

The Crusades have for a long time been considered a peculiarly characteristic phenomenon of the European Middle

Ages. This is a just description, so long as we know what we mean by it. Taking a wide view, it may be said that Europe in the high Middle Ages achieved a co-existence of opposite and conflicting elements and that this is evident in every department of life; the Crusades confirm, in the most obvious way and with a wealth of disparate manifestations, the fact of this co-existence, which seems to later generations as improbable as it is amazing. In every Crusade, and as often as not in the individual Crusader, there was a variety of conflicting motives connected with religion, economics, politics and class. Uppermost was faith, strong, sincere, solemn and naïve, in which politics and religion were mingled: by the light of faith the Crusade was in essence a pilgrimage to Jerusalem, a journey undertaken as a penance (the eleventh and twelfth century chroniclers do not speak of "Crusades" but of the "Jerusalem journey", the "journey to the Holy Sepulchre", the "pilgrimage to Jerusalem"). Penance was to be done for the sinfulness of a life corrupted by the wicked world, for killings and robberies; but there was longing too, longing to see the land which was the "ancient birthright" of God's son and, simply, there to die. Some were inspired by the desire to take home for themselves or their families relics and other such beneficent objects as were to be found in the Holy Land.

But peace of mind was only to be won through tribulation and war. The war was against the infidels, at first described as "God-hating dogs" (as were also any unpleasant neighbours in the West, Irish, Scots, Germans and Slavs, for example), though they were soon to be recognized, with serious wonderment, as "noble pagans". The Popes decreed indulgences for Crusaders; anyone who took up the Cross cast off all the burdens of his harsh terrestrial existence and could meet death freely and cheerfully, secure in the promise of eternal life. This was what brought the landless flocking to the East, chiefly the landless nobility, and also ordinary people escaping from the oppression of their masters. The élite among them, their leaders, were the nobility of the Norman kingdoms and northern France, intent on booty, which they indeed acquired in their Near Eastern *outremer*: castles, principalities and wealth.

Medieval religion was so complex that the Crusades could make their impact at many different levels. Even cynical and ruthless businessmen such as the traders and import and export merchants of Genoa and Venice, who made the biggest fortunes of their day out of the Crusades, were impelled by motives they themselves regarded as religious; they were as quick to seize on relics as on other treasures. The mentality of the Crusaders is in fact a striking expression of the whole range of Christian faith in the Middle Ages; material, even materialistic motives, such as the Crusader's quest for honours and estates, were not infrequently closely interwoven with others which in another age would be described as purely religious and idealistic.

An instance of how intimately and strongly the various motives—religious, social, political and economic—could become entangled can be seen in the dramatic history of the Military Orders which sprang up in the Holy Land. Starting as small aristocratic brotherhoods caring for pilgrims and the sick, they soon became powerful organizations. Their financial operations, which were on a gigantic scale (the Templars' especially), their wilful practice of power politics (sometimes in alliance with Islamic leaders), and the cheerful arrogance of their members, all combined to give them a double-edged reputation: if they were respected, admired and renowned, they were also feared, hated and envied. The first of these Orders was the Templars (founded about 1120 by a French knight); then came the Knights of St John, or the Hospitallers (they started to flourish in the mid-twelfth century, based on earlier foundations) and the Teutonic Knights (confirmed by Papal Bull in 1199). The Spanish Military Orders of Calatrava, Alcăntara and St James of Compostela, and later on Montjoie and Evora, are a special case, since the king reserved for himself the office of Grand Master and used the Orders to extend his rule.

The Military Orders were renowned for their medical care, their chivalry, their charitable works, and, as combatants, for their bravery in fighting to the bitter end; but against this must be set the record of their grand and petty political intrigues, their odious personal quarrels, and the collective egoism of these military corporations which turned them into competitive rather than co-operative brotherhoods, with no compunction about the betrayal of a brother of a different cloth and allegiance. The growth of these characteristics in that alien country was rapid; by the second generation the members of the Orders had often become so very much acclimatized in dress, manners and customs (both good and bad) that they struck newcomers from Europe as half-pagan at the very least. The power and wealth of the Templars were the cause of their tragic downfall; their extinction by the French king just after 1300 marks the end of the Crusading era.

How strong in numbers were the Crusading armies? The figures given by contemporary sources are products of the imagination. Moreover, the armies were always accompanied by non-combatants such as clerics and women. Knights sometimes took their wives and children with them (as in the case of Baldwin of Boulogne), and the wives had their own retinues. The camp-followers were almost an army in themselves. The ratio of mounted men to foot was probably about one in seven. For the siege of Jerusalem in the First Crusade there may have been from 1,200 to 1,300 cavalry out of a total strength of 12,000. The great lords, such as the kings and nobles of Western Europe (France, England and Normandy), each brought about 500–1,000 mounted knights; in the First Crusade the combined armies amounted to about 4,500 cavalry and 30,000 infantry. Later, the number of active combatants was often very much smaller.

From the beginning the Crusades were characterized by individual deeds of heroism, by great sacrifices and suffering, by hunger, disease and want. There were many who did not even survive the long outward journey, by land over the Balkans for Crusaders from Germany and Flanders, by sea for the English and French. There were heavy losses of material possessions and of men's lives. Heroic zeal and readiness to face death (as extolled in the *Song of Roland*) were at an early date yoke-fellows of a zest for atrocities and disaster. Consider for example the Crusaders' lust for blood as it was displayed at the capture of Jerusalem in the First Crusade. Western sources claim the slaughter of 10,000 Muslims; Arab sources put the figure at 100,000, including women and children. The impact of this on the Arab world was appalling. The Muslims had been as unprepared mentally for the Crusades as were the Byzantines, and it was only now, in reaction, that they learned to hate the Latin West, and to call the Franks "Christian dogs".

An Arabic poet, Mosaffer Allah Werdis, expressed his pain and bitterness:

We have mingled our blood and our tears.
None of us remains who has strength enough to beat
off these oppressors.
The sight of our weapons only brings sorrow to us

who must weep while the swords of war spark off
the all-consuming flames.

Ah, sons of Muhammed, what battles still await you,
how many heroic heads must lie under the horses'
feet!

Yet all your longing is only for an old age lapped
in safety and well-being, for a sweet smiling life,
like the flowers of the field.

Oh that so much blood had to flow, that so many
women were left with nothing save their bare hands
to protect their modesty!

Amid the fearful clashing swords and lances, the faces
of the children grow white with horror.

He continues with a call to resistance and to battle.

The blood-bath of the First Crusade was followed by the
debacle of the Second. Bernard of Clairvaux, its instigator
and spiritual leader, although accused of it, refused to accept the blame for this catastrophe; the real guilt lay, he
felt, with the sins of Christendom. In 1191, during the Third
Crusade, Crusaders quarrelled openly with each other, the
Germans with the French, the French with the Italians and
English, the English with the Germans. There was rivalry
between the Crusaders and the "native" Latin knights, who
already belonged more to the East than the West. Atrocities
continued. Because negotiations with Saladin dragged on too
long, Richard Coeur de Lion ordered the massacre of two
to three thousand Muslim prisoners. The entrails of the
corpses were searched for hidden gold, which had been
swallowed by the prisoners, and the bodies burned so that
the ashes might be sifted for it. Horrified at this atrocity,
the Islamic world became ineradicably suspicious of the
West. The Third Crusade did not succeed in recapturing
Jerusalem, despite an appalling loss of life in the attempt.
The casualties were put at half a million, and even a tenth
of this figure (which is probably too high) would represent
a fearful drain on the strength of Western Christendom,
whose resources in manpower were already small enough.

The Fourth Crusade brought the capture and sack of
Constantinople in 1204. More works of art and cultural
treasures were destroyed on this occasion than at any other
time throughout the Middle Ages, not excepting the Turkish
conquest of 1453. Villehardouin, an eyewitness, reported that
it was impossible to estimate the amount of gold, silver,

precious stones, silver vessels, silks, furs and rich clothing taken in the sack. After individuals had had their pick, there was so much booty left over that each Crusader could be assigned a share according to a fixed scale; for every foot-soldier's portion there were two for the priests and mounted sergeants and four for the knights.

It was this Crusade which set an unbridgeable gulf between Eastern and Western Christendom. The Fourth Crusade also gave the medieval Papacy the first premonition of its impending decline. Innocent III, the "strongest" medieval Pope, had entirely lost control of this, his "own" Crusade.

The atrocities and the disasters, the immeasurable suffering, the apparently meaningless sacrifices which accompanied the Crusades, all cast a heavy shadow over the West. But against these more sombre tones must be set the lyric poetry they inspired. These songs, quite impossible to translate into any modern idiom, gravely echo, with bell-like resonance and purity, the inner feelings of the many ordinary men who devoted everything they had to the Crusade, and either died during it, or, if they returned, brought back nothing but a great longing stilled at last—or a longing unassuaged, an incurable wound in the heart. The songs of German poets such as Heinrich von Morungen, Hartmann von Aue, Friedrich von Hausen and Walther von der Vogelweide, for example, are an unforgettable expression of all the varied emotional experiences of the simple crusading knight. He is shown taking melancholy leave of his home and family, in anxiety and hope, in renewed confidence in God, conscious of doing a duty, in fear of death, and longing for the Kingdom of Heaven. In the Crusading lyrics hearts and voices spoke freely. This was the "springtime of the *Minnesang*", when popular consciousness was first finding expression in vernacular song. It was to the great upheavals of the Crusades, with all their attendant dangers which were early and painfully recognized, that the earliest Minnesinger owed some of their noblest themes.

Faith at its purest and most innocent was inherent in one of the most horrifying and disastrous episodes of the whole epoch, the Children's Crusades. The magnates put their trust in the sword: a Christian used the sword to fight for the Kingdom of God. But in the twelfth century there were signs of a spiritual awakening, particularly among women and children, in which St Francis and some of the religious sects were also to play their part. The Cross took on a different complexion and became the sign in which love alone, and not force, could conquer. After a century of catastrophe, massacre, and continual defeat, the Crusading idea took on a new form in the hearts of simple people and of children, who dared to hope that where force had failed the power of naked love might yet succeed.

There is no discoverable connection between the two Children's Crusades, which started in the same year, 1212, one in the Rhineland, the other in the Loire valley. A ten-year-old boy, Nicholas, preached the Children's Crusade in Cologne and is said to have recruited about twenty thousand children. When they reached Italy, many of the girls were thrust into brothels and others taken into service as maid-servants. The Bishop of Brindisi tried to restrain them from crossing the sea. Innocent III, however, was deeply affected, and although he released the girls from their Crusading vows, left the boys to earn their own release when they should be of age. Those who did carry on with the journey were sold in the East as slaves. A remnant returned, ill-used and disillusioned. In France, a boy called Stephen from a village near Vendôme is alleged to have collected together about thirty thousand children. At Marseilles they fell into the hands of crooks and were sent to Alexandria to be sold as slaves; two ships foundered on the way.

The Children's Crusades should not be regarded merely as an episode, but as an echo of the deep-seated unrest which was disturbing the conscience of the masses. Innocent III, generally accounted one of the shrewdest and most ruthless political realists of his time, is supposed to have said: "These children put us to shame; whilst we are slumbering, they set forth gaily." Above all, the miracles associated with Stephen's Crusade (animals, birds, fishes and butterflies are said to have joined it) point forward to two other figures. St Francis and St Joan of Arc were borne on the stream of the same religious tradition, welling up from the same hidden depths. The Pastorelli movement of 1251 and 1320 shows how readily the sparks of this religious enthusiasm could be re-kindled over the centuries. The girl from Domrémy, Joan of Arc, the Maid of Orleans, was asked during her judicial examination, "Is it true that you and your banner go into battle in a cloud of butterflies?" Butterflies, anciently reputed to be the bearers of the soul (a belief already met with among the Egyptians), also fluttered about the heads of Stephen and the youthful Francis of Assisi. The naïve and young needed their butterflies if they were to rise above the bitter realities of the day.

The earliest Crusades and all the numerous small expeditions running parallel with them had led to heavy losses for minimal returns, doubtless due to the independent and headstrong leadership of the greater and lesser lords of the West European nobility. The mid-twelfth century saw Europe swept by recurrent moods of antagonism towards the Crusades. Before the century was out the Papacy had undertaken responsibility for their recruitment, organization and direction. This had important consequences for the internal development of Western Europe.

The building up of such an enormous financial organization made the Roman Curia the greatest monetary power in Europe. The collection of the Crusading taxes and the traffic in indulgences introduced a commercial element into the administration of the Church, which confirmed the people of Western Europe in their old aversion to Rome. Three things gave rise to particular indignation: the abuse of the power to absolve Crusading vows or to commute them (it was possible to buy oneself out of the obligation to crusade in person); the application of the Crusading taxes to other purposes; and the dishonest acquisition of revenues out of these taxes by rulers who were only sham Crusaders. The Curia was very often the dupe of such transactions. King Henry III of England and King Haakon IV of Norway are the classic examples of rulers adept in converting Crusading taxes to the benefit of their own pockets.

Recruitment to the Crusade, in which papal emissaries played their part, was made the occasion of religious-political propaganda aimed at the masses. Everything was there, atrocity stories, over-simplification, lies, inflammatory propaganda; it was small wonder that the masses often sought immediate relief from tension in pogroms against the Jews and in riots against foreigners, classing them all indiscriminately as enemies or heretics. The effect of this propaganda on behalf of the Crusades, much of which came from the preaching of the friars of the new Mendicant Orders, was heightened by the fact that it coincided with a change in the direction of the Crusading movement itself, which started in the mid-twelfth century and was completed by the beginning of the thirteenth. Crusades no longer set forth only for the Holy Land; they were launched as well against internal enemies, chiefly the Slavs of the German East

(Wendish Crusade, 1147), the Moors in Spain, and heretics (starting in 1179). The Albigensian Crusade (1209–1228) and the Crusade against the Stedinger peasants in North Germany led directly to the secularization of the Crusading ideal and its perversion for political ends which was to characterize the movement for the rest of the Middle Ages. In the first half of the thirteenth century the Popes were conducting Crusades whose purpose was the destruction of their bitter enemy, the house of Hohenstaufen. From that time on it became fashionable to launch a "Crusade" against one's most detested political opponents. The tradition was a long time dying; even in the time of Henry VIII and Elizabeth I attempts were made to restore England to its Roman obedience by means of a Crusade.

The canonists, the "crown lawyers" of the Curia, made a particularly fateful contribution by setting the seal of legitimacy on the gathering excesses of Crusading ideology and practice. The more the European laity hardened in their resistance to this degraded version of the Crusading ideal, an affront to conscience and intellect alike, the more uncompromising became the maxims of the papal jurists. They were labouring to fulfil the disagreeable task imposed on lawyers in every generation, that of finding justification for any war, and if possible of proving it "holy". Hostiensis, perhaps the most important canonist of the thirteenth century, taught that the Crusade of the Church against "infidels" was always a "just war"; it was a "Roman war", since the Church's war on paganism was a continuation of Rome's war on barbarism: "and Rome is the head and mother of our faith". It was the duty of Christians to "attack and overthrow the Saracens, since they acknowledge the sovereignty neither of the Church nor of the Roman Empire". The fourteenth century canonists further elaborated the point: the Pope was the unique legitimate heir of the Roman Empire, and had therefore inherited the obligation to fight its wars.

From the time of the Fourth Lateran Council (1215), the internal Crusade against "heretics" and other enemies of the Roman Church came to occupy an important place in the legal thinking of the canonists. Hostiensis is again typical: "Although public opinion looks favourably on the Crusade overseas—*crux marina*—nevertheless to anyone who judges according to reason and common sense the Crusade on the home front—*crux cismarina*—seems more just and more rational." In terms of consolidating its authority, the Church had much more to gain from Crusades at home than from Crusades in the torrid, stony wastelands of *outremer*.

The increasing incidence of *commutationes* reflects this development. *Commutatio* was a device by which a Crusader's oath could be "converted"; someone who had vowed to go to the Holy Land could have his vow changed and go Crusading instead in France, Spain or Prussia. The French and Spanish kings and the nobility of northern Germany made extensive use of this opportunity, which had a sound legal foundation. The canonists were particularly strenuous in their efforts to prove that the Pope had the right to lead crusading armies against the Roman Empire: that is, against the Hohenstaufen Emperors, particularly Frederick II. This, as opponents pointed out, in effect meant leading an army against himself; the two heads of the Holy Christian Empire were in tragic conflict, each fighting to subdue the other.

The ill-success which attended the crusading movement, and its diversion from its proper aim, unleashed a powerful reaction throughout Western Europe; waves of criticism, derision, indignation and impiety swept England, France, Germany, and Italy. In Germany the collapse of the Second Crusade had already aroused some sharp criticism. In France the tide of criticism reached its peak in a widespread revulsion provoked by the catastrophe of St Louis' Crusade, in which the leader's faith—the purest faith any Crusader ever brought to the enterprise—and the flower of French chivalry were alike put to shame. Blanche, the queen mother, a woman as able as she was cautious, had in vain tried to restrain her son from the Crusade, pleading that there were more important matters to attend to in France. As Regent of France during Louis' absence Blanche forbade all her subjects, under pain of confiscation of their estates, to join in the papal crusade of Innocent IV against Conrad of Hohenstaufen. St Louis himself had indignantly refused to crusade against Frederick II. Open criticism of papal crusading policy was common at this time. In Germany anyone taking the Cross at Regensburg was killed, and the Cathedral Chapter of Passau preached a little "crusade" against the papal legate who had come on a recruiting mission.

In France there even grew up a kind of "counter-crusade", supported at times by the queen, the towns and broad masses of the people: Jacob, the "Master from Hungary", called on the poor and lowly to go with him to the Holy Land.

These *pastorelli* were firmly anti-clerical and hostile toward knights, monks and priests. The poets of southern France described Crusaders as fools, criminals and madmen. Guillem Figueira protested that Rome had inflicted little damage on Saracens but had massacred scores of Greeks and Latins. Even after the elimination of the Albigensians, southern France was very receptive soil for remarks of this kind. The Cathars and a few other smaller nonconformist religious movements professed a religious pacifism reminiscent of the Greek Fathers of the Church: quite simply, a Christian was not allowed to take part in wars of any kind. The "left wing" of the popular religious movement of the twelfth and thirteenth centuries thus introduced the idea of religious pacifism which was to be carried further by the "Spiritual" Franciscans; it was to reappear in Wyclif's circle and from thence branch out into a dozen different rivulets leading to the pacifism of the Baptists and the Quakers.

We may recall that the great canon lawyer Hostiensis taught that the Crusade was in accord with reason. This was the voice of papal reason, the reason of the Curia at the height of its power. Another voice, the voice of bourgeois reason, speaks to us from an imaginary argument between a stay-at-home knight and a Crusader, written by Rutebuef, the great French poet of the people:

Am I to leave my wife and children, all my goods and inheritance, to go and conquer a foreign land which will give me nothing in return? I can worship God just as well in Paris as in Jerusalem. One doesn't have to cross the sea to get to Paradise. Those rich lords and prelates who have grabbed for themselves all the treasure on earth may well need to go on Crusade. But I live at peace with my neighbours, I am not bored with them yet and so I have no desire to go looking for a war at the other end of the world. If you like heroic deeds, you can go along and cover yourself with glory: tell the Sultan from me that if he feels like attacking me I know very well how to defend myself. But so long as he leaves me alone, I shall not bother my head about him. All you people, great and small, who go on pilgrimage to the Promised Land, ought to become very holy there: so how does it happen that the ones who come back are mostly bandits? If it were just a question of crossing a stream I would readily jump over—I might even wade through it. But the waters between here and Acre are broad and deep. God is everywhere: to you He may only be in Jerusalem, but to me He is here in France as well.

God in France, in Italy, in England, in Germany, in the heart and mind of every simple Christian: the crusading era coincided with the rise of the nations and of the vernacular languages, the awakening of an individualism founded on religious belief, and of an intellectual movement intensely critical in temper, all of which had violent repercussions on the crusading movement, which by about 1260–70 had completely lost its original form. From 1264 observance of the Feast of Corpus Christi had been made obligatory in Roman Christendom. Pope Urban IV commissioned Thomas Aquinas, the leading light of the new theology, to collect and compose appropriate liturgical texts and hymns. This festival, and the procession which was an essential part of it, proclaimed that Jerusalem was to be found in every township in the West. The people took a special delight in seeing the Host exhibited and the practice of elevating the Host began during this period. In every Host Christ was present. So too, was the Heavenly Jerusalem present in every Church, above all in every Gothic cathedral.

As Rutebuef's knight remarked, "the waters between here and Acre are broad and deep". On the other side of the water, under the burning Syrian sun, the small "Frankish" crusading states had achieved a remarkable coexistence with the Islamic world which endured for two centuries. The importance of this for the course of Europe's internal development has often been overlooked, as has also the eight-centuries-long coexistence of Muslims, Jews and Christians in medieval Spain.

Christians and heathens at Acre were not divided.
All the pilgrim might could not bring their brotherhood to
    nought.

This affirmation of the German poet Freidank (from his didactic poem *Bescheidenheit*) is echoed by a Frenchman, Fulcher of Chartres:

We who were once Westerners are now Easterners, a
Roman or a Frenchman in this country becomes a

Galilean or a Palestinian, a native of Rheims or Chartres
has become a native of Tyre or Antioch. For we have
forgotten the lands of our birth. To most of us they
have become territories unknown, or places never heard
mentioned any more. A man may possess here his own
houses and families and dependent tenants just as though
he had received and inherited them from his fathers;
another may have taken to himself a wife, not a
compatriot, but a Syrian or Armenian, or even a
baptized Saracen, and live together with all his wife's
clan. . . . He who was once a stranger has become a
native, the immigrant has become an inhabitant.

In the Frankish kingdoms of Jerusalem (1099–1185) and
Acre (1189–1291) the Western knights very quickly adopted
the customs of the country and entered to a considerable
extent into friendly and chivalrous relations with the neighbouring Muslim aristocracy. Barons and emirs entertained
each other with tournaments and exchanged gifts; they
praised each others' chivalrous behaviour in battle and war
was regarded as a feud between knights as it was in the
West. In such an atmosphere the two religions could live
side by side on almost friendly terms. Ricoldus de Monte
Crucius, writing in the mid-thirteenth century, praised the
fervour of the life of prayer he found in the Islamic
monasteries where he, a Western Christian, had been so
hospitably received; and above all, he praised them for their
charity and magnanimity. Such direct experience of the
"noble infidel" made a profound and indelible impression
on the West; it played an important role in the poetry of
the greatest of the German courtly epic poets, Wolfram von
Eschenbach, and became increasingly powerful with the
passage of time. Oliverus Scholasticus relates how the Sultan
al-Malik-al-Kamil supplied a defeated Frankish army with
food: "Who could doubt that such goodness, friendship and
charity came from God? Men whose parents, sons and
daughters, brothers and sisters had died in agony at our
hands, whose lands we took, whom we drove naked from their
homes, revived us with their own food when we were
dying of hunger, and showered us with kindness even while
we were in their power." Arnold of Lübeck puts the following words into the mouth of a Muslim: "It is certain, even
if our beliefs are different, that we have the same Creator
and Father, and that we must then be brothers, not ac-

cording to our confession but as men. Let us then remember our common Father and feed our brothers."

The Franks in the northern territories could not help knowing that in these parts Christians, Syrian Christians, had for centuries held high and honourable positions at the courts of the Caliphs and the Muslim princes as physicians, scribes, astronomers, interpreters and officials. The two religions which in the West were regarded as hostile by nature in the East, where the actual fighting took place, lived together in a certain degree of harmony. Some places of worship were used by both religions. At Acre the great mosque had been converted into a church, but a side-chapel was left free for Muslim worship. The major part of another mosque of the same city, the mosque at the Oxen's Well, was reserved for Muslims, but there was also a Christian altar. Muslims and Christians alike made pilgrimages to an image of the Virgin at the Saidanaja monastery at Damascus. As in many places in North Africa today, the prevailing atmosphere was such that even in the thick of the battlefields there were Christian monasteries and hermitages which were well known as sanctuaries for people of both religions. It could happen that Muslims would hand over to the Christians a man who had dishonoured the Cross and that a Christian bishop would concern himself about the fate of a large company of Muslim children captured in war and about to be sold into slavery.

The Emperor Frederick II who, after his excommunication by the Pope, carried on his Crusade by peaceful means, amazed his Arab friends by declaring Jerusalem a city of three religions, Jewish, Muslim and Christian. Under the peace he concluded as King of Jerusalem with the Sultan al-Malik-al-Kamil in 1229, the Holy Places of the city were divided between the two faiths: the Christians had the Holy Sepulchre, the Muslims the mosque of Omar, and both sections were kept open to pilgrims.

Each side had a profound respect for the other. The Emir Fakhr-ed-Din, sent by the Sultan of Egypt as his envoy, was as enthusiastic an admirer of Western culture as Frederick was of Eastern. From an early date many of the Frankish barons and bishops became bilingual, for example William of Tyre, Humphrey of Toron and Rainald of Sidon. The Templars were famed and respected for their amicable relations with their Islamic compeers. Personal contact between Frankish knights and Turco-Arab emirs could lead to genuine friendships, as for example between Fulk of Anjou, King of Jerusalem and the Regent of Damascus, and between Richard Coeur de Lion and the brother of Saladin, which imprinted themselves deeply on the memory of the West; their resplendent image has been immortalized in courtly epic poetry.

It is appropriate to conclude this chapter by considering a matter which is both part and parcel of the whole East-West conflict and the Crusades and at the same time extends far beyond them: the question of toleration in the Middle Ages. The fact that toleration can be discussed at all in connection with the Middle Ages is striking enough; it underlines the magnitude of the metamorphosis which transformed the "open" Middle Ages of the expansive twelfth century into the increasingly narrow and constricted later Middle Ages.

Toleration implied toleration of pagans and heretics, of men of different faiths living within or on the fringes of a Christian society. As with many other matters, the traditional teaching about toleration inherited from the Early Church was conflicting and ambiguous in the extreme. Great minds such as Origen and the majority of the Greek Fathers had completely rejected the idea of using force against pagans and "heretics", in which they were supported in the West by Tertullian, Lactantius and Salvian. They also favoured toleration in the case of individuals, as did Hilary, Ambrose, Augustine, and in fact all the great authorities of early Christian theology. It became an acknowledged maxim that no violence might be perpetrated on a man's conscience: "a man could believe only of his own free will".

But the case was very different when the Church was in conflict with "heretics" as a group—a "counter-Church"— and when heresy became treason, as it did from the time of Constantine's recognition of Christianity as the official religion of the Empire. One convert, Firmicus Maternus, displaying the zeal typical of the newly converted, demanded that the Emperor should take drastic measures to destroy pagan cults and root out unbelievers by confiscating their property and putting them to death: "even though it should be your brother, your son or the wife of your bosom". This was the beginning of the medieval and early modern practice of "liquidating" people of different beliefs, from which the political parties of modern times derived the methods and ideas of their own theory and practice of extermination.

Augustine, whose great authority dominated medieval

Christianity, changed his mind about toleration, with disastrous effect. Originally he was opposed to any coercion; but in his conflict with the Donatists of North Africa he publicized a maxim which was to remain current for a thousand years: "compel them to come in". The Donatists countered this with an argument which also had a long future, and which was invoked regularly by persecuted nonconformists from the twelfth century onwards: "the true Church is the one which is persecuted, not the one which persecutes."

Alcuin, the leading theologian at the court of Charlemagne, sharply criticized the great Emperor for his conversion of the Saxons at the point of the sword in the Saxon wars of the late eighth and early ninth centuries: Alcuin was a native of the British Isles, and his opinions may well be a remnant of the tradition of freedom associated with the "Celtic" Church. In the eleventh century Bishop Wazo of Liège attacked the brutal treatment of heretics in France. In the twelfth century the two great traditions of tolerance and intolerance came into direct conflict; in the thirteenth century, the age of scholasticism, of academic learning and of the exclusive Church as conceived by the canonists and the papal world politicians, intolerance triumphed, an intolerance as harsh in theory as in practice. Thomas Aquinas urged the severest punishment for heretics, and also for *relapsi*, back-sliders, on the grounds that heresy was an evil so infectious that its practitioners must be eradicated as thoroughly as possible. This argument overlooked, amongst other things, the fact that the "disease" was only spread still further by persecution, to become all the more virulent as the lower classes of the population became infected. One interesting consequence of the victory of the Western Church over the Eastern (in any case an illusory victory) was the way the more magnanimous Greek Fathers were now reinterpreted in the West: Thomas Aquinas alleged that St John Chrysostom had demanded that Arius be condemned to death, and that this was the origin of the death penalty for heretics!

In the "open" twelfth century there was a broad range of opposing intellectual and spiritual viewpoints to be accommodated. Christian philosophy and theology were forced to pay attention to three main groups; Jews, heretics and Muslims. For the first time there was serious consideration of the possibility of a plural society: could men of different faiths live together in a single state and society? This problem was complicated on the one hand by the tradition of persecution already described, and on the other by the fact that Judaism, Islam and Christianity, three very closely related faiths, were highly intolerant on points of dogma. So the question at issue was primarily the secondary one of whether intolerance about dogma necessarily demanded actual intolerance towards individual "unbelievers". Many subsidiary questions were bound up with this main issue: for example, whether it was permissible for one faith to recognize features of positive value in another, and what attitude and methods should be adopted by one faith in its conflict with another.

"There are Jews everywhere." The words are those of a thirteenth century chronicler, but they express summarily a problem recognized throughout the twelfth century. Rupert of Deutz, Bernard of Clairvaux, Peter the Venerable, Abelard, and many others had all discussed whether Jews should be tolerated in Christian society. Their answer was affirmative: Christ was of Jewish blood, the Jews would be saved at the end of the world, and therefore they should be spared. Bernard of Clairvaux, in a letter to Henry, Archbishop of Mainz, sternly condemned a monk named Radulf who had called for a persecution of the Jews in connection with the Crusade. For this was the liberal, open-minded Europe of the twelfth century. Gilbert Crispin (✝ 1117), Abbot of Westminster, reporting a disputation between himself and an educated Jew from Mainz, who had come to England on business, says that the discussion was conducted with the utmost courtesy. There are records of similar discussions from Spain, France and Italy. In the thirteenth century public disputations between Christian theologians and Jews were forbidden (as at Paris in 1208, at Trier in 1223 and by Pope Gregory IX in 1232); but medieval society, which took such pleasure in colloquies and arguments, was not to be cured of the habit so easily. Further disputations took place under royal patronage, at Paris in 1240 in the presence of Louis IX and at Barcelona in 1262 in the presence of James I of Aragon. Nevertheless, one notices a change of atmosphere. Candid speaking and discussion were being replaced by a chorus of abuse in which the Jews were castigated as a "depraved and perverse race". It was this later medieval attitude, together with a mass of vindictive sermonizing against the "damned race", that was bequeathed to later generations. Pope John XXIII only recently, at Easter 1958, ordered the deletion of the old references to the "perfidious" Jews from the prayers for Good Friday.

Although a measure of toleration towards Jews and "pagans", above all Muslims, was thus allowed by Western theologians and other authoritative writers it was infinitely more difficult for them to tolerate "heretics". Tolerating heretics set orthodox Christianity the impossible task of leaping its own shadow, a feat which even Luther, Calvin and their successors dared not attempt. The very idea was grossly repugnant to the mental and spiritual temper of the times. How could any man call himself a Christian and repudiate the Church? How could anyone who declared that the Church and the whole of Christendom were in error still remain a Christian? The intransigence of the theologians only increased as more and more people showed their sympathy with such heterodox teachings. The judgment of the theologians remained unbending: heretics must be annihilated, heresy deserved the death penalty. Starting from Bernard of Clairvaux, the canonists of the later twelfth and the thirteenth centuries wove their web of damnation ever more thickly. There were few Christian thinkers who dared to recall St Paul's great saying "heresies there must be". Peter Lombard, an important and temperate leader of twelfth century scholasticism who became Bishop of Paris, was one who was bold enough to draw his own conclusion from the Pauline text: "we need heretics, not because of their teaching but because they stimulate us as Catholics in our search for truth and for a proper understanding of everything in the world." Abelard, who championed the rights of an erring conscience, basing himself on St Paul, to some extent tempered the harshness of the contemporary view of heretics: people so afflicted had their rights too, and tender consciences should not be wounded, even if their owners were guilty of error. Abelard was the founder of a theological school of thought which upheld the right of an erring conscience throughout the twelfth and thirteenth centuries, and to which even Albert the Great and Thomas Aquinas partially subscribed. But in practice victory lay with the Augustinian tradition, with the intense fervour of the conservative Franciscans. Through the writings of Alexander of Hales and Bonaventura, this tradition became integrated into canon law studies and the practices of the Inquisition: there was to be no liberty for erring consciences, a heretic must either be converted or liquidated. They were to be liquidated "by the sword, by fire, by the militant learning of the new universities" (to quote the charter of the University of Toulouse, founded in 1229 to help pacify the defeated and heretical southern regions of France).

Our view of the Middle Ages would be entirely false if we allowed these harsh and exclusive doctrines to blind us to the contradictory picture presented by the colourful reality of life as it was lived. In practice there was both coexistence and toleration. In many of the towns of the western Mediterranean seaboard, in Spain, Italy and France, men of the three "fraternal religions" lived and worked side by side in peaceful co-operation. Jews, Christians and "infidels" were brought together in the ordinary course of business and by intellectual curiosity. In the Italian cities of the twelfth and early thirteenth centuries it was tacitly accepted that highly respected noblemen and women were "heretics"; indeed, in Italy at this time *nobile* was synonymous with "heretic". Ordinary people, in the day-to-day circumstances of ordinary life, were practising coexistence with "deadly enemies" long before, often centuries before, theologians and ideologists swallowed their scruples and their pride sufficiently to provide the intellectual basis for the religious toleration which the common people had already instinctively adopted.

In the twelfth century toleration was thus a matter of practical experience; but it was also something more. Among two groups of people, liberally-minded scholars with scientific leanings and devout laymen with a good share of common sense, toleration was a thought-out principle. We must again mention Chartres, which set the tone of Europe's intellectual awakening and expansiveness in the twelfth century. A Tierry of Chartres, a Bernard Sylvestris, a Herman of Carinthia (closely connected with Chartres) stood for that unprejudiced, objective, scientific mode of thought which looks first at the quality of a man's mind before passing judgment. They have had their successors in the small groups of "pure" scientists, bold enough to be tolerant, who have emerged from time to time in European society, for example the men of the early Royal Society (Europe's first scientific society) in the seventeenth century, and the international élite of atomic scientists of our own day. In the twelfth century there were Englishmen who travelled the world in search of a learning more liberal and cultivated than any they could find in the narrow confines of their native Christendom. Adelard of Bath journeyed in Spain and the Near East, Daniel Morley went to the "wiser masters of the world" at Toledo and brought back his library of Greek and Arab books. Under stress of provocation from the monks of his Breton abbey, Abelard had already voiced a plaint which would be echoed over the centuries by men for whom Europe had become too narrow: he would gladly forsake Christendom, he said, and take refuge with the heathens, amongst whom it might be possible to live a devout Christian life in peace. Heathens were after all much nicer people. The sentiment recurs: later generations were to find Indian and Chinese "pagans" equally attractive.

Next to these frank intellectuals were those aristocratic, knightly laymen who never lost sight of the humanity of their opponents, even in the heat of battle. Two outstanding examples must suffice. The Spanish epic, *Cantar de Mio Cid* (composed between 1140 and 1160), relates the heroic deeds of the Cid, the Spanish national hero of the *Reconquista*, a knight of the eleventh century. Based on the day-to-day narrative of one of the Cid's companions, the poem tells its tale with innocent candour and an air of veracity. It describes the Cid's exquisite courtesy in his dealings with the Moorish nobility, his gentle treatment of them and readiness to come to terms (he himself had spent many years in their service). Thus, for example, after taking a castle he would entrust it on his departure to the defeated Moors; and the Moors gave him their blessing as he left.

It is significant that Wolfram of Eschenbach, the greatest epic poet of the German Middle Ages and the creator of the German *Parzival*, should make a woman speak in impassioned defence of toleration in daily life, as he does in *Willehalm*. Gyburg, herself of heathen descent, is seeking to reconcile her pagan (i.e. Saracen) and Christian kinsmen; her argument turns on God's power to save men who are outside the Church. Pagans and Christians are equally invested with natural virtue; purity of heart is pleasing to the Creator and is independent of the waters of baptism. The "pure heart" of an aristocrat of the soul is more important than the colour of a man's skin or creed. To Wolfram, who was familiar with the situation in southern France and Spain, toleration meant the personal spirituality of a man mature and noble in spirit: toleration cut straight through the contemporary battle-lines to unite Christians, pagans, Jews, even heretics (called by Wolfram "publicans", tax-gatherers, a name often given to the Cathars).

Wolfram described an experience commonly met with by

Crusaders, particularly those who founded dynasties in the Near East: they came face to face with the "noble heathen". It was the general practice among the Islamic states to allow Christians to follow their own religion undisturbed. Islam felt itself under no obligation to save the souls of men of other faiths. Christians were not to be converted, merely prevented from molesting Muslims.

The appearance of the Mongols on the stage of world history opened up new perspectives for Western Europe, for the Crusaders and for the Christian East. Genghis Khan founded his Universal Mongol Empire in 1206; in 1258 the Mongols overwhelmingly defeated the Caliph of Bagdad and the last representative of the Abassid dynasty, for five centuries the leaders of orthodox Islam, was put to death. Once Western Europe recovered from the shock of the Mongol onslaught (1223–41), many political and ecclesiastical leaders realized that two unique opportunities had come their way: the chance of converting Asia to Christianity and the chance of defeating the Muslims, Turk and Arab, by means of a pincer movement, since the Mongols would be able to overwhelm Islamic positions from the East.

Throughout the late thirteenth and fourteenth centuries the West continued to be tantalized by the vision of a world empire governed by the Roman Church, dominated by Latin culture and under the protection of the Mongol rulers; the Popes, the kings of France, even the Byzantine Emperors (at one point an imperial princess was sent to be the bride of a Mongol ruler) all felt the attraction of this idea which also found a following in some monastic and crusading circles. The vision was never realized, but some discoveries were made. Western envoys to the Mongol Empire were astonished at the amicable atmosphere which prevailed at the centre of this world empire, based on universal toleration and the coexistence of the great religions. At the very moment when so many lights were being extinguished in Western Europe and the free discussion of religious beliefs in public seemed in danger, the East was discovering the potentialities of toleration.

Originally most of the Mongols had been Shamanists; but in the Mongol Empire Buddhists, Taoists, Confucianists, Muslims, Manichees, Jews, Nestorians, Catholics and numerous other sects all lived peaceably side by side. Each Church had its own statutes and its own jurisdiction. Genghis Khan's personal inclination was towards Taoism, and he hopefully expected a Taoist master to provide him with the elixir of eternal life. Many of his soldiers, his generals, his writers, and even the members of his own family (notably his favourite daughter-in-law) were Christians, members of the Nestorian Christian Church which had preserved its independence of both Rome and Byzantium despite all the turmoils which beset the East during the first Christian millennium.

Under Genghis Khan's successors the Nestorians became predominant at the Mongol court and the Nestorian patriarch of Bagdad founded an archbishopric at Peking. The great Khan Mangu, grandson and successor at second remove of Genghis Khan, son of a Nestorian princess and husband of two Nestorian wives, explained to the Franciscan William of Rubruck that he practised with equal fervour all the religions permitted at his court. Another Mongol prince admitted that since he did not know which of them was the true religion, it seemed sensible to cultivate them all. Rubruck had been sent to visit the Great Khan by St Louis in 1253, and his journey took him from Constantinople right across Asia; he was amazed to meet Nestorian Christians, very well-informed about European affairs, all along his route. On May 30, 1254, at Karakorum, in the presence of the Great Khan, he held a public debate in which the other participants were Nestorians and Muslims, whom as theists he quickly recognized as his allies, and Buddhist monks, whom he took to be atheists. The Flemish Franciscan found a miniature European community at the court of the Mongol ruler in the Altai mountains. There were men who had been captured in Hungary, a Lotharingian woman from Metz married to a Russian master-builder, a Parisian goldsmith (he was married to a "Saracen" from Hungary), whose brother still had a business on the Grand Pont in Paris, and the Hungarian-born son of an Englishman.

Another Franciscan, Giovanni de Pian-Carpino, the envoy of Innocent IV to the Golden Horde, had already brought back reports of the astounding tolerance prevailing at the court of Genghis Khan's grandson, Güyük Khan (1246). Western envoys were much struck at meeting European Christians at the Mongol courts who made no secret of the fact that they were Western heretics fleeing from persecution; one such, for example, had been a physician in Lombardy.

By the mid-thirteenth century, when Armenia, Russia and the Mongol lands were already receiving these outcasts from the West, Popes and Western kings were seeking the

Mongols as political allies against the Turks and the Arabs. The Mongols on their side demanded that the Western rulers should become vassals of the Great Khan, since "there is but one God in Heaven and one ruler on earth, Genghis Khan, the son of God". The Mongols had as sure a grasp as anyone in the West of the ancient ideal of unity: one God, one Empire, one King-Emperor, one Faith, one Church.

Italian traders made their first appearance in the markets of the Far East in the time of Kublai Khan. Among them were Nicolo and Maffeo Polo, who visited Kublai Khan at Peking in 1266; he sent a message by them to the Pope asking that one hundred scholars "learned in the seven arts" be sent to China. On their second journey (1271–75) the Polos were accompanied by their inquisitive and ambitious nephew, Marco, who remained in the service of the Mongols for fifteen years. In his celebrated account of the lands of the Far East he reports that Kublai Khan, Emperor of the Mongols at Peking, honoured Jesus, Muhammed, Moses and Sakyamuni, and allowed himself to be censed on his birthday by the priests of all four religions.

The Franciscan and Dominican missionaries who went as papal scouts to Mongolia and China were the first Westerners to bring back accounts of Buddhism and of the great piety of this "religion without God". "These monks live much more devoutly and ascetically than our Latin monks." Giovanni Marignolli, a Franciscan sent as the legate of Pope Benedict XIII to the Emperor of China in 1342, ended his report on the Buddhist monks by saying "these men lead a very holy life, although they lack faith". Westerners found the presence of Nestorian Christians in the Mongol Empire as confusing and surprising as the co-existence there of the world religions and the general lack of dogmatic belief. While some Westerners were strenuously defending the thesis that there could and should be only one Christendom, under the headship of the Pope of Rome, others were discovering that in the vast expanses of Asia there were highly educated and influential Christians who were very well-informed about European affairs but recognized neither the Papacy nor the forms proper to the Latin Church. Rabban Çauma, a man of good education, was sent to the West as the Nestorian ambassador of the Khan of Persia. At Paris he was received by Philip the Fair in the Sainte-Chapelle, that masterpiece of royal Gothic; he later visited Edward I of England at Bordeaux and, in 1288,

Pope Nicholas IV at Rome. The object of his visit was to negotiate an alliance with the West against the Mamelukes.

It was ironic that during the years between 1290 and 1350–70, when European Christendom was in decline and Europe was starting to shrink, new horizons should seem to open up in Asia, particularly in China, offering the promise of vast expansion for European influence. This irony is underlined by some striking coincidences. 1291, for example, was the year of the fall of St John of Acre, the last stronghold of the "Franks" in the Holy Land; it was also the year when Marco Polo returned to Europe. 1294 was the year of the accession to the Papacy of Boniface VIII, who was to bring the Church close to ruin, and also of the conversion by Giovanni de Montecorvino of the Mongol prince Öngut Körguz. As "Prince George" this Mongol chieftain was to become the mainstay of Catholic missions in Asia and China. In 1307 the liquidation of the Templars was set in train in France, while in the East Giovanni de Montecorvino became Archbishop of Peking. Between 1312 and 1314 Dante was writing the *Inferno,* exposing to the world a Europe torn by hatred, lethal violence and wickedness; in 1314 Odorico of Pordonore, among the most successful of the missionaries, was travelling in Eastern Asia. In 1338, while Europe was drowning in wars, epidemics and famine, Andalo de Sevignano, a Genoese in the service of the Emperor of China, came west on an embassy, and the Alans, the Chinese imperial guard, were converted to Catholicism. Around 1350, when Europe's population was decimated by the Plague, the signs in the East began to be less propitious. In 1368 Chu Yuan-Chang conquered Peking and founded the Ming dynasty, thus initiating a Chinese nationalist reaction which brought Mongol rule in China to an end, and with it the influence of Roman Catholicism, whose centre had been the archdiocese of Peking. The declining power of Genghis Khan's heirs and successors meant the decline of Catholicism and European cultural influences in Central Asia and China.

"I hold that the Holy Ghost can manifest Himself in Christians, Jews, Moors and all sorts of men, and not indeed only in the wise but also in the simple." This sentiment accords with the whole experience of twelfth and thirteenth century travellers, whether Crusaders, scholars or merchants. It comes from a letter of Christopher Columbus to the "Catholic kings". In the year when his Jewish kinsmen were expelled from Spain, Columbus set sail on his first voyage, which led to the discovery of the Americas. Columbus's aim, as he expressly declared, was to discover India and realize the old crusading dream of finally overcoming Islam by a huge pincer movement launched simultaneously from East and West. Later on, after he had been replaced as viceroy, Columbus was still collecting prophecies to help him prove that this was the time when Jerusalem should be delivered by Spain, by the grace of God and by Columbus's own strength and good judgment. For his great Indian undertaking, which was envisaged purely as a crusading enterprise, as a contribution to the evangelization of the world, Columbus invoked as patron a remarkable figure of the mid-twelfth century, Abbot Joachim of Flora, who—whilst Byzantine influences still lingered in Calabria and the Latin spirit there was face to face with the stubborn opposition of the Eastern Church—prophesied the coming reign of the Holy Ghost, the third millennium.

The discovery of America was thus itself a unique latter-day product of the European crusading movement, whose fervour was so quick to die down but was rekindled again and again, with consequences none could have expected.

CHAPTER 7

COURTLY LOVE AND COURTLY
LITERATURE

DURING the Second Crusade a scandal broke at Antioch. The wife of Louis VII of France wanted to separate from her husband and remain at Antioch with her kinsman the Prince. On the advice of Thierry Galeran, a eunuch who guarded the queen and her treasure, Louis had his wife arrested during the night and departed forthwith with all his retinue of knights, allowing the queen no time to take leave of her relatives.

This episode at once calls to mind the passage in Tristan and Isolde in which the crafty dwarf spies on the lovers and reports their love to Mark, the weak and jealous king. Queen Eleanor, the central figure in the Antioch story, was the richest heiress of Western Christendom. She had married Louis, who was one year her senior, at the age of fifteen. The match was a political one, arranged by Suger, Abbot of St Denis and chief spiritual and political adviser of the bridegroom's father, Louis VI, and was designed to bring back to the crown, now reduced to a narrow demesne, the vast territories of its greatest vassal, the Duke of Aquitaine. Eleanor's second marriage with Henry Plantagenet, Count of Anjou, brought into being the Angevin Empire, which stretched from Scotland to Toulouse and was the centre of French-speaking civilization in the twelfth century. Eleanor herself was the presiding genius of this courtly culture, which was extended by her daughters and grand-daughters to their own courts in northern France and Spain. Poets sang her praises in German, Provençal, French and English:

> "God save Lady Eleanor
> Queen who art the arbiter
> Of honour, wit and beauty,

Of largesse and loyalty." (Philippe de Thaun)

"Were all lands mine
From Elbe to Rhine
I'd count them little worth
If England's Queen
Would lie my arms between." (Anon, German)

The tapestry of courtly civilization was created from the interweaving of many different strands, Celtic, Moorish, Spanish and Oriental, together with material of magical, archaic, pre-Christian and anti-Christian (that is, Gnostic and Oriental) origin. And there were other strands too, which are very difficult to unravel. Dissimulation and concealment now gained wide currency as artistic devices, since lovers and religious sects had their secret languages and members of small esoteric cliques were made known to each other by signs and symbols, colours and passwords. This art found its master-practitioner in Dante.

In the north, where the ecclesiastical "establishment" was so firmly entrenched, the new courtly civilization was regarded with suspicion, fear and even hatred; courtesy was a child of the free south, and of the antique Greek delight in *eros* and freedom of the spirit. Bernard of Clairvaux abominated the Angevins, convinced that they were descended from the devil and would return to him again. The northern saint was correct in detecting a demon in them, the "demon of the south", but he erred somewhat in his prophecies, since two of Eleanor's grand-daughters became the mothers of saints; Blanche of Castile was the mother of St Louis of France, Berengaria of St Ferdinand of Spain.

Eleanor proved herself a true daughter of her forebears, those highly educated and immensely energetic Dukes of Aquitaine who had a finger in all the sacred and profane preoccupations of their age. Eleanor boasted of her Carolingian descent. Her family had founded Cluny, they had made Popes and anti-Popes. The seat of her inheritance was Bordeaux, whose schools, villas and ducal court still basked in the glory of Roman civilization. Eleanor's grandfather, Guillaume, seventh Count of Poitiers and ninth Duke of Aquitaine (1071–1127), is the first troubadour whose work has come down to us. He was a master of *savoir vivre*. A Crusader in the East and in Andalusia, he nevertheless incurred the wrath of the clergy on account of his obscene verses and innumerable tales about women. His poetry has echoes of both Ovid and Moorish Spain. Curious and eager to taste all that the world could offer, he immersed himself in the delights of secular love and yet longed to know as well the joys of heaven. At his invitation the preacher Robert of Arbrissel spent the decade 1105–1115 at his court. Three phases in the development of Guillaume's creative powers and interior life can be discerned from his extant writings. Those belonging to the earliest group parody the pious sentiments of the noble ladies who had been bewitched by Robert's preaching, and thus give indirect expression to that rivalry between knights and clerks for the love and favours of a grand lady which was to be a basic fact of courtly life. From the second group of poems it becomes clear that this ardent spirit, who cast such a spell on the world around him, was himself deeply influenced by the spiritual feelings he had parodied, since he introduces their latent mysticism into what was secular and courtly. In Guillaume's love-songs the vocabulary and emotional fervour hitherto ordinarily used to express man's love for God are transferred to the liturgical worship of woman, and vice versa. In the third group there is a harking back to the spiritual conflict between the courteous knight and clerk for the favour of a lady, but now the cup of life has been drained to the dregs, and all that is left for this man whom the Church has castigated as a pornographer and a cynic is melancholy and farewell, and the prospect of a pilgrimage to Compostela.

Eleanor's southern heritage burned in her blood, and the lands which went with it were baked by the southern sun. Extending from the Loire to the Pyrenees, from the Massif Central of the Auvergne to the Atlantic, they formed the richest and largest domain in Christendom, with Provence as its core. The courtly civilization which had its origin here went up in flames in the thirteenth century, and the Huguenot civilization, also indigenous to Provence, was all but consumed in the holocausts of the sixteenth to eighteenth centuries; nevertheless it is still possible for the traveller to realize how this landscape must have looked in the heyday of its splendour, when it occupied a unique position in the cultural life of Europe. Only Greece and Greek Sicily have ruins which can compare with the gold-yellow, honey-coloured stones of Provence. Amphitheatres, Roman arenas, Roman aqueducts and columns, façades, twelfth and thirteenth century sculptures all speak the same language and bear the same imprint of pure classical form, in the classical setting of cypress and bay, olive and broom.

Provence received its spiritual inspiration from Greece, Spain and the Near East. It was surely no accident that this region was so attractive to the men of the last days of classical civilization. Constantine the Great planned to make Arles his capital. Outside the gates of Arles is the Alyscamps, the medieval city of the dead, which figures in the poetry of both Dante and Ariosto. Between the ninth and thirteenth centuries this great necropolis was the most sought-after burial ground in France, chosen as their last resting place by princes, nobles and bishops. The Alyscamps was the earthly Elysium, a fairy-tale kingdom of the blessed dead. Today one may still walk its paths, lined with empty sarcophagi; anyone who does so in the light of the setting sun may well remember that the great Celtic poetry, which survived under the cloak of the romantic epic into the light of a new age, was also and always the poetry of death. Its theme was the journey to Avalon, the blessed land of the dead where King Arthur reigned for ever, lapped in the enchanted music which gave him eternal life.

The superb Romanesque church of St Trophime at Arles is in effect a summary of the Christian universe. At the end of the path leading to the Alyscamps stands the majestic ruin of St Honorat, sacked for the first time by the Saracens.

There had been noble ladies in Provence before Eleanor, pagan and Christian matrons of the Later Empire, whose exquisite names are preserved on the Arles sarcophagi: Julia Lucina, Cornelia Optata, Hydria Tertulla, Optatina Jacoena, Cornelia Sadata. The feminine arts and graces of courtesy were native to Provence; here the idea of the "lady" was born, here Eleanor was truly at home.

But her Capetian marriage took Eleanor far away from this congenial soil. Until the sudden death of his elder brother, it had been assumed that Louis would become a monk (which would have suited his disposition) and he had been educated in the cloister. He was a thorough northerner, fair-haired and blue-eyed. On returning to Paris after his marriage with Eleanor at Bordeaux, Louis at once immersed himself again in his studies and intellectual pursuits. The untamed young bride, brimming with vitality, who came to Paris in 1137 must have found the dilapidated capital sadly primitive and old-fashioned when compared with the wealth and luxury of the cities of Aquitaine. The king's quarters were in a gloomy Merovingian palace tower at the west end of the Ile de la Cité; at its east end lodged the Archbishop of Paris. A handful of poky old churches clustered nearby, together with the dwellings of the Jews, a few taverns and student lodging-houses. On the left bank of the Seine were the Schools, the embryonic Latin Quarter, noisy with argument and frequent rioting; it was already the noxious, filthy and disease-ridden place it would still be when Erasmus, Rabelais, Calvin and Ignatius Loyola were jostling among the crowds of the Collège Montaigu and Ste Barbe.

The young king was faced with permanent opposition from rebellious magnates, from the Church, which excommunicated him, and from the tempestuous and overwhelming Bernard of Clairvaux. Only Suger was loyal. It was a relief for the young couple to escape from the constrictions of Paris and set out on Crusade. Louis and Eleanor took the Cross at Vézélay, where they received their emblems from their great adversary, Bernard himself. There is a legend that Eleanor and her ladies appeared at Vézélay attired and armed as Amazons, mounted on white horses. Many chroniclers allege that there were women fighting with the Crusading armies. The Greek historian Nicetas describes one feminine contingent, whose leader, "the lady of the golden boots", he likens to Penthesilea, the Amazon queen.

A legendary glamour clings to this disastrous Crusade. It lives on in the tribal memory of the Khevsuri, a nomadic people of the Caucasus, who dress up in medieval armour to hold tournaments and duels, and have a song which goes: "The French warriors have a queen, Queen Eleanor, Queen Eleanor." Although the crusading Bull of Vézélay forbade it, troubadours accompanied the Crusade, to entertain the ladies with their singing.

The Crusaders were to discover two enchanted cities. The first was Constantinople; here the Emperor Manuel placed the Blachernae Palace at their disposal, withdrawing himself to the Boukoleon on the Bosphorous, where he still had between two hundred and three hundred rooms, not to mention numerous chapels, for his comfort. Memories of the gloomy tower in Paris receded. The Crusaders were dazzled by the splendours of gold and mosaic, by treasures from Persia and Cathay, from Bagdad and Mosul. Here they found all the refinements and luxury of the Orient. (A century later an attempt would be made to reproduce some of this splendour at Paris, in the Gothic Sainte-Chapelle.) But the festivities and feasting were brusquely interrupted by news of the catastrophic defeat of the army of the German king, Conrad III, whose presence in the same Crusade as the king of France had been a great triumph of persuasion on the part of Bernard of Clairvaux.

The Franks departed for Antioch, their second enchanted city, which proved even more perilous for the royal couple than the first. The urban civilization of Antioch in the twelfth century was compounded of many elements, Hellenistic, Roman, Persian, Sassanid and Byzantine, in a fruitful and stimulating combination. The population was a mixed one of Muslims and Greek and Frankish Christians, and the city contained churches, mosques and harems. Here, in great style, lived Raymond, Prince of Antioch, a man of the South and Eleanor's uncle. Many of the second-generation Crusaders living at Antioch were half-Saracen by blood and had adopted a semi-Muslim mode of life. Eleanor was deeply impressed by Antioch, which had such overwhelming similarities with her native Bordeaux, also an ancient southern cosmopolitan city, with Moors, Negroes and Jews among the population. Paris, the North, and the monkish ways of northern Christendom, must all have seemed very remote. Did Eleanor break her marriage on account of a liaison with Raymond? The flood of scandal which now gathered about her name continued unabated until her death and after. And this too has its place in the history of courtly love: Eleanor, its first and greatest patron, lived in the shadow of an ever-increasing notoriety and scandal. Bernard of Clairvaux found nothing in all this to astonish him. He saw in Eleanor the French king's evil genius, a demon-wife, sterile to the core—after ten years she still had not borne the king a male heir.

Louis, as we have seen, had removed his wife from Antioch by force. He proceeded to Jerusalem to make a joyous entry by the Jaffa Gate, preceded by the standard of the Templars, the *gonfanon bausent*, and the sacred oriflamme of France; Fulk, the Patriarch of Jerusalem, came to meet him with great ceremony. The party was received in the city by the half-French, half-Oriental Queen Melisande, together with her son Baldwin, the young King of Jerusalem, who came of Angevin stock. The chronicles make no mention of Eleanor at Jerusalem.

On their way back to France the estranged couple visited Rome, where they were reconciled by the Pope. During the winter of 1149–50, which was unusually severe in northern Europe, Eleanor bore a second daughter, and the Capetians were still without a male heir. Geoffrey, Count of Anjou, surnamed Plantagenet from his courtly custom of wearing a sprig of broom in his helm, now paid his addresses to the queen. It may have been to Geoffrey that she made the much-quoted remark, "I thought to have married a king but found I am wed to a monk". Eleanor was by now thoroughly antagonistic towards her husband, and felt herself the captive of barbaric northerners who could not even speak her sweet southern tongue, the Langue d'Oc. The Angevin saw his great opportunity: his son Henry (the future Henry II of England) could marry the queen and bring her rich inheritance to the house of Anjou. Henry was eighteen, Eleanor nearly thirty, but this discrepancy was no obstacle in medieval dynastic marriages. Geoffrey himself was fifteen years younger than his wife, the Empress Matilda, widow of Henry V.

The go-between in the important affair of the royal annulment was no less a person than Bernard of Clairvaux, who urged Pope Eugenius III, his former pupil, to grant Eleanor her divorce and so get rid of this shameless woman whose forebears had so often been such enemies of Rome. To Bernard she had been a perpetual thorn in the flesh. The Archbishop of Sens, who had presided over the condemnation of Abelard, pronounced the marriage dissolved on March 21, 1152, on the grounds of consanguinity. Eight weeks later Eleanor married Henry, who was as closely related to her as her former husband, and as Duke of Normandy was the vassal of the King of France. This marriage prepared the way for centuries of strife between France and England, the two rival Western powers which, for all their mutual antagonisms, stood jointly for "the West"; despite their differences and contrasts, they had in common their political systems, their ordering of society and their whole civilization. The two together formed a specifically "Western" culture.

Eleanor now made her home at Angers, the chief town of Anjou; for the first time she was able to organize her court and way of life after her own taste, as it had been formed in the South and the Near East. It was at Angers that Bernard de Ventadour composed in her honour some of the finest love-songs of the age. Bernard came to Angers as an exile from Ventadour, where his wooing of the countess had been over-ardent. His situation was typical of the troubadour's fate, later to be shared by the German Minnesinger: that of a poet who addressed love-songs to some highly-born married lady, legally beyond his reach, who nevertheless lent him a ready ear. The poet vows he would not change his lot—of endless suspense and alternating hope and despair—with that of any "king or duke or admiral". It is a commonplace among poets of this school for petty landless knights to rank themselves above kings and emperors, and for kings and emperors, such as Henry VI and Frederick II, to declare their readiness to renounce all the kingdoms of this world to win their lady's favour.

Bernard swore to Eleanor that Tristan never suffered for Isolde as he for her. This ancient Celtic romance of forbidden love was known to Bernard in its more primitive form, before its transformation by the Anglo-Norman Thomas and the German Gottfried von Strassburg. It must have seemed that the legend of Tristan and Isolde was being re-enacted as social reality, an edifying example to be admired and emulated by ladies of high rank. Eleanor herself had exchanged her sickly weakling of a king for a bold young knight. But Henry was now her husband. To separate Bernard from Eleanor, Henry summoned him to England. In the meantime Eleanor had borne Henry her first son, William, and at once designated him as her heir to the county of Poitou.

Whilst practising the art of love Eleanor was also learning the art of politics; here her teacher was the Empress Matilda, her husband's mother, who kept her court at Rouen. The Empress Matilda had brought up her son on a precept taken from the art of falconry. "Show your friends and allies their reward, keep it dangling before their eyes, but remove the bait before they can seize it; thus you will keep them devoted and eager to serve." There were obvious risks in following such advice, which imposed an intolerable strain on both parties to the sport; Henry died an exhausted and embittered man. Matilda also taught her son (she was the only woman he ever listened to) to test everything for himself, by sight, hearing or touch: weapons, precious stones, materials, women, musical instruments, hunting falcons, dogs, men and sports. Henry's political achievement did credit to his training; the acquisitive and self-assured young man went on to found a vast empire in the West.

Henry and Eleanor were crowned in Westminster Abbey on the Sunday before Christmas, 1154. A few weeks later, also in London, Eleanor gave birth to her second son, who was named Henry and designated Count of Anjou; on the death of his elder brother in the following year he became the heir to the English throne. The queen was to bear her husband six other children: Matilda in 1156; Richard, to be known by the courtly soubriquet of Coeur de Lion, in 1157 at the palace of Oxford; Geoffrey in 1158; two more daughters, Eleanor in 1161 and Joanna in 1165; and finally John "Lackland" in 1166.

Thomas's version of Tristan and Isolde contains a eulogy of London and its wealth: it was a city of industrious burgesses and seafaring men and merchants, stinking of fish, wool and beer, as yet quite untouched by courtly manners. Eleanor and her husband created a new social climate, an atmosphere in which courtly society could flourish.

Europe's conversion to the courtly way of life, the birth of the *roman courtois* and the flowering of troubadour poetry were all intimately connected with Eleanor and the rise of the Angevin Empire. The new literature was an attack, both open and concealed, on the old Franco-German idea of a Holy Empire with Charlemagne as its patron saint; it was also anti-Roman and anti-monastic. The day when monks and clerks were the custodians of a man's soul was past; a man's hope of felicity now lay in the hands of his *dompna* (Provençal for *domina*), his lady. With the lady as mentor, the two together could build up the inner kingdom of courtly love outside the bonds of wedlock.

The coming to England of Eleanor and Henry was a unique stroke of chance by which the *roman courtois* became linked with the political aspirations of the Angevin Empire. The main obstacles in the path of the Angevins were the King in Paris and the Pope in Rome. Up to this time the chief channel of expression for the cultural attitudes of aristocratic society and the chief vehicle for its imaginative powers had been the *chanson de geste*, which came to its fullest flowering between 1120 and 1160. Guibert de Nogent, writing about 1104, described the Crusade as "*Gesta dei per Francos*": God working on earth through the Franks, his chosen people. The Franks, i.e. the French, were the people of Charlemagne: at St Denis, just outside the gates of Paris, the cult of Charlemagne was steadily being fostered, largely by the superbly inventive genius of Abbot Suger (his part in the "invention" of Gothic will be discussed later). Charlemagne's standard, the oriflamme (another convenient recent discovery), had passed to his successor, the King of France, who like him went on pilgrimage to Compostela and carried on his war, the Crusade.

The *chanson de geste* was also cultivated at the abbey of St Denis. The *genre* served to boost the prestige not only of the French king, the descendant of Charlemagne, but also of the "old Frankish" chivalry. These epics (*Pélérinage de Charlemagne, Couronnement de Louis, Charroi de Nîmes, Prise d'Orange,* for example) all went back to the French *Chanson de Roland* and celebrated the noble Franks as invincible warriors in their fight against "infidel dogs"; in many of the *chansons* these "heathens" (i.e. the Saracens) become merged with the wicked Germans and English, in fact with all non-Franks who dared to challenge the *gloire* of Charlemagne and his heroes. The great success enjoyed by the *chansons de geste* outside the narrow demesne of the French king naturally had nothing to do with their latent propaganda on behalf of a French kingdom of God; their popularity arose from the fact that they so exactly matched the emotional attitudes and imaginings of the older generation of barons, their lack of sophistication and their joy in combat.

The *chansons de geste* and the whole Parisian culture as it was in the days of Louis VI and Louis VII were dismissed by Eleanor and her Angevin courtiers as primitive, provincial, "uncourtly" and ill-bred, of no interest save as objects of ridicule. The new courtly epic derived its "political" nourishment from three principal sources: Anglo-Saxon romancing, Celtic inspiration, and the doctrines of love and eroticism peculiar to Provence and south-western France. These three fused to produce a superb work of art which was the hallmark of the Angevin Empire, that loose-knit assembly of lordships stretching from England to the borders of Spain, itself the supreme example of political artistry the Middle Ages has to offer. The autumn of the Middle Ages was to see the emergence of another similarly distinct civilization, the kingdom of Burgundy, also a loose-knit assembly of individual lordships held together by the court and a handful of princes, set between France and the Empire and uniting all the rich lands from the Netherlands to the Swiss borders. Here was revived, and on a grand scale, the courtly romanticism and chivalry of Angevin times; in Burgundy originated the late medieval orders of chivalry such as the Golden Fleece. The Burgundian kingdom was more northern in temper, more serious and melancholy than Eleanor's world; to her preciosity was added the characteristically Burgundian cult of the dead and of death. New styles of court ceremonial and etiquette invented here were carried over into the Spanish and Austrian courts, to become, under Philip II, the attributes of a world power.

To return to Eleanor and England. She was singularly fortunate in the age she lived in. In England and the Angevin Empire there was a new interest in public and intellectual matters, which actively responded to the vitality and intellectual force behind Eleanor's and Henry's political aspirations. In the electric atmosphere of the years between 1160 and 1180 three poets of genius, Marie de France, Chrétien de Troyes and Gautier d'Arras, were at work, transmuting this potentially explosive material into literature of the highest order, which was to be the continuing inspiration of a great European tradition until the sixteenth century and after, right down to the nineteenth century.

As has been said already, the three most important sources of the new romantic epic were English romancing about the past, the Celtic genius, and the amatory doctrines of the Angevin courts of love. All three had their "public" aspect, and this will be treated first. But it should be noted that in common with the other elements which went to the making of the highly artistic and highly artificial literature of the age, and of the *roman courtois* in particular, they had other and more private aspects which could not fail to impress deeply those individuals who were in the process of waking to self-awareness and to the dawning power of imagination. These features will be discussed later.

To take first English romancing about the past. English chroniclers had for some time been turning their attention to the kings of remote antiquity; in so doing they laid the foundations of a particular fantasy which had a distinct ideological bearing. Writers such as Symeon of Durham (✣ 1130), Henry of Huntingdon (*circu* 1155) and above all William of Malmesbury (✣ 1143) concerned themselves with the Anglo-Saxon past. In Geoffrey of Monmouth's *Historia regum Britanniae* the sacred figure of King Arthur, the great ancestral archetype and exemplar of the Angevin kings and Angevin chivalry, appears aptly upon the hour.

Arthur, Celtic king and emblem of honour, the sun of the courtly epic, about whom his knights revolved like stars, fulfilled two important functions for the Angevin monarchy. This patriarchal figure, the epitome of all the old English kings who still commanded the allegiance of the English people smarting under the Norman yoke, linked these figures of the past with their true heirs, the new court aristocracy modelled on the Arthurian pattern. Secondly (and no less important), Arthur was of sufficient stature to stand in opposition to Charlemagne. The canonization of Charlemagne by Frederick Barbarossa's anti-Pope was a recent event. Another ostentatious gesture had been the translation of the relics of the Three Kings from Milan to Cologne, engineered by Frederick's Chancellor, Rainald of Dassel, who had acquired them as spoils of war. Charlemagne's Aachen was a favourite place of pilgrimage for the French kings. It is thus no surprise to find Richard I making a pilgrimage to the remains of King Arthur, which had been discovered at Glastonbury in 1191, at a time when the Angevin Empire had reached both its peak and a critical turning-point in its history. Richard caused these relics to be ceremoniously reinterred, together with those of Arthur's faery queen Gwenyver, another recent and significant "discovery". The ruins of Caerlon on Usk, the place where Arthur received the Roman envoys, had for some time been attracting pilgrims from among the young aristocrats of the court. The spell of pagan Rome and of the ruins of antiquity was just starting to be felt in the West, not least by a small number of the greater English lords.

The Abbey of Glastonbury had been richly endowed by the Plantagenets and was firmly entrenched in Wales and other Celtic parts of the kingdom, where many of its properties lay. Glastonbury was intimately connected not only with the Arthurian legend but also with the Grail. The "Matter of Britain", the collection of stories about King Arthur, Percival, Lancelot and the Grail, is an expression of the Celtic genius. It can surely be no accident that the area over which these legends and poems spread with such rapidity exactly coincided with the extent of primitive Celtic settlement in Europe, the region between Scotland, Thuringia and northern Italy. As they came flooding out from the British Isles, Arthurian literature and ideas found an eager welcome, for example at the court of the Landgrave of Thuringia, a court on the new model and the most considerable centre inside Germany of courtly poetry and culture; they were also popular at Vienna, a Celtic foundation, and in northern Italy.

The Abbey of Glastonbury and its wealthy sister-houses

could claim another merit based on their Celtic associations. At a much earlier date Irish-Celtic monasticism had been the means of incorporating the riches of pagan minstrel poetry and culture into Celtic Christianity. Now, in the twelfth century, when the Scots, Irish and Welsh were in active conflict with the English Angevin kings, there was once again the need to bring the exuberant vitality of the Celtic world into close harness with Christendom, the Church and secular authority, as represented by the new kings and their chivalry.

The "courtly" knight of the Angevin Empire was a man "reborn", a "new" man, initiated through the power of magic and myth into the company of King Arthur and his knights. His communion (in the sacramental sense) with the wonder-working heroes of the Celtic and Anglo-Saxon past gave him strength to face the great tasks the Angevin Empire demanded of him. The kingdom of the Plantagenets, which was orientated towards the south and east, looking towards the Mediterranean and beyond, needed England as a source of money and the breeding-ground of men.

The "public" implications of the third element in courtly literature and civilization, the amatory theories and practice of southern France and Provence, will become apparent as we take up again the thread of Eleanor's life-history. We have seen that the *roman courtois* derived from English and Celtic sources a tradition of antagonism towards the Holy Roman Empire, the France of the Capetian kings, and Rome. To these antagonisms, which it shared, the Provençal element added another, a proud and rebellious intolerance of the harsh authoritarian world of masculine kingship: Eleanor came into conflict with Henry II. The Queen's own public tragedy was closely bound up with the subsequent collapse of courtly civilization in Provence. The kingdom of courtly love was drawn into conflict with the greatest powers of the age. Its forces would undermine some enemy bastions, its scouts would penetrate deep into men's minds and lie there in ambush over the centuries; this much is proved by the enduring influence of *courtoisie* in Italy and other parts of Western Europe. But first the enemy must have his hour of triumph.

The Ballad of Fair Rosamund played itself out at Oxford and Godstow between 1166 and 1177. Many legends have been woven around this idyll. Stripped of its embellishments, Eleanor found nothing idyllic in the episode. Rosamund

Clifford was her husband's mistress. She had long been aware of her husband's waywardness, that none of the maids of her household were safe from him, and that the great vassals kept their wives and daughters out of his way. Nothing of this had disturbed her, for in this respect, as in others, medieval society was more tolerant than that of later periods. What turned Eleanor decisely against her husband was that his relations with Rosamund Clifford were public knowledge, and that they were permanent and serious. Eleanor now detached herself from her husband both formally and emotionally, and became his most dangerous enemy. Henry, a proud and masterful man, was later to imprison her and deprive her of her power; Eleanor, equally proud, and a woman of independent mind, was to rob him of his sons' affections.

About 1170 Eleanor took up residence in Poitiers. There she methodically set about constructing a commanding position for herself in Poitou, her own hereditary possession. She engineered a suitably ceremonious installation for her son Richard as Duke of Aquitaine, in the form of a symbolic marriage in the church of St Stephen at Limoges between Richard and St Valéry, the legendary martyr and patroness of the region. The saint's ring was placed on the young duke's finger in solemn token of his indissoluble union with the provinces and vassals of Aquitaine. In this action were combined the attributes of sacred kingship, sacramental initiation and the mysteries of archaic religion. We cannot hope to understand the atmosphere surrounding the courtly romances unless we accept as a fact this close union of the primeval and magical with hard-headed practical politics. At Venice an act of state of the utmost solemnity continued to be observed for centuries, the marriage of the Doge (who embodied the supernatural might of Venice) with the sea, the sacred mother of good and evil, a union also symbolized by the giving of a ring.

Eleanor's household and court at Poitiers became the chief academy of Western Europe for teaching the arts of courtesy. Here were educated several future kings and queens and numerous future dukes and duchesses, who formed themselves on the model of this powerful and passionate woman; they would later try to reproduce the atmosphere of her court at their own, just as Versailles, in the time of the Sun King, had its imitations in a dozen lesser courts. Prompted by motives of gratitude, curiosity or pure enjoyment, the offspring of the two rival houses, Capetian and Plantagenet, came to pay their respects to Eleanor. Her visitors included Margaret, the elder daughter of Louis VII by his second marriage and the wife of young Henry Plantagenet; Margaret's younger sister Alais, betrothed to Richard Plantagenet; Constance, Countess of Brittany, betrothed to Geoffrey Plantagenet; Alix, Countess of Blois; and Eleanor's own daughters, Eleanor, Queen of Castile and Joanna, Queen of Sicily. Presiding over all as mistress of the academy was Eleanor's daughter by her first marriage, Marie, Countess of Champagne. Marie had been very strictly brought up in the Paris of her father; at Poitiers she became the patroness of courtly love and poetry.

During the "season", that is, between Whitsun and St John's day (June 24), when there was an annual armistice in the permanent interbaronial fighting, the aristocratic young manhood of Europe foregathered at Poitiers. They came to joust and tourney, to enjoy courtly society and, above all, to look for a bride. Only by winning a wealthy bride could landless young noblemen hope to retain their rank in aristocratic society and climb higher. In some parts of France it was the practice to transmit fiefs laterally instead of vertically, so that on occasion an entire generation might be passed over, since all the collaterals inherited before the younger generation of the senior branch; this custom produced a restless, bellicose cadet nobility, a constant source of trouble to the magnates of their own houses and to the kings of France and England. They were also a matter of concern to the Papacy. What was to happen if these landless, penniless, proud young lords could no longer be despatched on Crusade or relegated to a monastery? Their precarious social status made them all the more critical and resentful of their "decadent" elderly fathers far away at home, not to mention the Father in Rome. There were thus men, as well as women, who were ready to welcome the new courtly way of life, and who appreciated the fluidity and frankness of this society which deliberately sought to free itself from the shackles of the "old world".

As they themselves must have realized, the ladies who were the arbiters of this society were in a situation at once enviable and perilous: what pleasure could be more exquisite than to form this young manhood after their own taste? Eleanor's daughter Marie had brought with her from Paris a court chaplain, Andreas Capellanus, to assist in the work of ennobling this turbulent, tempestuous crowd of young men by curing them of their uncouth habits and educating them to higher things by example, precept and ideals. Love was at once the goal and agent of their education. The essence of love, as taught at Poitiers, was not the indulgence of uncontrollable passion, but the moulding of passion by a man's lady, his "mistress".

Andreas, who addressed himself to his task with some reluctance, composed for Marie at her request a small treatise, *De Arte Honeste Amandi*. His literary examples were taken from Ovid, contemporary lyrics and Arthurian narrative poems. Andreas' scholarly treatise is a somewhat dull affair, and not only because of his formal manner of presentation. One can sense that the author, a clerk, educated in a thoroughly masculine environment, is torn between the desire of pleasing his highly-placed mistress and of following his own inclinations. In the last section, added later, Andreas renounces the ideas set out in the main body of his work just as Chrétien de Troyes, a more important protégé of the Countess Marie, was to cancel out his Lancelot with his Cligès, and in so doing disavow his mistress. However, the amatory handbook of Andreas Capellanus rapidly gained fame and respect throughout Europe as the first and only serious treatment of its theme; its theories were much debated and, in 1277, a century later, they were "finally" condemned by the Bishop of Paris.

The Code of Love in thirty-one Articles contained in Andreas' treatise is informed with the pulsating energy and passion which drove the women of Eleanor's entourage to create their own world and attempt the dethronement of masculine oppression and mastery. Courtly love was a practicable way of rebelling against the prevailing social *moeurs*, and was consciously adopted to serve this end. Marie de Champagne ruled that love had no power as between the two parties to a marriage, and justified her ruling on the grounds that in love everything depended on both parties giving themselves freely, whereas marriage implied obligations and coercion, which was the death of love. Andreas' comment was more cautious: "Marriage is no barrier to love." The new kingdom of courtly love was based exclusively on a state of tension, on the magnetic attraction between the two lovers. The poles of the older social order were Pope and Emperor, priest and people, the soul and God. The poles of courtly society were the lady and her "man", her lover, who owed fealty to her alone. Andreas declared "all action between lovers culminates in thought of the loved one", "the heart leaps up whén the beloved unexpectedly appears". Once upon a time it was manifestations of the Godhead that had made the heart (*cor* in Augustine, signifying the centre of a man) leap up in fear and trembling. Now the heart had become the last resort against the princes and powers of this world.

There is a tradition that "courts of love" were held by chatelaines of various Provençal courts, at Signe, Romanin, Purrefeu and other places in the far south. However that may be, the drama of this grand assize was certainly enacted, and in public, in the great hall of Queen Eleanor at Poitiers, before the scandalized gaze of old-fashioned feudal society. The judgments of the court, the *arrests d'amour*, concerned such matters as whether such and such a courtier loved his lady "lawfully", that is in conformity with the rules of courtly love. These judgments were clothed in current legal forms, which made them all the more piquant, since they were completely subversive of the accepted social order. The assessors of the court were a number of ladies, mostly between twenty-five and thirty years of age; Eleanor herself, Marie de Champagne, Isabella, Countess of Flanders (a niece of the Queen), Ermengarde, Countess of Narbonne, Emma of Anjou and others. These judges sat raised upon a dais; below them sat the men, the suitors to the court, prepared to hear lengthy and meticulous disputations on the essence and nature of love and an exposition of a man's duty of service towards his lady.

The great game played out in the courts of love at Poitiers reflected the tensions and tragedy (at times tragi-comedy) to be found in the courtly lyric poetry of the time, with its characteristic mingling of fantasy and passionate resentment. These noble ladies knew well enough that they were not mistresses of their situation, that men regarded them as loot or merchandise, as objects they openly and secretly traded among themselves, as prizes sometimes taken by stealth. Lands, men and crowns might flow from such golden booty. In feudal society marriage was an important political and commercial transaction, as it was to be in the bourgeois society which succeeded it. For a long time feudal society took no account of love as an emotion felt by individuals for each other; later it was thought of as something occurring in "literature". But these high-born ladies were also aware of the approaching dawn of a new age: an era for individuals, in which every man of breeding who understood the arts of love could organize his own life without reference to the "ego" of some royal superior. Woman would come into her own, educating men in the ripeness of her wisdom. Here at Eleanor's court in Poitiers, far from Paris, London and Rome, women were learning to exercise their power in novel and delicate ways. Men were to be captivated, guided, educated. Eleanor points the way to Beatrice.

Eleanor's court was the meeting-place of all the baronial rebels and malcontents who opposed Henry II. She conspired with her sons Richard and Geoffrey against their father; the heir to the throne, young Henry, also came over to their side. In 1173 the King crushed the rebellion of his sons and incarcerated his wife in the tower at Salisbury. For the next fifteen years, until the death of her husband, Eleanor remained in England as his prisoner, resisting his attempts to divorce her. Throughout her captivity her courage and sturdy pride never deserted her. She maintained relations with the bishops and magnates of her native land. When Henry died exhausted in 1189 she was ready to take over the government at a moment's notice.

All this while the feuds among the King, his baronage, and his sons had continued. One characteristic moment may be singled out for its illumination of this period, when the rougher manners of the past were becoming veiled under a courtly façade. The young Henry, Henry II's eldest son, crowned king in his father's lifetime, rebelled against his resplendent brother, Richard Coeur de Lion, the ruler of Aquitaine. Henry's resentment against his brother had been brought to boiling point by the political verses of Bertran de Born, lord of the castle of Hautefort, near Périgueux, who was a master of this genre. Such verses, called *sirvantés*, were a particular feature of troubadour poetry. Coruscating with wit, shot through with venom, they were a vehicle of propaganda against the Church and the magnates, and as they passed from mouth to mouth in response to the demands of an eager public, they also reflected all the current opinions of the day. Bertran's verses were spread all over Europe by his *jongleur* Papiol.

> I care nothing for months and weeks,
> For Monday or Tuesday devoted to peace,
> In April and March I do just as I will

> If enemies still remain for the kill ...
> Peace brings me no comfort,
> I live only for war
> My belief and my thought
> Has that creed for its star.

In the eleventh century there had been a movement, now revived, to institute certain days and seasons at times of truce, when all fighting was suspended; Monday, Tuesday, Easter, Christmas and Whitsun. Noblemen such as Bertran derided such things; but they clothed the old credo of the aristocracy in accomplished courtly verses. Bertran's songs breathe all the passionate hatreds of the South, now consciously committed to a way of life which flouted all convention.

Henry II died in 1189, worn out by the persecution of his victorious sons. They had allied themselves with the rising power of France, which was preparing to give the coup de grâce to that miracle of contrivance, the Angevin Empire. Henry was buried at Fontévrault, where Richard Coeur de Lion and Eleanor were later to join him (in 1199 and 1204). The Angevin vitality was wonderfully captured by the beautiful effigies which once surmounted their graves.

Eleanor's vigorous government of England as Richard's representative (from the time of her husband's death she styled herself "Eleanor, by the grace of God, Queen of England") belongs properly to political history. Richard, who in the presence of large cities felt that arrogance mixed with fear often to be found among aristocrats, had no use for London: "I would sell London if someone would show me a purchaser," he is reported to have said. On the Crusade which so absorbed his attention his conduct provoked much unfavourable criticism. Pope Celestine III's comments may be quoted as an example: "This man was surely not inspired by the fear of God or an access of remorse; all his enterprises were inspired rather by pride, conceit, and the lust for fame."

The songs he composed in his prison at the castle of Dürnstein on the Danube are the lament of the captured falcon, dreaming of the splendour and riches of his southern Aquitaine:

> No prisoner can tell his honest thought
> Unless he speaks as one who suffers wrong;

But for his comfort he may make a song.
My friends are many but their gifts are naught.
Shame will be theirs, if, for my ransom here
I lie another year . . .

They know this well who now are rich and strong
Young gentlemen of Anjou and Touraine
That far from them on hostile bonds I strain.
They loved me much, but have not loved me long . . .

Richard was justifiably suspicious of the plots being hatched at home. His youngest brother, John Lackland, in alliance with Philip Augustus, the heir to the French throne, thought of paying the Emperor 100,000 silver marks to get Richard into their own hands. When a man found himself in prison he voiced his complaint in song. Captive womanhood had not even this release. The death of Henry II freed from a twenty-five-years-long captivity at Rouen and elsewhere a sister of Philip Augustus named Alais, who had been given originally by her father Louis VII to Henry II as a bride for Richard; but she remained unwed and it was said that the covetous king preferred to keep her for his own use. Prematurely aged, she was now married off by her brother to one of his vassals. This tragic tale gives added point to Queen Eleanor's proud attempts to make woman, in her own dominions at least, mistress of a new spiritual dispensation.

The Angevin Empire disintegrated rapidly, and with it the elaborate world of courtly love. Richard Coeur de Lion was killed by an arrow at the close of the century, in 1199, leaving no sons; his assassin was a young man of low birth. Richard's successor, John Lackland, was to lose the Empire.

It has been necessary to paint in the political background against which Eleanor and her daughters and kinswomen moved because without it it is impossible to understand the rise of courtly culture and literature and its dramatic impact. The whole movement rode on the crest of a wave whose ground-swell could be felt long before and long after its climax, in fact long after the Angevin Empire and the civilization of Provence had vanished away. Troubadours, known in Northern France as *trouvères*, first emerge about 1080–90; they were poets of noble birth, like Eleanor's grandfather, Guillaume of Aquitaine. Their immediate influence was threefold. They gave the aristocratic ruling class a taste for formal elegance and the game of wit; they introduced a number of definite rules for the writing of vernacular poetry and rubrics for the liturgy of refinement; and lastly they evolved the courtly concept of love by applying their code of chivalrous conduct, based on a fusion of Oriental, gnostic and Islamic models, to the relations between men and women.

The *chanson d'amour* of the troubadour followed a set pattern. Its subject was always *amor*, that is, love itself and the art of expressing it in courtly and poetic form. The lady (*dompna*) was indicated by a symbol (*senhal*); she was married, concerned about her reputation (*pretz*), conscious of her worth (*valor*). Her lover was separated from her by a number of social and emotional taboos. There were many emotional variations upon the main theme: eulogy, desire, grief, hope and resignation. The main form of the courtly lyric was the *canzone*. Each new *canzone* required a new strophe or verse-form, and a new melody. The troubadour was expected to compose his own melodies, but his work would actually be performed by a *jongleur* in his employment; only somewhat penurious troubadours were their own *jongleurs*. In addition to the *canzone* there was the *tenzone*, the recital, strophe by strophe, of verses on two conflicting themes by two or more poets. The highest art was deployed and the richest emotional depths were plumbed in the *alba*, the watchman's warning to lovers of the approach of morning, enemies, spies, death himself.

About one hundred troubadours are known by name from the century between 1150 and 1250, including twenty or so women. Their literary ancestry was unexpectedly illumined by the discovery after the second world war of some enchanting *chansons* of Spanish provenance, bilingual lyrics written in Arabic and Hebrew, or in Arabic with the refrain in a very early form of Spanish. This prototype of the courtly lyric must have been in existence in Andalusia at least as early as the eleventh century. So far as Europe is concerned, however, Provence and the whole area covered by the Langue d'Oc must still be regarded as the cradle of this art form, the centre from which it spread to Northern France, England, Italy, Germany and Eastern Europe. We know that between 1175 and 1205 Peire Vidal was active as court poet in Provence, Spain, Italy, Hungary and Palestine. The Provençal lyric had its finest flowering between about 1175 and 1220. About forty troubadours of the first rank emerge during this period. Their involvement in contemporary politics, for example, the Crusades, the conflict between Henry II and his sons, and the Albigensian Crusade, gave point to their shafts and an astringent note to their poetry. Troubadour poetry, like other courtly literature, very soon became precious and artificial. Raimbaut de Vaqueyras, who was writing in the late twelfth century, on one occasion made use of five different dialects in the same poem (the Langue d'Oc, Northern French, Galician, Basque and Catalan). The inventiveness of twelfth century troubadour poetry, on both the intellectual and emotional plane, reveals intelligence and sensibility of a high order.

Until about 1200, Northern France knew the courtly lyric merely as an import from the region of the Langue d'Oc. After that date the genre was taken up by a number of poets native to the North, six of them troubadours of considerable merit; the next generation produced some fourteen more. In Italy, Provençal continued to be the language of polite literature up till about 1250: the Emperor Frederick II and Francis of Assisi, his spiritual antithesis, were equally in love with it. Provençal culture was exterminated by the Crusaders from Northern France during the Albigensian wars (1209–1229–1240). Many of the southern territories of the Angevin Empire passed into the hands of the French king, a latter-day triumph for the Capetians over Queen Eleanor. There were still some indigenous poets to voice the protests of the ill-used South: Peire Cardenal, a nobleman from Le Puy, only started his career as a poet about 1225 and continued until 1274, when he was nearly a hundred years old. But with him the voice of Provence was stilled. More than a century would pass before the civilization of the South became absorbed into that of France. The first considerable southern-born author to write in French was Antoine de la Salle (1388–1464).

The courtly epic or romance was just as much the product of courtly culture as the lyric, and was born at much the same time. The description *roman* or *romance* was originally applied to everything written in the vernacular as distinct from Latin; later it came to mean a narrative translated from Latin verse. About one hundred romances survive from the period between 1150 and 1220, during which three gifted poets already mentioned, Marie de France, Chrétien de Troyes and Gautier d'Arras, perfected the new form.

The name "Marie de France" probably conceals the Plantagenet princess who was Abbess of Shaftesbury between 1160–65 and 1190, and who wrote poetry dedicated to important personalities in the entourage of Henry II and Eleanor. She wrote romances of two types, fairy-tales and psychological studies (how closely these two were linked will be seen in discussing Chrétien de Troyes). For Marie love was all-powerful, the greatest force in nature, the presiding goddess and ruler of all. Is this an echo of the goddess Natura of the Chartres philosophers?

A few of Gautier's romances read like a Northern French protest against Marie de France and the world of Eleanor of Aquitaine. Gautier came from the family of the castle bailiffs of Arras. In his *Eracle* (which has a Byzantine background) and his *Ile et Galeron* (set in a pseudo-Breton atmosphere), he attempted to reconcile the austere tradition of the old heroic epics with the modern taste for non-Christian legends and fairy-tales from the East.

The master of the *roman courtois*, Chrétien de Troyes, reveals himself through his work (our only source of knowledge about him) as a classical writer of great power, quite without pretentiousness; he completely disguises his ultimate motives and beliefs. He may perhaps have been a heretic, a Cathar. All we know for certain is that his literary patron was Marie de Champagne, with whom he had some close personal relationship, and that he was also the protégé of various great lords in the entourage of Henry II and the Counts of Flanders. Chrétien made the "Matter of Britain" peculiarly his own. He found this archaic, magical, legendary world of King Arthur and the twelve Knights of the Round Table admirably suited for conveying to his courtly audience everything they needed to hear while at the same time concealing everything which could not be openly expressed for fear of offending against contemporary ecclesiastical and secular morality. There was the added attraction that all this could be wrapped up in material which would satisfy the prodigious appetite of this youthful society for novelties of every kind.

The giant-sized encyclopedic romances of the later Middle Ages, such as the Lancelot-Grail compiled between 1220 and 1235, which runs to four thousand printed pages, suffocate under the weight of their material. In them, the imagination which the romances themselves had brought to life is stifled. This cannot be said of Chrétien. In his great canvases depicting the ascensions and descents of the awakening soul.

of the ego struggling to be free, the colouring of the different parts has been most carefully weighed: a definite value is assigned to each of the sinister and wonder-working objects which make up the apparatus of magic, the raiment, the little dogs, the magical beasts and the horrific apparitions, as also to the finery, the feasting, the festivals, the heroic deeds and the marvellous adventures.

Chrétien's romances made a wide and profound impression just because they could be understood at so many different levels, a stratification no doubt reflected in his own personality: the adventures of his noble knights enter so many and such different dimensions. His works, produced under the many-dimensional driving force of his didactic purpose, taught by example, by setting up a standard: this is the guiding thread which runs through them all, *Erec* (1165–70), *Cligès* (1170–71), Lancelot (of supreme importance in this connection, written *circa* 1172–75), the crowning achievement of *Yvain, The Knight with the Lion,* his masterpiece, and *Perceval* or *Le Conte du Graal* (1174–80 or 1177–87). All these romances were educational in intention, aimed at the creation and moulding of a new type of man. They were addressed not only to the frivolous, superficial, inquisitive younger aristocracy but also to more serious and complex characters. Everyone alike had the duty of striving consciously to attain greater perfection in their daily lives. For all alike the highest values were to be found in *chevalerie* and *clergie*, in the courtly and chivalrous education of the individual. *Bravoure et justice,* true courage and a passion for justice, were the hallmarks of *chevalerie*, *clergie* entailed *elegance et culture*, right conduct, sensibility and the proper handling of human relationships, whether with a noble enemy, a friend, or a lady.

For more than five centuries the education of the laity in Europe meant in practice the education of the aristocracy. Later generations were to make the ideal aimed at more explicit, as in Castiligione's *Cortegiano* and its realization in the seventeenth century English gentleman and the *gentilhomme* of French classicism. But its prototype is to be found in the twelfth century, and Chrétien de Troyes was not least among its most luminous exponents.

I have already suggested that medieval civilization, particularly during its "open" period, is to be understood as a coexistence of highly improbable opposites, the bringing together of a number of elements greatly varying in age and ideological origin. This paradoxical civilization found in the figures, symbols and "adventures" of the *roman courtois* the artistic and formal expression ideally suited to it. As in a tapestry, the motifs intertwine in complex arabesques of meaning, drawn from many different worlds. Historians, theologians and philologists, champions of their rival disciplines, have all tried their hands at drawing out a single thread, be it of Christian, Persian, Gnostic, Cathar, druidical or Islamic origin. These invidious attempts are understandable, and can in a sense be justified. But they are an injustice perpetrated against the living reality of a work of art and the compelling power of its "symbolic" figures. It is, in fact, the veil of form and symbol that gives the *roman courtois* its power, for this veiling at once reveals and conceals the varied parentage of the figures and emblems of good and evil met with along the way. It is just because there has been such condensation of the various elements that the whole becomes so effective an exercise in depth psychology. There can no longer be any doubt that the theme of the great romantic epics (in France extending from the work of Chrétien de Troyes to that of Renaut de Beaujeu, in Germany from Hartmann von Aue to Wolfram von Eschenbach) is initiation, dedication, metamorphosis and absorption into a higher and fuller life, at once more human and more divine.

All Chrétien's work, indeed all Arthurian romances of the first rank, were attempts at expounding the processes of man's interior development. Here we have poetry, romance, dedicated to didactic and therapeutic ends. This explains why the same motifs and situations so frequently recur, just as they do in the course of a psycho-analysis. The remedies prescribed for the man who has strayed a thousand times into the jungle of his immature passions are woman, "nature", *mysterium*. In the *romans*, therefore, a woman is always at hand to transform and ennoble a man. Through his relationship with the woman the man gains access to his own soul, to the deeper layers of his "heart": his sorrowing quest for his "queen" makes him wiser, more sensitive, more scrupulous as a person. The success of a man's education is linked to the price he is prepared to pay for it: there will be many detours, byways and wrong turnings, adventures, journeys taken in error, descents into Hell, crushing defeats.

It was this insight which gave the courtly romantic epic its inherent superiority as an instrument of education over the scholastic and "Christian" manuals of pedagogy of contemporary and later date. The *roman courtois* did not ignore the energizing springs of life, the deeper layers of personality; they encompassed life as a whole. This is the literature of "wisdom": danger, temptation, error, sinning, lack of purpose and lack of achievement are all necessary if the inner core of a man's personality is to be truly and effectively unlocked, moulded and ennobled. The skill in "depth psychology" found in these romances is astonishing (at least to anyone ignorant of the wisdom that myths and fairy-tales habitually display in these matters). Embedded in them are all the father and mother motifs, used to illuminate the relations of the hero with his parents; and more than this, they often confront us with two sets of pairs in opposition to each other in a quaternity which brings to mind the researches of Jung: in *Erec*, Erec and Enide, Mabonagrain and his beloved, in *Yvain*, Yvain and Laudine, Gauvain and Lunete. (This quaternity is still adhered to in the *Commedia dell' Arte*.) The chief theme of *Yvain* is that eccentricity, even apparent madness, may be a stage in an individual's development, if such is demanded by inner necessity. But for this course to be successful, the man of nature (Yvain) needs to be supported by his natural instincts (the lion), and brought into relationship with the woman of nature (Laudine). Yvain and Laudine are thus a "natural pair". The opposing figure of Gauvain, standing for what is collective and conventional, is introduced as a yardstick to measure the progress of Yvain's evolution. Gauvain is the sun-member of a supernatural pair; the quartet is completed by a feminine moon figure, Lunete, who carries the development still further. Together the two pairs make up a quaternity.

The concept of the correspondences between the microcosmos (man) and the macrocosmos (nature) frequently occupied the forefront of twelfth century cosmological speculation. It had a similar importance in the ritual of Celtic Druidism, with its emphasis on consecrated objects and places. This cosmic concept was as important in the educational role of the romances as in the writings of Dante, where it informs and dominates the whole, bringing everything together under one roof. What it amounted to can be summarized as follows. Man is a being whose moulding and proper education can only be perfected in a spirit of complete candour, in full participation in all the elements of the natural and supernatural world. This is where the age-old wisdom of the poet, as midwife of the imagination, has its part to play, for it is only through images that man is fashioned into his own true image. These images, with their many layers of meaning, work on him unconsciously, to disturb, direct, arouse and satisfy the innermost core of his being.

In the great images of the *romans courtois* two currents merged in a powerful confluence: the stream of material flowing into Western Europe from the outside during the twelfth century, and the suppressed native springs of the underworld of Celtic and even more primitive cultures.

There is space here for only one example, the Grail, the holy vessel. In this symbol are contained memories and "fantasies" from the Orient (Hvareno, the Persian talisman, emblem of royal charisma, has a connection with "Waisen", the fabulous stone on the imperial crown of the Holy Roman Empire); there are also "memories" of ritual chalices and vessels which may have come down from the druids, the Cathars, the Gnostics and perhaps even the Order of Templars. Specifically Christian influences also play their part: twelfth century Cistercian mysticism, the yearning to see and gaze upon the Host, and the orientation of church buildings and liturgy towards the source and condition of illumination.

The ear of the individual listener (these romances reached their public through being read aloud; as with music, the audience was drawn into a weaving symphony of symbols and figures) could pick out from the whole whatever chimed with the temper of the times, the themes which met his own condition as he journeyed on his life's Crusade, whose perils he increasingly recognized. This raises the question of whether individual strands were consciously introduced by the poet into his tapestry. Where the weaving is densest, the likelihood that he knew what he was doing proportionately decreases.

To return to the Grail. One aspect of this symbol of redemption is by now generally recognized. The Grail, at its deepest level, is a feminine mother-symbol. In Chrétien's incomplete *Perceval* the hero's relationship with his mother determines the major part of the action, which turns on Perceval's expiation for his guilt in his mother's death, the failure of his encounter with the "mothers" and the lady. The Grail is borne by a virgin, and is flanked, in a necessary correspondence, by the masculine symbol of the Holy Lance (a phallic symbol like the rod of Moses, the royal sceptre, and so on). Integration, the ripening of the whole personality, entails the obligation of bringing to equal maturity both poles of a man's nature, the masculine and the feminine. In the romance, Perceval's quest for the Grail thus runs parallel with Gauvain's for the Lance. Gauvain had slain the father of a strange knight, Perceval was bound to expiate the death of his mother. Perceval and Gauvain are mirror images, figures of a single individual reaching his maturity as a human being.

Chrétien the clerk and Renaut de Beaujeu the nobleman wrote primarily for women, the objects of their special devotion. Both freely discuss erotic and sensual matters with a natural and unfussy warmth of feeling. There is a marked difference of tone between these passages and the Penitentials, marriage treatises and other theological pronouncements of the time, in which woman is still depicted as an impure, dangerous being, close kinswoman to the evil serpent and "filthy matter".

Renaut de Beaujeu's *Bel Inconnu* was written in the late twelfth or early thirteenth century. His theme is quite explicit: God created woman that man might honour and serve her; woman is the source of everything good. The denial of love is blind folly. Woman is endowed by God with everything good and those who speak evil of her fall under God's curse of dumbness. Underlying all this is a presentiment of evil, a plea and a warning: in the imprisoned Europe of the later Middle Ages the hatred and fear of woman were to break out with renewed force. Gwenyver, Arthur's wonder-working queen, was to be burnt as a witch, together with most of the other heroines of the *romans courtois*. Witch-hunting only came in with the heightened tensions and anxieties of the later Middle Ages; they were yet another sign that the education and refinement of personality had ceased to prosper.

Evidence of the importance Renaut de Beaujeu himself attached to such education is provided by his *Nekyia*, an account of the journey into the New Life, through Hell, death and the devil. This poem finds its place in a series stretching from Homer's account of Odysseus' descent into Hades, through the Descents into Hell of the early twelfth century down to Dante's *Inferno*. In Renaut de Beaujeu's version the hero comes to a castle with a thousand windows, a castle of spooks; at each window sits a musician, before him a burning candle; demoniacal music, pandemonium, fill the air. The knight encounters the devil in numerous incarnations. Around the enchanted castle lies the city of the dead, a fearful domain of death, an underworld. Living and growing are dangerous undertakings. Full growth can be achieved only at the cost of a painful transformation, wrought by death and the most rigorous trials. The depths of the abyss must be reached if a man is to rebound high enough to attain his salvation. In Renaut de Beaujeu the severities imposed by this process of salvation are symbolized by the serpent's kiss. Having come triumphantly through his trials, the knight is emboldened to allow the serpent to kiss him on the mouth, whereupon the beast is transformed back into a man; the work of perfection is complete.

Two of the most powerful motifs of courtly poetry, a strong oriental tradition and "depth psychology", are easily recognizable in *Nekyia*. Among gnostic sects the serpent had an important role as a sacred animal, the symbol of salvation. The liturgy of the Ophites, a gnostic sect which was widespread in later antiquity, culminated in the serpent's kiss. A Christian sect of our own day, the American "Pine Mountain Church of God", has a liturgical snake cult as one of its features. In the Europe of the twelfth and thirteenth centuries there were gnostic influences everywhere. Even more significant is the second motif, "depth psychology". This whole literature was nourished on the awareness by its authors and feminine public that the crisis in the consciences and instincts of the newly-awakened men of the twelfth century was already so acute that it could no longer be staved off by the old, devalued symbols which were all that the Church had to offer in its attenuated preaching and unsophisticated imagery.

Outside France and the Angevin Empire, the invention of courtly civilization and the birth of imagination made their profoundest impact during the twelfth and early thirteenth centuries in Germany. Between 1180 and 1220 the courtly literature of the two French civilizations found its richest, deepest and most creative echoes in the German-speaking lands, just as at a rather later date the grandeur and perfection of French Gothic sculpture at its height, the sculpture of Chartres, Rheims and Amiens, would be matched outside France only at Naumberg, Bamberg and Mainz.

This was no accident; in Germany too this new literature can be understood as a constructive response to the profound crisis in which society, the "state" and the existing political and ecclesiastical regimes were all involved. The two other great epochs of German culture were also times of abnormal psychological tension. The disintegration of society in the later Middle Ages and the decay of the Empire engendered anxieties and hopes in the German people which found response during the period 1480–1525 in the culture of the German Humanists and the age of Luther. Between the years 1770 and 1830, when the Germans were again the prey of hopes and fears, still overshadowed by the Thirty Years' War, still cooped up within the narrow bounds of their mutually hostile petty states and various religious confessions, an "answer" to their situation was provided by Goethe and the Romantics, who beckoned the German people into the light of a new day, summoning them, it seemed, to a mission of oecumenical grandeur.

By the mid-twelfth century, particularly in the south-west, Germany was beginning to emerge from its impassive and age-long self-sufficiency. The symptoms of upheaval were numerous: the rise of towns and of an aristocracy of service, the *ministeriales*; religious unrest; and the appearance of heretics of every persuasion, all the way from Cologne to Zurich. The people who witnessed the long-drawn-out struggle between Frederick I and the Popes perhaps sensed that the way was being prepared for the decline which overtook both Empire and Papacy in the thirteenth century. Moreover, alien ideas and materials were flooding in, from France in the west, from Byzantium in the east.

A tormented people, torn by the feuds of their spiritual and temporal masters, might well ask: "Where is God? What is the lord Pope doing, who seems interested only in extorting money from us stupid Germans? What, after all, does the lord Emperor really amount to?" It was to questions of this kind that the poets provided an answer, as often as not in provocative, even revolutionary terms.

The higher German nobility had long been connected with that of France by social and family ties; during the twelfth century these older connections became less important than links with England and southern France. "Matilda Empress", the widow of the Emperor Henry V, was the mother of Henry II. Another Matilda, daughter of Henry II and Eleanor, was to become the wife of Henry the Lion, the most powerful prince in Germany after Frederick Barbarossa, and a leading member of the great Welf clan. The family connection between the Welfs and the Plantagenets was one of the great facts of political life in the twelfth and early thirteenth centuries. One of Eleanor's grandchildren would become the Emperor Otto IV. As for southern France, the German kings and emperors had had close ties with the region since the eleventh century, on account of their privileges and estates there and in Burgundy. Provençal *jongleurs* now received an increasingly warm welcome at the festivities of the imperial court.

The rebellious aristocracy of Provence now had their counterpart in the new aristocracy of service which had emerged under the Hohenstaufen dynasty. Originally unfree, these capable and combative men had risen in the service of king and emperor to positions of responsibility, in particular the custody of the network of imperial castles which stretched from Alsace and the Hohenstaufen territories beyond Nürnberg as far as Eger, Cham and Nabburg, and would ultimately, it was intended, reach to Vienna. As castellans, the *ministeriales* administered castles and estates belonging both to the dynasty and to the Empire. Some of these *imperial ministeriales* rose to very high positions indeed; in Italy they were virtually viceroys or imperial commissars, responsible for the government of large tracts of country and wealthy cities.

The wares offered by the courtly civilization of the Provençal south were eagerly snapped up by this new nobility, these *homines novi*, who found themselves launched on the world without benefit of hereditary lands and traditions, and with no culture of their own making behind them. Looked down upon by the older aristocracy and the princes of the Church, secular and monastic, these new men were searching for new modes of thought and feeling to liberate them from their inner servitude to the old and established powers. These new lords and their ladies were offered by the Minnesinger the prospect of a "kingdom of love", a lofty realm with a wider range of vision than that of the existing "empires" which still had such a hold over the German people: the "empires" of politically-directed piety, of a ruling Church, the Holy Roman Empire itself. The foundations of the new kingdom consisted solely in the personal relationships of two individuals desiring one another in discreet indiscretion. The lovers hover between desire and its fulfilment: *sweben*, meaning "to hover", is a word which frequently recurs in the writings of the Minnesinger.

It is instructive and significant that the difference in phasing commonly noticeable as between western and eastern Europe occurs also on the literary plane. It took the Germanic East from one to two generations to absorb and refashion the material coming to it from the West; and the further east one looks, the longer is the time-lag. The courtly poetry of Provence and also to some extent that of northern France was only assimilated in south-western Germany after the lapse of a generation. During the years 1160–80, which saw the heyday of Marie de France and Chrétien de Troyes and when the songs of Eleanor's grandfather were already fifty years old, the type of lyric current in Germany was still strongly folk in character, resolutely innocent of the courtly convention which required the "lady" and her "lover" to keep their distance; courtly formalism was accepted only with great reluctance. In this "archaic" poetry, which excelled in directness and passion, men and women freely express their desire for one another without reference to codes and convention. The dominant note is one of joyous candour, at times even a little brazen, the expression of a primitive, naïve belief in the sympathy uniting man with the cosmos, God, nature and objects. These lyrics are artless and deeply felt, nourished by an unperturbed and unreflecting piety. Some of these poets are anonymous, known only as "Der von Kürenberg", "der Burggraf von Regensburg", "der Burggraf von Rietenburg"; others belonging to this group are Herr Meinloh von Sevelingen and Herr Hartwic von Rute. Poets like Heinrich von Rugge and Dietmar von Aist also merit inclusion, since when they are writing in earnest they strike the old chords, tearing to pieces their modish courtly façade. The same can be said of all the more important German courtly lyricists. These outbursts occur in crusading lyrics and in "unconventional" love-songs, for example love-songs addressed by a man to his wife or to some low-born light-of-love—unthinkable occasions for writing poetry according to the strict courtly canon.

But between 1180 and 1220 the courtly lyric held sway; the reign of *Minne* had begun. The German kingdom of love was modelled on the Provençal, but had some significant deviations from it; in Germany everything was more sombre, sometimes more profound, certainly more weighty and less limpid. What in the south had been a light-hearted sport, delicate, precious and ironical, in Germany became ponderous, an imposition of devotion. The lady's "grace and favour" was charged with all the potency which piety, ancient and modern, attributed to the grace of God and the Virgin. Implicit in the fealty (*triuwe*) which bound the courtly knight to his lady was the whole tradition of fealty and trust binding a vassal to his lord, and the Christian to God, his king. But it was reinforced by a serious recognition of the change which had come over the world: the relationship of two lovers is accepted as the only reality. They occupy the centre of the stage; God, nature, the world and time wait in the wings. God is made known in His "courtesy": the courteous God is the patron of lovers, and adapts Himself to them like the long sleeves fashionable in court society: "He falls into place and clings whichever way you try Him" (to quote a famous line from Gottfried von Strassburg). What do kings and emperors matter? The courtly poet knows himself more than their equal if he carries off the prize of his lady's favour.

As individuals, the foremost Minnesinger were men of widely varying character. Friedrich von Hausen, a retainer of Bishop Christian of Mainz who went to Italy on the affairs of Frederick I and Henry VI, was at bottom a knight of the old school who happened to make use of the new forms to express his thoughts and feelings. His well-known crusading song *"Mein Herz und mein Leib, die wollen sich scheiden"* is not just a new version of the poem by Conon de Bethune but a new creation, meeting something in his personal situation. He died on Barbarossa's Crusade.

Heinrich von Morungen, the most passionate among the poets of this circle, showed both in his life and his poetry an eccentricity powerful enough to flaunt the conventions of courtly etiquette. After completing his Crusade, he took himself off to India—bizarre conduct indeed, according to our notions of what was proper for twelfth century German knights. In his *Rückblickslied* he describes the courtly kingdom of love as a fiction, an illusion: *wân* as applied to the courteous knight's hopes of his lady's favour once meant folly; but as he sees now, it should really mean nothing short of disillusionment. Heinrich relates how formerly he would circle his lady as a falcon stalks its prey. But now he has lost all faith in woman's power to heal. Even the noblest lady has no consolation or redemption to offer. Full authority to free men and mankind is not hers to command. To whom then did it belong?

The Pope was a remote and alien power. The Emperors after the time of Henry VI, until the extinction of the

Hohenstaufen dynasty in 1250, were impotent, also alien, and usually equally remote. However, there were two princely houses in eastern Germany whose courts had become centres of the new culture; the Babenberger, who held court at Vienna, and the Landgraves of Thuringia, whose seat was on the Wartburg.

Vienna under the Babenberger was exposed to influences from east and west. There were Byzantine connections, arising from marriages and the continual passage through Vienna of parties of Crusaders. Contacts with eastern Europe and Russia were established by merchants; there had been a trade-route to Regensburg by way of Vienna from quite early in the Middle Ages. Vienna's links with the West were numerous and various: political, dynastic, religious and intellectual. Western influence in these last two by no means unimportant spheres was mediated largely by the twelfth century Cistercians and an early French schoolman, Magister Petrus. It was at this cosmopolitan court of Vienna that the poet who has been described as the "schoolman of blighted love", Reimar von Hagenau, was writing. His verse is precious, highly mannered and highly intellectual, revealing him as a master of sophistry who plays with emotion and the shades of emotion as with so many glass beads. It was here, too, at Vienna, in what was to become Austria, that the greatest German lyric poet of the Middle Ages, Walther von der Vogelweide, learned to "sing and say". He was to master and defeat all the conventions of courtly society.

By birth he belonged to the landless class of petty *ministeriales*; having no commitment, he was free to seek his board and lodging where he would, and passed his life in sojourns of varying length in a number of noble households. The great lords who became his patrons included three Dukes of Austria, Leopold VI, Frederick, and Leopold VII; Duke Bernard of Carinthia, the Landgrave Herman of Thuringia, the Margrave Dietrich IV of Meissen, Duke Welf VI; ecclesiastical princes of the Empire such as Wolfger von Ellenbrechtskirchen, Bishop of Passau and later Patriarch of Aquileja, and Archbishop Engelbert of Cologne; as well as many others of lesser rank. In the course of his life's journey Walther learned to know peoples and countries of all kinds as they really were. He found the world a nasty place. The princes snatched at fragments of the decaying Empire whenever they had opportunity. Walther's direct experience of popular misery, a misery afflicting body and soul alike, turned him into a great political and religious poet. In his *Sprüche*, or didactic and political songs, he attacks Roman greed and fraudulence in a way which not only reminds us of the impassioned protests of his Provençal confrères but also points towards the denunciations of a Hutten or a Luther. Walther foresaw worldwide catastrophe: Empire, Church and Christendom were falling apart, and even courtly civilization was no protection against destruction. Where then was salvation to be found? In a simple faith in the God of Love, manifest in the infant Christ of the manger, "young man and ancient God, meek in the presence of the ox and ass". Walther anticipated the vision of the *Poverello*, Francis of Assisi, who was to erect at Greccio the first manger-crib in Christendom, to chasten the pretensions of the mighty in Church and State.

The love of God imposed further obligations if its fuller depths were to be plumbed; it meant, for example, loving one's enemy as an equal, as a brother in Christ. Here, too, Walther was a "Franciscan" before St Francis, and far in advance of his own time and his own countrymen. However, all heart-felt love was rooted firmly in this earth. The folk inspiration of Walther's love-songs remained unmatched until it was recaptured in the bell-like timbre and purity of Goethe.

The social origins of Hartmann von Aue, the first German poet to write courtly epics, were similar to those of Walther. Hartmann "adapted" the *Erec* and *Yvain* of Chrétien de Troyes and in doing so refashioned both romances into a thoroughly Germanic mould. He is at his most original in *Gregorius* (1195–96) and *Der Arme Heinrich* (1199). Here the German poet has become the critic of German aristocratic society, which in *Gregorius* is depicted as stifling in incest and brutality; anyone sincerely trying to escape its toils must prepare himself for a strict and lengthy life of penance. In *Der Arme Heinrich* (whose magic inspired Gerhart Hauptmann to compose his own version of the tale), Heinrich is a knight suffering from leprosy; he is also the symbol of all that was best in chivalry. Heinrich, beyond the help of any great lord or ecclesiastical power, is rescued, healed and redeemed by the love of a pure village maiden; he is cured, above all, of his pride, his leprosy of the soul. The girl is willing to give her life for her lord, to sacrifice her blood for him, in an operation performed by a doctor from Salerno: "I am a woman and have the strength; only cut me and see that I can bear it." Her fortitude in making this sacrifice has its source in her love for her lord and for Christ. Christ appears to her in a vision under the form of a "free peasant", whose love for her, the little peasant girl, is as great as for any queen. It will be remembered that in *Piers Plowman*, written a century and a half later, William Langland sets the same vision of a "poor Christ" before the "poor people" of England for their consolation. The feelings of the German people had already reached the same critical situation around the beginning of the thirteenth century.

Two poems written about 1200, very different in form but alike in the vehemence of their attack on the political and ecclesiastical order as embodied in the Holy Roman Empire, indicate how rich was the vein of potentially explosive material in the Germany of that time, particularly in the West, which was exposed to the influence of its neighbours, France, Flanders, the Netherlands and Italy. In Alsace, the district between Strasbourg and Cologne, the danger had long been present. This was a region notorious for its heresy, its baronial rebellions, for bourgeois revolts against episcopal control of towns, and for monasteries which resisted reformation; it was in this perturbed region that the leaven of German mysticism at its most sublime and most active would later work. Here in Alsace the German brand of spiritual and intellectual nonconformism has always had deep roots; one sees it at Strasbourg, at the time of the Reformation, in the Pietists and Quietists, in the eighteenth century, and in our own contemporary Albert Schweitzer. This is not something confined to the cities; the small townships, the forests and remote green valleys, have all been touched by the breath, so gentle and seemingly so mild, of the rebellion of the "heart" against the "mighty".

Such was the background of the satirical epic *Reineke Fuchs*, written about 1181, and of Gottfried von Strassburg's *Tristan*, written some time after 1205. Official and semi-official court poetry and imperial propaganda hailed the Holy Roman Empire, revived by the Emperor Frederick I, as the kingdom of salvation and righteousness, the terrestrial representative of the Kingdom of God, and presented it as such to "truly believing subjects", that is, subjects faithful both to God and to the Empire (*Dei et Imperii Fideles*). This Empire was based on the maxim that the Emperor would reward loyal service in princely fashion, just as God rewarded His faithful servants. The virtuous would have their reward, the wicked their punishment. In Alsace, however, as was common knowledge, Frederick I had frequently found himself unable or unwilling to make good his promises, which in some cases had led to open rebellion against him. Heinrich der Glîchezare, the author of *Reineke Fuchs,* used the standard vehicle of medieval political satire, the animal fable, to prove that this Empire was a fiction. While artful scoundrels and flatterers were rewarded, loyal and honest subjects were being fleeced. Imperial propaganda presented the Emperor as the lion, the noble king of beasts, after the image of Christ, the Lion of Judah; but for Heinrich he was the image of the devil's lion, the king of wickedness. Faithless, miserly, fundamentally stupid, the lion is snared by the wiles of the fox, his cunning counsellor, and dies wretchedly. But the people still lament the "death of their noble king".

The "holy Empire" was not the only target of Heinrich's mordant and embittered ridicule; contemporary church dogmas and even courtly civilization came under attack. Frederick I, through the agency of his Chancellor, Rainald of Dassel, Archbishop-elect of Cologne, had engineered the canonization of Charlemagne as part of a general plan for exalting the saints of his dynasty. The king in *Reineke Fuchs* orders that the obsequies of the hen be conducted with the utmost liturgical ceremony; the hare then lies down on her grave and has a vision which he reports to the king: "the hen is in glory in the presence of God". The courtly world is just as surely unmasked. The crafty fox is a past master of courtly manners and uses these arts, amongst others, to achieve the rape of the wolf's wife, Frau Hersaute.

In his *Tristan* Gottfried von Strassburg presses into service all the formal arts of courtly literature to unveil the courtly world as a world of lies and delusion, of futile self-deception. It would be rewarding to compare his work with John of Salisbury's castigation of the malice and mendacity of the courtiers of Henry II. Gottfried first presents Isolde's husband King Mark as the prototype of all good, holy and courteous kings, Charlemagne and King Arthur rolled into one. Mark is pious, valiant, generous and just; the reputation of his court as a training-ground of courtesy is world-wide. He then allows this same Mark to traverse in slow motion a path leading to abject humiliation: from the time of his first encounter with Isolde he fails ignominiously. He allows himself to be foisted off on his wedding-night with Isolde's confidante, Brangane; later, when he cannot fail to notice his wife's love for Tristan, he shows himself a miserably feeble fellow, for whom no fraud or deception, not excluding self-deception, is too low if it will bring him to what he considers his right, possession of Isolde. The master of courtesy becomes a crazed, tearful creature, hopeless and helpless, the disgrace of his court and all earthly royalty.

This theme, implicit or explicit, is at the back of many of the *romans courtois;* with or without compassion, they lay bare the infirmities of a king in his mortal sickness, the thaumaturge who has lost his power to heal, an Amfortas, a Mark, even Arthur himself. Kingship remained a valid symbol only so long as the king could serve as an emblem of honour for his knights to justify their deeds; they found in kingship the legitimacy they craved. For in his own "kingdom", the kingdom of love, each of these new-fashioned knights was his own Pope, Emperor or King. Only Shakespeare, who could look back over the perspective offered by the Hundred Years' War and three centuries of troubled monarchical history, was capable on occasion of combining in a single vision the dual aspect of royalty: he exposes the mortal infirmity and sickness of all earthly monarchies, yet at the same time affirms that "not all the waters in the rough rude sea can wash the balm from an anointed king" (*Richard II*, iii, 2).

The German Gottfried von Strassburg, on the other hand, exposes in horrifying and meticulous detail just how thoroughly the waters of life washed away the royalty of Mark, to his complete undoing, until all that was left was the "unhappy Mark", a blinded and covetous fool, a burden to himself and the world, all from his incapacity to surrender what had never been truly his—his wife Isolde, who from the first had loved only Tristan. Mark's sight of the lovers alseep as he gazes on them through a small hole in their Lovers' Cave fills him with dread. This Lovers' Cave was the Church of the new Inner Kingdom. As Gottfried describes it, it was half Hohenstaufen palace, half Gothic cathedral, with Oriental and southern French overtones. It is with the description of the lovers' sojourn in the Cave that the poet mounts his main attack on monarchy, old and new, and on the hierarchical church and society of his time. With apparent composure, he explains that Tristan and Isolde have been anointed by their love. All other sacraments, the anointing of king and bishop, the consecration of the priest and the sacraments of marriage and communion, are superseded by this sacrament of love. This new sacrament, the entire involvement of two lovers with each other at the deepest level of intimacy, struck a fatal blow at all hierarchies, secular, ecclesiastical and social.

Gottfried makes his meaning quite clear. Through their carnal and spiritual union the lovers are made into the Grail and the Host, they administer to one another the sacrament of the new kingdom, the communion of flesh and blood. "Man was there with Woman, Woman there with Man. What else should they be needing?"

This was the only truth about life and reality which interested the poet and his public. The existential relationship of two human beings was the only measure by which honour, justice and morality could be judged. Morality was the fulfilment of the heart's desires. The world was governed by the lovers' "heart". Even the ordeal was powerless against it. Gottfried was writing in a Strasbourg which, because of the town's conflict with its bishop, Heinrich von Veringen, had for five years been deprived of all ecclesiastical offices; then in 1212 eighty heretics, men and women of both noble and non-noble birth, had been burnt, after failing in the ordeal of red-hot iron. The chronicles record the cheerfulness of these people, children among them, in the face of death. Gottfried's telling thrust at the ordeal, and the ordeal of red-hot iron at that, should probably be related to these events.

The major part of *Tristan* must have been composed between 1211 and 1215. The "Holy Empire" was *in extremis*. After the Battle of Bouvines in 1214 Philip Augustus of France, both friend and foe to Eleanor's sons, sent to Frederick II the captured imperial eagle. The radical individualism which was the hallmark of the Provençal atmosphere with which Eleanor had surrounded herself found its grandest expression in *Tristan*, the work of a German poet, a demon-king whose ironical pronouncements flash out in shafts of purple lightning: there is no holy empire outside the empire of love. And the empire of love consists wholly in the relationship of two lovers, who disdain all that God, the world and the social order can offer or deny them.

Gottfried's feelings with regard to his contemporary Wolfram von Eschenbach were deeply antipathetic. Wolfram, the greatest poet to write courtly romances in the German tongue, was a petty knight like Hartmann von Aue and Walther von der Vogelweide. We have already met him as the champion of toleration, in his *Willehalm*. In *Parzival*, his masterpiece,

Wolfram strove after the rehabilitation of the Empire, the nobility, courtly breeding and the nurture of personality on Christian lines. *Parsival* is thus at once the fulfilment of courtesy and its defeat. Parzival asks "Is God faithful?", and his query echoes doubts in the minds of people at large, the Crusaders and the "poor folk". Wolfram's answer is a qualified affirmative: God is faithful, but very often reveals His favour to men only through disfavour. "God can give joy and woe to whom He will: He may perchance thrust aside all my eager longings and turn them to tears, if He wills so to prove his goodness towards me." God's goodness is hidden in His wrath. Man goes astray, his life's journey leads him on through trials, sin and guilt. What is important is for man to know that these must be endured.

In Wolfram's hands, the adventures, the journeyings and joustings of the heroes of romance are elevated to the grandeur of baroque: here is a canvas which depicts the progress of man on his great pilgrimage into the depths and abysses of his own soul. Defeat must follow defeat if victory is to be achieved. Victory can be won only in the soul of the individual. He who in this way overcomes self-deception, false pride, factitious fears and the delusion of self-confidence, will be granted the vision of the Godhead, the "unending Trinity", as a deep mystery of power, love and spirit. Abelard's vision of the Trinity was the same.

CHAPTER 8

POPULAR RELIGIOUS MOVEMENTS

WHEN Henry II and Eleanor separated, the king had hopes that his wife would end her days as abbess of Fontévrault. Although Eleanor declined the position, it was at Fontévrault that the pair were eventually reunited. Eleanor rests there between her tempestuous husband and her no less tempestuous son, Richard Coeur de Lion. Her exquisite effigy shows Eleanor, the queen of courtly society, in the habit of a nun, a missal in her hands.

To this same Fontévrault a rich merchant of Lyons sent his two daughters to take the veil. He had been profoundly disturbed in spirit by hearing a minstrel's moving recital of the Alexius legend, which made him realize that a true Christian must abandon all his possessions and all thought of power and wealth to make his way through the world in poverty. The merchant's next step was to find someone to translate portions of the Scriptures into vernacular tongues. A poor scholar, Bernard Ydros, translated the Gospels and other religious texts for him into French, while Stephen d'Anse the grammarian, afterwards a prominent member of the cathedral chapter of Lyons, translated the Gospels into the soft tongue of Provence. The merchant was Peter Waldo (or Waldes), founder of the Waldensians, who, although destined to a future of blood, tears and persecution, never ceased from the twelfth century to the nineteenth to proclaim the Good News in their brotherhood, as laid down by their founder.

Waldensians were persecuted along with Cathars, and accounted arch-heretics. But it had been Waldo's intention to preach against Catharism and counteract its influence; he never dreamed he was on the way to founding a sect. This typifies the tragedy of the Church's situation from the middle of the eleventh to the middle of the thirteenth century. While Christianity and the Church were still "open", the Gospel could for the first time penetrate deep into the minds and consciences of individuals, captivating people of every degree, noblemen, peasants, townsmen, simple village priests, men, women and children. Seized by the spirit, laymen and monks turned itinerant preachers, proclaiming a Christ who came not with a sword and power but in poverty, and whose habitation was not in episcopal palaces and cathedral chapters, nor in opulent ancient monastic communities, but in the open air, on the land, in the fields and in the hearts of those who received Him. The *Cristo de los campesinos* of the Spanish proletariat (frequently alluded to in the Spanish heresy hunts of the sixteenth century) was already being preached in the eleventh and twelfth centuries by the inspired visionaries who initiated Europe's first revivalist movement.

There were numerous small groups of these "poor men of Christ" (as some of them called themselves) in southern and northern France, in Flanders, the Rhineland and northern Italy. They had no presentiment of what was to spring from their small beginnings. They regarded themselves as undisputed members of "holy Christianity" (in the eleventh and twelfth centuries "church" in popular parlance meant simply the church building).

One notices again and again that the fate of a group of religious revivalists seems to hinge on "accident"; that this should be so is one of history's grimmer secrets. Such a group may achieve ecclesiastical recognition as a reforming order or congregation, or as a group of laymen; or it may be caught up in the wake of denunciation and persecution and after a time become really "heretical". Forced out of the mainstream and pushed underground, such groups become infected with radicalism and are in danger of secularization; their range of vision contracts, and, equally damaging, they make common cause with the subterranean brotherhood already in existence all over Europe.

St Francis of Assisi has many admirers nowadays, among them pious Catholics, Protestants and non-Christians, attracted by his love for animals and all created things and by his pacifism. These pious, at times downright sentimental, devotees of the *Poverello* have rarely any notion of how close he came to the surrounding flames, which consumed some who stood nearest to him, his persecuted friends and brothers.

Let us recapitulate briefly some of the elements of early medieval popular piety which still retained their vigour: they were a provocation and a challenge, electrifying the atmosphere at the very moment when "awakened" men had come to realize how little of true Christianity the Christian world contained.

The sense of great joy and inward freedom which the early Church derived from its possession of the Good News (which every one could read for himself), and its sense of union with the resurrected Lord, had long since been overlaid by feelings of terror and estrangement. Men at their prayers no longer raised their arms and turned toward Christ, their rising sun, but folded their hands in the attitude of serfs, serfs of God and of their sin. Where formerly the priest had celebrated the Mass facing the people, in proof of his accessibility, now he turned his back on them and retreated to the fastnesses of the sanctuary, separated from the people's part of the church by a forbidding screen. Finally, the Mass was read in a tongue the people could not understand. As a prophylactic against spiritual harm the people concentrated on their love for a multitude of saints, invoked as the "friends of God", as advocates with power to heal, as channels of access to the dread and omnipotent majesty of God. Some of these saints were of mythical origin, others belonged to the ancestral kindred of important noble families. As late as the mid-twelfth century Pope Alexander III found it necessary to ask the Swedes to refrain from promptly honouring as saints "men who died in their cups" (at a sacral feast).

Mystery, the mystery of the Mass, ritual and liturgy, proliferated an outgrowth of the miraculous which eroded the edges of wholesome piety like a cancer. The supreme reality was no longer to be found in sober and sanctified participation in that mystery which proclaimed the transformation of mankind, "the putting on of the new man", but in the miraculous and marvellous. The mania for marvels was such that apparitions and visions were looked for, and found, on all sides; many of them were no doubt genuinely curious phenomena. Although in the twelfth century the fever for the marvellous found some relief through its eruption into literature, particularly the *roman courtois*, religion was still its chief field of action. We have already remarked on the critical attitude of the authors of *Reineke Fuchs* and the German *Tristan* towards the cult of the marvellous and spectacular.

This symptom, and the other manifestations of the headstrong growth and deformation of popular religious emotion, had two main underlying causes. First, Christ was no longer directly accessible to the people; direct contact with Him was first and foremost the privilege of monks and after them of the secular priesthood, who administered the power of Christ in the sacraments, particularly the Mass, which brought them daily into the presence of Christ the King, the great Lord of Heaven. Secondly, the Roman Church's veto on the translation of the Gospels and other religious texts into the vernacular was a most effective means of keeping the people at arm's length. The Greek Church, which had long been a missionary church, took an opposite view and had numerous translations of the Bible into vernacular languages to its credit: Coptic, Syriac, Old Latin, Ethiopian, Georgian, Armenian, Gothic and Old Slavonic. Byzantine missionaries were working among the Huns in their own language from early in the sixth century. The Roman Church, even to this day, has always jealously guarded the supremacy of Latin as the sacred tongue to the exclusion of all others. The price has been a heavy one. There was no "authorized" Christian translation of the Bible which could be read by the Berbers, the Celts or the Germanic peoples. The task of translating the Bible into the native languages would have presented no problem to the intellectual talent of the Church in Africa, the Church of Tertullian and Augustine. But it was not undertaken, and North Africa fell to Islam. From the twelfth century the Latin Church was starting to lose individual souls and entire peoples to religious movements which catered for their needs by translating the Bible and other religious literature into their own tongues. The later Middle Ages saw the defection first of England and Bohemia and later of Germany.

Catharism, the most powerful of the anti-Roman religious movements of the twelfth and thirteenth centuries, inherited from the Eastern Church and from Manichaeism the practice of conducting evangelistic work in the vernacular, with the assistance of vernacular texts. The record of the Manichees as translators equalled and indeed surpassed that of the Greeks. In the twelfth century they were assiduously carrying on this work in the West, having earlier produced translations into Asiatic languages, including Chinese, and into the African and Spanish Latin of late antiquity.

It was not until the twelfth century that popular religious movements began to be labelled by sympathizers and opponents as orthodox or heretical, "left" or "right". During the eleventh century, when the way for the full-scale movements was being prepared, accusations of heresy were at first levelled only at individual peasants and "illiterate" persons, and at certain clerics and noblemen. For example, about the year 1000 there was the case of a villager from Champagne called Leuthard; returning from the fields one day (perhaps, like Joan of Arc, he had had a vision there) he drove away his wife, dashed to pieces the crucifix in the church, refused to pay his tithe and declared he had no further use for the prophets of the Old Testament. In 1019 there were southern French "heretics" at Orleans, who succeeded in winning over a section of the nobility and educated clergy in the entourage of the French king, Robert the Pious (996–1031), who was a patron of church reform. Unmasked by spies as "heretics", they went cheerfully to their deaths on December 28, 1022, the first people to be burned as heretics in the West. They were confident that the entire population of France, including the king, would soon be captivated by their teaching.

About 1028 a group of peasants, clerics and nobles with heretical leanings established themselves at the castle of Monteforte, between Turin and Genoa, under the protection of the countess. This group seems to have had something of the gay serenity characteristic of the Franciscans. They taught that God the Father created all, that Christ was not God, remote and terrible, but the soul of mankind, in whom God delighted, and that the Holy Ghost was the proper knowledge and understanding of Holy Writ. Offered the choice between the Cross as interpreted by the Church and the stake, they unhesitatingly chose the latter. The ecclesiastical chronicles of the period, whose testimony on this point can surely be accepted without reserve, frequently remark on the cheerful eagerness with which "heretics" went to their death; this must have been the fruit of the inward freedom and joy, the liberation and integration of the innermost depths of being which came from the novelty of living by the light of a personally experienced faith. The intoxicating sense of joy and freedom one finds among the earliest Franciscans and Jesuits had its roots in the same experience.

During the eleventh century the most powerful promoter of popular religious emotion was the Papacy itself. When the Pope was the greatest revolutionary of his day, men who would otherwise have been labelled heretics became his most devoted followers. The Patarene movement, which started at Milan and Florence in 1057, found an ally in the revolutionary Pope Gregory VII, at that time in conflict with the "simoniacal" episcopate, strongly aristocratic in complexion, who refused to co-operate in his reform of the Church. Gregory thus mobilized the people in defence of the "freedom of the Church", since he needed to protect his reforms from the dangerous embrace of a feudalized and germanized Church. The people, in their longing for the "Christ of poverty", were themselves in conflict with their bishops and looked to the Papacy for aid. In 1077, for example, some fanatical Flemish laymen begged the Pope's protection against the Bishop of Cambrai, who had denounced them as heretics. In 1162 Flemish townsmen were again protesting to the Pope, Alexander III, on account of their condemnation as heretics by the Archbishop of Reims, who objected to their "apostolic" mode of life. In 1179 the same Pope embraced with brotherly affection Peter Waldo, driven by the threats of the Archbishop of Lyons to seek help from Rome.

Even so, Rome was too weak during the twelfth century to be capable of gathering these wayward souls into the Church, where they might have been protected and disciplined; the men and spiritual resources necessary for such a task were lacking. The problem was left increasingly to the bishops and the religious orders, old and new, whose view of the "innovators" was shot through with suspicion and dislike. The chief ground of complaint was the presumption of these "uneducated" men in preaching, and in reading and propagating translations of the Bible. Peter Waldo became a "heretic" because neither he nor his followers allowed themselves to be deterred from preaching. "The freedom of the Word of God" was for these visionaries a higher freedom than the "freedom of the Church".

Europe in the early twelfth century was swarming with hermits, wandering preachers and foot-loose monks. When they joined forces the resulting group might develop either into a new Order or Congregation, sealed with the blessing of the Church, or into a heretical sect. Robert of Arbrissel (already mentioned as the guest of Guillaume IX, the grandfather of Eleanor of Aquitaine and the first troubadour) was one such wanderer. He founded the congregation of Fontévrault, the place of refuge both of Eleanor herself and of the daughters of Peter Waldo.

Robert's foundation was an individual affair and there were other religious individualists about this time who formed the nucleus of a movement, sometimes large, sometimes small. They were particularly numerous in France and Flanders, though one finds them in northern Italy as well. They represented all ranks of society and included priests, monks, noblemen, smiths, artisans, peasants and urban patricians. The driving force behind all these manifestations of religious fervour was the urge to lead the apostolic life in imitation of the poverty and humility of Christ.

These twelfth-century "heretics" were convinced that their teaching was faithful to the teaching and spirit of the Gospels, while the Church, as it seemed to them, was in a state of apostasy, having denied God, Christ, the Holy Spirit and love itself; they were "true Christians". These "heretics" distinguished between "good" priests and "bad", from whom they refused to receive the sacraments. But their "anticlericalism" should not be misinterpreted. Even during the most "Catholic" periods, medieval society was sufficiently uninhibited and heterogeneous to tolerate very open criticism of the clergy, so that in this, as in other respects, the twelfth century "heretics" were in line with popular sentiment. If a few such groups did end by seeking for themselves a theoretical justification which took them further outside the Church of their own time, they were driven to it in self-defence by persecution and the opposition of individual bishops.

It is interesting to notice that as time went on women of noble birth became prominent as patrons of religious heterodoxy, a cause which had found sympathizers among their menfolk from an early date. Women were tired of the masculine ascendency, they disliked being chattels in the marriage market and the objects of monkish suspicion and contempt. Looking for a way of escape from this oppression they found it in education, of the mind and of the spirit. Courtly culture and Catharism both flourished under the protection of noble ladies, above all the noble ladies of Provence.

The arrival of Catharism in western Europe during the twelfth century marked a dramatic turning-point in the fortunes of "heretics" of every sort. Catharism itself originated outside Europe, in the East, and was at bottom a non-Christian religion. Initially it penetrated southwestern Europe subterraneously; but when it came out into the open its success was rapid and it was suppressed only after a civil war lasting thirty years. Cathars first appeared in western Europe about 1140 and the last Cathars of southern France were burnt at the stake in 1323–24. Even then their spirit lived on. The Huguenots of the sixteenth and seventeenth centuries were led by a sure instinct to recognize the Cathars as their spiritual kin, and their church as a figure of the archetypal church. Bossuet, the champion of an integrated Catholicism under the aegis of the Sun King, did not hesitate to describe the Cathars as the precursors of the Huguenots, adherents of that devil's church which flaunted its permanent challenge to the Church of Rome.

The drama and tragedy of the Cathars was closely bound up with the tragedy which overtook courtly civilization in the South and the fate of popular religious movements as a whole in the thirteenth and fourteenth centuries; there were always enemies ready to link this or that group with the Cathars, which by definition made them anti-Christian. Waldensians and Cathars were burnt at the same stake, despite the initial great antagonism of the Waldensians towards Catharism; Franciscans who refused to accept Bonaventure's victory over Francis had the Cathar label attached to them indiscriminately.

Catharism represented the first attempt by an eastern non-Christian religion to gain a foothold in the West. It had its roots in Gnosticism, which was Greek, and in Manichaeism, which came from Persia and the Near East. *Cathari* in Greek means "the pure". Purity of spirit and its liberation from the evil world and from matter was the goal of the Greek mystery religions and of Manichaeism. The chief characteristic of Gnosticism was its confident belief in the power of a pure spirit to attain direct communion with the Godhead; the Manichees were distinguished by their belief in the distinct and infrangible boundary separating the "children of light" from the "children of darkness". This dualistic doctrine, which could be regarded as both optimistic and pessimistic, made its appearance in Bulgaria during the tenth century. The Bulgars were at the time suffering a triple oppression, from the Russians, the Byzantines and the Roman Church. Bulgar society was sharply divided. On the one hand was the wealthy aristocracy and the wealthy church, on the other the lesser aristocracy, the lower clergy and the peasant. It was to this second group that the village priest Bogomil addressed his message, which can be summed up briefly: "the world is evil, let us therefore live like the apostles, in penitence, prayer and inward recollection." If simplicity of life was the ideal, then all ecclesiastical magnificence and secular might and riches were vanity. In this world the Christian could expect only blood and tears, since this world was the creation of Satan, God's elder son and Christ's brother, the "God" of Genesis and the Old Testament.

It is evident that Christian themes and non-Christian gnostic teachings were already starting to merge with each other. During the ninth century the Byzantine Emperors had forcibly transported to Thrace the adherents of two eastern gnostic sects, the Paulicians and the Messalians, who later joined up with the Bogomils, the "friends of God". After the conquest of the Bulgar kingdom by the Byzantines in 1018, the Empire was itself permeated by underground heterodoxy. In this affluent setting the Bogomils succeeded in gaining adherents among the higher nobility, a class much given to philosophizing and religious and intellectual enquiry, particularly into cosmological and philosophical subjects. Catharism was to have a similar attraction for the Provençal nobility in the twelfth century. The Bogomils even made some impression on the spiritually arid field of Byzantine monasticism. A split developed within the Bogomils themselves as a result of the extension of their activity into the alien political and intellectual climate of the Byzantine Empire. The old Bogomils styled themselves the Church of the "Bulgars", while the "new" Bogomils, taking their name from the Thracian district of Dragovitsa, became the "Dragovitsan" Church. When the Crusaders arrived in the Byzantine Empire in the early twelfth century they found the Emperor much taken up with the question of the expulsion of the Bogomils. Ejected from Byzantium (in 1110 and after 1140), the Bogomils wandered far and wide, carrying their teaching with them. Their missionary activity was deployed first in Serbia, Bosnia and Dalmatia, reaching Italy and France at a later date. In Bosnia Bogomilism was for a time the state religion; during the reign of Ban Kulin (1180–1204) it was the ideological mainstay of the country's resistance to the expansionist designs of Hungary, which adhered to the Papacy. In the Balkans, uneasily wedged between the two great

Churches and the two great Empires, between West Rome and East Rome, the Bogomils managed to survive until the Turks came to power in the fifteenth century. Even this was not the end. As an underground movement, Bogomilism divided into two branches: one was a radical and militant secret society, one of the roots of the secret fraternities of the nineteenth and early twentieth centuries which played their part in determining the course of the first and second world wars; the other branch was a pacifist brotherhood, equally radical, which from the sixteenth century joined forces with idealists from Western Europe in Transylvania, Poland and Moravia, and from there penetrated into Russia. The last remaining Bogomil clan, in Herzegovina, is said to have been converted to Islam in 1867. The whole character of the Balkan underground, in its religious, political and intellectual aspects, can only be understood in the light of Bogomilism, and the same can be said of the underground in Western Europe, where Bogomils were persecuted as "Cathars" and "Bulgars" (the generic name for heretics of all sorts).

Bogomil teachings were introduced into the Rhineland and northern France by merchants, and perhaps also by disillusioned Crusaders returning from the Second Crusade in 1149. Bogomils expelled from Byzantium also congregated in these regions. This was the "open" (some might say dangerously open) Europe of the twelfth century. The passage of these "heretics" to the West was "like a triumphal procession; they were made welcome everywhere, with a well-nigh incredible enthusiasm". The wealthy city of Cologne was particularly susceptible. Bernard of Clairvaux, the most eloquent champion of Western Christendom, fulminated against them unsupported and in vain. The main heads of his indictment were their pride and hypocrisy.

Catharism gained a hold on the region between the Rhine and the Pyrenees in just over two years. "The harmony between their lives and their teaching had an intoxicating effect". All classes of people were taken with the frenzy, all distinctions of rank were forgotten; Cathar adherents included both clergy and women. Europe was in the full flood of its first Revivalist movement.

Following Bogomil precedent, the Cathars founded bishoprics in the West. The first was in northern France, probably at Mont-Aimé in Champagne (*circa* 1150–60?). The next foundation, in the region of Albi in southern France, gave the movement a new name. Albigensian missions sent from France into Italy covered the whole country from Lombardy to Naples.

In 1162 a band of German Cathars led by a man named Gerhard arrived in England; they were probably peasants from the Rhineland and included women. They met with little success, and on the orders of an ecclesiastical Council held at Oxford they were branded on the forehead and expelled, accepting their fate with cheerful fortitude. The Assize of Clarendon of 1166, which has a clause against favouring heretics, is the first example of a secular heresy law to be found in medieval Europe. An English chronicler, commenting on the unsuccessful sortie of these heretics into England, remarks that this nameless movement had left its traces everywhere, in France, Spain and England, drifting and settling like the sands of the seashore. In 1210 there is again evidence of Catharism in England.

Catharism spread so quickly that even its own leaders were unable to control it. The administrative and spiritual weaknesses arising from this over-rapid advance produced fissures and cleavages within the movement, which in consequence lost some of its momentum. Eastern heresiarchs, who had been anxiously watching the turn of events in the West, decided it was time to intervene. Nicetas, bishop of the strictly dualist Dragovitsan church of Constantinople, came to Lombardy, probably in 1167, and consecrated as bishop a man named Marcus, who was deacon of the Italian Cathar church. As a result, Italian Catharism became much more radical; hitherto the Cathars of Western Europe, following the "old Bogomils", had taught a modified form of dualism (Satan helped God to create the world). Nicetas converted not only the Italian but also the French Cathars to his doctrines, and at the Cathar Council held at Saint-Felix-de-Caraman near Toulouse in 1167 reconsecrated three Cathar bishops, the bishops of Northern France, Southern France and Lombardy. By sheer weight of personality, this Easterner had succeeded in bringing together under one authority most of the Cathars of Western Europe, and in persuading them to accept the radicalism of his own extreme doctrines. Catharism was now much less Christian and less Western in temper; Oriental and non-Christian elements replaced poverty and the apostolic way of life as its dominating features.

In his great address to the Cathar Council Nicetas had warned his Western brethren to remain in peace and harmony among themselves. But this was asking for too much. The peculiar genius of European medieval civilization was to reveal itself, having been momentarily suppressed, just as clearly in Catharism, the anti-Church, as within the bosom of the Church of Rome itself. Catholic Christianity was already accommodating a wide range of very disparate elements. This feat of coexistence, to later generations wellnigh inconceivable, was if anything surpassed by the Cathars of Western Europe. The Cathars hived off into a number of deviating groups; and the beliefs of ordinary members of Cathar congregations contained a wide range of Christian elements, some of them quite orthodox. The Cathars later even evolved their own brand of Scholasticism; and in the course of argument they came closer and closer to the position of their adversaries, until they were posing the same problems, formulated in the same way. Catharism, in short, was a rich mélange of material taken from Gospel Christianity and of other beliefs, which were of Manichaean and Gnostic origin.

Later in the twelfth century the Cathars started to make inroads on eastern Europe, reaching out from the episcopal cities of the Rhineland along the Danube to Passau and Vienna. The Cathar "paradise" was Italy and Provence. In Italy they had six churches, of which the Lombard was the largest and the Florentine, where they had their own theological academy at Poggibonsi, the most sophisticated. All ranks of society were represented, but scriveners and weavers, members of those "sedentary and meditative trades", formed an élite. Between the twelfth and nineteenth centuries, in fact, weavers would be a constant element as the intelligentsia of the proletariat and the champions of proletarian intellectualism; they were always well represented numerically in nonconformist movements, whether religious or political. In towns the majority of Cathar supporters were artisans and day labourers. In southern France and Provence the movement had aristocratic protection. Here the wealthy nobility carried on a running feud with the wealthy higher clergy and monastic houses, whose properties they found tempting; the petty aristocracy were attracted to heresy for the same reason. Feminine interest in Catharism was on a more elevated plane. Ladies who openly declared themselves Cathars included *grandes dames* such as the wives of Raymond VI of Toulouse and Raymond-Roger of Foix, kinswomen of Queen Eleanor, ladies of high rank such as the famous Blanche de Laurrac, and nuns of noble birth; some ladies even maintained Cathar priests as their domestic chaplains.

What was it that so attracted the men of the twelfth century to the teaching of the Cathars, with its characteristic mélange of Gnostic and Christian elements? The idea of "purity" must always have held pride of place. It was a fundamental conviction of Catharism that there was an irreconcilable antithesis between the soul of the pure man and the evil world. Proof that this view of the world still has its compelling attraction for people of great intelligence and purity of spirit is provided by the case of Simone Weil, one of the most spiritual and single-minded of modern French intellectuals. Her thirst for the absolute was inextinguishable; during the second world war she made a pilgrimage to Toulouse, where neo-Catharism was being preached. The "Pure" were required to cleanse the world and themselves of everything unspiritual, which was by definition "impure". The ghost of Catharism hovers about the cradle of all later purifiers: of all Puritans. One of the first things to need "purification" was the Bible. The Old Testament was subjected to close scrutiny, from which only thirteen prophets, the five books of Solomon and the Psalms (later a great favourite with the Huguenots) emerged to be received into the Cathar canon. Christ was not God; He and the Virgin were spirits of a high order, their physical bodies merely appearances. The souls of men were "fallen spirits", corrupted by Satan in Heaven and thereafter flung down to earth.

There was a great divergence of views among the various Cathar groups over the origin of the cosmos and Satan's part in it. The most radical saw Satan as the evil God who created the cosmos, the terrestrial world and the flesh; the souls of men, imprisoned on earth, could be redeemed only by complete separation from the material world and progressive spiritualization. Among the Cathars of Spain and Italy this evil God became a coolly indifferent life-force, operating on the physical level. Doctors of medicine and others with an interest in natural philosophy found this idea of nature as an autonomous power particularly congenial. One of the later Cathars, who was teaching at Treviso in 1280, held that God left all things to take their course. It was not God, but the earth's own moisture which caused its fruits to grow and ripen; men died, just as cattle died.

There was equal lack of uniformity in Cathar views concerning the good God. One of the last Cathars to teach in southern France held that nature itself was the good God, that earth, water, and wind were the true trinity. This was an extreme case. The general line of teaching was as follows. The history of the world was to be understood as the conflict between the two Gods, the evil and the good. All man's sufferings were rooted in his ignorance: the "children of darkness" were fighting the "children of light". Blinded by Satan, the "children of darkness" addressed their prayers to the evil God, to Jehovah, Baal, Jupiter and the God of the Roman Church—seen as an institution ambitious for power—and so fell deeper and deeper into the toils of enslaving matter. Mankind could be redeemed through "true knowledge", through recognition of the true and good God. Christ was a teacher sent by this good God. After his death, Satan brought into being the Satanic Church, the whore of Babylon, the Church of Rome, which was now persecuting the "Pure", the poor, the true followers of Christ, and would continue to do so until the end of the world. One current doctrine (it had also been held by some orthodox reformers in the eleventh century) which found favour among some Cathars and also among some other heterodox Christians had momentous implications: namely that from the time of Constantine the Roman Church had succumbed to material attractions and the lust for power, and was ruling in unholy alliance with the princes of this world. Neither the Church nor the secular princes had the right to persecute and judge "heretics", still less to condemn them to death. (This belief was shared by the Waldensians.) The capital punishment of criminals and heretics was plain murder. All wars and all Crusades were sinful. Between the twelfth and the fifteenth centuries the Bogomil Church in Bosnia, true to its pacifist convictions, acted as peacemaker between the monarchy and the aristocracy, Catholics and Bogomils, Hungarians and Turks. Cathar propaganda against war and the Crusade was so effective that the Catholics were forced to reply; in their voluminous tracts justifying war and the Crusade as a means of "defending the social order" we find the theologians of the twelfth and thirteenth centuries using arguments similar to those of theologians in the twentieth.

This world is wicked and a man who seeks to be pure must renounce it. The "Perfect" (*perfecti*) renounced the flesh in all its forms, abstaining from sexual intercourse and mar-

riage; they practised the severest asceticism, living as nomads, dedicated to poverty and preaching and wholly without resources. The people were fascinated by this Cathar
élite, wondering if perhaps "true monks" had at last appeared to satisfy their yearnings. The Perfect demonstrated
what men who lived by "pure spirit" could achieve. Behind the teaching and exegesis of the Perfect (they relied
almost exclusively on the New Testament) lay a considerable
wealth of learning, which was more than could be said of
most popular Catholic teaching. Moreover, the Bible and
Cathar literature were offered to the people in the vernacular tongues, and here they need fear no rival.

The individual "Perfect" formed his whole life in accordance with the spirit, which became his understanding and
his will. One consequence of this was that he acquired the
right to bring about his own death, through suicide. The
favourite method was the *endura* or voluntary fast. The
glorification of suicide was something new in medieval
Europe; in the region of Toulouse, where there were so many
suicides of the Perfect during the twelfth and thirteenth
centuries, stoic and renaissance ideas were to come together
during the sixteenth and seventeenth centuries to produce
a similar phenomenon.

The radicalism of the "Church of the Pure" thus had
an equal appeal for the masses and for the educated. The
majority of those interested in the sect were content to lead
more or less ordinary lives, looking on the Perfect as
their ideal and aspiring to be accepted among them before
death. The fascination of Cathar ritual was a particular
source of anxiety to its opponents. Bernard of Clairvaux
and other preachers denounced the Cathars for their fur-
tiveness and secrecy: "like criminals ashamed of the light",
they celebrated their "abominable liturgies" in city basements, in outhouses and cellars, in forests and woodland
shacks. It was said that in districts where they were particularly influential, such as Toulouse, Milan and Florence,
they even used churches for their services. The shock for
Bernard and those who later preached the Albigensian Crusade would have been still greater had they realized that in
many essential features Cathar ritual reflected the practices
of the early, pre-Constantine Church. The whole drama of
the Albigensian Crusade, 1208–28, during which Cartharism
was all but annihilated, turns on this tremendous fact: the
drastically altered Christianity which had emerged from

centuries of barbarization, after exposure to late Roman, Celtic and Germanic influences, was now being confronted by a way of life and thought and worship so radical and fanatical that it came disturbingly close to reproducing the situation of the early Church. During its first four centuries Christianity had been in a state of chaotic ferment; it was a time when a hundred flowers bloomed (the metaphor comes from Clement of Alexandria), a time for the introduction of a variety of strains, classical, oriental, Hellenistic Greek, and Christianity of all shades; even if they were in conflict, there was benefit to be gained from their cross-fertilization. During the "open" and susceptible twelfth century there was a chance that Christian Europe might recapture this vitality.

The religious ceremonial of the Cathars was simple. Prayer, by day and night, was of its essence. Hymns and songs of praise had an important role in the actual services. There was a ritual feast, celebrated with thanksgivings, blessing and breaking of bread and participation in a communal meal, just as in the Early Church up to the middle of the third century, when the Agape (the love-feast) was still closely bound up with *Coena Domini*, the Lord's Supper. There would be a homily from one of the Perfect, usually based strictly on texts from the Gospels. Liturgical celebrations always ended with the kiss of peace; then the Believers knelt before the Perfect, calling on the Holy Ghost. Once a month the congregation confessed their sins in public to one of the Perfect, a rite known as the *apparelliamentum*.

The Church of the Pure had but one sacrament, the *consolamentum*, conferred by the laying on of hands. Through the *consolamentum* the Believer received back from one of the Perfect that "Holy Spirit" he had lost when the angels fell from Paradise. Before the sacrament could be received it was necessary to spend at least one year as a catechumen, a period of testing and penance. The *consolamentum* was at once baptism, confirmation, consecration to the priesthood and extreme unction. The candidate was addressed as "a living stone in the temple of God" (cf. the Templars and some of the rites of the Freemasons), as "disciple of Jesus Christ", and asked: "Do you give yourself to God and the Gospel?" This sacred compact, treated with the solemnity appropriate to a rite in preparation for martyrdom, was sealed by a solemn oath, promising steadfastness until death.

By means of the *consolamentum* the Believer was given strength to perform the works of Christ.

This ceremony in celebration of the spirit, which must have been very impressive in its own fashion, was the Catharist answer to the Mass and the other sacraments of the Roman Church, and to the importance attached by Catholics to the sign of the Cross, which for Cathars was the symbol of Satan's victory over Christ. The Cathars saw in the Mass a wicked and foolish perversion of the genuine "Divine Service", a degradation of the power of the Holy Ghost to superstitious use. It is said that Eleanor, the wife of Raymond VI of Toulouse, and kinswoman of that other Eleanor we have come to know so well, once secretly conducted a solemn *melioramentum* in the same chapel where the Pope was celebrating Mass.

The initial success of the Cathars was so great that the Roman Church could only arm itself for counter-measures after much uncertainty and delay. The first Crusade against the Cathars in 1181, an attack on Roger II, Viscount of Béziers and Carcassonne, led by the Cardinal-legate, Henry, Abbot of Clairvaux, attracted no great support and had little success. It was only two years since the Third Council of the Lateran had proclaimed the first indulgences for crusading against Catharism. Success came only when Innocent III called the Northerners to the Crusade, baiting his summons with the promise of confiscated Albigensian estates for the nobility and, for the king, the prospect of extending his rule over the South. The well-known affirmation of faith promulgated at the Fourth Lateran Council of 1215 is "an almost sentence by sentence refutation of Cathar doctrine". The Dominican Order, founded by Innocent III for the express purpose of converting the heretics, at first failed to make any impression, just as the Cistercians and the papal legates had failed. 1204 saw the last public disputation between Cathars and Catholics, at Carcassonne. A jury of twenty-six, on which each side was equally represented, watched over the proceedings, an arrangement typical both of the "open" twelfth century and of the willingness to differ in public over religion and other fundamental questions which was found in cultivated Islamic circles, and at a later date at the court of the Mongols.

"Action ranks higher than contemplation." This arresting statement comes from a letter addressed by Innocent III in January 1205, on the eve of the great war, to Peter de

Castelnau, his deputy in the task of recovering the South from its heresy, who was anxious to relinquish his post and retire to a monastery. Innocent's saying became the watchword of a now militant West: missions and campaigns to spread abroad the Kingdom of God on earth and bring culture and "progress" to benighted peoples were henceforth to be real wars, fought with real weapons.

The response of the nobility of northern France to Innocent's summons, at first hesitant, later became eager. The Pope called for the extermination of the heretics: *exterminare* is an ambiguous word, which can mean both "to exile" and "to execute". The war which raged from 1208–09 to 1229 was one of immense savagery and fanaticism. Even the dead were not safe from dishonour, and the worst humiliations were heaped upon women, the much-hated, much-feared and much-courted women of the South. Queen Eleanor's kingdom was dissolving in dust and ashes, and with it the feminine culture of the South and the "free spirit" of the troubadours. But as so often happened in the Middle Ages, the lines of battle became crossed, and, in this last effort of the South to maintain its independence of the North, there were Catholic noblemen who fought on the Cathar side. Men who in 1212 had been stoutly crusading against the Arabs in Spain, and had fought at the famous battle of Las Navas de Tolosa, were killed in the Albigensian wars by their former Northern comrades in arms. Among those who met their death in this way were King Peter of Aragon, the Lord of Astarac and many more. Conversely, there were Catharist chaplains in the entourage of that philistine ruffian Simon de Montfort, the leader of the Crusade. The war officially ended with the complete surrender of Raymond VII of Toulouse. It is ironic that the crusading armies of the North should have made their final onslaught just at the time when the third generation of Cathars was in process of developing into a peaceable and established church. It would have been a "Church of the middle road", in which many features of Catholicism were revived and the storm and stress and radicalism of the first and second generations transformed into something altogether quieter and more moderate, in fact a kind of Quietism, content to be itself without any thought of bringing revolutionary changes to the world.

The Inquisition was set up at Toulouse as soon as the Albigensians had been crushed in the field. All women over the age of twelve and all men over fourteen were required to abjure heresy. No one was to have in his possession either the Old or the New Testament, whether in Latin or the vernacular; the only books allowed, and they had to be in Latin, were the Psalter, the Breviary, and the Virgin's Book of Hours. The synod of Toulouse issued in 1229 the first of a long series of ecclesiastical prohibitions and restrictions on reading the Bible in the vernacular.

The papal university of Toulouse was also founded in 1229, the year of the great victory. It was planned as a centre of militant theology, to assist the Mendicant Orders, especially the Dominicans, in their task of running heretics to earth; once detected, heretics would be handed over to the secular arm for sentence. In Italy the Emperor Frederick II and the Pope vied with each other in evolving new codes of law against heretics, a singular form of rivalry. The Emperor, in typical fashion, took the lead: he was all for burning heretics, since he saw a heretic in every rebel against his rule. The Italian towns impartially resisted both laws, imperial and papal. The Pope decreed the introduction of his law into the papal territories in 1231, and in 1232 the burning of heretics became a law of the Empire. From 1233 the Pope made it his business to bring the Inquisition into the towns of Italy. The risings against the Inquisition which occurred in Italy, southern France and Germany throughout the later thirteenth century are evidence of popular opposition to this novel and unprecedented institution. With its appearance on the scene, the Middle Ages ceased to be "open", and the closed society, closed Church and closed state of the later medieval and early modern periods had come unmistakably into being.

This is made plain by the maxim which governed the Inquisition: "There must be no arguing with heretics. If a heretic believes, he should be received back, if he refuses to believe he must be condemned." The Inquisition had no use for "conversations between adversaries" of the kind which took place in the open world of the twelfth century; the Inquisition recognized nothing short of total surrender, the abject prostration of conscience and intellect.

All this had some serious side-effects: denunciation of heretics was imposed on orthodox believers as a duty, the identity of the person denouncing them was withheld from the accused, the estate and chattels of heretics were confiscated, to be divided in varying proportions among the monarchy, the informer and the Church. Resistance to the

Inquisition was gradually broken only by some iron-willed Popes, particularly Innocent IV, who again and again intervened to protect his Inquisitors, and by the fanaticism of religious obsessed with their mission; the procedure was built up slowly, piece by piece, to the point where it became a merciless machine. The Cathars died serenely, indeed cheerfully, true to their text: "Blessed is he who is persecuted for righteousness' sake." "There is no happier death than the death by fire."

Despite the Albigensian Crusade, Catharism remained a power in southern France until about 1244. In northern France, starting from 1233, the Cathar underground was ruthlessly exterminated. Survivors fled to Italy, only to be hounded down by the Inquisition's secret police. Cathars fled from Provence not only into Italy but also into Catalonia, a region which had close links with their homeland. Once the Inquisition had been admitted to Spain, it became a country of "two nations", a division which still exists: on the one hand there developed the freedom-loving, heterodox "Franciscan" Spain, with its centre in Catalonia, which sheltered sizable groups of Cathars and also some Waldensians; on the other was Castilian Spain, the Spain of St Ferdinand (a great-grandson of Queen Eleanor, incidentally), who carried on his own shoulders timber to stoke the heretic bonfires. In Germany during the first third of the thirteenth century there were Cathars at Cologne, Strasbourg, Goslar, Erfurt and at places along the Danube. Bohemia received a number of Cathar and Waldensian refugees whose presence there prepared the way for Hus.

The office of Inquisitor in France was held by the sinister Robert le Bougre, whose name suggests that there was heresy in his family (Bougre=Bulgar=heretic); he died in a royal prison. In Germany between 1231 and 1233 Conrad of Marburg was chief Inquisitor, leaving a trail of havoc behind him. Conrad, who burned heretics in droves, was father-confessor and spiritual director to St Elizabeth of Hungary, a Hungarian princess who had lived in Germany since childhood, and one of the most appealing and tender-hearted of all medieval saints. For three years Conrad raged up and down Germany in search of heretics, accompanied by his two lieutenants, Conrad known as Dorso, and the one-handed, one-eyed John.

Contemporary German sources, mostly of ecclesiastical provenance, give a horrifying picture of the reign of terror

24

The church was regarded as a fortress against Satan, God's stronghold on earth itself where he provides security and joy for true believers: Romanesque pilgrimage church at Vézelay

25

A potent influence in moulding men's lives; the ordinary village church of the people, which often survived unaltered by later Gothic influence: Iffley Church, Oxford

26

The twelfth century saw vivid, dramatic interpretations of popular religious beliefs: the creation of Eve on the bronze doors of Santa Sophia, Novgorod, 1132–54

27

The Madonna inspired art and hymnology during the twelfth century: the Madonna of Otzdorf, Meissen, shows Mary, Queen of Heaven, as a simple woman

28

The founding of new orders was a break with the aristocratic tradition and an attempt to invigorate Christianity. Characteristics of the Order of Fontévrault, founded by Robert of Arbrissel about 1100, were flight from the world and exaltation of poverty: the mother church at Fontévrault, c. 1119

29

Little enclaves of sanctity, committed to an agricultural economy in remote areas, their pure life was intended to redeem the sinful world. The Chapter House in the Cistercian abbey of Fontenay in Burgundy

30

Monasteries possessed huge libraries, both of Classical authors and the Church Fathers, often beautifully illustrated: calendar for February c. 1323, from a French breviary

Princes of the Church

31 and 32

The importance of the Church increased throughout the twelfth century: *(above right)* a bishop from a chess set. The sacred and magical powers of bishops were evident in their accoutrements: *(above left)* this German crozier (*c.* 1100) shows the administering of the Sacrament.

33

Typical of the aristocratic German bishops: the effigy of Bishop Wolfhard von Roth (*d.* 1302) at Augsburg

34

An Imperial bishop, Archbishop Frederick of Wettin. The Imperial
Church in Germany was rich, militant and powerful

35

Medieval towns varied greatly in legal status and importance. At Avila in Spain, the ancient walls still enclose the town

36

Internationally accepted standards of currency were of great value, particularly in banking transactions. Edward III's gold coinage: florin of 1344, noble of 1360–69

37

Industries flourished in the towns, where craftsmen joined together in guilds: a shoemaker at work

38 and 39

Towns were oases of peace and independence: (*left*) a rich French merchant's house at Provins. Italian townsmen favoured fine public buildings: (*below*) Palazzo dei Consoli at Gubbio, *c.* 1300

40 and 41

Civic pride of the German Hanseatic towns in northern Europe: *(right)* the splendid Schwarzhäupterhaus at Riga, *c.* 1400. Burgesses built their own independent churches: *(below)* Marienkirche at Stralsund, 1298

42

In the conservative tradition; Philosophy consoles Boethius in prison, from an English miniature, *c.* 1140

43 and 44

At centres of translating activity, such as Toledo, Montpelier, Cremona, the authentic Plato and Aristotle were discovered under the rubble of Latin literature: Plato and Aristotle, from a stained-glass window at Esslingen, Germany

45

Founders of the arts and their practitioners carved at Chartres; Pythagoras the mathematician with the figure of Music playing a lute and bells, and Bishop Donatus the grammarian with a schoolmaster and pupils

46

The earliest medieval centre of scientific learning was at Oxford, where the great scholar Robert Grossetest taught: an English astrolabe, *c.* 1280

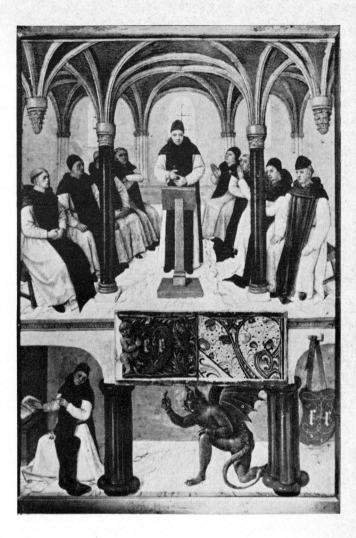

47

Amongst the greatest teachers of the age was Bernard of Clairvaux (1091–1153), whose eloquence was partially responsible for the meteoric rise of the Cistercian Order. A fifteenth-century portrait by Jean Fouquet

48

The monastery of San Giovanni in Fiore, Calabria, where the Abbot Joachim (*d.* 1202), one of the great historical scholars of the Middle Ages, wrote his philosophy of history

49

The collegiate system originated at Paris University but flourished best at Oxford: a late thirteenth-century foundation, Merton College, Oxford

50

Universities came into existence when teachers banded together in
associations as at Paris and Bologna: an Italian university lecture
and seminar depicted on a tomb at Pistoia

51

Moses, reverently depicted in an English miniature. In the liberal thought of the twelfth century there was remarkable tolerance of Judaism and Islam

52

Thirteenth-century Jewish persecution: the High Priests, paying Judas his thirty pieces of silver, wear special hats, obligatory for Jews at the time when this relief at Naumburg was carved

53 and 54

Disputation in the thirteenth century was concerned to convict the Jews of error: these statues at Strasbourg Cathedral contrast the vision and strength of the Church *(left)* with the blindness and broken powers of the Synagogue *(right)*

55 and 56

Matthew Paris, the English historian, made these two drawings of the Crusades. *(Above)* Two knights Templars share one horse, symbolic of the original poverty of the Order; *(below)* French prisoners of the Saracens are released by Richard of Cornwall in 1241

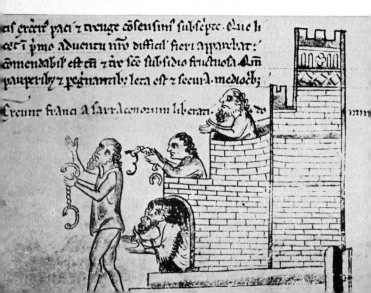

57

In the torrid, stony wastelands of 'Outremer', the Crusaders built their fortifications against the Saracens: Krak des Chevaliers in the Lebanon

58

Eastern influence in Europe: in Palermo Saracen craftsmen built the church of San Giovanni degli Eremiti with Arabian domes on the site of a former mosque, for the Norman kings of Sicily in 1132

59

Islamic influence at work in France: the church of St-Michel d'Aiguilhe, Le Puy

60

Hunting and hawking were favourite activities of the medieval aristocracy: a relief on the font in Perugia Cathedral

61

The magnificence of courtly life: Earl Richard of Cornwall was welcomed by this elephant in a triumphal procession at Cremona in 1241

62

Jousting was a great feature, particularly of the court at Poitiers, where knights fought for the favour of a lady. A French ivory casket shows the 'capture of the Castle of Love'

63 and 64

The presiding genius of courtly culture: *(above)* Eleanor of Aquitaine married secondly Henry Plantagenet, King of England and Count of Anjou *(below)*, and brought into being the Angevin Empire, extending from Toulouse to Scotland. Effigies from Fontévrault Abbey, Normandy

65

Eleanor's court at Poitiers was the chief academy in Western Europe for teaching the arts of courtly civilization: this French ivory mirror-back shows the mutual crowning of lovers

66

Civilized games such as chess were frequently played between men and women at court

67

Passion and covetousness: Herod and Salome. To many people, the practices of the court of Poitiers seemed equally wicked

68

In the thirteenth century the courtly cult shocked religious feeling: the debauched figure of Luxoria at Moissac

69

St Elisabeth of Marburg (1207–1231), the Hungarian princess renowned for her acts of charity, typifies the new religious emotion of abject service to the poor

70

Carved at Bamberg Cathedral, Germany, in 1237, the disputatious prophets, Jonas and Hosea, personify argument and dissension in religious matters

71

The repression of heresy: the fortified church at Albi, built 1282–1385, was a fortress of God against the hostile Albigensians

72 and 73

(Above) St Francis painted by Cimabue, *c.* 1280: his message was universal charity and love. He was renowned for his sympathy with the animal kingdom: *(left)* this English manuscript shows him preaching to the birds

74

The suffering and torments of popular religious feeling in the fourteenth century: the broken body of Christ on a Plague Cross from Cologne

of these three "madmen", intent on their mission of purging the world of vile heretics: they had undertaken the purification of the "pure". For example, this is what the *Chronica regia Coloniensis* has to say: "In various parts of Germany it has happened that many people, nobles and non-nobles, monks and nuns, townsmen and peasants, have been given to the flames by Brother Conrad because of their actual or suspected heresy after a trial which, if we may say so, was far too hasty. For a man may be sentenced without opportunity of appeal or defence and thrust into the fearful flames on the very same day on which he is accused; whether the accusation is justified or no makes no difference". Conrad was assassinated on July 30, 1233, by the followers of some noblemen he had summoned to appear before his court. After his death Archbishop Siegfried III of Mainz and a Dominican named Bernard sent the Pope, Gregory IX, full details of Conrad's reign of terror, his intimidation of prisoners, his false judgments and his atrocities. The Archbishops of Cologne and Trier had earlier brought similar charges. The Pope, shocked and bewildered, expressed his surprise: "We marvel that you allowed legal proceedings of this unprecedented nature to continue for so long among you without acquainting us of what was happening. It is our wish that such things should no longer be tolerated, and we declare these proceedings null and void. We cannot permit such misery as you have described."

For Germany the death of Conrad was like the vanishing away of a spectre. Suddenly it seemed absurd that an entire people, great men and small, should have for so long remained in terror of this little man, riding about on his tiny mule, and of his two gloomy-looking assistants; people wondered how it had ever been possible. This raises a question of some interest, not only from our own contemporary point of view, but also because of the light it sheds on some frequently overlooked features of the later medieval Inquisition, which can only be understood in the context of mass and group psychoses (for example, an infection spread by the Mendicant Orders). It was very often the masses, spurred on to "purge" themselves of all "uncleanliness" by a fervour in which hysterical devotion was mingled with fear (of everything alien and of Hell), who were both the mainstay of the Inquisition and its driving force. The aristocracy and the episcopate were hostile and in some places continued their resistance over several centuries, for the Inquisition infringed on their own jurisdiction and even set itself up as a superior authority. One finds such opposition in Germany during the thirteenth century and in Spain in the fifteenth and sixteenth centuries. Conrad had started his career in Germany by preaching the Crusade, in 1214. His oratory was impassioned and skilful: he kindled the ardour of the masses and stoked his own fires afresh at the flames. As with other demagogues of later date, in the course of time he became poisoned by his own venom; intoxicated with the power he had so demonstrably achieved over the popular mind, infected by the greed, hatred and envy of the populace, always glad at the prospect of striking a blow at the mighty, Conrad fell under the spell of the very people he sought to lead. The leader had become the led, and led into temptation. Every town, castle and cloister had its malcontents, people with an account to settle. Conrad acted in Germany as a catalyst. His highly neurotic personality touched off the neuroses of the masses and of individuals, and recharged them with new dynamite.

Conrad was buried at Marburg close to St Elizabeth in the new cathedral. This is the first German cathedral to be built in the Gothic style, and a magnificent example of it. In the south of France Gothic only appeared after the conquest of the region by the French king. This "assimilative" role of Gothic is one of the keys to its "invention".

In southern France, despite its occupation by the enemy and harsh repressive measures, a few embers still glowed, ready to flare up over and over again. The registers of the Inquisition are filled with the names of noblemen, clerks, monks, episcopal officials, lawyers, physicians and merchants, and some of the northern officials who had come south to combat heresy were won over to the Cathar cause. At Albi, Cordes and Limoux there was always a heretical party, though it might vary in strength. At Carcassonne two successful attempts were made on the archives of the Inquisition, in 1280 and 1291. The whole movement flared up again in the years following 1295, when Provençals who had fled to Como attempted the reconquest of their homeland. This revival was crushed by the Inquisition around 1310. But the "red South" (as it was later called) remained unquiet; it was soon to become the refuge of persecuted "left-wing" Franciscans, Joachimites, and Fraticelli. Here and in Catalonia such refugees created an intellectual and spiritual climate sufficiently disturbed to make possible the Spanish revivalist movements of the fifteenth and early sixteenth centuries.

During the thirteenth and fourteenth centuries, however, the main stream flowed in the direction of Italy. There are some similarities between the Langue d'Oc and the language of Friuli, and between the Ligurian and Sicilian dialects; some modern philologists ascribe these resemblances to the wanderings of the Cathars, who as time went on pressed further and further into southern Italy. There were well-organized escape routes for the Perfects leading from France and Germany into all parts of Italy. The safety of the routes and of the refuges along it was secured by a network of middlemen and guides, who could find a way through wild and pathless regions. The most desirable havens were wealthy cities, often in conflict with their bishops and cathedral chapters, where heretics might be sheltered by respectable citizens or even by the nobility. The Cathars had powerful friends at Florence, the Cavalcanti, the Baroni, the Pulci and the Ciprani; at Rome there was the house of Senator Brancaleone. It was not uncommon for Cathars to find advocates among nobles supporting the Ghibelline cause, men such as Ezzelino de Romano and Uberto Pallavicini. Italy was the only place where Catharism survived the persecutions of the thirteenth century. After 1300 the Italian Cathars fled to Sicily, to the Aragonese king, Frederick III (1296–1337). As late as 1412 the corpses of fifteen Cathars were exhumed and burnt at Chieri near Turin, so great was the fear that this "plague" might send out its poison even from the grave to putrefy the body of the Italian populace.

Some of the most energetic of the Italian Inquisitors had started out as convinced Cathars. There was the famous Raynier Sacconi, for example, and his colleague St Petrus Martyr, murdered by the Cathars. Petrus was a Dominican; his murder was plotted by a wide variety of enemies, including a Franciscan. His actual assassin, a man named Carino, made a saintly end in a Dominican priory at Forli, which was presided over by a brother of his victim. This episode illustrates the complexities of medieval animosities, the way the lives of adversaries so closely interlocked.

These complex situations could work the other way. During the later thirteenth century a certain Armanno Pungilupo was being venerated as a saint at the cathedral of Ferrara, where he was buried and where an altar had been raised in his honour. Proceedings for his beatification were set in train, only to end, in 1300, as a case for the Inquisition.

The "saint" was unmasked as a heresiarch. All his images were destroyed, and his altar and his corpse consigned to the flames.

Ecclesiastical sources even during the twelfth century are full of complaints about the "hypocrisy" of the Cathars, their remarkable talent for dissembling. The people, it was said, took the Cathars for saints; they had such an air of being thoroughly pious and right-minded men, capable of conquering the world by their learning, their charity and their innate attraction. Nicodemism, to give it its later name, soon became a fine art in Italy; Nicodemism meant outward scrupulous conformity with the norms of orthodoxy, whilst at the same time pumping them dry of all their original content and substituting in their place a new spirit and a new creed. The poetry of the *dolce stil nuovo* and of courtly love is drenched in Nicodemism; so, too, is the work of Dante.

A French cleric writing in 1215 named Milan as the main heretical stronghold. Pope Innocent III threatened the city with the same fate as had befallen the Albigensians. This pious wish could not be fulfilled, since in Italy itself the Papacy was weak. The effects of interdict and excommunication, the Pope's sharpest weapons in their struggle with the towns and city-states, were soon blunted: for if, as happened during the thirteenth and fourteenth centuries, great cities like Milan and Florence were left for years to languish under the Church's ban, with the complete suspension of the sacraments and all Church services that this entailed, "heretics" became all the more active in filling the vacuum. It was even possible for a declared heretic, Otto Visconti, to hold for a time the Archbishopric of Milan. There was scarcely a diocese whose bishop had not ranged himself politically against the Pope. Innocent III was acutely conscious of the deterioration among the clergy. In his *De Contemptu Mundi,* written before he became Pope, he complains of clerks who "by night embrace Venus and next morning honour the Virgin Mary". At the opening session of the Fourth Lateran Council, on November 11, 1215, Innocent painted a gloomy picture of Christianity and the Church in decay. "It often happens that bishops, by reason of their manifold preoccupations, fleshly pleasures and bellicose leanings, and from other causes, not least the poverty of their spiritual training and lack of pastoral zeal, are unfitted to proclaim the word of God and govern the people."

The country clergy were harshly oppressed by their noble landlords and patrons, and as poor as church mice. There were plenty of clerks who could not write and were scarcely able to read. Some priests kept ale-houses to support their wives and children. Superstition, magical practices (still common today in the South), soothsaying and astrology all exerted their baleful and seductive influence. Until well after the time of the Renaissance daily life was a close-woven tissue of habits derived from very ancient ritual practices, the dredged-up treasure of old non-Christian religions. Some Italian sorcerers had their training in Spain, until Siena became the centre of Italian sorcery, the Italian Toledo. The resources of magic were freely invoked in daily living, as a defence against the omnipresent perils of town and countryside laid waste by hatred, envy, wickedness and war. It was particularly useful in killing enemies on the field of battle.

In this turbulent Italy nearly every town was at war with its neighbour, and within the towns the parties were always at each other's throats: while at Rome the factions continually wrangled over the papal succession. Taking all the thirteenth century vacancies together, the Papal See was unoccupied during this period for more than nine years. A vacancy arose when the electors failed to reach agreement. Between Celestine IV and Innocent IV there was a gap of nineteen months (1241–42), a gap of two years and nine months between Clement IV and Gregory X (1268–71), a gap of eleven months between Honorius IV and Nicholas IV (1287–88) and another of two years and three months between Nicholas IV and Celestine V (1292–94). There were also several other vacancies lasting between three and seven months.

The towns and the people of Italy had long ago learned to cope with each other and their own problems without recourse to external authority. It is hardly surprising that heresy should have flourished among them. In a few towns the heretical party even temporarily captured the government. At Orvieto (not so very far from Rome) heretics in 1199 murdered the Roman *podestà*, who had only been imposed on the town by the Catholic faction after much difficulty; with the support of Innocent III the *podestà* had been taking active steps against heresy. More than two hundred noblemen were implicated as "heretics" in his murder. In 1204 the town of Assisi chose an excommunicate as *podestà*, and remained loyal to him despite papal objections. The town's resistance was broken only by an interdict.

And so we have come to Assisi, where, in 1204, the star of St Francis was already in the ascendant. This saint of the Catholic Church, venerated by his much-harried and devoted companions as the "second Christ", has won friends and admirers far outside his own Church and time; the power radiating from the *Poverello* has touched many different kinds of men and women, including the reformers of Luther's day, nonconformists of the eighteenth and later centuries, and people right outside Europe and right outside Christendom. We may wonder whether it was merely by accident that the earliest writings about him, the testimony of his earliest and closest companions, were rediscovered only at the close of the nineteenth century. It may also be significant that they were found in the archives of Poor Clares, Franciscan nuns, where they had been deposited to save them from destruction. And is it an accident that it is only now that Franciscan studies are sufficiently advanced to permit us to strip away the layer upon layer of false piety and sentimentality, sometimes deliberately superimposed, as in many early Christian paintings in the catacombs, so that the features which begin to emerge at last bear some resemblance to the reality?

Thomas of Celano's account of the saint's physical appearance is confirmed by the earliest portraits, still free of the idealization found in later paintings: the fresco in the Sacro Speco at Subiaco, the portrait behind the choir of San Francesco a Ripa at Rome, and parts of the Franciscan-cycle of Bonaventura Berlinghieri at San Francesco, Pescia.

"In stature he was rather on the short side, his head of moderate size and round, his face long and thrusting forward, his forehead smooth and low, his eyes of medium size, black and candid, his hair dark, his eyebrows straight, his nose even-shaped, thin and straight, his ears prominent but delicate, his temples unfurrowed. In conversation he was agreeable, ardent and penetrating, his voice firm, sweet-toned and clearly audible, his teeth were white, even and close together, his lips delicate, his beard black and rather sparse, his neck slender, his shoulders straight, his arms short, his hands small, with long fingers and narrow nails, his legs thin, his feet small, his skin tender, his flesh meagre, his clothing rough, his sleep brief and his bounty most liberal."

The portrait is clear and precise, free of any suggestion of sickly suffering. In 1260–63 the General Chapter of the

Franciscan Order commissioned its Minister-General, Giovanni da Fidanza, otherwise known as Bonaventura, to compose an official life of St Francis. After it appeared an attempt was made to track down and destroy all biographical writings emanating from the saint's personal circle.

Neither Celano nor Bonaventura reveals to us the authentic saint, the man who radiated both joy and sorrow, who united serenity and grief, quietude and turbulence, who rejoiced in all men, animals and things, yet was austere with the fortitude of the Desert Fathers, whose spirit was born of love out of fire, whose countenance was veiled in blood and tears: a man crucified. The appearance on Francis's body of the *stigmata*, the wounds of Christ, is the first recorded instance of this phenomenon among Christians of the West. The Eastern Church knew nothing of such miracles and had no wish to know them. Christ's Passion was not much dwelt upon in Eastern Christendom. What counted there was his Transfiguration; Christ was the lord of the cosmos; He was caught up as man into the circle of light radiating from the "triple sun of the Godhead, which shed on man its benign radiance". This was the teaching about the humanity of Christ current in the Eastern Church.

But God became man, and wholly man, born a naked infant and laid in the manger. Francis set up his Crib at Greccio not as a pretty toy but to be a dread and solemn warning to the mighty, to theologians and to ordinary Christians: "Behold your God, a poor and helpless child, the ox and the ass beside Him." (Walther von der Vogelweide had uttered the same admonition.) "Your God is of your flesh, He lives in your nearest neighbour, in every man, for all men are your brothers".

The Crib, the *stigmata*, the preachings to the beasts, St Francis's whole life of dedication to his bride, Lady Poverty, were all messages addressed to those great powers who in this fateful hour were struggling in Italy and Europe for the possession of mankind. To the Cathars the message ran: God is not only "pure spirit" but also wholly man, vulnerable, helpless, bleeding flesh, the blood of brother men, too precious to be shed in warfare of any kind. To Byzantium and the Eastern Church it said: even in his Transfiguration, Christ still appears to us poor men in His crucified body (Francis's vision on Mount La Verna). To Rome, the Church which claimed to rule the emperors and kings of this world, it said: Christ came to earth to be the servant of His own.

The war-mad Italian towns, standing for embattled Christendom as a whole, were reminded that Christians were called to be peacemakers. Francis brought the wolf into the town as his brother. *Homo homini lupus*, man is as a wolf to other men; such was the pessimistic wisdom of antiquity, and the political "realism" of rulers and governments in the Middle Ages. Francis, who preached to the animals and made friends with "brother wolf", dissented from this view, protesting that all creatures and all men were created by God to be brothers.

But it would be quite wrong to describe the Catholic saint as any kind of "protestant". A protestant protests against something; Francis was "against" nothing. The "poor little Francis" was not found preaching against Cathars and Waldensians, although he knew very well what they were. Nor did he preach against the Emperor and the imperial party in Italy, just entering on their last great struggle with the Papacy at the time when Francis was at his most influential. Francis was also a silent witness of the conflict between Assisi and the Pope in 1204, as already mentioned; in fact he had just returned to Assisi from Perugia, where he had been imprisoned for his part in the war between Perugia and Assisi. Nor did he preach against the Pope, but rather submitted himself wholly to him, to his own bishop and to all priests. Francis the layman (he had only minor orders and never became a priest) declared his continuing faith in priests in his Testament: "If they should persecute me, I would yet wish to have recourse to them". Francis knew no "against", no boundaries; he was as ingenuous with the Sultan as with his brethren in Italy.

Francis taught the good news for what it was: a message of joy and love, God dwelling at peace with men, mediated by Christ to his brother men. His experience of the being of Christ was something concrete, a historical fact. Contemporary medieval society, whose daily life was warfare, unrest, tumult, hatred, envy and the lust for power, all those sinister beasts of prey whom Dante saw stalking through the world, was confronted with its greatest challenge. Francis knew that in such a world an open heart meant a heart ready to accept the world in its entirety, to transform it by a life of unsullied sacrifice. "Toleration" meant for Francis what it had meant for Paul and Christ: submission to the death of the Cross, and before that a life spent until its last hour in bearing the cross of this world.

Giovanni Bernardone was born in 1181 or 1182 at Assisi, the son of Pietro Bernardone, a wealthy cloth merchant whose business took him frequently to the south of France; he was, it seems, attending a trade fair there when Giovanni was born, and on his return gave his infant son the additional name of Francesco, in honour of the sweet South. Francis's mother may have been French, a native of Picardy. Francis's youth was like that of any other rich young man in a wealthy and licentious town. It was a spell of illness and imprisonment that released his particular genius for seeing all things as though for the first time through the eyes of the Creator, and revealed to him that his first duty was to cultivate a serene self-detachment from everything rooted in warfare and the perpetual commotion of the city; in fact from envy and hatred. "Listen everyone and understand it well: until now I have called Pietro Bernardone my father; but now that I intend to serve the Lord I am returning to this man all the money which has caused him such a pother, and all the clothes that were his property; and from now on I shall say 'Our Father which art in Heaven', instead of 'my father, Pietro Bernardone'."

The world was cheerfully abandoned that the world might be served; Francis took to the road in complete poverty, earning his daily bread by the labour of his hands or by begging, and as he went, he preached. He has himself summarized the substance of his message: "Fear and honour God, praise and give thanks to Him . . . Father, Son and Holy Ghost . . . Do penance . . . for you know that we must soon die . . . Confess all your sins . . . Blessed are those who die penitent, for they will be in the Kingdom of Heaven, while the unconfessed . . . will go to the everlasting fire. Guard yourselves from all evil and persevere in goodness till the end".

Francis was not thinking of founding an Order. With his brethren he begged and preached his way through Italy, southern France and Spain. The people flocked to him, seeking peace and joy, seeking a new image of God and a new brotherhood.

What was it that distinguished these "penitents from Assisi" as they called themselves, all of them laymen, from the sundry heretics, hotheads, "Poor Men of Christ", *Humiliati,* Waldensians and Albigensians who also thronged the roads of south-western Europe, preaching where they could? One main difference was that Francis was persuaded

of the need for papal approval and a Rule if his brotherhood was to escape being swept away in the wake of persecution. Heretics menaced by this danger, particularly Waldensians, were quick to seek shelter under the wing of the
new community, which grew at a fantastic rate; by 1282 the
Franciscan Order possessed 1,583 houses in Europe. But
Francis himself desired no "house", no safe stronghold, no
cloister, no possessions, no privileges: all these things he
saw as fetters, links with the affairs of the world. His
brotherhood was to be defenceless, exposed. He forbade the
brethren to go to the Pope for letters of protection and
privileges. Christ's friends and disciples on earth should remain in complete poverty, without possessions and without
legal protection. Such complete abnegation created a new
kind of asceticism, a new appreciation of the world, a new
kind of joy: serene and unencumbered, the friend of holy
poverty was set free to live and rejoice in the love of his
fellow men without obscuring or violating his own personality. Francis's Testament (which is not mentioned in Bonaventura's official life of the saint) shows that he did not
waver from this position: "I strictly command all the
brethren on obedience that . . . they shall not dare to ask
for any letter from the Roman court . . . neither for purposes of preaching nor because of any persecution of their
bodies."

There is an episode which illustrates how consistent was
Francis's belief in uncloistered Christianity. In 1220 he
ordered the abolition of the house of studies at Bologna,
founded by Pietro Staccia, Provincial-Minister of the Franciscans and a distinguished lawyer. "You are trying to
destroy my order; it is my desire and will that my brethren,
following the example of Jesus Christ, shall give more time
to prayer than to study." Francis cursed Staccia, it is said,
and to his dying day refused to abrogate the curse. Francis
knew what he was about. The new theologians were impris-
oning God within their philosophical system, bending divinity to their own wills and objects. The canon lawyers, the jurists
of the Church, were endeavouring to transform the Roman
household of the Pope into a stronghold of power. In the
course of this struggle to assert the rights of the Curia and
the Church the medieval Papacy fought its way up to its
highest eminence and to its ruin.

The household was a basic unit in the medieval world—
fortified houses, in other words castles, patrician houses in

towns, manor houses, bishops' houses, monastic houses. It is understandable that such a society should have tried to bring some order into the growing horde of "lesser brothers", "friars minor" as they called themselves from 1216, congregating around St Francis. And so an Order was founded. Francis and his earliest and closest companions had been laymen. By 1219–20 the brotherhood was definitely a Religious Order. Some years before his death Francis was forced by illness to give up his leadership of the Order; however, he tried to see to it that the principles of poverty, itinerant preaching and manual labour were retained and incorporated into the revised Rule he was asked to compose about this time, although in other respects he had to compromise. In the Rule which finally received papal approbation (by Honorius III in 1223) known as the *Regula Secunda* or *Bullata,* the all-important poverty clauses were struck out or modified; complete poverty was henceforth to be practised only by individuals, and there is no mention of haphazard itinerant preaching. The Franciscans were now an Order, like all the other Orders prepared to fight for their privileges in every town in Christendom; their chief rivals were the Dominicans, their closest contemporaries. Inevitably, the friars minor became entangled in the affairs of bishops and parish priests and of men of all kinds; and they were drawn into the academic atmosphere of the universities.

Francis spent his last years in the crucifying knowledge that his ideals were being mutilated. Through his perpetual contemplation of the crucified Christ he became deeply identified with Christ's suffering; shortly before his death he discovered on his own body lesions corresponding to the five wounds of his Lord. He took the utmost care to conceal this terrifying happening from the small group of loyal companions with whom he was now living and whose protection he made his last concern. The dearest of them was probably Leo, the subject of the only two surviving documents written in the saint's own hand. One is a letter: "Brother Leo, your brother Francis sends you his greeting and peace. My son, I am talking to you like a mother, summing up in this letter all the words and advice that passed between us on the way: in whatever way it seems to you that you can be most pleasing to the Lord our God, and best follow in his footsteps and imitate his poverty, do it, with the blessing of the Lord God and in my obedience. And if it is necessary for your soul's sake or your own consolation that you should come to me, and if you want to do it, then, Leo, come."

The other document contains on one side a blessing for Brother Leo and on the other a hymn of praise:

Thou art holy, Lord and God, Thou art the God of Gods, the God that doest wonders. Thou art strong, Thou art great, Thou art the highest, Thou art almighty. Thou art the holy father, king of heaven and earth. Thou art the only and the highest good, the one and true Lord God. Thou art love and charity, Thou art wisdom, Thou art humility, Thou art patience; Thou art beauty, Thou art security; Thou art rest, Thou art joy. Thou art our hope and our gladness; Thou art justice and temperance, Thou art strength and prudence, Thou art riches and sufficiency. Thou art meekness, Thou art our defender, our guardian, our protector, Thou art our shield, our refuge and our virtue. Thou art our faith, hope and charity. Thou art our greatest delight. Thou art infinite goodness, great and admirable. O my Lord, almighty, merciful God and Saviour.

This is utterly free from complaint and recrimination, as indeed were the last years and days of the saint's life, when he was bequeathing to the world his most precious and most personal legacy, adding a new note to the scale of humanity: joy born of perfect and explicit surrender to suffering, willingness to taste the bitterest of this world's fruits. At Assisi, in the garden of the Minoresses of San Damiano, the dying man who had seen his work destroyed could yet sing the *Canticle of the Sun*. This originally ended with the praise of God in "our sister, mother earth". But now, when civil war was once again threatening Assisi, Francis sent the contending parties a hymn of peace, which became the penultimate verse of the *Canticle*:

"Be praised, my Lord, for those who for Thy love forgive, Contented unavenged in quiet to live.
Blest those who in the way of peace are found—
By thee O Lord most high shall they be crowned."

When the enemies heard it they begged pardon of one another and exchanged the kiss of peace.

As death drew nearer Francis allowed his brothers to write down his praise of "sister death":

"Be praised, my Lord, for our sister bodily death
 From whom none can escape that hath drawn breath . . .
 Praise ye and bless my Lord and do Him service due
 With humblest thanks for all He has done for you."

Very close now to death, he had himself laid on the bare earth, and with his left hand on the wound in his side said "I have done what I had to do; may Christ teach you what is your part." He died soon after sunset on October 3, 1226, at the small hermitage of the Portiuncula near Assisi.

Francis's town of Assisi was hailed by his fellow-countryman Dante as the birthplace of the *Canticle of the Sun*:

"Upon that side
Where it doth break its steepness most, arose
A sun upon the world, as duly this
From Ganges doth: therefore let none who speak
Of that place say Ascesi; for its name
Were lamely so delivered: but the East,
To call things rightly, be it henceforth styled . . ."

Francis had loosened the tongues and opened the eyes of the Italian people, dispersing the choking fumes of anxiety and hatred which surrounded them. Francis's appeal to the masses is echoed in the Italian vernacular poetry, secular and religious, known as *laude* and in the sublime paintings produced under Franciscan inspiration in the thirteenth and fourteenth centuries. Here at last a valid reconciliation was achieved, the reconciliation of man with himself, with his brother men and with sister earth, an acceptance of the fact that all alike were rooted in the God-given reality of all created things.

Friars minor took a leading part in the "Great Halleluja", a peace-movement which captured many Italian towns in northern Italy: at Parma, Brothers Benedict and Gerardo, at Piacenza Brother Leo. The "Great Halleluja" swept through the whole region like a spring storm, a clap of Whitsuntide thunder. Ancient feuds were healed, warring adversaries became reconciled; everyone was filled with brotherly love and did penance in an access of tears and joy.

Then the spring ran dry. The daily warfare continued. It is evident that the great Franciscan religious poetry (a high-water mark of European achievement in this genre) was the work of men convinced of the reality of endless suffering. The *Dies Irae, Dies Illa*, still the core of the Roman Church's liturgy for the dead, comes from the heart of a Franciscan shocked by his saint into proclaiming the sufferings, fears and hopes of mankind. Suffering and joy are inseparable in this Franciscan hymn, or rather poem—it is both secular and religious. The greatest writer of folk-inspired *laude* may also have been the author of another of the great medieval Latin hymns, the *Stabat Mater*. This was Jacopone da Todi (born 1230, died 1306), a lawyer of noble birth and worldly habits, who became a lay-brother of the Franciscan Order after the death of his wife at a banquet as the result of a horrifying accident. Jacopone delighted to praise the holy poverty of Francis. As a friar minor and open supporter of the Colonna, he was imprisoned for five years by Pope Boniface VIII and only liberated on the Pope's death.

As one looks upwards towards Assisi from the slope of Mount Subasio, covered with olive trees and crossed with the little walls of numerous smallholdings, the eye is met by serried tiers of masonry. On the summit stands the Church of San Francesco, the burial place of St Francis, fortified by its massive substructure of other buildings thrusting boldly outward from the mountainside. The two churches, the enormous convent with its pillared courtyards, the twelve turrets, together make up one tremendous citadel. It is true that all this was not built in a day. But it was the building of this vast burial church and the collection of the correspondingly vast sums of money needed for it that first brought out into the open in 1230 the conflict between the two opposing parties within the Order, which was to continue for centuries although the name and style of the factions might change. In the first half of the fourteenth century it seemed that the Order would disintegrate into a number of heretical groups. By the fifteenth century this danger had been averted, only to be replaced by the threat of fresh dissensions between the Observants, who wanted to return to Francis's original ideals, and the Conventuals, with the "neutrals" as a third force. The building of the basilica had been a symbol of the victory of the Conventual faction over the "Spiritual", that is over the party which appealed to Francis's Testament and its demand for absolute poverty.

Those who claimed to be St Francis's spiritual descendants were to meet with little success. While the saint's closest and

dearest companions, a Leo or a Giles, disappeared from the
public gaze into the silence of small remote country communities, the *zelanti,* the Spirituals, became a party of fanatics,
who throughout the thirteenth century competed with the
Conventuals for the control of the Order. Elias of Cortona,
leader of the Conventuals, who presided over the building
of the basilica at Assisi and was from 1231 Minister-General
of the Order, was relentless in his harrying of the Spirituals;
their leader, Caesarius of Speyer, was even imprisoned. By
1239 the burden of Elias's dictatorship had become intolerable to the Order; he was deprived of his office by the Pope
and afterwards became a political partisan of the Emperor
Frederick II. The first Minister-General to represent the
Spirituals was John of Parma (between 1247 and 1257). During his Generalate, however, there appeared the first omens
of the catastrophe which was to overtake them. In 1255 a
friar from Pisa, Gerard of Borgo San Donnino, was condemned to life imprisonment. Gerard had written an Introduction to a treatise of Abbot Joachim of Flora, and published the two together in Paris. Gerard's Introduction related Joachim's third Dispensation, which was to supplant
the carnal Church, to the coming of the Spiritual Franciscans. The Order now came to have a distinctly Joachimite
wing, who looked on themselves as the chosen men of the
future, the predestined successors of the papal Church. The
highly significant ideas about history entertained by these
men will be discussed further on, in a broader context. What
is relevant here is to notice that their compromising association with ecstatic prophecies made the Spirituals the victims
of successive persecutions, which continued to dog them until
well into the later fourteenth century.

There grew up around the Spirituals an atmosphere of intellectual and religious unrest and speculation, capable of
fostering the scientific studies of a Roger Bacon and the
philosophical and political theorizing of a William of Ockham, the late medieval Franciscan whose political sympathies lay with the Empire. Persecuted Spirituals fled from
Italy to southern France, Spain and the East. In the last year
of the thirteenth century, for example, we hear of some going
to Armenia.

These "left-wing" Franciscans, unlike Francis himself, were
protesting against the world as they found it; against the
growing worldliness within their own Order and its involvement in politics, against domination of the Order by the

papal Curia, which turned it into a willing tool in dispensing papal propaganda and in bolstering up the Inquisition.

The defeat of St Francis within his own Order was not without its therapeutic effects. It meant that in some Franciscan convents there was always a welcome for radical thinking, in religion, philosophy or politics; the prevailing opinion in such houses was compounded of animosity towards Rome and loyal veneration of the memory of the Poor Man of Assisi as the leader of a new age for Christianity and mankind, Christ born again to free his brothers from the chains of the Law. In Italy, southern France and Spain, and later in Germany too, this permanently restless Franciscan element, in which the Minoresses were strongly represented, united with remnants of Waldensian, Albigensian and other heterodox movements, now driven underground, to form what was virtually a separate Church, with its own saints and martyrs, who were none other than Spirituals executed by Rome. For example, four Spirituals condemned at Marseilles in 1318 were venerated as "catholic and glorious martyrs" throughout southern France and Catalonia.

The majority of the Order, however, kept in line with the victorious Conventuals. They found they had to battle on three fronts: against the infiltration of their houses by Spirituals, against heretics of all kinds, and against the restrictive practices of the universities, where Mendicant professors were unwelcome.

Although the other great Mendicant Order, that of the Dominicans, had been founded at much the same time, its position was in some ways very different. Dominic, a Castilian by birth, had learned to recognize and fear heretics in Languedoc whilst he was still a young man. His Order became the sword of the Church, to be brandished against both its internal and its external foes. Dominicans, *domini canes,* the bloodhounds of the Lord, found their particular vocation in the Inquisition. From the time to Gregory IX they occupied a special position at Rome as the Pope's most trusted aides in all problems concerning the orthodoxy of doctrine. Thomism, from 1286 the official theology of the Order, has now become, after a struggle lasting from the thirteenth century to the twentieth, the guiding theology of the Catholic Church. Dominicans were also useful agents of the Popes in their disputes with bishops and with local ecclesiastical institutions.

The Order founded by St Dominic (✝1221, canonized

1234) never had to contend with the inner temptations which afflicted the sons of St Francis; emotionalism and ecstasy, prophecy and eschatology were all matters quite foreign to the Dominican temper. The Dominicans were exposed to a different temptation, that of intellectual curiosity, the urge to explore the "heights and profundities of the Godhead" by the exercise of powerful and self-confident reason. However, the achievement of Meister Eckhart and of a number of other French and German Dominicans shows that in them too the spirit was in the end enfranchised of all boundaries and limitations.

Both Orders took particular pains to attract the laity and women, the very people whose lack of any positive religious commitment had also greatly facilitated the rapid spread of the Cathar, Waldensian, and other unorthodox religious movements. Francis founded as the Second Order of his society the women's order known as the Poor Clares, after St Clare of Assisi, who had taken vows of perpetual poverty and chastity at Portiuncula in 1212. Dominic was from the beginning resolutely opposed to the foundation of a women's section of his Order. His thoroughly masculine temperament jibbed at the thought of coping with women's souls. As a result, when several well-endowed houses of Dominican nuns did come to be established, the male branch of the Order tried to avoid the responsibility of their spiritual training and direction. In Germany, however, after they had been ordered to assume this task, there blossomed that mysticism which is one of the finest flowers of German and Christian spiritual achievement.

The "Third Orders" of the Franciscans and Dominicans were designed to gather in the laity, and were a suitable refuge for members of extinct brotherhoods and the battered remnants of lay companies in danger of persecution. As semi-religious, these tertiaries sought to realize the monastic ideal while living in the world. They included some distinguished names, St Elisabeth of Hungary, St Louis of France, St Hedwig of Silesia.

The fate of the Beguines, who during the fourteenth century often sought the protection of the Dominicans to avoid loose accusations of heresy and actual persecution, illustrates how rapidly, in the varying circumstances of contemporary life, a popular religious movement could change its character, moving from "left" to "right" wing, from "orthodox" to "heretical". The first Beguinage was founded at Liège about 1170–80; it was a feminine community, in a region of surplus women, dedicated to leading a common life under spiritual direction while working at weaving, spinning and similar crafts. From there the movement spread rapidly along the Rhine to France and Germany and also to the Latin countries, and acquired a male branch. From the beginning the Beguines were suspected of heresy, or at least of being very close to it, and they were nearly always under fire. Their very name aroused suspicion. Modern scholars incline to the view that *begina* is derived not from *beige*, after the grey-brown colour of their habit, but from Albigenses. Beguine was again and again used as a simple synonym for heretic. "Right" and "left" wing Beguines were persecuted indiscriminately. In 1311 Pope John XXII excommunicated all Beguines and Beghards; a few years later he was forced to make a drastic modification of this omnibus condemnation. Mystics, both orthodox and heretical, found in Beguinage a rich and congenial soil.

CHAPTER 9

INTELLECTUALISM AND THE UNIVERSITIES

A FEW great medieval institutions are still with us: constitutional monarchy, parliaments, trial by jury, the Roman Catholic Church, and universities. The university, and the intellectualism it nurtured, is a specifically European phenomenon. In the universities were laid the foundations of the scientific culture of our modern world, in them grew up the habit of disciplined thinking, followed by systematic investigation, which made possible the rise of the natural sciences and of the technical civilization necessary to large industrial societies. Nevertheless, the university, typically medieval and typically European, borrowed freely from outside, from institutions of the ancient and Islamic worlds. Although it was much else besides, the intellectual life developed in medieval Europe was a positive response to the broad stream of classical, Arab, Islamic and Jewish influences to which it was exposed, particularly in the south and north-west.

A Spanish scholar, J. Ribena y Tarrago, has maintained that the medieval university owed much to the educational system of the Arabs. There is no doubt that Islamic Spain was a stimulating influence. In the century between 632 and 732 Islam had become master of the region between Persia and Spain, which thus became and remained "the Islamic world". By the end of the eighth century Islamic ritual and doctrine had reached their full development, and Islam had become a closed society, in which temporal and spiritual authority were coterminous and jurisprudence meant a knowledge of the practical precepts of religion. The world was sharply divided between the *dar-al-islam,* the people living under Muslim rule, and the *dar-el-harb,* the lands of the unconverted, potential battlefields. However, this closed society was like the filigree work characteristic of Islamic decorative art: it was full of minute holes, cracks and apertures, through which alien influences could find an entry. Much to the consternation of the orthodox, it was possible in Islamic states for Jews and Christians to rise high, sometimes right to the top, in the service of the government or the financial administration: as "People of the Book", fellow-worshippers of Holy Writ, they and their religious congregations enjoyed definite rights secured to them by treaty.

There is an apocryphal saying of Mohammed which runs: "My communion will be divided into seventy-three *firaq* (heresies), of which only one will be saved." Islam did in fact produce a number of sects, a multiplicity of religious, mystical and philosophical undercurrents, each in their own way reflecting what they had absorbed from the peoples of the conquered territories. In the eleventh century the numerous little courts of the rival Muslim chieftains in Spain, the *reyes de Taifas*, made a fine show, with their sparkling and thoroughly secular culture: Seville, Cordoba, Malaga, Valencia and Saragossa all competed for the best writers and minstrel poets. Some of the rulers were themselves distinguished poets, such as al Mu'tamid ibn 'Abbad of Seville (1069–91). In the Christian part of Spain this civilization was an object of fear and wonder. During this period the Castilian language took over a number of Arabic words which had to do with government, technology and cultural matters in general. The cultured Hispano-Arab princes of the Taifas had their latter-day successors in Frederick II, the Hohenstaufen Emperor, and the Spanish and Portuguese "pholosopher" kings of the twelfth and thirteenth centuries. The atmosphere of these courts was such that culture was equated with argument; public disputations were staged between scholars and theologians of the three religions, Islam, Judaism and Christianity. The envoy of the Emperor Otto I was amazed at finding Christian prelates and Jewish rabbis and physicians holding positions of importance at one of these courts.

Islamic orthodoxy, already vehemently opposed to such tolerance, was powerfully strengthened by the arrival of fresh supporters from the heart of the African desert and the High Atlas. During the eleventh century the Almoravids, a nomadic people from the Sahara, burst upon the scene; their first success was the conquest of Morocco (1056), their aim to make an end of the "godlessness" of a few Berber princes. The native religion was exterminated and a large empire set up in north-west Africa, all in the space of twenty-five years. The absolutism of the jealous God from the fiery wastes seemed vindicated when the Arab kinglets of Spain, who squabbled among each other yet had remained in amity with their Christian neighbours, called on the Almoravids for help against crusaders from the North. It is interesting to find even at this early date contention arising between Spanish crusaders and those from France and Northern Europe: the Spaniards were disinclined to see their Islamic enemies indiscriminately slaughtered like so many "mad dogs".

The advent of the Almoravids in Spain was the signal for the escape northwards into France, Germany and Italy of numbers of Jews, fleeing from the primitive Islamic and African fanaticism of the invaders; they took with them an intellectual culture which Islam itself had done much to enrich.

The rule of the Almoravids collapsed in the middle of the twelfth century, leaving a significant legacy, the close connection between Spain and Morocco; from this powerful liaison sprang the rebirth of Hispano-Moorish culture. The Almoha, Berbers from the High Atlas who succeeded the Almoravids, championed the cause of political and religious reform, and like their predecessors felt the call to purify Islam from unwholesome intercourse with the wicked, unbelieving non-Islamic world. However, the Almoha speedily adapted themselves to the prevailing intellectual and cultural climate, and went on to create the impressive civilization of the mid-twelfth century. Their marvellous mosques still stand as witness: the Kutubija at Marrakesh, the Giralda at Seville, the Hassan mosque at Rabat. The walled fortifications of their towns, with their monumental gateways, were the model for Norman strongholds in Sicily, Naples and England, and for crusading castles in the Holy Land. Literature, philosophy and science were revived. Poets, historians, philosophers and theologians gathered at the court of Marrakesh; Almoha princes had Ibn Tufail and Averroes (Ibn Ruschd) as their tutors. In this setting there flourished, particularly during the twelfth century, an Islamic brand of scholasticism, hammered out originally in the debates of the law schools. The methodology of legal-theological and political disputation had already become fixed during the ninth century. If the Word of God made no direct reference to the subject in hand, there must be recourse to a *hadit* or dictum: this in effect was an appeal to the patriarchs of Islam, to a saying of

Mohammed or one of his contemporaries, an appeal to "authority", as later Christian scholars would term it. In the absence of such a saying it was necessary to turn for an authoritative pronouncement to the writings of a great teacher of more recent date, or, if there were no direct statement there, to analyse in all its possible extensions any adducible precedent implicit in his argument. The chasing after authorities, the hunt for conclusive pronouncements from the great teachers of antiquity and the Church, so characteristic of European Christian scholasticism, here found its own precedent and authority.

The internal tensions and conflicts of Islam (tensions which also affected Western Europe) were pointed by the division of learning into two categories: on the one hand were certain subjects which were regarded as indigenous to Islam including jurisprudence, traditional lore, grammar, lexicography, history, the study of literature, poetry and metrics; and on the other, those such as natural science, philosophy and mathematics which were held to be intrinsically alien, a danger to Islamic orthodoxy.

Arab scholars and religious philosophers always had to work under the watchful and suspicious eyes of the champions of orthodoxy and of a people jealous of the purity of their faith. Dredging up the treasures of antiquity was perilous work on such volcanic soil, in a society which though closed was yet multifariously porous. The finds included the religious and scientific writings of the Neo-Platonists, Hellenistic authorities on medicine and the natural sciences, and, most precious of all, the works of Aristotle. Plato and Aristotle were first encountered buried in a waste of "Platonic" and "Aristotelian" literature, in which the "original" matter had become thoroughly enmeshed in a mass of very different material. Over the centuries a small army of enquiring scholars, some of them seekers after God, others of them agnostics or downright sceptics, penetrated by their critical endeavours to the "authentic" Aristotle, the master of a "world-centred" philosophy and of a rational scientific method, which dispensed with "God" and transcendental faith. Such was the difficult road traversed by al-Kindī (✣ circa 873), al-Fārābi (✣ circa 950), Avicenna (✟1037), Avenpace (Ibn Bājja, ✟1138/39) and Averroes (Ibn Ruschd, ✟1198), and they followed it to the summit. Their orthodox critics were convinced that such rationalist philosophy was destroying the integrity of Islamic faith.

Between the eighth century and the twelfth a number of thinkers were accused of heresy and atheism and even persecuted on that account. Their lives were often a perpetual migration, from Spain to North Africa, to Egypt, to Syria and Persia. They fled eastwards, like many of those Christians of the sixth and of the twelfth and thirteenth centuries whose religious and philosophical ideas deviated from the accepted norm. Their writings were suppressed and burned and they themselves condemned to exile or murdered.

There are remarkable parallels to all this in Christian and Jewish history. "Enlightened" Jewish thinkers and religious deviationists suffered the same fate; so did some Christian scholars and religious. Still more remarkable is the survival of this attitude into modern times. Even nowadays, a student at a Talmudic school will only read Maimonides' *Guide for the Perplexed* (Moreh Nebukim) in secret: Maimonides marks the culmination of "enlightened" Jewish philosophy and piety, and is today the object of as much suspicion, fear and curiosity as in the twelfth and thirteenth centuries; and he died in 1204, the year when the Crusaders captured Constantinople. Again, there are today orthodox theologians at the Al-Azhar University of Cairo who still resist the invasion of Islam by elements of corrosion they fancy they can detect in the great thinkers of the Arab scientific renaissance of the twelfth century. Finally, much heated controversy still rages, both within the Christian West and outside it, around the great figures who, continuing the work of Averroes, made up the Aristotelian "left wing" in Paris during the thirteenth and early fourteenth centuries, men such as Siger de Brabant, and also around "right wing" mystics like Meister Eckhart, just as it did during their lifetimes.

The Arab scholars were not alone in their quest. A similar spirit of enquiry and passion for knowledge was stirring in the West; Eastern and Western scholars met each other half-way, figuratively and literally. Cosmopolitan Toledo, with its mixed population of Jews, Moors and Spaniards, both Muslim and Christian (it was under Muslim rule from 712 to 1085 and Arabic was still being spoken there in the twelfth century), was especially attractive to the new intelligentsia of Western Europe on account of the school of translators founded there by Archbishop Raymund I (1126–51). Raymund was fortunate in securing as his chief assistant the archdeacon of Segovia, Domingo Gundisalvo, a converted Jew. The entire Aristotelian corpus was translated from Arabic into Latin and this was followed by translations of the chief works of the great Islamic and Jewish philosophers and religious thinkers, al-Kindī, al-Fārābi, al-Battāni, Avicenna, Ibn Gabirol, al-Ghazālī.

It was from the example of Toledo that Europe first learnt to understand that learning knows no frontiers, that it is universal, global, and "human", that it concerns mankind as a whole, without respect of race or religion. At Toledo Arabs, Jews and Greeks worked with Spaniards, Frenchmen and Germans, with Slavs from the Balkans and, last but not least, with Englishmen. Adelard of Bath, one of the first scholars in Western Europe to study nature at first hand, was probably a visitor there, to be followed by Robert of Chester, Daniel Morley and Alfred of Sareshel. From Italy came Plato of Tivoli, Gerard of Cremona and John of Brescia. Flanders was represented by Henry Bate and Rudolf of Bruges, France by the emissaries of Peter of Cluny and the scholars of Chartres; from the Balkans came Hermann of Carinthia, from southern France a number of Provençals and some distinguished Jews, Armengaud, Moses ibn Tibbon, and Jacob Ben Mahir ibn Tibbon. From Spain, amongst many others mention may be made of John of Seville and Hugh of Santalla, It was in this suitably cosmopolitan setting that the first attempt was made, by Gundisalvo, to reconcile Avicenna with Augustinian theology.

Toledo was not the only intellectual clearing-house; there were whole regions, such as Provence, Northern Italy and Sicily, which because of their "open" character became a forum for the exchange of ideas and texts, and certain "open" cities, Milan, Pisa, Montpellier, Salerno, Naples and Palermo, which were important vitalizing cells in the steadily mounting bloodstream of European intellectual life.

But when these "open" areas themselves became closed, and their contact with the Muslim world, also suffering from hardening of the arteries, was broken, the whole structure of Europe's intellectual life was profoundly modified. Whereas during the twelfth and early thirteenth centuries the lines of communication had been kept open, during the later Middle Ages they were cut.

Loaded down with a tantalizing and perilously rich burden of knowledge, conscious that a whole array of further problems awaited solution, European thinkers withdrew into a territory whose limits were now bounded by Oxford, Brussels, Cologne and Basel, though it would later extend eastwards to take in Cracow, Prague and Vienna. Its centre was Paris. It was no longer possible for men to sharpen their brains by those extensive journeyings about the world which had formerly delighted scholars, leading some of them even deep in to the Orient; the life of the intellect was now concentrated in certain places: universities. Public disputations with Cathars, Waldensians, Jews, or theologians of the Eastern Church were no longer possible either, in view of the change in the ecclesiastical and social climate; but in an altered form, and under strictly defined conditions laid down by the Church, there was still a place and scope for such exercises in the scholastic disputation, an essential feature of the medieval university. As an institution the university was at once a restraining and a liberating influence. In its restraining aspect the university was a stronghold of the Faith, the bulwark of the Papal Church, the instrument of kings, prelates and religious orders, who drew from it a new clerical estate of academically trained experts and officials. Learned in both canon and civil law, such men become valuable adjutants of the rising power of the Papal Church and the Western monarchies, the first civil servants.

But the universities were also oases of freedom, where all those questions which elsewhere were suppressed and forbidden were discussed with what hostile critics described as brazen impudence. One would be hard put to it to think of any thorny problem touching God, the world, the Church, Christianity and dogma, which was not posed in its basic and essential form in the universities of the thirteenth and fourteenth centuries.

For the Popes the universities were the object of their highest hopes and the occasion of their deepest disappointment. Two dates and events may serve as a preliminary illustration of this point. The University of Bologna received from the Pope the right to style itself "the teacher of Europe". In a Bull of 1220 Pope Honorius III gratefully acknowledged that from Bologna had come "rulers to rule the Christian people", an allusion to the canon lawyers for which Bologna was famous. In 1290 an ecclesiastical council at Paris had to listen to a scorching address from a papal legate in which the University of Paris was thoroughly trounced. The legate was none other than Benedetto Gaetani, the future Pope Boniface VIII. He chided the professors of the university for their folly in imagining they had any reputation for great wisdom at the Papal Curia. "At Rome we account them more foolish than the ignorant, men who have poisoned by their teaching not only themselves but also the entire world. You masters of Paris have made all your learning and doctrine a laughing-stock . . . It is all trivial . . . To us your fame is mere folly and smoke . . . We forbid you, on pain of losing your positions, your dignities and your benefices, to discuss the privileges of the Mendicant Orders, whether in public or in secret." Gaetani was incensed at the support given by the university to the French bishops in their opposition to the Bull *Ad fructus uberes* which confirmed the right of the Mendicants to hear confessions, a pastoral office the secular clergy considered their own preserve. Gaetani insisted that the masters of Paris had no business to meddle with such matters: "Rather than revoke this privilege, the Roman Curia will utterly destroy the University of Paris. We are called by God not to acquire wisdom or dazzle mankind but to save our souls."

The University of Paris looked its great adversary in the face. Refusing to be shaken, it became in the later Middle Ages the most powerful enemy of the Roman papacy, the protagonist of the Gallican policies of the French kings and the French church. When the Church entered on its democratic phase with the Conciliar Movement of the early fifteenth century the University of Paris, at the Councils of Constance and Basel, set itself up to be the judge of Popes.

In the Middle Ages the word *universitas* meant primarily an association, a corporation of the kind already frequently found in urban life; the name is applicable to any guild of merchants or craftsmen, or indeed to any organized group. The university in its narrower sense originated as an association of teachers or scholars for their mutual benefit during their sojourn in foreign parts. As aliens they were virtually defenceless, and came together for the sake of protection and security. At Bologna the *universitas* originated as an association of German, French and English students. At Paris it was the teachers who came together in this way (at Bologna they were mostly natives and thus in no need of protection). Paris and Bologna, both of which had their beginnings in the late twelfth century, are the two archetypes of the European university: student-universities were modelled on Bologna, universities of masters on Paris. The school of Salerno, where medicine was taught, was even older than Paris and Bologna, and for two centuries had a prestige as great as theirs. Founded in the tenth century at the latest,

Salerno was already famous as the repository of Greek and Roman medical knowledge when Constantius Africanus added to its resources by the introduction of Arab medical science, some time late in the twelfth century. Salerno maintained steady connections with Constantinople, whose impressive hospital organization has already been mentioned.

Bologna was the great centre of legal studies, Paris was the centre of theology. Bologna owed its success as a university to two circumstances: Italy had a long tradition of lay education (the Lombard nobility had their sons taught to read and write, whereas the nobility north of the Alps held book learning in contempt); and the towns, becoming increasingly important in Italy, were in constant need of lawyers and educated men to carry on their government and administer their laws. There had been eminent law schools in Italy before Bologna, at Rome, Pavia, and Ravenna. Indeed, around the year 1000 Bologna was famous not as a law school but as an academy of the seven liberal arts. It was in the twelfth century, under Irnerius, that it first acquired prestige as a law school teaching Roman Law. Four teachers of law from Bologna, Bulgarus, Martinus, Jacobus and Hugo, were present as advisers of Frederick I at the famous Diet of Roncaglia. About 1140 Gratian established Canon Law studies at Bologna; working on the same lines as the civil lawyers, he produced his textbook the *Decretum,* a systematic concordance of canon law judgments. His work also owed something to Abelard's *Sic et non.* Alexander III, the greatest of the twelfth century Popes, was a pupil of Gratian's and his first commentator, and Innocent III was a pupil of another canonist from Bologna, Uguccio of Pisa.

The canonists of Bologna aimed at creating for the Church a law worthy of it as *societas perfecta;* canon law should be as complete, as perfect and as free from loopholes as Roman Law. It was the canonists who built up the new hierarchy of the Papal Church: from the thirteenth century onwards the leading positions in the Church were occupied by lawyers rather than monks, pastors and theologians. It was the canonists, too, who evolved the theory of the universal dominion of the Papacy, which came to embrace the claim to political supremacy over all the peoples of the world.

It would be wrong, however, to imagine that Bologna was a "clerical" university; in the Middle Ages at least it was precisely the reverse. Once again we find the co-existence of opposites. The people who counted were the students, secular in their interests and completely self-assured, the majority of them already mature and experienced men. These students of civil law would tolerate no sermonizing, whether from Rome or from their university professors; the university belonged to them. A professor at Bologna was really a kind of private tutor, employed by an independent group of students whose ages might be anything between seventeen and forty and who owed their masters no moral or spiritual obedience. As the dominant element in the university, the students could exert powerful pressure on the city and on the professors, who at first were only loosely organized into a "college". The students negotiated with the city over the price of lodgings and food and conducted the continual lawsuits.

The medieval student took to quarrelling as readily as he took to drink. If no agreement could be reached with the town or with the professors, there was always the formidable threat of secession: Bologna and Paris both set an example here. Other towns were eager to welcome an academic migration for easily understandable motives, both economic and political. In fact the majority of the Italian law-schools and universities originated in secessions of students and/or teachers no longer able to tolerate the conditions in their own towns. The most important secession from Bologna took place in 1222 and resulted in the foundation of Padua, which in turn produced Vercelli in 1228. Vicenza, founded in 1204, was probably another offshoot of Bologna.

From about the middle of the thirteenth century the law students at Bologna were organized in two "universities", one of Italian students, the *universitas citramontanorum*, the other of all "transmontane" students, from whatever part of Europe. Germans, and also Poles, Czechs and Hungarians, were quite important at Bologna from an early date. The students, who had the whip hand, kept their professors to a punctual observance of the lecture timetable, under threat of financial penalties, and revenged themselves on unpopular teachers by boycotts. Naturally enough, the masters sought to protect themselves from such oppression. Like the students, they adopted the idea of a corporation and it was their guild which determined who should be licensed to teach, by the conferment of the *licentia docendi*, which made its holder a doctor. A chair at Bologna was much coveted as a rarity (at Paris there were more). The regular lectures took place in the mornings, special lectures in the afternoons. The academic year began on October 19. The order of graduation as laid down by Pope Honorius III in 1219 set a precedent followed all over Europe. Since every promotion to the doctorate now required the assent of the archdeacon of Bologna a certain degree of ecclesiastical control was assured. However, the students of Bologna would have nothing to do with papal privileges. Papal influence became pronounced at Bologna only in the later Middle Ages, when the Papacy had gained political control over the city.

In addition to its schools of canon and civil law Bologna also had "universities" of the liberal arts and of medicine. Philosophy and medicine were closely linked, an arrangement typical of Italy; the fundamental authorities were Aristotle and other classical texts which dealt with the theoretical aspects of medicine. As is well known, practical medicine, including surgery, long remained an inferior art, the province of manual workers such as the surgeon-barbers and army doctors. Bologna also had a chair of astrology, a fact of some significance: its most famous occupant, Cecco d'Ascoli, was burned in 1327, a victim of the Inquisition.

The organization of intellectual and academic life in Italy was directed to political and social ends. Pride of place was given to the two laws and to medicine and the philosophical studies ancillary to it. It was a matter of papal policy that theology should be reserved primarily for England and France, and this arrangement suited the Italian temper. Bologna later acquired a faculty of theology, but it was never of much consequence. The colleges founded at Bologna for "foreign" students (an "Avignon" college in 1267, a "Brescia" college in 1326, a "Spanish" college in 1367) were also not very important features of university life.

The medieval University of Paris was the battlefield of all the most significant intellectual conflicts of the age; it was also the place where thinkers of the later Middle Ages started to lay some of the important foundations of modern scientific thought. As an institution, it throve on conflict; perpetually at odds with officialdom (episcopal, papal and royal), for a long time obdurate in its resistance to the Mendicant Orders, during the thirteenth and fourteenth centuries the University of Paris became a power in Europe of an entirely different order of magnitude from the universities of today. Medieval Paris was a world within a world; its interior life will later be explored from the inside; we are concerned here only with its outward appearance and structure.

It will be recalled that towards the end of the eleventh century or the beginning of the twelfth the business of teaching was passing from the monks to the secular clergy; this was a distinct revolution in intellectual matters. Abelard, although he knew nothing of universities, was the first teacher to attract large crowds of students to Paris from every country in Europe. There were three important schools, cells from which the future university developed: the school of the collegiate church of Ste Geneviève, the monastic school of St Victor, and the cathedral school of Notre Dame. The university grew up between 1150 and 1170, with the Chancellor of the cathedral church of Paris, Notre Dame, as its "ecclesiastical superintendent", empowered to confer the *licentia docendi* on all eligible applicants. The Chancellor also claimed to be the *judex ordinarius* of the scholars. For a long time the most important teachers at Paris were foreigners; it was their guild which made up the university. It is important to notice that during the decisive years of conflict between the university and the Chancellor appointed by the bishop, the Pope sided with the university (1200–20). Rome was anxious to win Paris for itself as a centre of theological studies, and this was the reason why in 1219 Honorius III forbade the teaching of Roman Law at Paris. The Pope was afraid that the young theologians studying at Paris might be seduced from their proper studies by the attractions of careerism, the prospect of advancement in the service of Church and State available to those who had studied the law. This prohibition also suited the French kings, who feared Roman Law because of its associations with the Empire.

By far the largest faculty in the university was that of arts, the "philosophical" faculty. The curriculum was based on the seven liberal arts, grammar, rhetoric and dialectics, which made up the *trivium,* and music, arithmetic, geometry and astronomy, which were the *quadrivium.* In the thirteenth century interest was concentrated on the subjects of the *trivium,* that is on philosophy and its ancillary disciplines; by the fourteenth century it had shifted to the more "scientific" subjects of the *quadrivium,* largely in consequence of ecclesiastical sanctions against the free-thinking philosophy of the "artists".

Study in the faculty of arts was really intended as a

prologue to the study of theology. The only "full" professors at Paris were the doctors of theology, who had completed sixteen years of study, of which the years spent in the faculty of arts were only a necessary preliminary, to be looked back on with contempt in after years. Nevertheless, the theologians tended to regard the "artists" with disquiet and displeasure, often not untinged with envy. This is understandable when it is realized how greatly the artists increased in numbers in the second half of the twelfth century, so that the young masters of arts came to constitute a university on their own. By 1362 there were 441 masters in the faculty of arts as compared with 25 in theology, 25 in medicine and 11 in canon law.

At Paris the masters of arts were the permanent element of intellectual unrest and the driving force of intellectual revolutions. The quality and historical importance of the "full" professors, the theologians, can be measured by their response to the perpetual challenge of the artists: whether, that is, they stood their ground on the battlefield of disputation or removed themselves in cowardly flight. Thomas Aquinas and his teacher Albertus Magnus both stood their ground.

The intellectual restlessness of the artists was closely connected with the uncertainty of their status. On the one hand they were teachers; all the students had to pass through their hands. But they were students as well, engaged in further studies leading to doctorates in theology and professorships. Just because they were so numerous, many hundreds of them were denied any hope of a chair, which only added to their unrest. Quite a few, including some of the best, had no wish to become theologians: they preferred the greater intellectual freedom and mobility afforded by philosophy. With a foot in both camps, at once teachers and students, the masters of arts came to occupy a key position in the university. The crisis came about the year 1220. Before 1200 the Chancellor of Notre Dame had restricted all lecturing to the Ile de la Cîté, where it would be under the close control of the bishop, whose representative he was. But about 1210 the masters of arts withdrew themselves from the Chancellor's jurisdiction and settled on the left bank of the Seine, in the Rue du Fouarre, "the street of straw", so-called because of the straw-covered entries to the schools. The Latin Quarter was now in being. Jurisdiction over the arts faculty was assumed by the Abbot of Ste Geneviève, a rival of the Chancellor and the cathedral school.

A few minutes' walk from the Ile de la Cîté brings one to the tiny group of houses which is all that remains of the old Rue du Fouarre. They are a picturesque, typically Parisian jumble of buildings, a mixture of the styles of the last few centuries, cheek by jowl with the more venerable survivals from the Paris of the early Middle Ages which stand nearby. This maze of streets and houses, a great favourite with painters, is the monument to a past age of intellectual heroism: in this place the intellectual life of medieval Europe found its greatest freedom, here the love of controversy was extended to the limit.

Dante, in the *Divine Comedy,* puts his eulogy of Siger of Brabant, chief of the artists, into the mouth of Thomas Aquinas, chief of the theologians and Siger's great adversary:

> ". . . the eternal light of Sigebert
> Who escaped not envy, when of truth he argued,
> Reading in the straw-littered street."

Condemned by the Church, Siger died wretchedly in prison. Dante, however, makes Aquinas sing his praises in Paradise, an illuminating comment on the undercurrents of medieval intellectual life.

From the beginning life among the arts students at Paris was a turbulent affair. In the early years of the thirteenth century a cell of "pantheists" and "freethinkers" was uncovered, and several priests and clerks from the schools were burned or imprisoned in consequence. Their heresy had been inspired by Amaury of Bêne and David of Dinant; in 1215 the papal legate forbade all lecturing on Aristotle's books of natural philosophy (i.e. the *Physics* and *Metaphysics*), and ordered all arts students to abstain on oath from reading the works of David of Dinant and other heretics. By 1255, however, practically all the known works of Aristotle had become required reading for students in the arts faculty. In the meantime the artists had gained control of the university, with their Rector as its head, and the oath of obedience to the Rector became the foundation of the whole academic structure.

The artists reached this position of strength as the leaders of the "Nations", the students. There were four "Nations", usually mutually antagonistic, three French (the French, Norman and Picard) and the English, which included all students from Germany and other northern countries (in the fifteenth century it came to be called the "German" Nation). From the beginning of the thirteenth century there were also the three faculties, of arts, theology and canon law (medicine belonged to the arts faculty).

From the early thirteenth century the university as a whole (i.e. both teachers and students) was in conflict with the Chancellor and the city of Paris. The first and largest migration of students and teachers from Paris (in 1228–29) was occasioned by carnival riots. The emigrants dispersed to Oxford, Cambridge, Angers, Toulouse, Orleans, and Rheims, there to escape the vigilance of Parisian officials, ecclesiastical and lay. (The city and its citizens had no doubt suffered much from the university, with its numerous special corporations and large crowds of students.) Rome was alarmed at the exodus. Gregory IX, whose attempt to bring the wanderers back was only partially successful, in 1231 promulgated the Bull *Parens Scientiarum*, the "Magna Carta" of the University of Paris: Paris was recognized as the mother of the sciences, and the jurisdiction over it of the Chancellor and the Bishop of Paris was severely curtailed.

After the dispersion of 1228/29 there was a partial truce between the artists and the theologians, brought about by their common opposition to the Mendicant Orders, who had taken advantage of the upheaval to extend their teaching activities. The secular clerks regarded the Dominicans and Franciscans, bound as they were by the strictest obedience to their own Orders and the Papacy, as undisguised enemies of the university. In 1253 the university imposed an oath on all masters, binding them to observe the university statutes. This was something the friars could not and would not tolerate. In 1255 a Papal Bull threatened the university with excommunication if it failed to admit friars as doctors. Thereupon the university formally dissolved itself. Such a dissolution, together with secession and cessation (i.e. suspension of all teaching), was the universities' most formidable weapon, and it could be used with impunity. A university possessed no buildings of its own; it could keep its "open house" anywhere, and its teachers and students would find a welcome everywhere in Europe.

In the course of this conflict each side denounced the other as "heretics", "atheists" and so forth. The progressive overclouding of the intellectual climate, which became more ominous as the thirteenth century went on its way, is closely connected with this quarrel. A temporary truce was reached in 1261 through the good offices of Pope Urban VI, who had studied canon law at Paris: the university as a whole agreed to admit the friars, but they were to be excluded from membership of the faculty of arts, which was preserved as an area of freedom. In addition, no religious college was to have more than one doctor acting as a regent of the university (a member of the governing body, normally composed of fully qualified Masters and Doctors), with the exception of the Dominicans, who were allowed to appoint two. This was really a victory for the university, whose corporate spirit had by now become well established; the struggle with the friars had made the university set its own house in order. In 1318 the oath of obedience was at length imposed on the friars.

As a political power the University of Paris reached its maturity in the fourteenth and early fifteenth centuries. The "eldest daughter of the French monarchy", it prided itself on being above all secular jurisdiction, including that of the *Parlement*, the king's court. In 1398 Gerson became Rector, and during his time the university soared even higher, to become judge over Popes and anti-Popes. The Council of Constance was organized into four Nations (French, English, German and Italian), a device aimed at reducing the dominant influence of the Italians and modelled on the organization of the University of Paris.

But now the strain of so much self-confident intellectualism and striving after power began to tell. The university revealed its inner weaknesses in its posthumous condemnation of Joan of Arc as a heretic and a witch, two years after her death. It was finally brought low after a prolonged struggle with the French monarchy during the reigns of Charles VII, Louis XI and Louis XII. In the last year of the fifteenth century Louis XII rode armed into the university precincts, revoked the right of cessation, and thus finally brought the university to heel. By his action Louis had brought to an end a great variety of liberties, some of which we have failed to recover.

From the beginning the University of Paris had particularly close connections with English intellectual life. During the twelfth century the English contingent made up the majority of non-French students. It was in Paris, not in England, that the collegiate system originated, a fact often overlooked. The first college-foundation at Paris was the Collège des Dix-Huits, lodged in the Hôtel-Dieu, opposite the west front of Notre Dame: the college occupied a room purchased for it from the hospital by a London burgess returning by way of Paris from a pilgrimage to Jerusalem. Later it acquired a house of its own. About 1186 Count Robert of Dreux founded a hospice for "poor clerks" in the neighbourhood of the Louvre. In 1208 a Parisian burgess, Etienne Belot, founded with his wife the college of "The Good Children of St Honoré". Their example was followed not only by other citizens of Paris but also by great abbots and other princes of the Church, for example the abbots of Clairvaux, Prémontré and Cluny. The most famous college of all, the House of Sorbonne, which bequeathed its name to the whole university, was founded about 1257 by Robert de Sorbon, chaplain to St Louis, as a college for masters of arts who intended to proceed to a doctorate in theology. Provision of this kind was necessary if new generations of secular clerks were to be trained up in theology; otherwise theology might pass entirely into the hands of the friars, whose students were not prevented by financial considerations from undertaking this lengthy and expensive course. Another famous and distinguished college was the College of Navarre, founded in 1304 by Joanna of Navarre, wife of Philip the Fair.

There were, however, significant differences between a college at Paris and a college at Oxford: the Paris colleges were essentially colleges for students, under the direction of a head who was also a teacher. They were in a much weaker position than the Oxford colleges. The church authorities in Paris had the right to send their representatives, the Chancellor or his deputies, to conduct visitations of the colleges. The Oxford colleges were autonomous corporations, headed by a principal elected by his fellows to administer the internal affairs of the college. The head ruled with the assistance of the senior members and on issues of importance it was necessary to secure the assent of all the members; he had no power in academic matters.

In the Paris of Erasmus, Calvin, Ignatius Loyola and Rabelais the colleges had taken over most of the teaching; some of them even became small universities in their own right. But even in the early sixteenth century the atmosphere of, for example, the Collège Montaigu, attended by all four of these ill-assorted scholars within the space of a few decades, was still inhospitably medieval: a harsh disciplinary regime, filth and stench, appalling food, and, among the students and young masters, wretchedness and poverty. Many of the Paris colleges faded away at an early date, and the rest were swept away by the French Revolution. In England the continuity was unbroken: nearly all the colleges of medieval Oxford and Cambridge still exist, in one form or another.

England's ancient universities and colleges have preserved something of the splendour of their medieval liberties. Oxford was the mother of them all; Cambridge started with a migration of scholars from Oxford in 1209; Northampton, which may have had a continuous existence as a university between 1238 and 1264, was made up of migrants from both Oxford and Cambridge; an exodus of Oxford scholars to Salisbury in 1238 led to the setting up there of a *studium generale* which may have lasted until 1278; and as late as 1334 another band of Oxford migrants were trying to set up a university at Stamford. As for Oxford itself, the nucleus of the university was in all likelihood formed by the exodus of English masters and scholars from Paris in 1167. In the course of Henry II's struggle with Becket, Oxford was raised to the status of a *studium generale*. The site was a favourable one for a university, particularly since Oxford was not the seat of a bishopric and thus had no cathedral school; it was in the diocese of Lincoln, whose bishop lived 120 miles away, which made it much easier for the university to achieve independence. As at Paris, the Chancellor of the University was originally an episcopal official, but during the conflicts between the university and the bishop which developed during the thirteenth century the Chancellor became increasingly identified with the interests of the university. In the early fourteenth century the bishop's authority was finally and completely shaken off.

There were "Nations" at Oxford, as at Paris, but after the early years they ceased to be important. The relatively rapid unification of England into a nation made it possible to dispense in 1274 with the "northern" and "southern" Nations which had formerly vied with each other as fiercely as the Nations of Paris.

Although there were close links with Paris through individual masters and scholars, Oxford went its own way. The natural sciences won an early ascendency there, and the university had a strong Franciscan contingent. These two features gave Oxford its characteristic intellectual complexion. The best mathematicians of the thirteenth century came out of Oxford, for example John of Holywood (Johannes de

Sacro-Bosco) and the Franciscan John Pecham, who became Archbishop of Canterbury. For a long time the friars lived unmolested in Oxford. The Dominicans settled there in 1221, taking a house right in the centre of the town, on the eastern side of the Jewry, for as a trading city Oxford had large numbers of Jews. We shall discover how important was their intellectual influence, not least because of their connections with Spain and the East, when we come to consider Roger Bacon; it was, in fact, through Jewish translators that the store of Arab and Greek knowledge accumulated in the Mediterranean lands became available to Oxford scholars. The Dominicans of Oxford regarded the conversion of the Jews as their special mission.

The Franciscans settled at Oxford without any difficulty in 1224, the Carmelites in 1256 and the Augustinians in 1268. The conflict between secular clerks and friars, which at Paris had left its mark on the whole character of the university, was at Oxford virtually unknown until the early fourteenth century, though then for a time there were serious disputes between the friars and the university, similar to those which had disturbed Paris. In the course of this quarrel, which involved litigation, royal letters patent were issued, in 1314, which settled the general principles of the university constitution and confirmed the democratic nature of its governing body, the Great Congregation. In time the university gained complete control of the town, and all the more important disputes were reserved for the court of the Chancellor.

The fame of Oxford is inseparable from the fame of its colleges, so much so that it is worth giving a very brief account of some of the more important foundations, although it is impossible in such a short space to show them in their proper light as intimate communities exerting a potent influence in the moulding of mind and character. University College owed its foundation (*circa* 1280) to a legacy from William of Durham, who had been a master of Paris; it began as a very small self-governing society of four masters living together in a hall under the direction of their senior fellow. Balliol College was founded as a penance for his sins by Sir John de Balliol; it was originally intended as a hostel for poor students on the Parisian model and only fell into line with the prevailing English pattern in the fourteenth century. Walter de Merton's foundation was already in existence *de facto* and *de jure* in 1264, and Merton

College has the "best claim to be the earliest Oxford college". The first eight students were all nephews of the founder, and even when their number had grown to twenty they were still all founder's kin. Their superior was a warden, but at first he ruled from a distance, residing at the house in Surrey which provided their endowment. His authority over the scholars derived from the fact that he was *in loco avunculi* (and a rich one at that), and not from any academic status. All the members of this family foundation wore a uniform dress. The regulations drawn up by the founder in 1270 and 1274 and incorporated into the college statutes became exemplars for other English university foundations: exact rules were laid down for the conduct of life in college and for the courses to be pursued. The freedom of the continental student was unknown in England. Later foundations (Exeter 1314, Oriel 1324, Queen's 1341, New College 1379) followed the pattern already laid down.

Italy during the thirteenth and fourteenth centuries had a host of smaller universities, many of which were little more than municipal schools of law, possessing their own buildings and with a civic rather than an ecclesiastical character: for example, Reggio, Vicenza, Siena, Piacenza, Perugia, Treviso, Verona, Pisa, Florence and Pavia. The University of Naples, founded by Frederick II as an answer to Bologna (which was a Guelph and therefore a papal university), was in a special position. Padua, which was started by a band of emigrants from Bologna in 1222, reinforced by other migrations in 1306 and 1322, rose to be unique among the universities of Europe. Under the protection of the Republic of Venice Padua became a centre of scientific and left-wing Aristotelian thought, attracting scholars from all over Europe, including large numbers of Germans, Poles and other Central Europeans. Copernicus and Galileo built on foundations laid by generations of Paduan doctors, mathematicians, astronomers and natural philosophers. Shielded by Venice from the Inquisition, Padua was famed for its tolerance. It was the first Western university to confer a doctorate in medicine on a Jew, in 1409. Even in the eighteenth century there were a number of English, Scottish and other Protestant students coming to work at Padua.

In Spain and Portugal the universities were royal foundations and maintained close links with the crown. They often had a royal official as Chancellor and were closely connected with the local cathedral school, which might mean considerable interference from the diocesan bishop. The names at least of the Spanish and Portuguese universities deserve to be set on record (Valladolid in the mid-thirteenth century, Salamanca *circa* 1227, Palencia in 1208–09 and Lerida in 1300 for Spain, Lisbon and Coimbra in 1290 for Portugal), although their heyday was in the sixteenth century, when they acquired a European reputation.

The peculiar eminence of the University of Paris, which had such an important influence on Europe as a whole, should not blind us to the lively existence of a number of other French universities, which as they grew came to exercise a considerable influence within France itself. As an example of their specific contribution, one may suggest that Calvin owed his particular cast of mind more to the humanism and jurisprudence he learned at Orleans than to anything he was taught at Paris. Bologna, rather than Paris, was the model of most of these French universities, though they were sometimes a mixture of the two. During the fourteenth century the students of several universities succeeded in winning a voice for themselves in university affairs, for example in the election of the Rector. And even where they were unsuccessful, they were able to establish their own powerful corporations alongside the university proper. Nearly everywhere the bishop had more power and influence than at either Bologna or Paris and it was only at a later date that the municipalities intruded their influence, when the question of paying fixed salaries arose. Many of the smaller universities had a system of colleges or hostels for housing poor students. The study of law took pride of place.

The greatest law school of medieval France was Orleans, which as early as the twelfth century had been a flourishing centre not only of legal but also of humanistic studies, classical literature, grammar and poetry. The best-known stylists and poets of the age had had their education from Orleans; so had all the secretaries of Popes Alexander III and Lucius III. When Chartres fell into decline, the classical humanist tradition of the twelfth century was still continued at Orleans. A thirteenth century writer ranked Orleans with Paris, Bologna and Salerno. In the fourteenth century the university took a revolutionary step, in other countries postponed for centuries (in Germany it was delayed until the seventeenth and eighteenth centuries): the professors began to lecture in the vernacular, giving courses in French as well as the obligatory lectures in Latin.

Toulouse was founded by Pope Gregory IX in 1229 as a move in the campaign against Catharism. As a singular example of political and pastoral reasoning it is worth mentioning that in order to increase the prestige of Toulouse Aristotle's teachings on scientific subjects, at that time prohibited in Paris, were made freely available there. Many a scholar must have gone out from Europe's higher institutions of learning with a store of knowledge and experience very different from what the founders intended. Toulouse was one of the few great European universities where all the faculties were represented.

The smaller French universities included Angers, Avignon (founded in 1303 by Boniface VIII), Cahors, Grenoble, Orange and Aix, these last all established between 1332 and 1409. Montpellier, where Arabs, Jews and Spaniards were still living side by side in the thirteenth century, was an intellectual world in itself. It preserved something of the spirit of resistance native to Provence and the South of France generally. Arab influence here was immediate and potent, particularly marked in medicine (regarded as a major branch of science) and in various speculative sciences. The university had three Nations, Provençal, Burgundian and Catalonian. Montpellier was a university of masters, governed by a Chancellor appointed by the bishop and by three masters. The bishop had his seat at Maguellone, quite close at hand: much closer than Lincoln was to Oxford, closer even than Ely was to Cambridge; and at Montpellier the bishop retained his jurisdiction over both masters and students. However, the students succeeded in securing some rights of practical importance, worth attention from modern university reformers: twice a year students and masters met to arrange the lecture timetable for the coming semester and to discuss grievances and other matters affecting both sides.

Until the middle of the fourteenth century Germany looked to Paris and northern Italy to cater for its intellectual needs; for example, the Emperor Charles IV (1347–78) was educated in France. Prague, founded in 1348, was at once the first German and the first Czech university; it was modelled on Paris, and so was Vienna, founded in 1365, the first university to be established on German-speaking soil. The influence of Oxford is also discernible in both cases. The first teachers at Vienna were masters from the

English nation at Paris. Paris also provided the model for Erfurt (1379–92), Heidelberg (1385), Cologne (1388) and for the earliest universities of Poland (Cracow, 1364–97) and Hungary (Pecs-Fünfkirchen, 1367, Buda, 1389–95, Pressburg, 1465–67). It will be noticed that for all the more easterly universities, except Vienna, two dates are given. The reason is that in this part of Europe an initial foundation usually failed to flourish and a fresh start had to be made a few years later. There was not as yet any great need in these regions for educated clerks, nor any particular interest in creating an intellectual élite.

The medieval universities trained up and moulded a new class, and what might almost be described as a new type of man: the academic and the intellectual. The two terms are not automatically interchangeable. Some members of the new class spent from fourteen to sixteen years as students. The minimum age for entry was usually fourteen, and most of the students coming to the universities were between thirteen and sixteen years old. A very large percentage had their studies paid for by someone else, a wealthy relative or patron, an important cleric or some student foundation. Many were very poor. Their miserable lodgings were poorly heated and ill-lit. Their life was turbulent and often dissipated; brawls with the townsfolk and artisans, assassinations and excesses of all kinds were a regular part of it. Discipline in the colleges was often harsh and gloomy, distinctly parsonical in tone, and accompanied by a highly-developed system of informing. At the biennial meetings of the chapter the students were obliged to denounce one another's faults. This system affected men in different ways, according to their disposition: while an Erasmus or a Rabelais found it intolerable, Calvin adopted it as part of his own spiritual discipline.

Lectures started at a very early hour, six o'clock in winter, in summer even earlier, and often lasted for three hours. Famous teachers attracted large crowds, which the antiquated rooms serving as lecture-halls could barely accommodate. There were very few of the size and beauty of the late medieval lecture-hall at Salamanca which still survives for our admiration.

Contemporaries seem to have found the throng of students so overwhelming that they were driven to making wild estimates of their numbers. For example, it is said that in 1287 Paris had 30,000 students and Bologna 10,000. In fact Paris probably averaged about 2,500, rising to six or seven thousand in its heyday. At the end of the thirteenth century Oxford may have had between fifteen hundred and two thousand students.

It is highly significant that the medieval universities gave their students no spiritual training or instruction. This was something only introduced later by teachers whose personal religion had a strong emotional backing, the reformers Wyclif and Hus for instance; when it came, it marked the dawn of a new age. Strong religious and national feelings—the two were often combined—later came to affect both students and teachers, particularly in Eastern Europe.

Clerks trained in the university law schools became indispensable functionaries of the newly-developing and rising states of the high Middle Ages, particularly France and England. Kings, Popes, princes, prelates, towns and corporations all competed for the services of this new class. The *clerici* were the equivalent of our "managerial class". They were administrators and bureaucrats, often the only people capable of manipulating the levers of power. Their steady rise from the twelfth century onwards, which now excites such interest, at the time went almost unobserved. Chroniclers could hardly be expected to notice it: their record is of battles and of the endless quarrels of Popes, kings and barons. But in the background the men of the new class were doggedly and systematically building up and enlarging the structure of the state, in France, in England and in the territorial principalities of Germany; no less important, they were turning the Church itself into a bureaucracy. They went serenely on their way, unperturbed by the misfortunes of their masters, unshaken by the frailties of kings or the *hubris* of Popes. Even their own setbacks failed to dismay them: if one of their number fell from grace, plenty were left to carry on with the work of bringing reason to bear on the exercise of power. The ablest of them were completely absorbed in their mission. Church and State should be fashioned into works of art, creations constructed with the same intellectual care as went to the making of a Gothic cathedral. The State, the Church and the administrative apparatus were ends in themselves; for those who served them the old boundaries dissolved and became meaningless.

The education of this new class had a legalistic and intellectual bias. The grandeurs and miseries of the European intellectual have their origin in the medieval university, with its almost complete concentration on the education of men's reason, a task it admittedly performed to admiration. But there were whole areas it left untouched: it failed to reach the affections and emotions, failed to instil manners of a deeper sort, failed to mould the elemental forces of personality, failed to provide the nourishment of true religion. Medieval intellectuals often show symptoms of a split personality: their intellects might be highly developed, but their manners were vicious and uncouth, their personalities spiritually immature. They also had to cope with the occupational disability of their calling, homosexuality; it was not merely this, however, but the defectiveness of their personalities as a whole which so aroused the indignation of sensitive and genuinely devout men. The Paris of the intellectuals was Babylon to Jacques de Vitry, as it had been to Bernard of Clairvaux. Bernard exhorted teachers and students to flee from it and save their souls. To other people, however, Paris was paradise itself. The goliards and wandering scholars, intellectuals after their own fashion, had already sung its praises: "paradise on earth, the rose of the world, the balm of the universe". The hypercritical intellectuals of Europe made it their capital. They criticized everything, each other, the bureaucratic Church, and above all the monks, whom they stigmatized as slothful, gluttonous and lewd. The later attacks on monasticism coming from Valla and Erasmus belong to this acrimonious tradition. Typically urban, the intellectuals of Paris looked down on everything rustic and provincial, including the peasantry. The aristocracy they regarded as at least their equals if not their inferiors: what counted was the "inner nobility" of the intellect. One could fill a long catalogue with these shortcomings and vices. Their vocation made these men very vulnerable. If they were remorseless, it was in the nature of their calling. Robert de Sorbon asserted that "nothing is fully known until it has been chewed to shreds in argument". The pursuit of knowledge by way of logic imposed an endless process of dissection, analysis, categorization, clarification, distinction and elucidation. Not a few of them lived in the confident hope (and illusion) of becoming capable of all things: of being able to understand and comprehend everything under a precise formulation, logically arranged. They had their own version of Faust's dream: the world and all reality might be controlled if only man could arrive at a proper grasp of them, that is, if everything could be formulated in the correct way.

It is timely now to turn to the great achievements of medieval intellectuals. Boetius of Dacia, outstanding among their number, names *magnanimatas* as the intellectual's foremost virtue. Abelard had already celebrated the same quality as the supreme virtue attending all philosophical enquiry, the passion which inspires hope. Imbued with this spirit, which was a legacy of the noble philosophers of antiquity and an attribute of contemporary chivalry, man could take up with enthusiasm the proper study of mankind, which was to plumb the depths of reality, nature and man, reaching to the heart of the Godhead itself, in the light of reason and understanding.

The great intellects of the later Middle Ages demonstrated their audacity in every department of knowledge and achievement, art, politics, the affairs of Church and State. Even if some medieval intellectuals indulged themselves by dabbling in trivialities, it should never be forgotten that from among this horde of the nameless and the known who from the early thirteenth century thronged the cities, courts and chanceries of Europe—their enemies said they descended on them like locusts—there arose a few lofty figures whose achievement has become a permanent part of man's heritage. They tower above the mass of their less talented fellow-toilers as surely as the Gothic cathedral, that most intellectual of all medieval works of art, dominated the lowly dwellings of the men who built them.

CHAPTER 10

INTELLECTUAL WARFARE IN PARIS

FROM the twelfth century onwards Paris was the acknowledged intellectual capital of Europe; during the thirteenth and early fourteenth centuries it was the arena of combat for the ablest and most daring minds of the age. The Dominicans arrived there in 1217, the Franciscans in 1229. Roger Bacon was a master of Paris and lived there between 1240 and 1247. Albert the Great taught there between 1245 (or perhaps 1242) and 1248, the year when the Franciscan Bonaventura began to teach at Paris, to continue until 1255. The Dominican Thomas Aquinas was teaching at Paris from 1252 to 1259, a period almost coterminous with the height of the battle over the friar doctors (1252–57). In 1265 he started work on the *Summa Theologica,* a year later Roger Bacon wrote his *Opus Maius.* Siger of Brabant must have come to Paris between 1255 and 1260, and was lecturing there when Aquinas returned in 1269. Siger's propositions were first condemned by the Church in 1270, a condemnation reiterated in 1277, when 219 theses were censured by the Bishop of Paris, including a few held by Aquinas, Siger's great adversary.

This first round of conflicts, which had culminated in ecclesiastical censure, was followed by a brief breathing-space. But battle was resumed at the beginning of the next century. Duns Scotus was teaching in Paris between 1303 and 1308, Meister Eckhart from 1300 to 1303 and again from 1312 to 1314. And it was between 1312 and 1314 that Dante, far removed from Paris in body but very much there in spirit, was writing the *Inferno.* In 1325 the university revoked its condemnation of Thomism: what in 1270 had been revolutionary was now conservative, an urgently needed ally against the radicalism it had helped to produce. Meister Eckhart was condemned by the Pope in 1329 and in 1337 the University of Paris issued its first condemnation of Ockhamist teaching. William of Ockham taught at Oxford between 1318 and 1324.

Thus set out, these names and dates crowded into the space of little more than a century are mere cyphers. It is time to investigate what lies behind them.

As a prelude, there is a dramatic episode to record. In 1210 the body of Amaury of Bêne, teacher of philosophy (and therefore a master of arts), who had died four years previously, was burned; the same fate overtook ten living "Amauricians". Amaury had studied at Chartres (Bêne was a village close by), a school whose confident intellectualism has already been described. Before Amaury there had been Clarembald of Chartres (✝ after 1170), later to be attacked by Aquinas and cited by Meister Eckhart as one of his chief authorities. Clarembald had taught that in principle everything is knowable; the essence of matter is flux, movement; mathematics discovers the laws governing the alteration of matter; thus by exercising the most powerful resources of the intellect, God is also knowable. Amaury taught: Hell is ignorance, Hell is within us, "like a bad tooth in the mouth"; God is identical with all that is; even evil belongs to Him and proves his omnipotence. A man who knows that God works through everything cannot sin, since every human act is then the act of God; such a man's recognition of truth puts him already in Heaven and is the only possible resurrection. There is no other life; man's fulfilment is in this life alone.

One can detect here the origins of that earth-bound humanism which the Averroistic Aristotelians worked out decisively and clearly in the thirteenth century, to make it the base of further advances. It has been the foundation of militant, non-Christian humanist thinking ever since, right down to Gide, Sartre and Camus.

Even among the Amauricians, this brand of humanism already had a markedly political content. Amaury and his disciples expressed in an actively political, not to say explosive, form, ideas which originated with Joachim of Flora. Their political message can be summarized as follows: all three Persons of the Trinity were creatures and had their own incarnation; the kingdom of the Father was the kingdom of the Old Testament, the kingdom of the Son that of the Church of the Sacraments, whose reign was just drawing to a close; the kingdom of the Holy Ghost was dawning, newly incarnate every day in the individual believer, making him God. The idea of identifying the Holy Ghost with the spirit working as "activating intellect" (*intellectus agens*) in every man, a deduction eventually made by the left-wing Aristotelians basing themselves on Averroes, was probably the most important contribution made by this school. The Amauricians seem to have had some measure of protection from the royal court. Amaury is said to have been the tutor of the son of Philip Augustus, the heir to the throne, who, according to Amaurician belief, would appear as the saviour in the last days of the world and make an end of Empire and Papacy.

David of Dinant, whose teachings were condemned together with Amaury's, was an out-and-out Aristotelian, basing himself on pure logic. He seems to have taught a materialistic pantheism: God is matter and no reality exists outside matter, outside God. All that is known of David personally is that he had an interview with Innocent III in Rome.

In their intoxicating enthusiasm for Aristotle and the Arab commentators, above all Avicenna and Averroes, these young masters saw God and nature, matter and spirit all on the same plane. Certain teachings acted like a habit-forming drug: thus, matter is eternal and perpetually in motion; there has never been any creation in time; there is but one intellect, the power of thought which all men have in common; there is but one world soul subsisting in all living things; there is no personal immortality; faith and knowledge must be kept severely apart; science is concerned only with nature and natural processes; and theology is not a science. The discovery of free-thinking and pantheistic cells touched off a series of chain reactions at the University of Paris: no less than six decrees were issued between 1213 and 1241 forbidding clerks to engage in the study of the natural sciences. No one "in bad repute" was permitted to lecture (statutes of Robert de Courçon, Cardinal-Legate, promulgated in 1215). In 1231 the Church forbade scientific discussions in the vernacular: Galileo was also to be censured for bringing "dangerous propositions" before the masses.

Nevertheless, during the period 1230–50 the main writings censured by these prohibitions, the scientific treatises of Aristotle and his Arab commentators, were gaining ground at Paris, where interest centred on Averroes. Roger Bacon's lectures on Aristotle, given as early as 1245, frequently refer to Avicenna and Averroes. A little later it becomes evident that there was a strong minority of heterodox Aristotelians among the artists. The leading intellects among them were all northerners, from northern France, northern Germany and Scandinavia: Siger of Brabant, Boetius of Dacia (he was a Dane or a Swede) and Goswin of La Chapelle from the Netherlands. Their fundamental position as philosophers is summarized by a saying of Siger's: "We are not discussing God's miracles; what we have to do is to discuss what is natural in a natural way." Someone who heard Boetius of Dacia lecture described him in his lecture-notes as *naturalis*; his interest was confined to "things, their motion and matter". Boetius was silenced by the condemnation of 1277; so little is known of him personally that it is not certain exactly where he came from or when he died. He was the author of one of the most interesting medieval treatises on grammatical theory (*De modis significandi*) and of a small work *On the Sovereign Good* (*De summo bono*), which Mandonnet has described as the "purest, clearest and most resolute rationalism one could possibly find". Boetius's conclusion is that the greatest beatitude is to be found in the practice of the good and the cognition of the true. Man's intellect must guide him to the discovery of both the good and the true, for if there is anything divine in man then it is the intellect, and it is by the exercise of intellect that truth and justice are discerned and practised: intellect, truth and right conduct make up the trinity of human beatitude. For the purpose of this treatise Boetius makes a sharp distinction between belief and knowledge; he represents the much-debated thesis of "double reality" at its purest. Faith and knowledge are governed by different principles, and always have their own validity.

There is still as much heated controversy around the figure of Siger of Brabant (born *circa* 1240, murdered by a madman while under some form of papal detention at Orvieto *circa* 1282) as there was in the thirteenth century. East and West both claim him as their own. One contemporary manuscript alludes to this young man, who had mapped out the whole scheme of his life's work by the time he was twenty-six, as "Siger the Great". Duns Scotus, however, considered that anyone who had erred so grossly was quite beyond the pale of human society. Petrarch described Averroes, Siger's principal authority, as a "mad dog, baying with insensate frenzy after Christ his Lord and the Catholic faith". Siger was at the heart of the intellectual storm raging in

Paris during the second half of the thirteenth century, his party, the "party of Siger", for some years refused to accept the result of the rectorial election of 1271. Siger fascinated students and scholars as the unequivocal champion of the autonomy of reason, of "pure" knowledge free of any theoretical limitation. The man of knowledge is made to appear as the true prophet: "Be alert, study, read, and if any doubt remains let it stimulate you to further study, for a life without knowledge is death, the grave of an inferior being." "Pure reason" could know nothing of providence or free will, but must recognize the world as an uncreated eternity and that men shared a unique intellectual soul; individual souls had no immortality. Religion was necessary for the masses, but not for educated people. Dogmas were beneficial for faith, but reason often taught the contrary. Siger adhered to the idea of cycles, which had been common in antiquity: history was cyclical, everything recurred, including legal systems and religions. The world was almost entirely self-propelled by its own mechanism; it was only on its periphery that the stars, the celestial intelligences, could exert some influence. Matter, motion and time were eternal. Individuals were the only transitory things; they, however, shared in the intellectual soul common to all mankind. "Free will", strictly speaking, was an empty phrase. The life of every individual was predetermined by the existing laws. Good consisted in anything useful to the human race, evil in whatever injured it.

The year before Siger's teachings were first condemned, 1269 saw the recall of Thomas Aquinas to Paris for a second spell of teaching, despite the university statute which allowed friar doctors only one such period; Aquinas was needed to support the tottering anti-Averroist front. The dispute between Siger and Aquinas has been described as the most important intellectual episode of the thirteenth century. When Aquinas died exhausted in 1274, Albert the Great, his teacher and friend, carried on the struggle.

A prayer of St Thomas Aquinas which has been preserved shows him asking God to keep him in cheerfulness without levity and in wisdom without pretension. The "Sicilian Ox" (as he was called in admiration by his brother friars) plunged into the intellectual affray of his time with a good humour and calm which today seem almost uncanny. Throughout all his prodigiously extensive writings there are very few lapses into personal polemics. He remained controlled, sober and patient, giving a full hearing to his opponents. In his hands the methods and temper of disputation and academical debate were refined to a delicacy rarely achieved by scholars before or since. Aquinas, working within the university and in the context of philosophical enquiry, was able to preserve a tradition no longer observed in the world outside, that of candidly discussing the most knotty issues with the most intractable adversaries.

Aquinas was obliged to fight on at least four fronts, two on the "right" and two on the "left". The station on the right was occupied by the conservative university theologians and the Franciscans, that on the left by free-thinkers and radical Averroists, the men of Siger's party. Bishop Tempier's condemnation of 219 dangerous propositions in 1277 put Aquinas in the same boat with Siger and other "free-thinkers", not to mention Amauricians and sundry political and religious fanatics.

To the men of the right Aquinas was a revolutionary and a thoroughly dangerous man. The men of the left saw him as a thinker who had stuck half-way. The traditionalists and the Franciscans reproached him for having introduced the sinister figure of Aristotle and his still more sinister commentators into the theology of the university and the Church, for having, indeed, opened the door to the whole rabble of Jewish, Arab and Classical philosophers. The Franciscan attack on Aquinas was mounted between 1265 and 1270; in a course of instruction given by Bonaventura at Paris in 1273 Aristotle and Aquinas both came under attack.

In relying on St Augustine, Franciscan theologians and philosophers remained loyal to one of the older schools of traditional theology: their theme was of grace and love, and the conflict between the "natural" and the "supernatural", between spirit and flesh. Pride of intellect meant the corruption of Christian humanity. This way of thinking had a strong emotional colouring, a legacy of St Francis's own resistance to soulless learning based on reason, and of the Order's bitterness at the humiliations heaped upon it in the conflicts of the day. Moreover, Bonaventura was attempting to retain within the Order at least a remnant of those Franciscans who were caught up in prophetic and historical speculation. Aquinas was attacked from this quarter for having betrayed Christ and the Church to the unfettered play of intellect. It cannot be denied that Aquinas, the son of one of

Frederick II's most loyal vassals (he was actually related to the Emperor), and brother to a courtly *minnesänger*, was much closer in spirit to Siger of Brabant than to the Franciscans and the traditionalist school. Avid for knowledge, Aquinas immersed himself in the newly discovered texts; he read Averroes and Avicenna early in his career (though at first without appreciating the tremendous implications of what he read) and steeped himself in the growing number of classical, Arab and Jewish texts daily becoming available in translation. Aquinas, Albert the Great and Meister Eckhart were all, for example, deeply indebted to Maimonides, the grand master of neo-Judaism, the Jewish "Enlightenment".

But while the "right" was suspicious of Aquinas as an Aristotelian and a pioneer of enlightenment, as the worshipper of reason and master of a dispassionate rational and speculative philosophy firmly committed to its "scientific" method, the "left" accused him of timidity in refusing to follow his thinking to its conclusion; they were scornful above all of his attempt to house Aristotle, the Arabs and all rationalist philosophies under the protective roof of a wholly unnecessary theological superstructure, which could only distort what it shielded.

The key to Aquinas's predilection for the middle road is to be found in his own temperament and the circumstances of his age. Sir Henry Slesser has called Aquinas "the first Whig". Whether consciously or unconsciously, Thomism has had its attraction for English philosophers whose thought has tended towards creative compromise and living conservatism, Hooker, for example, and other early theologians of the Church of England. Aquinas was perfectly clear about the limits and dimensions of human understanding, and never altered his opinion. Everything terrestial is a fit object of investigation, and there can be speculation about much that is celestial. The world is good; it was created by God. Man, as the child of God, was created good; but his intellectual soul has become clouded, largely as the result of sin: "the first-born daughter of impurity is blindness of the intellect." With God's help, however, man can still unfold all the powers of his mind and spirit and henceforth, as master of himself, and therefore master of his intellect and his will, is free to do good, to fashion his life in a wholesome and rational manner in the light of intelligent humility. God's help is available to man through four channels: the

Church, society, the exercise of the powers of understanding, and argument with opponents. All four are a means of education, which implies opening oneself to reality as a whole in accepting obedience. Thomas, the nobly-born, subjected himself in all humility to the discipline of these four "schools". He followed Aristotle in acknowledging that in every respect the "common will" takes precedence over individual wills; in the "school" of Church and society the individual was therefore obliged to submit to the prevailing social order. Aquinas accepted *in toto* the traditional hierarchy of aristocratic Europe, as it had existed from Homeric times up to his own day: slavery, warfare, capital punishment were all a natural part of it. His favourite simile for this static human society was that of a city, a city informed by reason, in which every man was equally at home and the friend of his neighbour. Friendship imposed its own duty, the duty of educating oneself and one's neighbours. Aquinas's tireless intellectual endeavours, his two great *Summae,* his university lectures, had their roots in his personal experience and conviction: he had seen the young intelligentsia of Paris, indeed of all Europe, reeling under the intoxicating influence of the new thought from the Near East (not to mention the oriental gnosticism which originated yet further east, coming from Bagdad and Persia). These young men seemed to hold that everything was permissible, and that everything was within the scope of human thought and invention. For Aquinas this was going much too far, and his rejection of such extremism was the main reason for his quarrel with the "left".

Massive both in physique and intellect, Aquinas yet retained an essential modesty; the intellectual arrogance of later scholastic theologians in attempting to embrace God, the world, man and nature within the grasp of their hybrid speculations was quite alien to him. This is why on occasion he was bold enough to attack even Averroes, from whom he had learned so much, as the "perverter of Aristotle", for Aquinas was convinced that Aristotle had a natural humility and piety which restrained him from delving into the ultimate secrets lying at the heart of reality.

While Aquinas was warning left-wing thinkers that they had gone too far, the right were denouncing him in almost the same terms: or even suggesting that he should not think at all. The merit of being attacked from the right has made of Thomas the "father of the Enlightenment", the direct ancestor of rational philosophy, of Descartes and of Kant. Not only was Aquinas opposed to all obscurantism, he was also against any submergence of reason in a sea of emotion, or indeed, "faith", and this was also important for Europe's progress towards self-discovery. Here Aquinas joined issue, for the first and only time, with the greatest of western theologians, Augustine. Augustine taught the primacy of the "will", of the "heart", of the forces of emotion. Aquinas taught the primacy of intellect. God is the "most perfect of intellectual beings". What is essential about the being and existence of God is that He thinks, understands and observes Himself. That is the great Magna Carta of an open-minded European rationalism.

The better the use man makes of his intellect, the more open he becomes, accessible to God and himself. A well-ordered society is that in which free and reasonable men, speaking a common language, set up a community on the basis of common understanding. But Aquinas realized that men in fact no longer understood one another. The first and most urgent obligation of scholarship was the specifically political task of evolving a basic language, by which men's thoughts could be reduced to a common denominator. Scholasticism for Aquinas meant training in clear thinking, in the use of terminology which was both unambiguous and unemotive. Thomas' personal and religious concern coincided with his didactic aim, that of expressing himself at every turn as precisely and clearly as possible. This explains why he cultivated the art of disputation. The *disputatio legitima,* that is, a disputation which followed a prescribed form, dominated the formal teaching of the universities in the thirteenth century. The stages of the argument proceeded as follows: question, answer, thesis, agreement, refutation, argument, suggested proof and final resolution. Aquinas made this the basic framework of his work (in fact all his writings are in this form) and as a teacher favoured particularly that form of disputation where the theme was left to the audience to decide: this was the *disputatio de quolibet,* a form which reflected his fundamental conviction that in intellectual argument the common interest demanded the victory not of one side or the other but of truth. One should be grateful even to those proved to be in error, since error has its part to play in making truth plain. The greatest benefit a man could bestow on his neighbour was to lead him towards truth. "We must love equally those whose opinions we share and those whose opinions we reject. For both have made the effort to discover truth, and both, in so doing, have assisted us."

Aquinas had great skill in mastering the arguments of his opponents. Indeed, where necessary, he made a point of recasting them into clearer form. Paul Valéry had a famous maxim: "The first task of anyone who would refute an opinion is to master it a little more surely than its ablest defender."

In his writing and lecturing Aquinas aimed at building an edifice which could contain both rational thought and faith: and for both he contrived more spacious premises than either his left or his right wing opponents realized. He held that the created world, which embraced nature, man, society and all objects, was available to rational investigation and should be so investigated. But there remained, as the primary duty of theology, the obligation to surround God with silence; here Aquinas was in agreement with the oldest traditions of Christian theology. "For we cannot understand of God what He is, but only what He is not, therefore we cannot see how God is, but only much more how He is not."

There came a day, to be precise the Feast of St Nicholas (December 6) in 1273, when Aquinas returned from Mass and pushed aside his work on the *Summa Theologica,* saying "I cannot do it". When Reginald of Piperno, his friend and secretary, made some motion of troubled protest, Aquinas again said "I cannot do it. Everything I have written seems so much chaff", and then, after a pause, "compared with what I have seen and what has been revealed to me". This silence lasted for the rest of the winter. Then, on the instructions of the Pope, Aquinas set out for Lyons to attend the Council, travelling on foot. He was a Mendicant, and it was his habit always to travel in this way. Reginald tried to encourage him: "If only you can reach the Council, much good will come from it, for the whole Church, for our Order, and for the kingdom of Sicily." Aquinas answered, "Indeed, may God grant that something good may be accomplished there." On the way to Lyons he died. The last words to come from his pen are a letter in answer to a monk of Fosse Nuovo who had asked for an exposition of the Song of Songs.

This was an end in more ways than one. Did Thomas realize what assumptions were necessary if his synthesis of intellect and feeling, knowledge and revelation, rational philosophy and Christian theology was to remain viable and permit of further extension? This marvellous edifice of thought assumed, amongst other things, a pre-arranged harmony between Church and State, and the existence of "reasonable" and civilized men, disposed to friendly argument. Moreover, these same reasonable and disciplined men must also be filled with a sincere and deep-seated faith, a faith which accepted the dogmas and truths of revelation as easily as their understanding accepted the laws of logic and of knowledge. There were two sentences that Aquinas found completely convincing. "Our resurrection will be in the same kind as that of Christ," and "Man is a thing of nature" (*homo res naturalis est*). But they brought little comfort to his contemporaries, and still less to later generations; the *societas humana* as they knew it was one in which the great powers fought one another instead of coming to terms. Aquinas never so much as mentions the conflict between Empire and Papacy. Nor does he comment on the burning of the Amauricians or the persecution of his junior colleagues in the faculty of arts. These were matters the succeeding generation could no longer ignore: there was a chill wind blowing in Paris then, with Aquinas and Bonaventura dead and Siger and his friends expelled and in prison.

Pope Boniface III (his invectives on the subject of the masters of Paris have already been mentioned), having once again tried to assert the supremacy of the Papacy over the princes and peoples of Europe, was humiliated by Nogaret, minister to the king of France, and died of the ignominy. Between 1309 and 1377 the Popes resided at Avignon, more or less committed to serving the interests of the French monarchy. The weaknesses of the Papacy were plain for the world to see. Moreover, men who stood for the religious life at its purest often found themselves not only at odds with the Papacy but even the objects of papal attack. Pope John XXII was as ready to condemn the Spiritual Franciscans, who preserved the ideal of poverty laid down by St Francis, as he was to anathematize Marsilius of Padua, William of Ockham and Meister Eckhart. Division was the order of the day. In the light of this experience shared by the intellectual and religious élite, Aquinas's idea of synthesis seemed scarcely tenable. The universities now became dominated by a more rigid and mechanical type of Thomism, which claimed to represent orthodox theology; and with this development the forces opposed to Aquinas gathered strength. This latter-day Thomism used the concepts of the master's philosophy as though they were tools of thought valid for all time. A two-tiered theological structure was erected. In the top drawer reposed the ideas, facts and data concerning the "supernatural" world, always available in their invulnerable perfection; this category included all the doctrines and dogmas of the Church. There was no point in arguing about these matters further; all that was required was to defend them. In the lower drawer were the objects and data of the "natural" world, which were fit subjects for argument. And argued they were, in endless disputations conducted in accordance with the rules of formal logic, which took to pieces everything coming within the scope of scholastic dialectic (and which in fact frequently encroached on the "supernatural" world). The dialectic itself was purely verbal, and remained so, refraining from any dealings with objects, reality, history or the actual political situation facing the Church.

This scholasticism which "knew" everything but could make no positive or reliable contribution in any concrete situation was challenged by some of the outstanding intellects in the generation that followed Aquinas. This protest expressed itself on the one hand in a search for the "concrete" and on the other in a realization of the depth of the abyss running through the Church, society and man himself. The general conclusion was that formal logic-chopping must be swept away and "reality" admitted in its place. There were for example the political thinkers, Henry of Ghent, Godfrey of Fontaines, Marsilius of Padua, John of Jandun and others, who sought for a definition of Church and State in concrete terms. Their radical ideas will be discussed further in the chapter "The New State and the New Church". Then there were thinkers who concerned themselves with human history and with the natural order, much-discussed topics, particularly among Joachimites and Franciscans, both before and after the time of Aquinas. The natural sciences and natural philosophy, as they were developed between Roger Bacon and the fourteenth century scientists of Paris and Padua, also owed much to this phase of the anti-Thomist movement.

The third line of attack began where St Thomas, deeply troubled, had halted. It was realized that no one philosophical definition could ever contain the One and Triune God, but to search for one was considered the primary and self-imposed obligation of the intellect. Thomist boldness found eventual fulfilment in the mysticism of Meister Eckhart, who was persuaded that man, whose soul retained some sparks of the divine intelligence itself, experienced actual divinity through the union of his intellect with that of God.

The fourth line of attack on Thomism provides the most vigorous expression in philosophical and theological terms of the prevailing sense that an irremediable flaw existed at the heart of things. This attack, which had its origins in Franciscan resistance both to Thomism and to the Papal image of world order, took two forms: Scotism, and Nominalism or Ockhamism, so-called after its "founder", the Englishman William of Ockham. Both he and Duns Scotus were Franciscans.

According to Scotus (*circa* 1270–1308) God is infinitely remote from His creation. He repudiated the Thomist synthesis, finding it insufficiently penetrating. For one thing, God was not worshipped enough in it; the contrast between God on the one hand and man in his individuality and freedom on the other was insufficiently marked. Scotus held that God and man, faith and knowledge, theology and philosophy are first of all separated from each other by a great gulf. God is freedom, his is the freest of all wills, bound only by the laws of logic and the first two commandments of the Decalogue. But God is not tied to creation, redemption or the moral order. He could have left the world uncreated and man unredeemed. On the other side of the gulf, confronting this "God who is quite other", stands man, inhabiting in "utter loneliness" a harsh world of nature, governed by immutable laws. Man fulfils himself in his actions, in his response to the perpetual demands made on him by freedom of choice, and by love; God, the world and all natural objects confront him from the outside as things external. In a sense one might describe Scotus as the first Christian existentialist.

Scotus discusses the nature of existence in terms of existence "here in the thisness" (or *haecceitas,* a concept invented by Scotus). Human life is a matter of serious and formidable effort. Man is continually forced to make decisions, challenged to conduct himself correctly in four different spheres. God demands of him love, unconditional surrender and sacrifice; the philosophical principles underlying the metaphysical world extend his intellect to the limit, if he is to avoid perverting the purity and grandeur of its system by loose or feeble thinking; the moral order is no less demanding and from first to last, since he inhabits the earth, man must recognize the laws of nature.

Scotus was both an intellectual and a mystic. He demanded absolute purity both of the intellect and of the heart. His "golden treatise" *De primo principio* is at once a geometrically precise exercise in logic and a glowing outpouring of mystical love. God in unity, as the unique first principle, declares Himself in the Trinity; and the Trinity demands from man the supreme exertion of his intellect and the fulness of his love: "Thou living and noblest thing, thinking and willing, blessed be Thou . . . clear vision of Thyself, most excellent love."

It is barely possible even to suggest in this brief sketch how great were the demands laid on man in Scotus's philosophy: man must temper his mind and spirit through constant self-purification, as a sacrifice to God; he must educate himself to a humble acceptance of the unyielding and autonomous laws of nature and of ethics, and at the same time surrender himself in pure love to God and his fellow-men, even though separated from them by an abyss. Scotus found his own way of bridging this gulf in his devotion to the Virgin. Aquinas's attitude to the cult of the Virgin, which had been rapidly gaining ground since the twelfth century, was one of great reserve; he had no need personally for this emotional bond as a means of reconciling God, the world and mankind. He would have dismissed as absurd the idea of the Virgin current in certain Catholic circles today, which honours her as co-redeemer. It was otherwise with Duns Scotus, with whom "mariolatry" in its modern sense may be said to originate: Mary as the "great mother" unites what man in his extremity of anguish sees only as an unbridgeable chasm.

William of Ockham (born before 1300, ✠1349–50) shows how rapidly Scotus was overtaken by the still more radical thinking of a younger generation. Ockham's nominalism was the most fertile of the later medieval philosophies and the parent of "modern" thought.

From Plato to Aquinas people had taken the act of thinking as evidence of being. Words, the substance of thought, were types of the "universals" for which they stood; human thought reflected the order and ultimate reality to be found in the cosmos. "Right" thinking meant thinking in harmony with the "right" ordering of the world. Ockham, however, introduced in opposition to this view a new language, new terms, a new way of thinking: speech is a convention democratically arrived at by free and separate individuals, who have to come to an agreement among themselves about the meaning of each word. Thinking is no longer a matter of saying over the God-given words and of discovering the God-given sense of each separate thing from its roots in the universal. The term "universal" is simply a conventional sign for a majority. The language of man was no longer a type of the language of God and of creation, but a human convention.

This "democratic" philosophy is reflected in Ockham's political ideas. Ockham was a Franciscan, and a defender of the Spiritual position. After spending some time in papal custody at Avignon, he fled together with Bonagratia of Bergamo, a fellow Spiritual, and Michael of Cesena, the General of the Order, to the court of Louis of Bavaria, having first subscribed to Cesena's protest against the decretal of John XXII condemning the Franciscan doctrine of absolute poverty.

Philosophers and theologians were beginning to lead their lives outside the universities and university polemics; Ockham and others like him, Wyclif, Hus and Luther, were personally involved in the great political issues of their day, in fact were making history. The entire corpus of Ockham's philosophy is shot through with political ideas. His censure of the "gluttony, avarice and ambition of professors of theology", of the "illiterate and covetous Inquisitors" who understood neither orthodoxy nor heresy, and of the papacy "lusting after power", is one aspect of his theology and philosophy and all of a piece with it.

"Every thing is individual, unique." The whole is made up of such individual entities, existing side by side. God is free, and man is free, and they confront each other in their utmost singularity. The individual, at bottom completely isolated and free, arrives at his own natural morality. Morality is what is reasonable. The majority of existing political and religious institutions and social arrangements have nothing whatsoever to do with God and the cosmos but are simply enacted "positive law", conventions which could be altered at any time. Ockham, who in many ways is the father of democratic political thought and latter-day views on the "rights of man", did not so much want to vindicate the radical freedom of the individual as to uphold the liberties of leagues, associations, peoples and states. Citizens should come to an understanding among themselves by rational agreement and they have both the right and the duty of electing their superiors, whether in Church or State.

If one asks what place God has in this scheme, the answer is that God has nothing at all to do with human arrangements. God is the utter other, infinitely remote, incomprehensible and unimaginable, right outside the affairs of men (and certainly far removed from the politics of the Church), withdrawn from human contact (and also well beyond the grasp of theologians). Ockham regarded a large part of the older theology as fiction, an unwarrantable playing upon words; God eluded the theologians, and men deceived themselves if they thought otherwise.

With the fragmentation of the "Nominalist" and "Ockhamist" schools in the succeeding period Ockham's own originality and daring were almost completely lost. This is characteristic of the way the "open Europe" continually had to surrender to the closed Europe of the later medieval and early-modern periods. Moreover, once the Dominicans, after a few decades of open-mindedness, had officially adopted Thomism and the Franciscans had adopted Scotism, the two philosophies became the labels of academic factions, bitterly and mutually antagonistic. Both groups declared themselves "realists", that is followers of the *via antiqua*, as opposed to the men of the *via moderna*, the Nominalists and the Ockhamists. There was often as little of the grandeur, creative originality and independent spirit of Aquinas, Duns Scotus and Ockham among the partisans who ranged themselves under the various philosophical banners as there was of the greatness of an Innocent III or the imperial self-assuredness of a Henry VI or Frederick II among the Guelphs and Ghibellines at loggerheads in the Italian city-states.

As often as not bitter adversaries were divided only by their labels; the more they came to resemble each other in the strength of their bigotry, the more acrimonious grew their disputes. Although Aquinas, the revolutionary of 1270, was canonized in 1323 Thomism suffered something of an eclipse during the fourteenth century; in the succeeding century its chief stronghold was at Cologne. But after the heyday of the city-states and the Conciliar Movement was past, Thomism made a triumphal comeback with the victory of absolutism and the Counter-Reformation. Scotism, often combined with nominalist elements, revealed its revolutionary potentialities in the Oxford of Wyclif and the Prague of

Hus. Even in the sixteenth and seventeenth centuries there were considerable Scotist groups at Rome, Padua, Salamanca, Alcalá and Coimbra. Ockham, excommunicated in 1328, conquered Paris with his nominalism about 1340, and from there it spread to the German universities. A neo-Ockhamist, Gabriel Biel, taught Luther his philosophy (by way of Staupitz and Nathin). On the eve of the Reformation the universities of Erfurt and Wittenberg were strongly Nominalist in complexion.

CHAPTER 11

HISTORY

SUSTAINED historical writing, philosophical, apocalyptical, and straight narrative, was the offspring of the open Europe of the twelfth and early thirteenth centuries. The writing of chronicles, historical narrative, called for an open mind, ready to reflect on a wealth of experience. The urge to write history in philosophical and apocalyptical terms sprang from an oppressive sense of anguish and foreboding, which led to the posing of anxious questions about the deeper meaning of contemporary events, for example the collapse of the great powers. In short, it was inspired by a troubled desire to read the signs of the times.

The most important chroniclers of this period were Anglo-Saxons, Normans, and Frenchmen. Their especial concern was to explain to themselves and their contemporaries the prodigious rise in influence and importance of their own peoples and the various internal conflicts which had troubled their history. Philosophical history was largely a German preserve; the favourite subjects for discussion were the decline of the Holy Roman Empire, the frailties of the Church and the horrifying consequences of disunity. Material for meditation on this last point was provided by the Eastern Church and the Eastern Empire and the existence of heresy. Behind all this was the larger problem of reconciling the idea of history as a redemptive process with the symptoms of progressive evil and decay everywhere apparent. Histories in apocalyptical form were written both by Germans and by Italians, moved by the agony of the Spiritual Franciscans and the sufferings of the "poor people of Italy" under alien and oppressive rule. Great hopes were born of this agony, the expectation that an "angel Pope" or "holy Emperor" would arise.

278

In the constricting conditions of the later Middle Ages the uninhibited vigour of historical writing degenerated into religious-political *schwärmerei* and soothsaying, strongly censured by the Church. History had no place among the learned disciplines recognized by the universities, and visionary champions of a new universal history were brushed aside with ridicule. Even the Jesuits, when they drew up their curriculum, still classed history with rhetoric. Straightforward narration also suffered a decline during the later Middle Ages, whose chroniclers were often ill-educated and usually lacked the necessary temper of eagerness and impartiality.

It was, in fact, in just this frame of mind that the Anglo-Norman historians of the twelfth century approached their work. Ordericus Vitalis (✝ *circa* 1154), whose *Historia Ecclesiastica* is a universal history in the old style, covering events in Western Christendom from the birth of Christ down to his own day, saw history as the divine plan for the education of mankind. But his sympathy and interest were primarily engaged by the rise of the Normans and their fortunes in England after 1066. Himself a monk, he kept a sharp look-out for signs of decay in the morals and learning of the pre-conquest Anglo-Saxon church; he was just as quick to recognize the harsh lot of the common people under their new masters. He illustrates the energy, audacity and political aptitude of the Normans, comparing them with the Roman senate, and at the same time draws attention to their pride, their cruelty and overbearing lust for power. Through all his writing there breathes a lively sense of actuality; he was clearly a man personally involved in his subject, a man engaged.

The work of Eadmer (✝ *circa* 1124), a contemporary of Orderic's, reveals a high level of technical competence in the writing of historical narrative. The pupil and biographer of Anselm of Canterbury, Eadmer recognized that the service of truth was chief among the duties of a historian. Dispassionate and lucid, he set himself to work only within his own range; his most important work, the *Historia Novorum*, deals largely with events of his own lifetime. His affections lay with his own people, the Anglo-Saxons, and he saw the Normans as their enemies. William of Malmesbury (✝ *circa* 1142) belonged by birth to both races, the English and the Norman; he can already look back with contempt and some self-congratulation on the "ignorant" historians of the past. Although his sympathies belonged wholly to the Western world, and the Anglo-Normans in particular, he was at some pains to give a coherent account of the tragic history of the Empire in the eleventh century. He was deeply impressed by the political and military importance of the German imperial church (he tells us that the Abbot of Fulda provided the Emperor with sixty thousand men!), and was capable of objective remarks about the Saracens, acknowledging their natural humanity.

Malmesbury's younger fellow-countryman William of Newburgh (✠ circa 1201) has been described as the father of modern historical criticism, because of his sturdy scepticism over Geoffrey of Monmouth's "discoveries" concerning King Arthur. William of Newburgh and other English historians, notably Roger Hoveden, Gervase of Canterbury, and Matthew Paris (a monk of St Albans), are all distinctly "modern" in their use of documents as historical sources. Roger had close links with the English court, where he served the king as judge, counsellor and chancery clerk. This sober and empirical English way of looking at history, with its emphasis on contemporary happenings, was paralleled by the preference shown for mathematical problems and the natural sciences at the embryonic university of Oxford.

Characteristic of this attitude is the important part played in English historical writing by biography, in which the writer traces the course of events as influenced by some prominent personage personally known to him. Roger Hoveden's account of Henry II and Richard I was written from this standpoint. Suger's *Life of Louis VI* is not quite of the same character, since Suger stylized his subject, turning Louis into a type of exemplary Christian king, who protected his people from the depredations of the nobility and was the incarnation of peace and justice.

Crusading chronicles occupy a special position among Western histories. Guibert of Nogent, the historian of the First Crusade, Fulcher of Chartres, William of Tyre, William of Malmesbury and others who wrote of the Crusades were by no means uncritical of the Crusaders. The Crusades and increased familiarity with the East whetted the appetite of a wider audience for new material, a demand increasingly met by vernacular histories. Up to the end of the fourteenth century Englishmen still wrote in French, the language of the court and the nobility. The first production of note is Wace's *Roman de Rou* (Rou=Rollo), written *circa* 1170, a glorification of the early Dukes of Normandy and the Norman Conquest. The most important of the vernacular histories is Villehardouin's account of the capture of Constantinople; there are also a couple of agreeable and lively biographies written by laymen, an anonymous history of William the Marshal and Joinville's life of St Louis.

Alfonso X of Castile, the Wise (1252–84), set himself to educate his people, and commissioned for the instruction of his warriors, herdsmen and peasants a vernacular history which included a history of Spain (*Grande e General Estoria*) together with a legal textbook and encyclopedia (*Las Partidas*). He made Castilian the official language of the country, the first Romance tongue to be so dignified. Alfonso's deliberate and scholarly encouragement of education, science and history brings him into line with the cultural tradition of the Islamic and other orientalized states, a tradition formerly represented in Spain by the *Reyes de Taifos* and recently revived in Sicily by Frederick II. It is not out of place here to mention that this liberal and oriental culture had its grand finale under Mongol patronage, with the unique appearance of a new species of universal history, the *Collection of Histories* of the physician and scholar Rashíd al-Dín (1247–1318); he may have been a converted Jew. Rashíd rose to be chief minister of Ghāzān Mahmūd, the Mongol ruler of Persia, who commissioned him to write a universal history. The work was continued under Ghāzān's successor. The panel of scholars Rashíd assembled to help him included two Chinese, a Buddhist hermit from Kashmir, a Mongol (as an expert on Mongol genealogy), a "Frankish" monk and a few Persians. The scope of this history, extending from China to England, is remarkable; another five centuries had to elapse before Europe could produce anything of comparable range.

Germany, like the West, had its chroniclers and annalists, but what was more significant was the German predilection for a philosophy of history. The prevailing outlook in Germany was markedly conservative, even as late as the twelfth century; the old institutions—the Holy Roman Empire and the imperial church—were staunchly defended, and the archaic notion of the underlying harmony between God, the world, man and all wholesome things was preserved. But in the very act of explaining and justifying the *ancien régime* new and even revolutionary ideas were generated, as is so often the case. As they reflected upon history,

German monks, theologians and prelates elaborated ideas and drew conclusions which led far beyond what they themselves understood or intended.

The ultra-conservative Rupert of Deutz, a monk of Cologne, who was writing early in the twelfth century, saw universal history as the unfolding of the Trinity. Hugh of St Victor, a German by birth though he worked in Paris, was already wrestling with the idea of progress. He asked whether there could really be a beneficent impulse secretly working through the constant fluctuations in human affairs, the rise and fall of great empires. He ended by convincing himself of the slow but sure advance of Christ's kingdom. Was it then right to see universal history in terms of progress? This hypothesis was emphatically denied by Catharist thinkers, whose ideas were gaining ground in the Rhineland. They saw history in general as a process of continuous decay, with the history of Western Europe as a conspicuous example. Ekbert of Schönau found this early version of the myth of the "corrupt West" so alarming that he composed a comprehensive defence of the West, the Empire and the Church, and submitted it to his former fellow-student, Rainald of Dassel, Chancellor to Frederick I.

Nevertheless, the pessimism of the heterodox "left" found powerful support in Germany even among unimpeachably orthodox thinkers. It had, after all, been sanctioned by Augustine, transmitted by Orosius to the Middle Ages (his history written in the fifth century provided the basic classical material for medieval world histories) and was long to retain its hold over German philosophers and minds sensitive to spiritual values, right down to Luther: one might indeed say down to Spengler. "The history of the world is the judgment of the world" (Kleist): the peoples are perpetually being judged, and the judgment is a judgment of terror. This pessimism has at all times played an important part in confirming the Germans in their well-known reluctance to engage in political activity and to resist, as individuals or as a group, the policies of great men and great powers.

Among those who wrestled with the problem were two writers of the mid-twelfth century, Gerhoh von Reichersperg and Otto of Freising. Both were horrified by the effects on the world of the unholy and mutually destructive conflict between Empire and Papacy which had started with the dispute between Henry IV and Gregory VII in the late eleventh century. There was no denying the magnitude of the distress and disorder brought to the people and the Church in Germany by this struggle. The only debatable question concerned the future. Gerhoh, the querulous provost of Reichersberg in Bavaria, saw universal history as an uninterrupted decline and fall. The work in which he develops these ideas is called *De quartuor vigilia noctis* (On the fourth watch of the night). Through the long night of barbarism, with faith all but extinguished and moral corruption rampant, there were very few to bear witness to the light, watchmen chosen by God; the fourth watch had begun with Gregory VII and would continue until the Last Judgment. It was during this last watch that the Church was most threatened by internal strife: avarice and the lust for power would tempt even the Popes to err. The watch was being kept only by a few "Poor Men of Christ", a handful of lowly monks and laymen.

Gerhoh's views were shared by Hildegard of Bingen, another prophet of decline, whose fame even in the twelfth century spread far outside Germany, to reach England and Iceland. The graphic talents of this seeress tinctured her apocalyptic utterances with a lurid golden light. She saw history as the progress of man, under the guidance of God, towards the Judgment Seat. After five epochs of world history had been run through, and the gold of man's character refined in the fires of time, then would come the final reckoning and fulfilment. Each epoch had its animal emblem: the fiery hound for naked power, the golden lion for the misery of war, the cream-coloured horse for frivolity and luxury, the black pig for lechery and schism, and finally the grey wolf for Anti-Christ (shades of the Fenris-wolf of Voluspa, the Nordic apocalypse!). When all these ages were done the cosmos would expire in a blaze of light. Before this could happen Empire and Church, Emperor and Pope, must fall, the kings of the West become independent and heresy spread throughout every land. Protestant historians of the sixteenth century found in Hildegard of Bingen a cardinal witness for their case.

Otto of Freising, the greatest of the German medieval historians, was the son of Leopold the Pious, Duke of Austria. After studying in Paris under Abelard he became a Cistercian (which did not prevent him from adopting a somewhat sceptical and critical attitude towards Bernard of Clairvaux) and was later appointed Bishop of Freising. Both as a reforming bishop and as the grandson of Henry IV and uncle of Frederick Barbarossa he was deeply shocked and distressed at the tragedy of the Holy Roman Empire. The subject of his universal history of *The Two Cities* (*Historia de duabus civitatibus*) is the conflict between the children of light and the children of darkness, as it can be traced through history; underlying the whole is the idea that all that mattered in the history of the world was already a thing of the past. But Otto does not abandon himself completely to pessimism: the Kingdom of God continues to grow slowly, gradually and in secret, amid all temporal disasters. New men, for example, the religious of new Orders, had already come forward to bear aloft the light of the good future that lay ahead, the "new age" of the last days.

Otto lived on into the early years of Barbarossa's reign, and derived much comfort from them. A happier note enters his writings: throughout his *Deeds of Frederick Barbarossa* (*Gesta Frederici*) runs the conviction that the coming of this strong and just ruler had arrested the process of decline.

There are traces in Otto of the three-phased law of universal history later developed by the historical philosopher Anselm of Havelberg in his *Dialogus*. Anselm's varied life, in which he was continually journeying about on horseback, by ship or on foot, made him well-acquainted with the sharp contrasts to be found in the twelfth century world. He was a member of the Premonstratensian Order; he was employed on diplomatic missions by the Emperor; he was Bishop of Havelberg in the still semi-pagan East; and he ended as Archbishop of Ravenna. He thus had personal experience of Rome, Byzantium and the Slavonic East, of the new monastic orders and of the old centres of Greek and Roman culture. All this is reflected in his view of universal history, which he saw as a long process of divine education. God was slowly leading man on towards complete truth, which was Christ; man's first instruction came through the images and customs of heathen prehistory, then from the Church. Anselm's optimism was based, as that of the Greek Fathers had been, on divine inspiration, the operation of the Holy Ghost. For him historical change had a positive value, since it was a means used by the Holy Ghost to further the education of man. Modern man could have a better grasp of Christianity than was possible even in apostolic times. The Holy Ghost was the agent and driving force of all progress, and gave Himself to everyone, particularly those of the "new religions", by which Anselm meant the new religious Orders.

One founder of a new Order in the later twelfth century was Abbot Joachim of Flora, who had formerly presided over a house of Cistercians in Calabria. He was treated by the Cistercians as a renegade and by the theologians of Paris and members of other Orders as a heretic. The verdict on Joachim of a prominent late Scholastic, Henry of Langenstein, is typical and was for centuries the stock attitude adopted by Scholastic and other university philosophers (not excluding Aquinas), who were either indifferent to history as a subject or actively hostile towards it. "The school of Paris (which is the summit of learning in all the civilized world) knows well enough what kind of person he was. There he enjoys no good reputation or authority, but is reckoned a fraud, a dabbler in the future." There can, in fact, have been few individuals as influential as this "dabbler" in stimulating Europeans to an interest in philosophy. Dante placed him in Paradise, in the circle of the sun, a luminary of Christian wisdom, "imbued with the prophetic spirit". Columbus harked back to his ideas, his writings were printed in the Republic of Venice during the Renaissance and Reformation periods. Through Lessing Joachim's theories were reintroduced into German historical thinking during the eighteenth and nineteenth centuries.

Joachim died in 1202, in the remoteness of his mountain monastery. The immense success of the Joachimite movement of the thirteenth and fourteenth centuries, which appealed to his authority but in many ways misinterpreted him, has obscured the details about his own life and work. The sources differ in their accounts of his origins: one says he was the son of a notary, another that he came of unfree peasant stock, a third that he was of Jewish descent. All that is known for certain is that he grew up in Greek Southern Italy, where the Norman kings and their Hohenstaufen successors fought the Papacy for mastery, and that from an early age he had a burning interest in political and ecclesiastical affairs. He had connections both with the court at Palermo and with the papal curia, and enjoyed a high reputation at both. He may well have had some contact with the various German philosopher-historians already mentioned. The imperial monastery of Monte Cassino, so bitterly fought over during the second world war, was at that time a strongpoint of German ecclesiastical and cultural influence. Rupert of Deutz spent several years there and Anselm of Havelberg was thoroughly familiar with the Italian scene.

Joachim's authentic writings constantly allude to the sufferings of the Italian people under the oppression of alien rule. This was highly important in forming his view of history. For him the dawning of a new era, the era of the Holy Ghost, was necessarily preceded by the break-up of the old Church under the weight of a barbarian reign of terror. The old clergy and the old Church had shown themselves incapable of moulding and guiding the "new man" to become perfect in love and spirit. The old hieratic priesthood and the rule of the Church were being brought to an end in a struggle which was actually in progress—Joachim was thinking of the record of the German rulers and princes from the time of Henry IV.

There is an air of caution and reserve about Joachim's statements concerning the transition from the Second to the Third Age of the world. His First Age is that of the old covenant, the Old Testament, ruled by a strict and materialistic legality. The Second is the "Middle Ages"; Tertullian had already coined the expression *tempus medium* in the second century, and twelfth century German philosopher-historians speak of a *status mediocris*. For them, as for Tertullian, this meant a time when old and new, barbarian and Christian, mingled together but were yet in conflict: a time of mixing. Joachim's "Middle Age" is the age of the West, of the Roman Church, governed by power and violence and terrestrial law. But even while it reigned supreme, the way was being prepared for the Third Age, that of the Holy Spirit. Some of the signs of its coming were to be found within the Second Age itself, for example the appearance of martyrs and of new religious orders; but it was also being brought into being from outside, by the direct intervention of the Holy Spirit.

There are still many orthodox Christians cherishing the belief that there can be nothing new or good under the sun. Christ belongs only to the Last Days. Everything important has already happened; all man can do is to wait in humility for the Last Judgment, for the punishment of all the many evil-doers who persecute God's kingdom, and for the reward of the virtuous. We have seen that though the general tenor of historical thinking in twelfth-century Germany was conservative and deeply pessimistic, the great wall of fear erected by a predominantly dualistic conception (in the last analysis Manichaean) was pierced in places by anticipations of joys to come. Joachim went much further. Man's future is not past (apart from the heroic age of the Early Church and the elucidation of Christian doctrine in the first five centuries); it lies before him, and may bring him times of joy as well as times of suffering. Joachim's particular achievement, and it was an achievement of quite unusual merit, was to unlock the possibility of an "open" future, the counterpart and fulfilment of the openness of the twelfth century as a whole.

However, he was quite clear that the dissolution of the hieratic church and its replacement by the new society of "new men", living under a new order of freedom and love and guided by the spirit, would demand heavy sacrifices. "The man of the flesh persecutes those who are born of the spirit." Peter now bears rule, but John is already at his side: the spiritual church of the future, the new society of new men, is already growing up through the Papal Church of the present. Joachim by no means rejected in their entirety the forms, traditions and laws of the old Church; they had their part to play both in temporal history and in the history of man's redemption. Once they had fulfilled their function they would be done away with, "when that which is perfect is come". That day was already at hand. Joachim regarded the foundation of his own new contemplative order as a cell from which the new mankind of the future would develop. The Rule he drew up is applicable to all men. His Epistle, "to all believers in Christ", is really a manifesto, reminiscent of papal encyclicals and imperial charters which were addressed in similar terms. Successive generations of revolutionaries have made the same appeal, though with most of them the echo of Joachim has been quite unconscious: the Puritans and the revolutionaries of the late eighteenth and early twentieth centuries addressed themselves "to all mankind".

It is not clear from the original writings of Joachim still extant whether he ever went into details about the nature of the "Everlasting Gospel", the Good News of the Holy Spirit which was to abolish the old Church and the old kingdoms of this world. But even if he did not, the seed fell on richly fertile soil. It took root, for example, among troubled Franciscans who saw their founder's intentions concerning absolute poverty flouted by the Papacy and the majority of their Order.

In their spiritual isolation and distress of soul these "Spiritual" Franciscans had already evolved their own view of history, even before coming under Joachimite influence. By claiming that Francis was Christ reborn, the saviour and redeemer who would initiate the long-awaited New Age, they satisfied their consciences and justified their resistance. They also committed themselves to a battle on three fronts, against the Dominicans, against the Emperor Frederick II and against the Pope. The superiority ascribed to the Franciscans over the Dominicans in the Spirituals' scheme of history is not merely to be regarded as an instance of rivalry between two religious Orders, which was common enough in the Middle Ages, but also as the confident affirmation of a fundamental conviction. God had appointed one Order alone to lead men into the New Age of the Last Days, and that was the brotherhood of St Francis. The rejection of St Francis's testament and the modification of the Franciscan rule was the first and decisive occasion of an open breach between the Spirituals and Rome. In the late thirteenth, and above all in the fourteenth century, Spirituals are found forming significant alliances as part of their struggle against Rome, which they aimed at possessing. They became the instruments of princes and Emperors (for example, they were used as political propagandists by Louis of Bavaria), they associated with various popular groups and took up with the new learning. There were Franciscans in the entourage of Joan of Arc. Between the thirteenth and the sixteenth centuries Franciscans continued to be burnt as heretics.

A direct link was forged between the Spirituals and the Joachimites (or rather the neo-Joachimites, who were developing Joachim's historical and cosmological ideas along their own lines) when in 1241 the abbot of the Joachimite Order fled to the Franciscan convent at Pisa, fearing the destruction of his own house by Frederick II. He brought with him many Joachimite writings. Both the Spirituals and the Joachimites saw the Emperor as Anti-Christ, or at the least as a type of Anti-Christ. The Franciscan Gerard of Borgo San Donnino went from Pisa to Paris, where he published in 1254 his "Introduction to the Everlasting Gospel", an edition of the three principal works of Joachim with his own introduction and glosses on what he considered salient points. From this modest title the work sounds straightforward enough, but it seems (no copy has survived) that Gerard was not expounding the "Everlasting Gospel" text by text, since this was impossible: "the letter killeth", and the Gospel was in any case implicit in Joachim's writings taken as a whole.

The spiritually adept could discern it there for themselves. What he did say was that the Everlasting Gospel transformed the gospel of Christ, eliminating the need for signs and symbols and riddles, all of them things of the past. "Now will all images cease and the truth of the two Testaments stand revealed." The dispensation of the old Church was drawing to its close. The new era would start in 1260, and those already inspired by the spirit to become members of the new Church of the Holy Ghost could rejoice.

Gerard expressed publicly and in writing thoughts that had long been incubating in the minds of Joachimites and Spirituals in Italy, southern France and Spain. But he happened to do it in Paris, at a time when the struggle over the friar doctors was boiling up to its first crisis. The secular professors immediately snatched at this golden opportunity for making a *cause celèbre*. Here, in black and white, was proof that the Mendicant Orders were infected with heresy, that they were a spawning ground of fanatics and the corrupters of students and of the people at large.

In 1255 Gerard was condemned by the Church. There is no space here to describe the subsequent persecution of the Spirituals by the Church, which continued for another century and a half. It is important to notice, however, how radically their view of history altered once they were driven underground. Their ideas became more markedly political and increasingly secular. The image they built up of themselves as the perpetually victimized "poor men of Christ", in constant conflict with the powers of Rome and of the world, had a long future before it.

In 1298 there died at Narbonne (formerly a centre of Catharism and of Provençal culture) Petrus Johannis Olivi, a Franciscan who had on several occasions been condemned by the Church. His *Letter* to the sons of Charles II of Naples and his *Commentary on the Apocalypse* are an exposition of the Spirituals' view of history. The history of the world must run through three sacred cycles: the kingdom of the Father, the kingdom of the Son, and the kingdom of the Holy Spirit. What is new comes into being only in travail, attended by suffering and persecution. The "third kingdom", the kingdom of the Holy Spirit and of freedom, will be ushered in by the Spirituals, and in persecuting them the Roman Church stands revealed as Anti-Christ. The Church of the Popes, greedy for power and possessions, was the new Babel, still just capable of suppressing "the poor little Francis", but soon to be forced to yield to him. For Francis was "the new man", the new leader of humanity made new.

This idyllic picture was soon tarnished as the persecution of the Spirituals increased in strength. In writing his history of the tribulations of his Order Angelo Clareno was also describing the sufferings of mankind. Throughout southern Italy, particularly in the district round Naples, the Spirituals were growing more and more secularist in their attitude, not least in the sect of Fra Dolcino. This was the first group to consider the expediency of permitting a secular ruler to preside over the inauguration of the "New Age". At first the most likely candidate was the Angevin ruler of Naples; later he was succeeded by the Aragon rulers who ousted the Angevins from power. But the Spiritual Franciscans were not the only religious eccentrics patronized by the court of Naples. This was a period of a growing cult of Messianism. Cola di Rienzo, known to many people nowadays only as a figure of Wagnerian opera, made a bid to become master of Rome under the style "Tribune of the People". At his "Synod" of Italian national freedom held in 1347 he proclaimed the special mission of the Italians as the people of salvation. He saw himself as a second Francis, called to continue and complete his work by giving it a political basis. In succeeding centuries much revolutionary historical thinking and much revolutionary action had a Franciscan colouring.

It became increasingly clear that the New Age had not in fact dawned, either in 1260 or in 1300, another date suggested. The old rulers and the old powers were everywhere triumphant. And the outlook would become darker yet, as Dante, the disciple of the Spirituals, was soon to make clear. Some hoped to find an escape overseas. In 1299 Angelo Clareno set out on a mission to Armenia. Others fled to Africa or the Far East, travelling even to Mongolia to claim the protective toleration extended to all religions by the greatest Empire of all time.

Other Spirituals sought to escape into an interior world of thought, to conquer for themselves a new kingdom in the natural sciences. At the Franciscan convent of Hyères near Toulon, the intellectual centre of Provençal Joachimism, Hugh of Digne presided over a group of physicians, notaries and other educated men whose main purpose was to study the Bible and to read together the works of Joachim. These pious laymen in their turn aroused the interest of the Spirituals in the natural sciences. Petrus Johannis Olivi, already briefly mentioned, was also interested in the investigation of nature; his theory of impetus and his concept of the inertia of mass were the first steps towards the modern theory of motion.

The study of natural science was one means of "remaking" the world in the Spiritual Franciscan sense. In Roger Bacon and his pupil Arnold of Villanova the prophetic enthusiasm of the Spirituals was diverted to the acquisition of the knowledge which could alone enable its possessors to remake the world. The only true learning was that of the man learned in nature; it was he who truly understood the spirit, since he uncovered it where it lay at the heart of nature; he would usher in the New Age, the age of Man, whose spirit would conquer the earth.

CHAPTER 12

SCIENCE

ABOUT the middle of the fourteenth century John of Rupescissa, a Franciscan, complained that there were so few genuine and pious natural philosophers; most of those who pretended to pursue the sciences were magicians, sorcerers, swindlers and false coiners. "It is of no avail to strive for perfection in this art if a man has not first purified his mind by a devout life and profound contemplation, so that he not only recognizes nature for what it is but also understands how to change what can be changed; but this is given to all too few."

John's own scientific knowledge came to him "through divine enlightenment", during a stay of seven years in prison. His subjects were medicine, chemistry and alchemy, and he attracted much attention in his own day by his prophecies of changes in Church and State. He foretold that the Papacy, then captive at Avignon, would lose its power and worldly possessions and return to apostolic poverty. His years of imprisonment were passed first at Toulouse, as the prisoner of the Franciscan Provincial of Aquitaine, and afterwards in a papal gaol at Avignon. Primarily "a seeker out of the secrets of nature", he falls, with other Franciscans, alchemists, soothsayers and astrologers, into that line of European natural philosophers which leads through Dr Faustus, Boyle and Erasmus Darwin down into the nineteenth century and indeed into the present.

This "seeking out of the secrets of nature" should not be regarded as something set apart from the religious and political preoccupations of the moment; it was intimately bound up with the prevailing outlook on the world. Those most active and most activating in this field were attempting nothing less than the transformation of the "elements of nature" and of society, the metamorphosis which should alter the age itself and all human relations. A high value has often been set on natural science as the coadjutor of religious and political advancement. Eramus Darwin, for example, the grandfather of Charles Darwin, was at once a doctor of medicine, a religious reformer, a man of the "enlightenment" and a revolutionary. It can be shown that the reforming ideal of using science to "make the world a better place", which in the nineteenth century is associated with Haeckel on the right and with the revolutionary speculations of Engels on the left, and which in the twentieth century is bound up with the two great questions of the relationship of science and religion and the social and political uses of atomic energy, has a long ancestry. In Europe the pedigree reaches back at least into the twelfth century, though it was mainly in the thirteenth and early fourteenth centuries that the natural sciences began to emerge in their own right, and even then in a peculiarly ambiguous role. Anyone who concerned himself with the "secrets of nature" and was bold enough to seek them out by experiment was committed to a perilous association with magicians, sorcerers and alchemists, that is to say with underground conspirators dedicated to uncovering the secrets God had veiled in mystery, impelled by motives of ambition and vanity or in consequence of a sworn compact with the devil. Gerbert of Aurillac, the tenth century scholar with mathematical and scientific interests who on his election to the Papacy took the name Sylvester II, was famous in the Middle Ages not for his pontificate but as a magician and a sorcerer. As late as the seventeenth century the same German word still served both for "spirit" and for "gas" and the distinction between the two was arrived at only very slowly. Boyle, friend of Newton and the "father of modern chemistry", was a practising alchemist, and Newton himself derived some of the basic elements of his colour theory from the natural philosophers of the thirteenth and fourteenth centuries.

During the Middle Ages those who pursued the natural sciences had no legitimate niche in society, nor were they recognized by the Church. The universities eschewed technical activities (the necessary basis of experiment and of empirical research) as "illiberal arts", banishing them to the backrooms and workshops of small craftsmen and persons of dubious reputation. Theology frowned on any attempt at reaching into the secrets of nature, an unlawful invasion of the sacred womb of the Great Mother. Even in the nineteenth century the Spanish Academy of Sciences could reject on these grounds a proposal for controlling the river Manzanares. Anyone who persisted in flying in the face of public opinion by meddling with science was forced to consort with outcasts of all kinds: with Provençal Jews, because they could translate Arabic texts dealing with alchemy, chemistry, medicine and astrology, and with eccentrics who lived out their lives in dark secluded basements, dedicated to their quest for the "philosopher's stone", the transmutation of quicksilver into gold. Anyone who like Roger Bacon was bold enough to convert his monastic cell into a cell of early scientific endeavour had to be prepared to exchange it for a prison.

The pattern of development in medieval ideas about the natural sciences provides as conspicuous an example of that broad co-existence of opposites as any we have yet met with: it can never be sufficiently stressed that medieval society, medieval piety and medieval learning were all compounded of numerous contradictory and diverse elements. Scholars who engaged in scientific pursuits did so from a mixture of motives, rational and irrational, scholarly and superstitious; their methods were a combination of empiricism and bold speculation. The stresses of contemporary political and religious pressures were such that although these activities may have made a satisfying life's work for an individual, what emerged from them was certainly not science. The different subjects went together in pairs, some of them so closely linked as to become hybrids. Chemistry went with alchemy, astronomy with astrology, mathematics with cosmology (numbers were regarded as sacred cyphers in which were hidden all the secrets of the macrocosm and the microcosm), technology with magic, medicine with philosophy and optics with mystical ideas about light.

The earliest centre of scientific learning to shed its light far afield was the Oxford of Robert Grosseteste. Grosseteste (born *circa* 1170, died 1253), a native of Suffolk, was a student of Oxford and Paris. Returning to Oxford to teach, he became the mentor of the Franciscan school and rose to be Chancellor of the University; he died as bishop of Lincoln, a position from which he still had the right to watch over the fortunes of his native university. The light which radiated from Oxford during his lifetime was the light of Greek learning and of pure reason, and its influence soon spread far afield; even before Grosseteste was dead, Witelo in Silesia was already making advances on the work in optics begun in Oxford.

Plato had seen light and numbers as closely related elements, basic structures of the cosmos. The Middle Ages inherited this theory by way of Augustine and the neo-Platonists. While the Dominicans were Aristotelian in outlook, the Franciscans, especially at Oxford, were Platonists and staunch adherents of Augustine. Grosseteste taught that extension in three dimensions and the properties of space were determined by the properties of light and its laws of operation. Light, and light-energy, were the basis of all causality in nature. For this reason the laws of optics were fundamental to all explanations of nature. The cosmos was the self-unfolding of the light-principle according to laws immanent in itself. These laws were reflected and expressed in numbers and in the simplest and most obvious of geometrical models. Grosseteste claimed, as Roger Bacon and Galileo were to claim after him, that nothing could be understood in natural philosophy and empirical investigation (the two were inseparable) without mathematics, by which he chiefly meant geometry.

Grosseteste made his theory that light was the universal principle serve to illustrate the relations between the three persons of the Trinity, to "explain" the operation of grace through free will. Light was the agent through which the soul worked on the body; it was light that gave beauty to the visible creation. These highly conjectural ideas, inherited from the Greeks, were combined with experiment in a fashion characteristic of Oxford and indeed of the English talent for what is empirical and "practical". It is this combination, as Crombie has remarked, that makes Grosseteste's career of such "great strategic importance". Western thinkers were now submitting Greek views to the test of experiment, which meant making use of those manual arts the Greeks themselves had disdained as servile. The Platonic rationalism of twelfth century Chartres, with its veneration of Natura, was now harnessed to the task of investigating light, which, as Grosseteste saw it, was the essence of nature.

The scientific tradition founded at Oxford by Grosseteste was maintained by Roger Bacon, John Pecham, Duns Scotus, William of Ockham, John Bradwardine, John Dumbleton and others less eminent, and its influence extended overseas to reach Germany, Padua and Paris. The problems raised and the positions upheld by the natural philosophers and experimenters of the thirteenth and early fourteenth centuries held a deep attraction, not always consciously realized, for later generations of scientists, for Leonardo, Galileo, William Gilbert, Francis Bacon, Harvey, Descartes, Newton and Leibniz. It is striking and significant that this should be so.

New scientific methods were developed by the Oxford school: inductive investigation allied with the application of mathematical and philosophical principles (as in the acutely relevant problem: do our senses tell us the truth?). The ardour with which they pursued the practical can be amply illustrated from the work of some of the mathematicians and experimenters of the fourteenth century. Richard of Wallingford (*circa* 1292–1335) developed measuring instruments and trigonometrical techniques. William Merle (who may have belonged to the same family as the twelfth century scholar Daniel Morley) kept a meteorological diary at Oxford between 1337 and 1344, and used the data he collected to write a treatise on weather-forecasting, as an aid to farmers. The combination of first-hand observation with exact methods of reckoning made meteorology one of the strongest subjects at Oxford in this period. The scholar known as "Perscrutator" (probably Robert of York) confidently dismisses ancient writers as the purveyors of fairy-tales. He took from them only a few rules and methods, and for the rest relied on the grace of God, his own judgment, and experiment. Richard Swineshead (Suiseth) in his *Calculator* (which even Leibniz wanted to re-edit) adumbrated some of the theoretical principles for applying mathematical methods to physics.

Oxford was distinguished by its combination of Platonic cosmology, native empiricism and research into fundamental mathematics (a subject in which Oxford led Europe during the thirteenth century), and its achievements stimulated advances in Paris, Padua, and later on in Germany. But Roger Bacon, that figure whom later centuries liked to see as the first "modern scientist", is there to remind us that Oxford was still rooted firmly in the medieval world. A Franciscan, Bacon sold his patrimony for the sake of his scientific studies, which made him the laughing-stock of Spanish students at Oxford; his superiors in the Order sent him to prison. Roger Bacon looked towards the South, where Arab, Jewish and Christian learning mingled: this was the fount of saving knowledge, mathematics, astrology, biblical exegesis and philosophy. There could be no true theology without an understanding of natural science. In the course of his work Bacon cites over thirty Islamic and Jewish authorities. There was a Jewish community at Oxford which may have had a stimulating influence on Bacon and indeed on the university as a whole. Bacon aimed at total knowledge, which was to purify Christendom and transform and convert the world.

With this in mind, he carefully studied the reports of Franciscan missions working in the Far East and suggested to the Pope, his patron, that it was desirable to have the whole world surveyed; he himself drew a map of the world (now lost) showing the sea-route westward from Spain to the Indies, and this suggestion came down to Columbus, by way of Peter of Ailly.

The Pope in question was Guido de Foulques, an open-minded southern Frenchman who had taken priest's orders only on the death of his wife, having already been a soldier, a lawyer, and secretary to St Louis of France. He subsequently became Archbishop of Narbonne and finally, in 1265, Pope, taking the name Clement IV. This Provençal Pope went behind the back of Bacon's superiors and asked him to send secret reports of his scientific discoveries to the Curia. Avignon, later to become the seat of the Papacy, was already a byword as the resort of astrologers, alchemists, would-be gold-makers, sorcerers and necromancers. Necromancy was a favourite form of magic and even kings and bishops did not shrink from attempting to dispose of their enemies by this means: Hugh Gerard, Bishop of Cahors, tried to kill Pope John XXII by magic, and Philip IV, King of France, used spells against Boniface VIII and the Templars. Pope John XXII was kept perpetually busy with trials of the clergy on charges of sorcery, and in 1318 he set up a commission to enquire into the magical practices of the clergy at the papal court. In the Bull *Super illius specula* it was alleged that large numbers of Christians had given themselves over to sorcery and made pacts with demons. The Pope called a conference of all available scientists and alchemists to discover whether these arts had any natural foundation or rested entirely on black magic; the alchemists replied that they had, the scientists that they had not. This was the climate in which the natural sciences developed in Europe, emerging but slowly from the clouds compounded of witches' brews, ecstatic spells and political wishful thinking.

Bacon's major work is contained in the treatises addressed to his "Angel Pope" Clement IV, the man he hoped would revive the Church, "purify" learning and liberate theology. Bacon held that all the sciences had their particular usefulness, *utilitas*, which could be steered towards a definite aim, that of making Christendom fit to compete intellectually and morally with pagans and infidels. Bacon considered it better to confound unbelievers by wisdom and true learning than to conquer them in wars conducted by pugnacious illiterates whose successes could only be ephemeral. Military Crusades had failed and must be replaced by crusades of learning, to win over minds and souls.

Bacon, who belonged to the Spiritual party among the Franciscans, was filled with rage and disgust when he saw Christendom so patently unfit to undertake crusades of this kind. Everything about Rome and the Curia was corrupt, and pride, avarice, sensuality and debauchery were the ruling passions. All the Orders were corrupt, so was the whole clergy (Bacon is emphatic about this, *totus clerus*). The princes and laity were corrupt, destroying one another in their constant warfare. The universities, particularly Paris, were corrupt. Men might delude themselves that the age was one of great learning, an apogee of scholarship; but in fact the schools were threshing empty straws and their dialectical sham-battles in formal logic nowhere touched reality. Bacon knew universities from the inside but yet felt himself an outsider; it was the insight of this Spiritual Franciscan that made possible the first comprehensive criticism of the European university system and of intellectualism.

This isolated figure demanded nothing less than the purification of Christendom, to be achieved by the purification of learning. The universities must therefore be cleansed of sodomy, and delivered from their homosexual professors. Theology too stood in need of purification; among its seven deadly sins were concentration on formal philosophy and the neglect of the natural sciences, philology and textual criticism. These last two had a bearing on eschatology, since the meaning of every word and syllable of the Bible had to be weighed, as keys to the history and future of the Church from the beginning to the end of time.

Bacon was wholly dominated by the historical vision of the Franciscan Spirituals, on which he explicitly based himself. "Nature is an instrument of that divine plan of operation which is discernible in the history of the world." This pinpoints the moment when apocalyptic prophecy was abandoned in favour of astrology, a trend from now onwards increasingly marked among the Spiritual Franciscans; for astrology, using science as its handmaid, could foretell the future with exactitude.

From the twelfth century astrological ideas and practices, some of them handed down from classical antiquity, others of Jewish and Arabic origin, had been flooding into Western Europe. Horoscopes were cast by astrologers of all religions, including that described by Bacon as the *"secta Christi"*, and by Pierre Dubois as the *"secta Catholicorum"* (Dubois was an important pamphleteer for the French government and a pupil of Siger of Brabant). The rise and fall of the Christian West were the subjects of earnest calculation. It is not unreasonable to include as alumni of this school those obsessed thinkers, from the thirteenth century down to Nietzsche and Spengler, who have plotted the life-span of cultures, world empires and "Western civilization". There was, for example, the astrologer and physician Pietro d'Abano, educated at Constantinople and Paris and responsible for bringing Averroism to Padua. He pointed out that Christianity, Socrates, Plato and Aristotle, not to mention numerous poets, all flourished under the planet Mercury. Cecco d'Ascoli drew the horoscope of Christ, holding that the whole course of his life, including his Passion, was determined by the stars, and that nothing happened of his own free will. This was radical, left-wing, "scientific" astrology, characterized by aggressive anti-Christian and anti-Roman tendencies. Pietro d'Abano categorically pronounced that there could be no such thing as "prophecy", since nature followed its own unalterable laws, which could be calculated by scientists, above all by astrologers. Hence miracles were impossibilities, and no one could claim to have miraculous powers at his disposal, an assertion which robbed the Papacy, and indeed the whole idea on which the Church at that time rested, of much of its efficacy. Astrologers were not "false magicians" but people who measured nature; for them the real practitioners of "false magic" were people who busied themselves with religion, any kind of religion. The Church and the clergy were just as ready on their side to prove that the "scientists" and astrologers were fraudulent magicians and sorcerers: a matter of some difficulty since the clergy were themselves so deeply involved in alchemy, magic and astrology. Astrologers of the "right wing", which included Bacon, had a different idea of the function of astrology. Bacon hoped to compute astrologically the destruction of Islam, and to introduce a reformed calendar on astronomical principles.

Bacon's scientific studies and speculations were informed by his conviction of the imminence of the new and last age, the age of the spirit. This age was to be ushered in by "spiritual man", persecuted from time immemorial. For Bacon, however, and this brought a momentous twist to an idea which in essence was that already held by the Spirituals, this man was none other than the enquirer into nature, the pure scientist. He it was who should bring enlightenment and universal peace to the Church and the world. It was in keeping with Bacon's creed to acknowledge that the new burning-glass had been invented "by God's grace". It will help us to realize how fundamental was this change of outlook if we recall that the previous agents of God's grace and the bearers of salvation had been Emperors, Popes, kings and rulers of every degree: now it was machines. In opposition to the occult and archaic world which Bacon knew so well (he mentions magical incantation, spells for healing and the ordeal) the "spiritual man", the scientist, could invoke the new work of grace, that is to say the "miracle" of technology and investigation of the "marvels" of nature.

Giovanni de' Dondi (born in 1318), professor first of astronomy at Padua and later of medicine at Florence (his father was a physician and had been professor at Padua), who worked for ten years over the construction of his clock with a striking mechanism, wrote: "There are so many marvellous coherences to be found in every natural object: these are *mirabilia*, not *miracula*, wonderful phenomena accessible to understanding and thought, capable of being investigated, in no sense miracles." Giovanni appealed to Aristotle and his own experience when he said: "We are surrounded daily by marvels; when we become familiar with them through use many objects lose their quality of being miraculous and incomprehensible; hence I am no longer filled with wonder and terror as once I was, but have trained myself to look carefully at everything marvellous, to reflect on what I see and never to allow myself to become unduly astonished."

De' Dondi's famous contemporary, Nicole Oresme (who died in 1382 as Bishop of Lisieux), wrote attacks on astrologers in French, his native tongue, translated the scientific works of Aristotle into the same language and was the lifelong foe of "erroneous belief in miracles" among the people, as he called it. His psychological critique of the human love for the miraculous is comprehensive; he made experiments on himself to assess the effects on the human body of imagination and fantasy. This enlightened prelate complained of the number of clerics who were themselves gluttons for marvels, and of those others who deceived the people by ingeniously fabricated miracles and wonders to get money for their churches. Oresme was in favour of research into the wonders of nature, and an enthusiastic champion of the rationality of the Bible, of the Gospels, and of the Christian faith as a whole. "Everything contained in the Gospels is highly reasonable *(rationabilissima)*." We can see from this that criticism of the cult of the miraculous started actually inside the framework of orthodox medieval theology and learning. Criticism would continue, taken up now by the Reformers, by men of the "enlightenment", and, above all, by natural philosophers and investigators. The line stretches down through Toland, Hume and his intellectual descendants to the critical self-analysis characteristic of modern thought. The rational, "explicable" "wonders of nature" are played off —this is always the central feature—against the "irrational" wonders of the old Church, the superstitious credulity of the "uninstructed" masses. Scientific criticism of the miraculous is always charged with emotion and always related to certain contemporary political attitudes and ways of looking at the world. This was as true of the thirteenth and fourteenth centuries as it has been of the nineteenth and twentieth.

To return to Roger Bacon. This Oxford Franciscan attacked both the superstitions of the masses and the hostility towards science of the Paris schoolmen. He called for the empirical investigation of nature and urged men to experiment, although he himself was unable to achieve very much in this field. It is important to remind ourselves that scientific experiment was at this time still deeply entangled in magic and sorcery; experiments were still thoroughly Faustian—trials perhaps, but trials which led to the temptation of good and evil spirits, formulations maybe, but as likely as not ending with magical formulae. This was so in Bacon's time, and things were still much the same in the time of Leonardo da Vinci. Here, for example, is Bacon posing a "scientific" problem: "If deer, eagles and snakes can prolong their lives by using toads and stones, why should the discovery of an elixir of life be denied to mankind?" Until well into the nineteenth century there were European princes who continued to maintain "scientists" of a certain stamp in the hope that they would produce for them the means of transmuting quicksilver into gold, potent machines useful against enemies, the philosopher's stone and the elixir of life.

Bacon had his own vision of the technical world of the future: ships without oarsmen, submarines, "automobiles", aeroplanes, small magical gadgets for releasing oneself from prison, magical fetters (for use on other people) and devices for walking on water. Many sources of inspiration helped to nourish his vision: the magical techniques of primitive peoples, the wish-fulfilment of the masses, the apocalyptic frenzy of the Spiritual Franciscans and, not least, an unfettered curiosity into the marvels lying concealed in the womb of nature. Whoever mastered these could be lord of the world and of the future. This realistic curiosity was something new.

Bacon's plans and vision brought great illumination to his "pupil", Arnold of Villanova (born *circa* 1238), who often borrowed directly from Bacon's work. Bacon died in prison: "his" Pope had died too soon. Arnold held his own against the Inquisition, secure in his position as court physician to Popes and kings. He was a Catalan who had studied at Naples, Barcelona, Montpellier, Paris, Rome and Avignon; his studies covered medicine, alchemy and astrology, his active life was spent in diplomacy, social reform and writing on the relations between theology and history. A Spiritual Franciscan like his master, he wrote an anti-Thomist manifesto entitled *The Sword of Truth against the Thomists*. Arnold aimed at retaining the characteristic vision of the Spiritual Franciscans and their religious and scientific endeavours within the bosom of the Church. An "angel Pope" should preside over the coming rejuvenation which would transform the cosmos, the Church, society at large and all the elements. Arnold searched for a medicine which would cure all ills—a panacea in fact—and which would rejuvenate man in body and soul. His scheme of things made natural science the most potent ally of the Spiritual Franciscans in their aim of remaking the world.

As physician and alchemist Arnold directs our attention to certain specific aspects of the chemistry and medicine of the age. He was famous in his own day and for several centuries afterwards as the supposed author of manuals on alchemy. At this date chemistry and alchemy were inseparable, and alchemist texts from Arab sources had been circulating in Europe since 1144. The aim of alchemy-chemistry was to metamorphose the elements of nature, turning them into something better, more spiritual and more divine. In one of the tracts ascribed to Arnold the Passion of Christ is compared to the "passion" of the elements: chemical metamorphosis is analogous to the transmutation of the bread and wine into the flesh and blood of Christ. Quicksilver is led like a lamb to the slaughter and "sweats blood to free mankind from poverty and distress".

The chemical elements, first regarded as coadjutors, were later expected to perform saving works on their own account in providing "man's daily bread". The alchemists, however, whose terminology remained current until the eighteenth century, meant only that the chemical elements prepared the way for metamorphosis. These monkish scientists hoped by transmuting the elements to assist and accelerate the work of Christ in His transformation and transmutation of the world. Scientific activity of this kind was animated by a spirit of ecstatic impatience (it has its practitioners today): objects must be "radically" transformed by working outwards from their roots, their essential substances, and man must "radically" transform himself to match, by renouncing those arbitrary authorities by which the old, unregenerate world was governed. Chemistry and alchemy were thus made to serve a religious-political vision of the world's redemption which in the minds of the radical Franciscans who had been expelled from Avignon and found refuge in Germany and Bohemia was already linked with the liberation of the awakening masses from the dominion of Rome.

Medieval medicine was equally bound up with a particular view of the world. Medicine in Western Europe was the offspring of classical medicine and of the medical philosophy evolved by great Arab and Jewish doctors. The two great thinkers of the twelfth century "enlightenment", Ibn Ruschd, otherwise Averroes, and Maimonides, his exact contemporary, were both of them great physicians, and practising physicians at that. The same is true of Ibn Sina, otherwise Avicenna. Every medieval doctor was in some degree an astrologer and expected to practise as such. By the mid-thirteenth century there was a standard collection of classical, Arabic and Jewish medical texts, which was found in all the great libraries, Montpellier, Salerno, Paris, Granada, Toledo, Cairo, Damascus and Bagdad.

Any serious student of medicine was forced to spend at least some part of his life in the "free-thinking", "enlightened" atmosphere of the lands bordering the Mediterranean. Here the two branches of medicine, theoretical and practical, grew up side by side. Practical medicine, involving as it did the invasion of that most secret of all the wonders of nature, the human body, was particularly daring. Today it is barely possible to imagine just what this invasion must have meant to people of the time, when every man's body was the image of Christ's body, Corpus Christi. Dissecting a man was tantamount to dissecting God. Nothing could be more impious, godless and inhuman than the study of anatomy. In the thirteenth and fourteenth centuries Petrarch and the humanists mounted an attack on "godless physicians" which was aimed particularly at the Averroists of Padua. This antagonism has lasted for well over five centuries and is still kept alive in the undisguised mistrust of "doctors" commonly displayed by humanists, artists and other creative individualists, who imagine doctors capable of all manner of infamy: they are aggressors against man, the "holiest" thing on earth.

The study of anatomy made some progress during the Middle Ages, despite this resistance. Pigs were used as subjects for dissection at Salerno in the late eleventh and early twelfth centuries, and later on the bodies of criminals. However, the great age of anatomy began only with Mondino de Luzzi in the fourteenth century. Surgery made some advance with the appearance of Bruno da Longoburgo's *Chirurgica Magna* at Padua in 1252. In Western Europe the main advances in medicine were the achievements of the despised army doctors and surgeons, that is to say of manual workers, "outsiders", held in contempt by the university professors. In the universities medicine was entirely a matter of book learning, with especial reference to classical texts.

Clinical medicine found a home among the Arabs and the Jews, with whom the practice of medicine tended to be a family affair; we know of some medical dynasties which retained the tradition unbroken from the twelfth down to the fourteenth or even the fifteenth centuries. Averroes' friend Ibn Zuhr (Avenzoar), probably the greatest of the Islamic physicians, was the most distinguished member of the best-known medical family of Islamic Spain, whose descent has been traced through six generations. There were also

Suffering and Mysticism

75

No longer King and Lord, but the sufferer of intense grief and pain: Pieta at Bonn, *c.* 1300

76

(Below) Refuge from suffering was found in the peace of mysticism: Germany developed new devotional themes such as Johannesminne: Christ and the sleeping St John

77

Frederick I, Barbarossa, and the Bishop of Freising. From the time of its foundation by Charlemagne, the Holy Roman Empire was the supreme protector of Christendom

78

Head of Henry IV, tragic and immense, whose lifetime saw the crisis of the Holy Roman Empire; from the shrine of Charlemagne at Aachen Cathedral

79

Symbol of Empire: the orb, part of the Crown jewels of the Holy Roman Empire

80

'Stupor Mundi', the Emperor Frederick II of Germany and Sicily, whose quarrel with the Papacy was the greatest scandal of the age

81

Constantly travelling his domains, Frederick II built numerous castles to house his court: most famous of all, Castle del Monte, on the Apulian uplands, built *c.* 1240

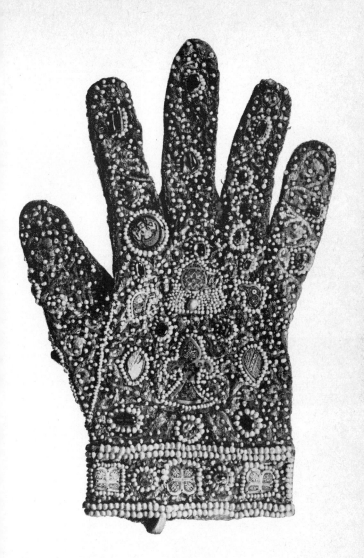

82

Part of the Sicilian regalia of Roger II: the glove in which the Sicilian kings were crowned

83

Boniface VIII, *d.* 1303, a splendid autocrat, had a vision of universal Papal domination

84

The new relationship between kings and bishops is shown by the proportions of these figures: Archbishop Siegfried III von Eppstein crowns two minor kings in this relief from his tomb in Mainz Cathedral

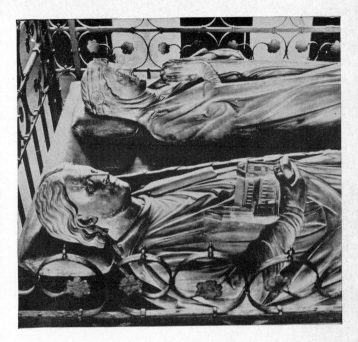

85

The great lay princes rivalled the Emperor himself: tomb in Brunswick Cathedral of Henry the Lion, a vassal in name only of Frederick I, and his wife Matilda, daughter of Henry II of England

86

Edward I of England, holding the sword of secular power defies the Papal legates

87

Canonization of a saintly king could add lustre to a royal house: St Louis (Louis IX 1214–1270) of France leaves for a crusade

88

Medieval art reflects regional and social divisions: San Miniato **al** Monte, Florence, has a classical simplicity derived from **Roman** antiquities (11th century)

89

Northern Romanesque, built on the model of Cluny: the Cathedral at Worms, *c.* 1100

90

Romanesque churches were drenched in colour. The marble pulpit of San Pante-leone at Ravello near Sorrento, has black and gold, scarlet and turquoise mosaics

91 and 92

Highly conscious of the supernatural, Romanesque artists carved devils and grotesques; lions were a defence against evil spirits: *(right)* Easter candlestick from San Paulo Fuori le Mura, Rome, and *(below)* font, Bremen Cathedral

93

Romanesque painting was ecstatic, apocalyptic, magical: Christ in Majesty at Berzé-la-Ville, showing the symbolic and sacramental significance of the use of colour

94

Salzburg produced remarkable illuminated manuscripts in the twelfth century, showing Byzantine influence in their colour and images

95

One of the most typical examples of English Gothic, Salisbury Cathedral was built in 1220–1258

96 and 97

Gothic architecture originated in the Ile de France: the style soon became an architectural *lingua franca* valid throughout Europe: *(above)* Chartres Cathedral (*c.* 1220). The west facade of Chartres Cathedral is the earliest example of Gothic sculpture *(below)*

98 and 99

Gaieth and naturalism, two characteristics of early Gothic sculpture: *(right)* smiling angel from Rheims Cathedral and *(below)* capital from the Marienkirche, Gelnhausen

100

Sculpture gained in humanity and comfort what it lost of the magical power of Romanesque art: *'Le Beau Dieu'* (*c.* 1230), Amiens Cathedral

clans of Jewish doctors, found in Spain, Provence and Italy, where Jews often served the Popes as their personal physicians and astrologers. This continuity, which gave practitioners self-assurance and permitted the building up of a tradition, is important.

The experience of these doctors was such that nothing human was alien to them. They stood equidistant from all religions. Critical judgment, detachment, and "enlightenment" throve in such a climate. On their many journeyings they had come to know both East and West for themselves. They travelled incessantly, in search of further training, to take service at the courts of foreign princes, and from necessity, as refugees.

Other Jewish families made the translation and interpretation of texts their speciality. For example, Jacob ben Mahir ibn Tibbon, the Provençal mathematician, astronomer and zoologist and one of the greatest of all the translators of scientific works from Arabic into Hebrew, came of a famous family of educated and "enlightened" Jews, and was himself a leader of the party of Maimonides against the old Rabbinical orthodoxy. His work was still quoted by Keppel and Copernicus.

The natural sciences thus throve in the margins of Europe and among the marginal groups of society. They were carried on by people working outside the university disciplines and who held heterodox religious beliefs, Jews, Muslims and Spiritual Franciscans. One important branch, practical mechanics, was pursued by men of the lower orders, manual workers engaged wholly in the "illiberal arts". Admittedly this indispensable foundation of technological advance did receive some attention from more educated people, such as Jordanus Nemorarius in the thirteenth century, and an anonymous disciple of his who has been described by Duhem as the "forerunner of Leonardo". Gerard of Brussels, Roger Bacon, Petrus Johannis Olivi and a few others, isolated individuals working in Padua, Oxford, Flanders and Silesia, occupied themselves with certain problems which might be described as "technical" in the narrower sense. But several centuries still had to elapse before there was any genuine and fruitful collaboration between academics and artisans of the kind to be found in the early days of the Royal Society, in the Netherlands and in France in the early eighteenth century. One has only to think of the mental gulf which still all too often yawns between "humanists" and "technologists" to appreciate something of the difficulties attending experiment in the thirteenth and fourteenth centuries.

In the year 1600 William Gilbert (who was Queen Elizabeth's personal physician) published his book on magnets, the first printed book written by an academic which deals exclusively with a scientific subject on the basis of experiment and observation. Gilbert was very proud of having drawn on the experience of simple miners and mariners. He attached particular importance to the work of Robert Norman, a retired sailor who had studied methods of making compasses and put his observations into writing. But as early as 1269 Peter the Stranger, while he was with the Angevin army besieging Lucera dei Pagani in Calabria, wrote a treatise on magnets which is one of the most remarkable monuments of medieval experimental research since it refers to a whole series of experiments on magnetism.

The hope and vision of medieval science and theology, of the medieval Church and state, were united in the life and work of Ramon Lull (1235–1315). The writings of this remarkable man are still read and commented upon, and not only in his native Spain. Large in mind and generous in spirit, ready to embrace the whole world in his sympathies, Lull held that conversion to Christianity, as the sum of earthly truth, would inevitably follow from the spread of enlightenment: in fact that true enlightenment and conversion to Christianity were identical. Faith and reason, mystery and rationality were indissolubly wed. Lull was a prodigious traveller. He visited the papal curia, frequented the lecture rooms of Paris and Padua and went the round of royal courts and councils in France and Germany; he was to be found deep in conversation in the streets and market places of North African cities and perhaps also in Asia. Long after his death he still cast his spell over men such as Nicholas of Cues and those great humanists Bessarion and Pico della Mirandola, over Giordano Bruno, Gassendi and Leibniz. Lull was already forty when he had his first vision of that all-embracing logic, his *Ars Magna*. It came to him while he was alone on Mount Randa (hear Palma in Majorca, his birthplace) and was the visual incarnation of his dream of universal knowledge. It took the form of what can only be described as a computing engine, which linked up the basic principles or "ground-words" of all knowledge by a mechanism consisting of concentric circles segmented by radii and of geometrical symbols. It seems to have been what might be called a cybernetic machine, prepared to unravel every problem, every science, even faith itself. Here in rudimentary fashion were anticipated the great universal formulae of Einstein and Heisenberg, which have provided man with the mathematical keys to the problems of matter, light, energy, and the fundamental laws of the cosmos. A miracle machine: or, as later scoffers were to say, a wind machine, tossing empty words about. Leibniz however was not among the mockers; Lull's vision came too close to his own dream of finding a universal, scientifically viable language, which should enlighten all men impartially: the prerequisite of universal peace.

Lull was the author of a didactic romance, *Blanquerna,* which was a favourite with the men of the eighteenth century Enlightenment and is also, incidentally, the first European travel book to describe the Sudan, Abyssinia, Turkey and Georgia. There is a passage which relates how the Pope appealed to the cardinals to support a project Lull himself advocated: "Help me, I pray, in my endeavour to reduce all existing languages to one. For if there is but one, the peoples will understand one another and through understanding learn to love each other; they will adopt uniform customs and meet each other on common ground." Such a man, it will be objected, was a Utopian dreamer. He was indeed. But he was also a universal genius, a bold anticipator of the thoughts and problems of the future.

Although already middle-aged at the time of his visionary experience, Lull nevertheless set himself to learn Arabic and, like Bacon, urged the establishment in Europe of academies in which the basic studies would be Hebrew, Arabic and Greek. Lull had a great appreciation and love of his Islamic adversaries and would have liked to revive the disputations formerly held between representatives of the three great religions. In his *Libro del Gentil* (which appeared first in Arabic, in 1272–73, at Majorca), a Jew, a Muslim and a Christian expound the chief points of their respective faiths. In his *Liber de Sancto Spiritu* a Greek and a Latin converse in the presence of a Muslim, while in his *Liber Tartari et Christiani* (Rome, 1285) a Tartar questions a Jew, a Christian and a Muslim. Lull thought it an advantage for the children of Christian Europe to gain some insight into the Jewish and Islamic worlds. He was convinced that European Christendom needed to be educated afresh so that people's eyes might be opened to the beauty of alien worlds.

The age of military crusading was past. The Church's foes

would now surrender only to pure learning and a purified faith. After much hesitation Lull became a Francisan tertiary. He had a good deal in common with St Francis—a love of ordinary people (he was one of the greatest vernacular writers of the Middle Ages) and of children, and a capacity for loving his enemies. He was also thoroughly Franciscan in his rejection of the intellectualism of Thomist Paris and Averroist Padua. At the age of eighty he achieved his longed-for goal of martyrdom. Few visitors to Majorca are aware that the vast cathedral of the island's capital is the last resting place of this great European, for whom Europe was always open, exposed to rewarding influences on every side.

Cardinal Nicholas of Cues (1401–64), the most considerable thinker of the waning Middle Ages, mathematician, scientist, philosopher and churchman, possessed forty-five of Lull's works. Under their powerful stimulus Nicholas projected his thoughts and his political aspirations well outside the accustomed medieval boundaries, even, one might say, beyond the habitual frontiers of modern Europe. He was daring enough to think that coexistence might be possible even with those dread and well-armed enemies who year by year were striking fresh blows in their invasion of Christendom: the Hussites and the Turks.

CHAPTER 13

JEWS AND WOMEN

THE reader may find it odd that the medieval Jew should share a chapter with medieval woman. There are any number of surveys of the Middle Ages in which neither appears at all, or at most they are dismissed with a brief mention. This silence is no accident: for although during the "open" Middle Ages Jews and women made a positive contribution to culture and to society, both were later relegated to the life of the Ghetto, and it was they who suffered most when society closed its ranks during the later Middle Ages. Witch-mania was a catching malady in a world made schizophrenic by masculine anxieties and masculine fears. The witch-hunting of the later Middle Ages, which continued at least into the eighteenth century (a witch was burnt in Germany during Goethe's lifetime), is telling proof that with increased tension society was becoming nastier and narrower, though the gloom of the general picture is somewhat redeemed by isolated and short-lived instances of a more generous morality.

There can be no denying the unifying and unique contribution made by Jewish learning and piety to the intellectual and religious culture of earlier medieval Europe, above all during the twelfth, that most "open" of the medieval centuries. Jewish doctors, translators, philosophers and theologians, and Jewish financiers in the service of lay and ecclesiastical princes, all played their part in creating the bracing intellectual and emotional climate which roused Europe from its torpor. Avencebrol (Ibn Gabirol) had a great influence on Franciscan scientific thought, Maimonides (Rabbi Moses as he is called by Aquinas) was an even more conspicuous influence on the Thomists and the Dominicans generally. It is as difficult to imagine Meister Eckhart, the greatest of medieval German philosophers and mystics, without Maimonides and the Jewish neo-Platonists as it is to think of Dante shorn of the knowledge of Sufite Arab mysticism, Gnosticism and cosmological and numerological ideas transmitted to the world of the Western Mediterranean by the Jews of Provence, Spain and Italy.

Jewish culture, a culture both of the intellect and of the emotions, reached its dazzling peak of perfection in the shadow of impending catastrophe. The persecutions of the Jews which accompanied the first two Crusades, in 1096 and 1146, sounded a warning note. Until that time outbursts of anti-Semitism in Western Europe had been rare and sporadic. But now the omens were unmistakable; although the Jews were only finally expelled from England in 1290, there had already been a massacre of English Jews a century earlier. France expelled its Jews in 1306, Lithuania in 1395, Spain in 1492, Portugal in 1497. Jews were not readmitted to England until the time of Cromwell, in 1655: the Puritans building the new "Israel" were mindful of their spiritual fathers.

In 1215 by a decree of the Fourth Lateran Council the Church, then at the height of its power, took a leaf from the Caliphs' book and ordered Jews to wear a distinguishing form of dress. The distinctive yellow patch, horned cap and other emblems of Cain invited the hostility of those who saw the Jews as the "murderers of Christ". In 1233 a papal Bull forbade any argument on religious matters between Christians and Jews. Such disputations had been common in the open twelfth century; now, if they still took place, it had to be under the especially privileged auspices of the kings of Spain or of recognized missionaries. Even then they usually degenerated into undisguised slanging matches or worse. The twelfth century saw the beginnings of the Ghetto system and the isolation of Jews from their environment. Jews ceased to live in the Christian sectors of towns and settled in a specifically Jewish quarter, hoping to find protection among their own kind when persecution struck suddenly and unexpectedly, just as the German merchants of Novgorod walled themselves in behind palisades and ditches for fear of the Russian mob.

Who were the persecutors of the Jews and who their protectors? It was the fanatical zeal of small undisciplined crusading contingents which was largely responsible for the earliest outbreaks of persecution, in which monastic preaching unhappily played a part. At a later date the Franciscans joined the hunt. But large sections of the population would have no part in it, recognizing their common brotherhood with their Jewish neighbours. There were individuals, knights, townsmen and peasants, who sheltered Jews in their own houses. We find German townspeople siding with the Jews while the commons of France and England worked on their kings to secure their recall, in France with success. Letters of protection and privilege for Jews were obtained from popes, emperors and kings, while both lay and ecclesiastical rulers kept Jews to look after their household affairs, prizing them as valuable chattels. During the latter Middle Ages Jews were sometimes the objects of complicated business transactions. Louis of Bavaria sold "his" Jews or pawned them to princes for a limited period. Taken all in all, it is as difficult to generalize about the protection of the Jews as it is about their persecution. As an indication that another point of view could exist, it is worth noting that the Third Lateran Council of 1179 called for toleration of the Jews "on grounds of humanity alone", *"pro sola humanitate"*.

Anti-Semitic feeling for a long time remained largely confined to the lower levels of the population, the underdogs of town and country. It was the preaching of the Mendicants and of other religions that spread the infection, particularly in the towns. The failure of Christianity to cure the peoples of Europe of their deep-seated hatreds and anxieties, in itself perhaps the most momentous fact about Europe's inner history during these avowedly Christian centuries, weighted the odds still further against the Jews. Popular tension was all the more dangerous for being wedded to ignorance: every abortion, animal or human, every fatal accident to a child, every famine and epidemic, was presumed to be the work of an evil-doer. Until they had been eliminated the Jews were the obvious culprits; afterwards it was women, witches. Many Jewish communities were massacred in the aftermath of the great pestilence which struck Europe from 1348–50.

There is no space here to give an adequate account of the sufferings of the Jews from the twelfth century onwards, but the graph of persecution can be roughly sketched. It started in the towns of France and the Rhineland, where entire communities were put to death, singing Psalms as their synagogues burned over their heads. Suspected Jews resorted to suicide; married and betrothed couples killed one another, as the last office of their love; mothers murdered their children. Measured in terms of duration, magnitude and conscious suffering there is nothing in the history of Europe, or even of the world, to compare with the martyrdom of the Jews of medieval Europe. Non-Jewish and Christian historians should feel it their solemn duty to put the facts on record.

The internal history of Europe was much influenced by the chain of migrations set in motion by persecution. Jews in southern Spain escaped northwards (to Castile, where they knew they had friends), fleeing before the fanaticism of North African Muslims at the time of the Almoha and Almoravid invasions. Jews who migrated from Provence into France and Italy brought the Jewish intellectual renaissance with them. The great eastward migration began after the First Crusade, when German and Central European Jews fled into Poland, Bohemia, Moravia, Silesia and Hungary. This West-East migration ran parallel with German movement in the same direction. Germans and Jews both moved East simultaneously, and Poland became known as "a colony of German Jews". English Jews fled from England to France, Germany, Spain and Italy. Jews from France went to Italy, Spain, Jerusalem, and the Islamic lands. Jews left Germany for France, Spain, Poland and Italy. This constant migration did much to create that mobility so characteristic of medieval society. Even when they were not fleeing from oppression the Jews were constantly on the move, impelled by a variety of motives. Consider the itinerary of Abraham Judaeus (Ibn Ezra), born *circa* 1090 at Toledo. In 1140 he was in Rome, in 1141 at Salerno, in 1145 at Verona, in 1148 at Lucca, in 1156 at Beziers, in 1158 in London, in 1160 at Narbonne, and he probably died at Calahorra in 1167. A distinguished translator from Arabic into Hebrew, Abraham Judaeus was one of the greatest of medieval commentators on the Bible, and a forerunner of modern biblical criticism; his work was much admired by Spinoza. Abraham's fellow-countryman Pedro Alfonso, who died in 1110, was personal physician to Alfonso VI of Castile; a convert to Christianity, he later became court physician to Henry I of England. The more than thirty tales attributed to his pen were translated into many languages and were drawn on as plot material by Chaucer, Shakespeare and other European writers. Two important twelfth century travellers, Benjamin of Tudela and

Petahiah of Regensburg, have left accounts of their journeyings through Europe and the Near East.

There is a close internal correspondence to be observed between Jewish thought and belief and Christian philosophy and theology. At first the Jews were often a couple of generations in advance of the Christians, as when in the twelfth century they helped to make the cultural achievement of antiquity and the Arabs available to the West. In the thirteenth century Jewish thinking and piety expressed themselves in ways similar to those of contemporary Christianity, scholasticism, orthodox theology and mysticism. Finally, with the decline of Jewish communities in Spain and Germany in the fourteenth and fifteenth centuries, Judaism showed symptoms of rigidity remarkably similar to those afflicting Christian thinking. The Jews now entrenched themselves within a narrowly exclusive orthodoxy which neither recognized nor wanted to recognize the existence of windows to the world outside. In France and Spain in the thirteenth century there were internal disputes within the Synagogue over the orthodoxy of the philosophers of the "enlightenment", the followers of Maimonides, which were the counterpart of contemporary disputes within the Church.

In the twelfth century, it was in Islamic Spain that Jewish poetry and philosophical and religious speculation reached their apogee. From there this Golden Age spread its benign influence into Provence, and the liturgical and intellectual life of European Jewry has continued to draw nourishment from it ever since. In this corner of Europe two Jewish writers of the eleventh century had already marked out the path of future development, the neo-Platonist Ibn Gabirol (called Avencebrol by Latin writers) and Ibn Pakuda, the title of whose book *Guide to the Duties of the Heart* sums up his approach. There is evidence of a religious and spiritual awakening. Two poets, Moses Ibn Ezra and Jehuda Halevy, gave arresting expression to the particular experience of their own people, their sense of grief and of greatness. "Israel is to other peoples as the heart is to other parts of the body; it suffers for the whole and is more acutely pierced by grief than any other member. It was not for nothing that God spake unto Israel 'I have known thee among the nations; therefore will I seek thee above all others'."

This passage is an explicit statement of one of the fundamental motifs of Jewish thought, which has had its effect both on Jewish intellectualism and, often concealed, on Jewish wit and irony. This Jewish sense of suffering was quite un-paralleled in Europe. The passion of the Jews was continuous and contemporary, they experienced in all its enormity the suffering prepared by man for man. "Why?" they asked—and the cry arose both from the torments of those led like beasts to the sacrifice and from the reflections of philosophers —"Why does God inflict such suffering upon us? Why does He allow such wickedness against Himself, against His Chosen People?" Great Jewish poetry was born out of this suffering, in Spain and above all in Germany. Vernacular poetry frequently has its roots in suffering: one has only to think of the poetry of the Franciscan Jacopone da Todi, the despairing poetry of Walther von der Vogelweide, with its lament for the misery of the Empire, the Church, the entire world "where injustice stalks the streets", and the elegiac poetry of the German-Jewish poets of the twelfth and thirteenth centuries at once falls into place.

Some basic features of the German mentality are charac-teristically reflected in the life of German Jewry. The German Jews contributed to Jewish culture and spirituality an intense experience of suffering, and a rigid and narrow-minded Talmudism (with martyrs ready to leap to its defence); this last produced its own reaction, a quietistic mysticism. In the fourteenth century German Rabbis who had gone to southern France and Spain are found taking the side of law and order against the more liberal spirituality of the disciples of Maimonides.

Maimonides, Rabbi Moses ben Maimon, "the second Moses", born in Cordoba in 1135, died in Cairo in 1204, stands pre-eminent among Jewish philosophers and liberal thinkers. He is significant both as an influence on European philosophy, a man who left his mark on generations of thinkers from Aquinas down to Spinoza and Kant, and as a stumbling-block to Jewish Orthodoxy, still an ambiguous figure, stationed at the parting of the ways. Born into a medical family, he was himself a doctor, a believer in em-pirical methods, and at the same time a philosopher and the-ologian. His personality contained two equally vital strains: a serene intellectualism based on Aristotle and the thought of his own Arab contemporaries and compatriots (Aver-roes also came from Cordoba), and complete assurance in matters of religion. He aimed at reconciling the thought and feeling of his own people with the great traditions of classical and more recent philosophy: at gathering all reason and all piety within the hospitable bosom of the Synagogue. This openness of mind struck a responsive chord among the Jewish intellectuals who had made roots for themselves in the alien worlds of Provence and Spain. The Jews of this circle, doctors, translators, wealthy townsmen, court officials in the service of the kings of Spain, advisers of bishops, financiers to great secular lords, recognized that they had an opportunity of making a legitimate contribution, as Jews, to the whole body of scientific and philosophical thought.

These disciples of Maimonides aroused the opposition of those strongly orthodox Rabbis who wanted to preserve the integrity of Judaism by the complete exclusion of all outside influences. They even denounced adherents of Maimonides before the Inquisition, as for example at Montpellier in 1233; this marks the beginning of a universal campaign to keep Judaism pure. The publicly announced intention of the Orthodox to "destroy, burn and root out" shows a startling similarity to the outlook of Catholic heresy-hunters. Persecution only made Jewish Orthodoxy more rigid and gloomy. By the fourteenth and fifteenth centuries, when the pitiful remnant of Jewry had come to accept the restraints imposed by life in the Ghetto and by an exclusive and jealously-guarded theology, the triumph of Orthodoxy was complete.

Although this account must necessarily be brief, two interesting phenomena should not be allowed to go unnoticed. First, the tragic role of converted Jews as informers and persecutors. The annihilation of Spanish Jewry after the "Holy War", the massacre of 1391, could never have been so complete without the co-operation of the *conversi*, who, inspired by the hatred typical of renegades and the newly-converted, aimed at the wholesale conversion or extermination of all Jews.

But the traffic was by no means all in one direction, a fact often overlooked. Medieval Christians were very susceptible to the attractions of Judaism. Admittedly, there are only isolated instances of individual conversions (not infrequently of clerics, who found in the God of the Old Testament a more perfect incarnation of their own idea of God); and there is no record of the mass conversion of entire populations and peoples, such as occurred later in Eastern Europe and on one occasion in southern Italy. The constantly re-iterated warnings of Councils and Synods against the dangers arising from contact with Jews and Jewish customs must clearly have been taken seriously. The reasons for the barrier separating the Jews from their Christian environment were often those advanced by a papal legate to the Council of Breslau in 1267: "Since the Poles are a new plantation on the soil of Christendom, we must continually be on our guard lest the Christian population here, where the Christian religion has not as yet taken deep root in the hearts of believers, succumb to the influence of the counterfeit faith and evil habits of the Jews living in their midst." The rapid spread of heresy had already demonstrated clearly enough that Christian beliefs had only a very precarious hold on the souls of the masses. In 1270 (three years after the legate's speech at Breslau) three Jews were killed at Weissenberg in Alsace; two were Christians converted to Judaism, one of them "formerly a prior in a Mendicant Order".

The Jews were at once too close and too remote from their Christian neighbours. They attracted Christians by their sturdy piety and intense faith, and repelled them by being at once too archaic and too advanced. Their tribalism made them appear so very primitive—as though they had still not shaken off the dust of the desert and the burning ashes of Mount Sinai; and yet their "enlightened" doctors and educated élite were so very daring and progressive.

The sombre tones of the general picture are alleviated by one ray of light, the Statute of 1244 granted to the Jews by Duke Frederick of Austria, which became the model for similar privileges in Poland, Bohemia, Hungary and Silesia. The tradition was carried on in Austria by Duke Albert II, reviled by his enemies as "protector of the Jews", and was still a reality in the sixteenth century, when it found expression in the toleration laws of Ferdinand I and Maximilian II, a code copied in other parts of Europe, including non-Catholic countries.

The most important and most fruitful legacy of twelfth century Judaism to non-Jewish Europe was the Cabbala. This intellectual form of mysticism, whose origins are lost in remote antiquity, is first found in Provence; from there it spread to France and Spain and can be shown to have been an important influence from the early Renaissance period onwards. Humanists and speculative thinkers, including Reuchlin, Pico della Mirandola, Jacob Böhme, Fludd and others, found its attraction unusually compelling.

Expelled from England, reduced to living as self-contained communities cut off from their environment in France and Germany, the Jews still retained a large measure of freedom in Italy, and not least in Rome, where they were protected by the Popes. There was even a partial renaissance of Jewish intellectual life in Italy, stimulated no doubt by this freer atmosphere. Rome produced Immanual Romi (*circa* 1270–1335), the "medieval Heine", an admirer of Maimonides and a humorist. The chief centre of Jewish learning was Padua, where strict Talmudism, an import from Germany, was gaining ground and winning new recruits, as had formerly happened in Spain. At the other extreme Padua was also the home of the Cretan-born philosopher Elias Delmedigo (*circa* 1460–97), who taught at the university under the protection of the Republic of Venice, and was tutor to the youthful Giovanni Pico della Mirandola, Count of the Empire. The title of his little treatise *On the Value of Man* epitomizes the main theme of European humanism.

It is odd that the only two medieval Jewish personalities at all familiar to the modern public should both be women, and one wonders if this is entirely fortuitous: in England the beautiful and fictitious Jewess of *Ivanhoe*, in Germany the "Jewess of Toledo", who was a historical character, but is known only because she appears in the eponymous drama of the Austrian writer Franz Grillparzer.

The position of medieval woman is much less easily defined in general terms than that of the Jew. There was much less uniformity about her status, which varied according to class and also to some extent according to place and time. But by the close of the Middle Ages one social axiom had become firmly established and was long to remain in force: "Woman's voice is not to be heard in public." A grossly overworked saying of St Paul condemned her to keep silence in church; the law was men's law, man was the sole authority in the family, in society at large and in the state. The time was past when great women rulers, abbesses, patrons of courtly society, poets and mystics could leave a mark on their generation.

Some illustrations from French history will help to show the extent to which woman's position declined. The Merovingian era had been dominated by forceful, not to say formidable, women; Brünhilde, although the most memorable, was by no means unique. The mother of Charlemagne and Hildegard, his third wife, were women of considerable influence, while the Empress Judith, wife to Louis the Pious, his successor, was a stronger and more effective character than her husband, a worthy namesake of the great heroine of the Apocrypha. In the disorders of the succeeding centuries, when monarchy was weak and the baronage powerful, widows of apparently superhuman strength frequently fought to preserve their children's inheritance intact from the depredations of vassals and neighbours. Although a ninth century council held in the diocese of Nantes forbade women to attend political assemblies, there is evidence that in the south of France women took part in elections to the *commune,* the municipal government. From the eleventh century it seems that there was something like equality between the sexes in this region. Still later, in 1308, we hear of certain women in the Touraine who were apparently eligible to assist in the election of deputies to the assembly of estates at Tours. The town charter of Beaumont, which served as model for over five hundred small towns in Champagne and eastern France, has a regulation requiring the assent of the vendor's wife to any sale of goods or property.

There were still great ruling ladies in the France of the twelfth and thirteenth centuries. Eleanor of Aquitaine, the Empress Matilda and Blanche of Castile at once spring to mind. This period opens with the elder Matilda, wife of William the Conqueror, firmly in control of Normandy during her husband's absences in England. Then there was Ermengarde, Countess of Narbonne, who ruled her lands and her troops for fifty years and was the leader of the French royalist party in the south of France in opposition to the English—a nobly-born Joan of Arc. Ermengarde was married several times, but her husbands took no part in the government. She fought numerous wars in defence of her territories, was a patron of troubadours and a protector of the Church, and had great renown as an arbiter and judge in difficult cases of feudal law.

At the time when Philip Augustus was engaged in unifying the country under the crown, large tracts of France were governed by women—Eleanor of Aquitaine, Alix of Vergy in Burgundy, and the Countesses Marie and Blanche in Champagne, where they fostered the growth of the trade fairs and of urban settlement. Flanders, the other great centre of economic activity in north-western Europe and a much fought-over territory, was ruled by women for sixty-five years, first by Joanna and after her by her sister Margaret, who rehabilitated the country after its devastation by war.

Margaret regarded herself as the vassal of the French King and of the German Emperor in her own person, and did all in her power to promote urban independence. She was the first ruler to adopt French as the official language of her chancery. This was in 1221; it was not used at Paris until some years later, in the time of Louis IX. The growth of the vernacular languages owed much to feminine influence, as is clear enough from religious and literary sources.

Blanche of Castile impressed her personality on every department of French life in the first half of the thirteenth century. Her political contribution as regent for her son, St Louis, has already been described. She also made a significant social contribution, as protector of the Jews and champion of the poor. St Louis was persuaded by his Franciscan advisers to adopt a most unhappy policy towards the Jews, and it was during his reign that the first burnings of the Talmud took place. When some Jews came to plead their cause at the royal court in Paris they found the Queen-Mother in charge; she treated them with far more wisdom and understanding than her son in his agony of mind had been able to show. Blanche appears as protector of the poor in an anecdote told by the chronicler of St Denis, who praises her for shielding them from the cruelty of affluent clerks: the cathedral chapter of Paris had imprisoned large numbers of tenants (both dependent and free) from the villages of Orly, Chatenai and other neighbouring places because of their refusal to pay a special tax. The Queen came in person to open the doors of the prison and set free the men, women and children suffocating from the heat inside.

Blanche had a worthy successor in her daughter-in-law, Margaret of Provence, though the two had little liking for each other. A woman of great strength and courage and the mother of eleven children, Margaret made Philip, the heir to the throne, swear to remain subject to her advice until he was thirty years old.

The rise of France in the twelfth and thirteenth centuries thus owed something to the achievements of its great ladies. But then a masculine era set in; in 1317 an assembly of notables meeting in Paris under Philip V declared that women were excluded from succession to the crown. The career of Joan of Arc at the close of the Middle Ages seems to promise a return to women's former political status and prestige. Almost at once, however, she was turned into a figure with largely supernatural associations and made the subject of legend. This was characteristic of the age: what had once been sober reality was now felt to be impracticable and improper.

We have already noted the considerable positive contribution made by noble and other women to Catharism. For the first time women had been admitted to a leading role in a religious society. Women were eligible to become Perfects and were authorized to preach and to dispense the *consolamentum*. A Countess of Foix left her husband to become head of a feminine Albigensian community. The women and girls of Toulouse fought alongside their men against the masculine array of crusaders from the North led by Simon de Montfort, the epitome of brutal and ambitious manhood, who met his death under a hail of stones hurled at him by a band of women.

There had been women troubadours as well as women Perfects. Five songs have survived by the Countess Beatrix of Die, an open and unashamed expression of her love for Count Raimbaut of Orange. Other women troubadours included Beatrix's daughter Tiberga, Castellox, Clara of Anduse, Isabella of Malaspina and Marie of Ventadour. The celebrated poetess Marie de France says of herself, with proud and serene assurance, *"Marie ai nom, si sui de France"*. This simple statement, "Marie is my name and I come from France", finds its echo in the equally proud and unaffected avowal of Joan of Domrémy, who withstood the examination of some fifty crabbed theologians only to be broken by imprisonment: "My name is Joan and I came to France from Domrémy".

Around the year 1250 there were some five hundred nunneries in Germany, with a total population of between twenty-five and thirty thousand religious. Even so, it is evident that the Church had not succeeded in giving full scope to the religious energies of women. Hildegard of Bingen, who lived in the twelfth century, had already appreciated the seriousness of the situation. She held that the decadence of Church and society was chiefly caused by masculine weakness: women therefore must act where men had failed; this was the *tempus muliebre*, the era of woman. Since the clergy would not, it was left to women to go and preach against heretics and make missionary journeys up and down the Rhine and the Nahe. The Abbess Hildegard in fact had many masculine traits to her character and for a long time yet the life of the female religious would continue to be ordered along the lines laid down for men. The *Speculum Virginum*, for example, a handbook for nuns composed about 1100 and still extant in versions in Latin, Middle Low German and Swedish, has no section devoted to love, private prayer is not mentioned, nor is there any hint of concern for the soul of the individual nun. The spiritual regime prescribed is harsh and unyielding. No penance could be accepted from the fallen, though all the world knew how easy it was for young nuns to fall from grace, seduced as often as not by clerks.

Heterodox and heretical groups offered women much greater freedom and a wider field of activity. The Waldensians and Cathars, and other sects as well, encouraged women to preach and propagandize and to cultivate their own souls, both actively and passively. When these groups were suppressed—not before many women and girls had gone cheerfully to their deaths, serenely confident, inwardly set free —a number of passionately devout and spiritually awakened women sought refuge in Dominican and Franciscan convents and in Beguinages. But there they often found themselves in little better case, and their position became increasingly difficult during the thirteenth and fourteenth centuries. Men were reluctant to assume responsibility for the spiritual direction of women and evaded it wherever they could; the Church continued to distrust women who were spiritually restless, suspecting them all the time of heresy. For a brief space the omens were more propitious, when Meister Eckhart, Tauler and Suso were bringing their mysticism into the Dominican convents of Germany. They succeeded in absorbing and deflecting much of this restless yearning after personal communion with God, channelling it into forms of expression recognized by the Church; but this was a passing phase.

The increasing gloom and anxiety which spread over Europe in the later Middle Ages, when nations, churches and minorities drew further and further apart, to eye one another with mutual hostility and envy, is closely bound up with the failure to harness to the social and religious needs of the age that feminine spiritual energy which had burst forth so dramatically in the twelfth century. The embers were banked down, but they still smouldered. Cast spiritually and intellectually adrift, women were confronted with the closed ranks of a masculine society, governed by a thoroughly masculine theology and by a morality made by

men for men. The other half of humanity came into the
picture only when specifically feminine services were needed.
Aquinas's ethical system related entirely to men. He speaks
blandly of "making use of a necessary object, woman, who
is needed to preserve the species or to provide food and
drink". "Woman was created to be man's helpmeet, but
her unique role is in conception . . . since for other purposes men would be better assisted by other men." True,
some relaxation of this suspicious fear is evident in a few
thirteenth century books of penitence and in some scholastic
writers, but the great mass of homiletic literature is still
pervaded with hatred and distrust: woman is portrayed as
"sin", without qualification. The tradition is an ancient one,
going back to Augustine and the early Fathers, above all to
St Jerome, the patron saint of misogynists: "woman is
the gate of the devil, the path of wickedness, the sting of
the serpent, in a word a perilous object."

The inner schizophrenia of the waning Middle Ages is
clearly shown up in the gulf between prevailing theories
and social reality. Women, feared by monks and theologians
and disdained as the least valuable of all human material,
contributed largely by their labours to both urban and rural
economic life. Women worked in the fields and sometimes,
as among the Germans, were responsible for the entire
agricultural routine. Townswomen were active in a wide
variety of trades and industries. The women of Paris are
known to have been engaged in more than a hundred different occupations. They worked as weavers, embroiderers
and retailers; when their husbands died they carried on their
businesses with resource and courage, proving themselves
master craftsmen in their own right; they were teachers,
doctors and merchants, capable of handling the large-scale
affairs of foreign trade. In all these fields they acquitted
themselves like men. The decline of the German towns in
the late Middle Ages is bound up with the suppression of
flourishing feminine industries and the replacement of skilled
women by men, which created a large female proletariat. This
class of distressed women was much augmented by the
appalling growth of public prostitution and the moral collapse of Beguinism. We know the extent of the disproportion
between men and women in some of the larger towns during
the later Middle Ages: for every thousand men Nuremberg
had 1,207 women, Basel 1,246 and Rostock 1,295. There

was no suitable outlet for their great abilities and no satisfaction for their spiritual and intellectual yearnings.

The women who grew up in the courtly civilization of the twelfth century had learned to "sing and say", to use their minds and their imaginations, to conduct their lives and loves on a highly-civilized plane. In the later Middle Ages there are a few ecstatic figures, burning with a prophetic flame, who stand out sharply against the undifferentiated mass of oppressed women forced to accept life and men and misery as they found them: these were exceptional women by any standard, women such as Catherine of Siena, who threatened the Popes with dire penalties if they refused to return to Rome from Avignon. The Middle Ages had conspicuously failed to solve the problem of woman's place in society; it was left as a heavy mortgage on the future.

CHAPTER 14

THE NEW STATE AND THE
NEW CHURCH

THE cathedral of Palermo is the last resting-place of a man described by his contemporaries as "the terror of the earth", "the wonder-working transformer", the Emperor Frederick II. His lion-throned sarcophagus of blood-red porphyry is a monument so classical, so proud and so unapproachable that it involuntarily calls to mind Napoleon's tomb in Paris. Six medallions carved in relief bear the figures of Christ, the Virgin and the symbols of the four evangelists.

This man whose mortal remains lie buried in stone which burns like ice was condemned by Dante to suffer for his sins in Hell, in a fiery tomb among the heretics. Frederick saw himself, however, as the terrestrial incarnation of divine justice, the supreme representative of God's will in the sphere of political order. Frederick's political ideas are expressed in the Code of Laws drawn up for the Sicilian kingdom under the title he himself chose, *Liber Augustalis*. These "Constitutions" of Melfi (1231) were designed as a model for the states of the future, states constructed as works of art by exalted rulers guided by divine reason, monuments of the intellect and of adamantine political purpose. If a state was to conform to this aesthetic ideal nothing in it should be left to chance: there must be loyal public servants, a state police, a fully-formed system of justice and an army, to serve as watchdogs against internal unrest and external aggression.

The Emperor thus proclaimed to the Christian world that just as God revealed himself to the faithful as a Trinity, the Emperor manifested himself to men as absolute justice. The Emperor was the foundation of the state, just as Christ was the foundation of the Church. Men needed the Church for the salvation of their souls, the state for the preservation of human life on earth. Without the state man was nothing, since life was impossible outside the framework of law and order which the state provided. The state, indeed, was a natural phenomenon, ordained by God and necessary in nature. The state was the temple of justice, its officials were the hierophants, and the Emperor as head of the hierarchy dispensed the high mysteries of his highpriestly office. He was omnipresent and infallible. It was sacrilege even to discuss the "judgments, decisions and edicts of the Emperor".

"Passing over his other faults in silence, we affirm that the Emperor is guilty of four great crimes: he has perjured himself on many occasions, he wantonly broke the peace between himself and the Church after it had been restored, he committed sacrilege in ordering the capture of cardinals and other prelates journeying to attend the council called by our predecessor, and is justly suspected of heresy." Such was the indictment that prefaced Innocent IV's sentence of deposition on the Emperor, pronounced at the concluding session of the Council of Lyons, July 17, 1245. The actual formula of deposition ran as follows: "After careful consideration among our brothers and in this holy synod of the wickednesses of this prince, both those already named and many others, we pronounce and declare, in virtue of the power to bind and loose entrusted to us by Christ, whose representative on earth, though unworthy, we are, through the authority transmitted to us by St Peter: that this prince who by reason of his sins has proved himself unworthy of Empire and kingship as of all honour and dignity, is rejected by God as Emperor and king and is deprived by God of all honour and dignity. By this sentence we remove them from him . . . and in virtue of our apostolic authority forbid anyone henceforth to render him obedience or allegiance as Emperor or king. We decree that anyone who in future gives him counsel, help or favour shall be excommunicate without further formality. Those who have the right to elect an Emperor shall proceed without hindrance to elect a successor. We ourselves will make disposition of the kingdom of Sicily after consultation with our brethren."

The Pope and the fathers of the Council then dashed their burning candles to the flagstoned floor of the cathedral, in token that the Emperor's blaze of glory was extinguished. Thereupon all joined in a solemn *Te Deum*.

This marked a climactic moment in a conflict of universal

dimensions. To all appearance the Papacy had completely crushed its greatest and most dangerous rival, the Emperor of the Holy Roman Empire, or, to use the title given currency by sixteenth-century German humanists in imperial court circles, the Emperor of the Holy Roman Empire of the German nation. Once the Emperor had been deprived of his power and dignity and of his aura of sanctity, the way was at last clear for the rise of new young states in Western and Eastern Europe and for the Papal Church to establish itself as the "perfect society", with the Pope as overlord of all Christian princes and judge of the nations. Vigorous new growths sprang up round the corpse of the Holy Roman Empire, the new states and nations and the new Church, its hieratical organization now brought to a pitch of perfection. The old Empire and its rulers entered the realm of legend and nourished dreams of wish-fulfilment in later generations. The dismembered but still valuable *disjecta membra imperii,* the limbs of the carcass, were to be wrangled over for another five centuries among the Empire's heirs and successors.

It would be inappropriate here to trace back over the centuries and through successive changes of dynasty the earlier stages of the struggle between the Empire and the Papacy, the two supreme powers of the medieval order. But it may be helpful to touch on a few of the main trends to explain the situation as it was in the middle of the thirteenth century.

From the time of its foundation by Charlemagne the Holy Roman Empire was regarded as the supreme protector of the Church, that is of "Christendom". During the Middle Ages and even later the German people had a clear-cut picture of the roles of the two earthly upholders of the divine world order. Pope and Emperor sat enthroned in brotherly amity, both of them watching over Christendom, which meant mankind; the spiritual sword belonged to the Pope, the secular sword to the Emperor. As defender of the Church the Emperor waged God's wars on earth and was responsible for maintaining peace and justice. Individual Emperors and their adherents were convinced that this responsibility included the establishment of "right order" in Italy, "the beautiful garden of the Empire" as Dante called it, the preservation there of imperial rights, the protection of the Pope in Rome and the "reformation" of the Church whenever this seemed necessary.

The authority of the Emperor and of the Holy Roman

Empire was most effective in the tenth and early eleventh centuries under the rule of the Saxon or Ottonian Emperors, who really were the protectors, guardians and leaders of the Church and Christendom. They reformed the Church and the monasteries, made and unmade Popes, and intervened decisively in those grave conflicts which had turned the Papacy, politically enfeebled and spiritually degraded, into an object of booty wrangled over by the cliques and clans of the Roman nobility.

The very idea of "domination by barbarous Germans" over Italy and the Church filled the Italians of the thirteenth and fourteenth centuries who were zealous for Church reform with anger and dismay; the prospect seemed to promise only unmitigated oppression, and they attacked Frederick II as anti-Christ. German clerics, however, looked back on the Saxon Emperors with admiration. Frederick I and his ecclesiastical advisers made the revival of Ottonian splendour a maxim of their policy. The cathedrals and imperial palaces of the Rhineland were planned as conscious revivals of the Ottonian style.

The level of art and civilization reached during the Ottonian epoch made it the one period of European history in which the Germans could be said to have been the undisputed leaders of the world. No other country (certainly not Italy) and no other people produced anything which could compare with German art in its sense of having found favour with God and man, its assured, monumental quality, and its radiant spirituality; in architecture, building techniques, sculpture, illuminated manuscripts and religious poetry the Germans stood supreme. In view of this it is pardonable to conclude that the Holy Roman Empire, as conceived by the Germans, was no mere chimera; it was not an illusion, nor an act of *hubris* and violence, despite the contradictory assertions and behaviour of its later detractors and many of its political successors.

In the eleventh century, under the leadership of monastic reformers, a revolutionary Papacy rebelled against imperial tutelage. Gregory VII battled for "the freedom of the Church" against "worldly and carnal prelates", against "simonists" who had purchased their offices from secular lords or held them as fiefs of secular lords, and against the German king who as Emperor had "usurped" the government of Italy and the pontifical throne.

In its attempts to free itself from the leading-reins of the early Middle Ages the revolutionary Papacy found allies who later revealed themselves as enemies: the spiritually awakened masses, new monastic reformers, and even lay princes, both within the Empire and without, who saw alliance with Rome as a means of reducing the Emperor to a position where he was at most an impotent *primus inter pares*.

Roman Catholicism still bears some of the scars of the battle fought by Gregory VII and his reforming allies against the "laicization" of the Church and against Henry IV, that "unchaste king". Gregory aimed at making celibacy the rule for all the clergy: free of the "flesh", unhampered by a family and the demands of kindred and clan, a clerk could devote himself wholly to the service of God and St Peter, which meant in practice St Peter's successor, the Pope in Rome. The impact of this proclamation of a unique fatherhood was revolutionary: at a stroke all temporal fatherhood and lordship were desanctified and rendered powerless, including the specific authority of the "Lord Emperor": as *christus domini*, the Lord's anointed (in virtue of his unction and coronation), he had hitherto possessed quasi-episcopal rank and through the device of the honorary diaconate had had a seat in numerous cathedral chapters, including that of Rome, all of which had given him a secure and consecrated position within the sacerdotal hierarchy itself.

The Gregorian reformers had initiated a programme which was to be systematically extended during the twelfth and thirteenth centuries. The dismantling of the Emperor's sacerdotal powers was paralleled by the Pope's accumulation of the titles, ranks, offices and duties of the Emperor and the Empire. The Roman curia was using formulae of the imperial chancery as early as the eleventh century. The Pope assumed (or usurped) sacred vestments which surpassed the Emperor's in magnificence; and he trumped the imperial crown, that symbol of universal dominion, with the ace of the three-tiered papal tiara, abandoning in its favour the simple cap which had been the Pope's traditional headgear. The canonists now brought increasing precision to the juridical theory which was the ideological basis of Papal claims: the Roman Church was the unique legitimate successor of the Roman Empire, the Empire of ancient Rome. Only Rome, Papal Rome, could be Rome's heir. The Pope was the only lawful inheritor of the rights and authority of the Roman Emperors. He was entitled to choose who should afford him temporal assistance and bear the sword of temporal power, which meant that he was free to appoint the ruler of Germany and of all Christian principalities. It is understandable that lay princes, both within the Empire and in Europe at large, were wholly agreeable to this emasculation of imperial power and were willing to offer the Pope their assistance, so long as they were not themselves drawn into a similar conflict with the Curia over the control of their own "territorial" churches. It will also be appreciated that the Emperor resisted this development with all the resources at his disposal. An attempt at compromise was finally successful, and a concordat was reached at Worms in 1122, thanks to the legal ingenuity of a French churchman and the weariness of both parties after a struggle which had already lasted half a century. The terms were that the Emperor, as King of the Germans, was to be left a free hand in Germany proper, even in church matters, but that in Italy the Pope's primacy should be acknowledged when it came to appointing bishops, which in effect gave him control of the Church there.

Each renewed attempt at an accommodation between Emperor and Pope foundered, because both parties were driven by their conception of their task and status to make fresh inroads on each other's position; they always confronted each other in Italy, the field of battle which neither could avoid. Whenever an Emperor was strong in Germany, his thoughts always turned to the recovery of former greatness, to *renovatio imperii,* which above all else meant recovering his authority over imperial possessions in Italy, whose connection with the Empire was becoming more and more tenuous. The Popes knew that in the long run they had no chance of withstanding the military and political pressure which would be applied once the Emperor had a firm foothold in Italy. The marriage between Constance, heiress to the Norman kingdom of Sicily and southern Italy, and Henry VI, the son of the Emperor Frederick I, a hard, cunning and ruthless politician cast in the true Norman mould, offered a grave threat to the Papacy. The Hohenstaufen eagle was soaring with unerring aim to the empyrean heights of world domination, and its beating pinions cast their shadow over Rome from both North and South. All lesser lords, both lay and ecclesiastical, who dared resist its rise had reason to fear the sharpness of its talons. Rome lay helpless in the trap.

Frederick II, Henry's youthful son, had been the ward

of Pope Innocent III. Shortly before his death Innocent made Frederick promise that once he was crowned Emperor he would renounce Sicily in favour of his own infant son Henry, who should rule it with the Pope as regent. Frederick in fact had no intention of surrendering Sicily, the island kingdom where he had been brought up, and whose cosmopolitan society of Saracens, Greeks and Normans and distinguished élite of professional administrators and technologists was admirably suited to his purpose. Sicily, with its Norman administrative system as a foundation, was the one place where Frederick could build up his ideal state of the future: a fool-proof state, governed and regulated by officials, experts, judges, policemen and a highly-developed system of taxes, and whose material wealth would be exploited to the full. On the mainland of Italy, where Frederick was hemmed in by powerful city-states and the lordships of his allies and adversaries, there was little room for experiment. In Germany, where the lay and ecclesiastical princes had gained the initiative, there seemed no room to build up a direct imperial lordship. It was not until the last years of his reign that such a chance presented itself in the eastern part of the *Reich,* when the last Babenberg duke of Austria died. Frederick planned to create an Austrian kingdom which would combine with the old Hohenstaufen territories to form a bastion of independent power in the south-eastern part of his Empire, stretching from Alsace across south-west Germany via Eger to Vienna. It was in precisely this region that the Hapsburgs started building up their power some thirty years later.

Excommunicated, outlawed—killing Frederick was not merely permissible but a Christian duty—proclaimed as anti-Christ by papal emissaries up and down Italy, battling his way from one place to the next, harried by traitors and would-be assassins, often defeated, briefly victorious, the Emperor died exhausted in 1250. This was the end of an epoch in world history. In Germany the Holy Empire collapsed in a welter of civil war: the time of terror had come, the "age without an Emperor".

Conradin, Frederick's grandson and the last of the Hohenstaufen, met his death by execution in 1268. The sentence was carried out in the market-place of Naples, where Frederick II had founded his imperial "anti-papal" university, to be a centre of "enlightenment" and an advanced training school for administrators from all over Europe. Conradin, attempting to recover his Sicilian inheritance, had fallen into the hands of the kingdom's new master, Charles of Anjou. The papal party in Italy was jubilant: the last of the eaglets had been blotted out and the devil's brood exterminated.

The public execution of the last of the Hohenstaufen in the market-place of Naples was a revolutionary event, without precedent in the history of Europe; until it had happened anyone would have said it was unthinkable. In terms of "the logic of history" it may seem the "right" conclusion to the papal revolt against the Emperor. It was only papal approval and the tenor of papal propaganda over the past two centuries that made the deed possible. The Popes, by diminishing the status of imperial descent, had prepared the scaffold for future princes of noble birth (or of "divine descent", according to popular belief): for the execution of Charles I and Louis XVI. It was fruitless for Popes of more modern times, from the sixteenth to the nineteenth centuries, to set themselves up as the sworn allies of "Christian princes" in the task of crushing "infamous rebellions" instigated by heretics and "the scum of society"; it was fruitless for papal ideologists to try to breathe fresh life and meaning into post-revolutionary attempts at restoration. The Papacy had encompassed the destruction of the Empire only by a revolutionary breach of the continuity of European history; the transformation of the popular image of the Christian monarch from a sacred and sacrosanct figure into a diabolical object of execration had called for the most blatant techniques of propaganda and political manoeuvring. Scarcely a generation elapsed after the execution of Conradin before the Pope was forced to pay the first instalment of the penalty for having degraded and dishallowed the highest office in Christendom apart from his own. In 1303 Boniface VIII was taken prisoner at Anagni by William of Nogaret, Councillor to Philip IV of France. Subjected to all manner of ignominy, the Pope's pride and self-confidence were mortally wounded and he died in Rome only a few weeks after his release.

Only a short time before Boniface had excommunicated the King of France. This "splendid autocrat" (as Previté-Orton described him) had attempted to take over the role assumed a century earlier by Innocent III as overlord of all Christian princes and arbiter of the nations. Long before he became Pope, Boniface had been convinced that the papal mission was to lead mankind, the whole of mankind, to God. In his great Bulls (*Clericis Laicos, Ausculta Fili,* and above all *Unam Sanctam*) he proclaimed to the world his sacred conviction that the laity were subject to the clergy, that the Pope had the right to command Christian kings and was supreme judge over them, and that all Christians owed him political and religious obedience. The Bull *Unam Sanctam* could be described as a programme of universal domination; it was never amended from the papal side until the late nineteenth century, in the time of Leo XIII.

Boniface, a highly-trained jurist, commanded an organization capable of making mass propaganda and staging spectacular attractions. The invention of the Jubilee Year, proclaimed in 1300, provided an excuse for bringing all Christendom to his feet in Rome, a spectacle which satisfied his own inner yearnings. The decrees of indulgence proclaimed for the Holy Year attracted the common folk to Rome in their thousands. Mass demonstrations of this kind are usually thought to be a phenomenon of a later period of European history, but this assembling of the people at Rome is perhaps the first example of the manipulation of the masses for a political end, in this case the demonstration of the power of the papal theocracy and the full authority of papal rule over all Christian people.

The invention and staging of the Holy Year throw into relief some other features of this "new Church" of the "new age". This was a Church in which the lay masses were strictly controlled by the clergy; it was centred on Rome, it was absolutist in tendency, governed by Canon Law and moulded by the exigencies of litigation and finance. The organization of the Holy Year was itself a financial operation of some magnitude. This vast extension of the Church's activity on the material plane went hand in hand with other manifestations which reveal just how false, anachronistic and altogether unreal was the whole image of the Church as it moved into its new age in the later medieval and early modern periods.

Proceedings were opened against Boniface in France in 1303, and Philip's legal advisers prolonged them over the next ten years, in fact long after the accused was dead. The deposition of the Pope was demanded on grounds of heresy. The prosecutors included French prelates and crown lawyers, always ready to curry favour with the king, and the Cardinals of the Colonna family, implacably hostile to Boniface. The supporting "evidence" they produced is of little interest today. What is interesting is the historical situation in which such proceedings were even possible. Boniface, who fancied himself as a realist, had completely overlooked the substantial transformation in the religious and political climate which had occurred since the time of Innocent III: new states, France and England, were emerging in the West, and they were not at all disposed to surrender control over "their" territorial churches to Rome. The people, when they looked towards Rome, felt disillusioned and cheated; Rome's misfortunes were a matter of indifference, malicious pleasure, or even positive distaste, evoking only anger or sorrow. We can now see that a highly significant process was at work. The Church was out of step with the times, and was continually at odds with the new states of the West. The Church of the later Middle Ages was becoming completely institutionalized and completely clerical: the laity were regarded as little more than serfs, as slaves even, "instruments" whose function was to yield willing obedience. (It is interesting that this word "instrument", used by Aristotle with reference to slaves, is still retained, for example by Catholic Action, to describe the distinctive role of the laity.)

While the Popes were finding it in practice increasingly difficult, even impossible, to coerce the rising nation states into recognition of papal rights and claims, canon lawyers and other papal theorists were redoubling the Pope's claim to possess "fullness of power" over the Church and all Christendom. This *plenitudo potestatis* made him the fountain of law and justice, whose secrets were locked in his own bosom, *"omne jus in scrinio sui pectoris habet"*. "He rules and disposes all things, orders and governs everything as he pleases. . . . He can deprive anyone of his right, as it pleases him . . . for with him his will is right and reason; whatever pleases him has the force of law." This account of the Pope's *plenitudo potestatis* was written in 1332 by a Spanish Franciscan, Alvarez Pelayo. Another tract emanating from curial circles at much the same date ridicules the Emperor for his impotence: "it is said that the Emperor possesses all things; but in reality he possesses virtually nothing."

But much the same could be said of the Popes. When steel struck on steel, as in the struggle between the Popes and the monarchs of the West, particularly the kings of France and England, it became appallingly evident how little real power the Pope possessed, except when he could play one prince off against another.

It is not difficult for us to pick out the weaknesses and self-delusions in the personality of Boniface VIII, whose pontificate was such a decisive turning-point in the history of the medieval Church. It is more difficult to recognize in him the traits of greatness, of inner strength and of courage (which was not merely a matter of pride). These traits only become obvious when we are bold enough to admit that many of the anachronistic features of Boniface's policy and outlook are already to be found in the pontificate of the man who is commonly regarded as representing the highest point of achievement reached by the medieval papacy and as the greatest Pope of his age: Innocent III.

Innocent, while admitting that the Pope was inferior to God, nevertheless held that he was something more than man: God spoke and acted through the Pope, hence whatever the Pope proclaimed as law was divine law. The Pope interpreted the will of God. In political terms this meant that Innocent saw himself as the one true *Imperator;* the superior of kings and Emperor, he had the right to arbitrate in all important disputes between the peoples. In ecclesiastical terms this meant that bishops were subject to the Pope and had no autonomous power, that they were papal officials; through his legates the Pope could intervene in the Church government of the various countries.

Many of Innocent's much-lauded triumphs (still much admired) can be shown to have been precarious, accidental or empty, while other policies he initiated were to prove disastrous for the Church and Christendom as their effect became plain over the centuries. For example, the Pope saw himself as the head of a league of Christian states. True, a number of weak kings and pretenders owed their crowns to him and declared themselves his vassals to gain a political advantage. The rulers of Portugal, Aragon, Poland, Hungary, Galicia and Lodomeria, Serbia, Croatia and Bulgaria were all indebted to him in this way. But these were momentary and vulnerable successes. Innocent's intervention in English affairs shows how seriously he could overreach himself. Although he could force John to receive back England as a papal fief, his opposition to Magna Carta was quite unavailing. His meddling in the affairs of France and Germany only aroused implacable hostility, expressed in the political songs of Walther von der Vogelweide and long nursed in France, whose thirteenth and fourteenth century kings revenged themselves by their anti-papal policy for the interdicts and excommunications and other coercive measures heaped on their predecessors in time of weakness. Innocent's cherished project, the Fourth Crusade, met with complete disaster; he was responsible for the barrage of propaganda which accompanied its launching and for its finances, but completely lost control of its direction, since he could not lead it in person, though many of his contemporaries pleaded that he should. The sack of Constantinople and the conquest of the Byzantine Empire aroused the undying hatred of the Greeks and the Eastern Church. No less disastrous was the injury inflicted on Western Europe by the Albigensian Crusade and the subsequent extermination of Provençal culture. Admittedly, the Fourth Lateran Council of 1215 brought a moment of triumph. But it was also the occasion on which Innocent publicly acknowledged the weakness and corruption within the Church, the venality of the bishops, the illiteracy of the clergy and the impiety of the laity.

The key to the Pope's steadfast urging of his absolutist claims may be found in the title of one of Innocent's best-known works, *De Contemptu Mundi*. Although Innocent's successors were not all his equal as personalities, they shared his pessimistic view of man as a creature so debilitated by sin that his salvation could be achieved only by coercion; unless they submitted to that perfect government which the Church alone could offer, the masses were doomed to damnation. The Church was the world's supreme court, *ecclesia judiatrix*, the judge of kings, nations and individuals. The comforting image of Mother Church, indulgent of her children's whims and aberrations, was receding, to be replaced by the forbidding figure of a prosecuting tribunal made up of lawyers and financiers.

Admittedly, theologians like Godfrey of Fontaines and Augustinus Triumphus of Ancona (both died early in the fourteenth century) could still debate the question whether the Church was better governed by a lawyer or a theologian and decide in favour of the latter. But during the thirteenth and fourteenth centuries the Papacy was being remorselessly turned over to the lawyers, and the Church as a whole was declining into a state of "canonist petrifaction", to use an expression coined by Heimpel, one of the greatest authorities on the later Middle Ages. It became generally accepted that the leadership of the Church was best entrusted to lawyers, preferably those learned in both Canon and Roman Law, to administrative officials, and most important of all, to men with a talent for finance.

Throughout the thirteenth and fourteenth centuries canon lawyers were bringing further refinement to the doctrine of the fullness of papal power, on which the Pope based his claim to be the Church's ruler and law-giver. Clerks of all nations were involved, though the leading canon lawyers were mainly Italians, Spaniards and Englishmen: Boniface VIII relied on the authority of Alanus the Englishman and English canon lawyers and jurists were prominent at Rome in his time. "The Pope can do whatever God can do." As the "Emperor sent by heaven", *coelestis imperator*, the Pope could absolve men from binding oaths and depose kings and emperors. Heresy was *lèse-majesté* and resistance to papal policies, whether political or religious, was heresy and rebellion. The "rebels" were excommunicated and papal armies sent to do battle with them. It was on this pretext that papal troops fought in and for Italy.

During the fourteenth century the Popes entrenched themselves within the massive and uncompromising walls, several feet thick, of their fortified palace on the chalk cliffs above the Rhône at Avignon. Philip the Fair of France, victor over Boniface VIII, was mainly responsible for this removal, which took place in 1309, and Avignon remained the seat of the Curia until 1377. There were contributory influences from the papal side: the Pope's anxiety over the trial of his predecessor, which was still in progress with the object of unmasking Boniface as a heretic, and his hope of quashing the scandalous proceedings initiated by the French king against the Templars.

Here at Avignon the Papal Church put on the armour of stone walls, whose chilly angularity symbolized the triumph of undeviating correctness and of overweening dominion. But this was all external. In the great hall within, lightness and luxury abounded. The frescoes and tapestries which contributed to this effect have now almost vanished, with the exception of the graceful and delicate sylvan frescoes adorning the Pope's robing room in the Tour de la Garde-Robe: with their frankly sensuous portrayal of earthly pleasures, they remain as witness that the hard outer shell concealed a soft centre.

St Bridget of Sweden had a vision of Avignon in which it was revealed to her as a "field of tares". "It must first be weeded with an iron hoe, then purified by fire and finally smoothed again with the plough." The "tares" were pride, envy, ambition, lust and simony; everything at Avignon had its price. Other contemporary writers describe Avignon in the most opprobrious terms. It was a "sink of iniquity", Hell, Babylon.

The streets of medieval Avignon, squatting beneath the papal residence which was palace and fortress in one, were narrow and filthy. The stench was such as to cause at least one foreigner, an ambassador from Aragon, to swoon. Rents were high, accommodation limited (few houses had more than one storey) and the city thronged with people: petitioners, envoys, money-changers (by 1327 there were already forty-three Italian money-changers in Avignon), notaries, lawyers, officials of the Curia and of other European courts, craftsmen, painters, builders, and a host of adventurers— thieves, money-lenders, prostitutes, astrologers, sorcerers, necromancers and men taken prisoner. The papal administration was growing at a prodigious rate and provided employment for a large staff. One of the main departments was the *camera apostolica*, under its director the *camerarius*, who was always a cardinal; as the Pope's finance minister and most intimate adviser, he was the most important personage of the Curia. The *camerarius* had under his control the secretaries who conducted political correspondence, the treasurer, and the papal mint, in fact the whole financial apparatus in all its ramifications.

Another important department was the chancery, made up of seven distinct offices, all under the direction of a vice-chancellor. Yet another department was that of justice, which in the last resort was directly under the control of the Pope and cardinals in Consistory, though there were occasional courts presided over by cardinals and a series of inferior courts. The energies of the Church were increasingly concentrated on litigation and raising money. The upkeep of the court and its army of officials, together with the wars in Italy (which dragged on throughout the fourteenth century), ate up huge sums of money. It was essential to find and build up new sources of income to replace the crusading tithes formerly paid to finance those wars officially designated as Crusades and which most states now refused to pay. Supplying this financial need presented no problem to a centralizing Church, and taxation and centralization marched forward hand in hand. Anyone who needed anything from the Church had to pay for it, and go to the Curia to do so. Bishops and other high church dignitaries had to pay *servitia* on appointment to their offices; churches and abbeys had to pay a tax for recognition; every document and privilege cost something; annates, the first year's income from a benefice, was a further new source of revenue; however, the clerical tax known as "tenths" often had to be shared with the lay ruler of the country concerned. John XXII was the chief architect of this comprehensive system. Chroniclers of many nations, Italian, German, English and French, not to mention Petrarch and Dante, were loud in their complaints over this financial machine, and the harshness with which it was operated aroused general hostility. Anyone who failed to pay was excommunicated. On July 5, 1328, for example, there was a mass excommunication on these grounds of a patriarch, five archbishops, thirty bishops and forty-six abbots.

The men at the head of the papal bureaucracy were largely French in origin. Of the 134 cardinals created by the Avignon Popes, thirteen were Italian, five Spanish, two English, one was a native of Geneva, and the remaining 113 were French. There was thus not a single German among them. The exclusion of Germans dated from the time of Gregory IX, and was only brought to an end under the stress of the Great Schism, when Urban needed the help of the Emperor. The Avignon papacy, generally suspected of being anti-German and pro-French, sowed some of the seeds which were to germinate in the German and English Reformations.

As individuals the Avignon Popes were often more attractive than their reputation allows. The first of them, Clement V (1305–14), formerly Archbishop of Bordeaux, was a man of culture and learning; he ordered the institution of chairs in Hebrew, Syriac and Arabic at Paris, Bologna, Oxford and Salamanca, and his friends included doctors of medicine and some early humanists. But he was dogged by ill-health and incapable of meeting the political challenge presented by so formidable an adversary and master as Philip the Fair; it was he who moved the Papacy to Avignon. His successor, John XXII (1316–34), who came of a wealthy bourgeois family from Cahors in Provence, made the Curia the world's leading financial power. Reserved, avaricious and irascible in his personal character, in his policy John showed himself the determined enemy of the Emperor and of heterodoxy. He excommunicated not only the Spiritual Franciscans (for their stand in the matter of poverty) but also Waldensians, Cathars and Beguines; he censured twenty-eight propositions of Meister Eckhart and sixty of Johannis Petrus Olivi. But he himself came close to heresy in the views he propounded concerning the fate of the soul after death. He set out these ideas in three sermons. The souls of the righteous, he maintained, will not enjoy the Beatific Vision of God until the time comes for the general resurrection of the body; nor will Hell have any occupants until the Last Day. This confused doctrine was a gift to the Emperor's theologians, Michael of Cesena, Ockham and Bonagratia of Bergamo, who were quick to expose the heresy of this heresy-hunting Pope. The choleric and tenacious old man (he was already seventy-two when he became Pope) half-recanted of his heresy before he died; he had been generally hated and a great nepotist.

His successor Benedict XII (1334–42) was one of his protégés and as professor at Paris and later as Bishop had helped him by writing pamphlets attacking Franciscans, Joachimites, Meister Eckhart, Ockham and Olivi. As Pope, Benedict was renowned as "the scourge of heretics"; those whom he so relentlessly persecuted, Waldensians and Albigensians, execrated him as a "devil", "the spirit of evil". A man of lowly birth, his aim as Pope was to eradicate all wickedness from the Church. His drastic measures of reform and his campaign against the Mendicant Orders (he himself was a Cistercian) brought him some partial success. Harsh and uncompromising in character, he was castigated by contemporaries for his avarice, his hardness of heart and his egotism. When he died the cardinals showed their desire to bring about a change of atmosphere at Avignon by the election as Pope of Pierre Roger, Archbishop of Rouen, an open-handed and affable *grand seigneur*, who ruled as Clement VI from 1342–52. During his pontificate the number of clerks seeking papally provided benefices rose to a hundred thousand. His court was the acknowledged centre of high society in Europe, attracting the pleasure-loving and cultured aristocracy by jousts and grand parties; his three immediate successors were all to complain of his inroads on the papal treasury. Clement VI was also a patron of learning and the arts; in some ways he foreshadows the Popes of the Renaissance, for he gathered round him painters from Germany and Italy, poets and architects from France, and physicians and scientists from all over Europe. But if he was open-minded he was also open-handed; during the peak period of the Black Death he dispensed charity on a grand scale. Under Innocent VI (1352–62), the wind shifted to a different quarter. The new Pope had been an Inquisitor, a remorseless persecutor of Spiritual Franciscans.

In the early years of the fourteenth century Pierre Dubois, one of Philip the Fair's propagandists, wrote: "It would be salutary for the whole world to submit to France, for the French make better use of the power of rational judgment than do any other people." Dubois argued in favour of a European federation under the hegemony of France. For him the supremacy of France was equivalent to the supremacy of political reason; and to France had fallen the task of diminishing the pretensions of the Holy Roman Empire and the papalized Church. Dubois describes the Empire as German, not Roman, and the Church as the *secta catholicorum*. He thus robs the two great powers of their old and hallowed titles, a fact highly significant of the altered temper of the times. The Crusades he regarded as a means of promoting trade and colonization, of making Oriental products cheaper in the West and of securing the Mediterranean trade-routes. He had some interesting ideas for the reform of teaching and about education generally, which is seen as one of the important tasks to be undertaken by the projected federation. Dubois in fact anticipated UNESCO by some six centuries. The supremacy of the West in the world at large could be secured only by education, superior knowledge and a rationally ordered way of life. Dubois specifically mentions the education of women as being something in need of attention.

Secta catholicorum: Dubois' casual use of this expression simply put into words an idea which had long been held as axiomatic by politicians and officials, not excluding ecclesiastics, who served the state in France and England. The "Church" meant on the one hand the Curia, with which one must continually bargain or quarrel, particularly over the steepness of its financial demands (though there was always the chance of keeping the lion's share for oneself). But the "Church" also meant the church and clergy in one's own country, slowly but surely becoming subject to the political authority of the national monarch. The centralized, bureaucratic autocratic administration characteristic of the Curia at this period was being duplicated in France, where the royal bureaucrats were "making the Civil Law their gospel". In the light of what was happening in France and England, the apparently aggressive papal policies and the ideological propaganda which went with them should be seen as a defensive reflex. Rome and Avignon adopted the maxim that attack was the best form of defence in order to maintain the *status quo*. But it was becoming increasingly difficult for the towering façade of papal and curial claims to conceal the harsh realities of political events. The kings continually gained ground at the expense of the Pope, building up their new states with the help of a corps of officials, in France known as the *chevaliers du roi*, drawn from the petty aristocracy and the bourgeoisie.

The astonishing rise of France, however, was the direct achievement of its kings. In this they were much assisted by the belief in monarchy prevalent among the people. At the beginning of the twelfth century the monarchy was still weak, maintaining itself only with difficulty in its own immediate domain, the Ile de France (the region around Paris). As early as 1124, however, the vigour of French resistance to a German invasion reveals the existence of deeply-rooted national feelings. This patriotism was fostered by Suger of St Denis, chancellor and chief counsellor to Louis VI. Aegidius of Corbeil (1140–1224?) could already sing the praises of France as "the only land which makes men human: all barbarous lands should suck thy nectar, all need thy salt and thy sweetness". This sense of cultural superiority was soon matched by a growing pride in national identity. This emerges from some remarks addressed by Louis VII to an envoy of his rival Henry II, who far exceeded him in splendour and power and was in possession of a large part of France. "The Emperor of Byzantium and King of Sicily pride themselves on their gold and silken raiment . . . Your master, the King of England, wants for nothing. He has experienced soldiers, horses, gold, silks, jewels, choice fruits, game worth the hunting, and everything the heart could wish [the order in which these luxuries appear in the list is revealing!]. In France things are different. We have only our bread, our wine, and our simple pleasures."

Louis VII was a man of reserve and circumspection. His favourite pastime after his day's work was to play chess; as he grew older it became his habit to take his meals in the monks' refectory. Patient by nature, he knew he could wait for time to carry away his rivals and enemies, until the rich lands of western and southern France fell into his lap like ripe fruit. To recover the whole of France for the monarchy was the work of centuries. But it was always worth making minor advances here and there, particularly in the region closest to the royal domain, by a process of patient manoeuvring on a small scale: a few great lords would submit, lands might fall in on the death of a vassal, and the king could make himself loved as the protector of clergy and people. Three great kings built up the French state in the course of a century: Philip Augustus (1180–1223), Louis IX (St Louis) (1226–70) and Philip the Fair (1285–1314). They all consciously fostered popular confidence in kingship, which Suger had already made the ideological basis of his policy. The "most Christian king of France", anointed with the holy oil of St Rémy, was the authentic successor of Charlemagne, whose sacred sword and standard, the oriflamme, he bore with him into battle against the "barbarian" enemies of God and the Church. The Church in France, Rome's "eldest and most obedient daughter", remained loyal to the King, who upheld peace and justice and healed the sick by his thaumaturgic power (a king crowned and anointed at Rheims could heal scrofula—confirmed royalists confidently expected the restored Bourbon king to do the same after the defeat of Napoleon), who protected the weak, sheltered the persecuted and forgave the poor their debts.

The fact that one of the kings instrumental in the rise of France was also a saint was a tremendous advantage, demonstrating to the world that the people's belief in their monarchy was no idle fancy but a well-grounded act of faith, justified by historical events. This faith was to be rekindled later by Joan of Arc at a critical stage of the Hundred Years' War, when France seemed on the verge of ruin.

Alongside this belief in the monarchy there emerged what might be described as a peculiarly French trait, the habit of applying reason to politics: in some individuals faith and reason mingled. This rationalization was the specific contribution of the royal officials, loyal servants of their master. The administration of the nascent state developed from methods used in the administration of the crown estates on the royal domain and in the dispensing of royal justice. Crown estates previously administered by hereditary provosts were placed under the control of officials appointed by the Crown, the *baillis* (south of the Loire they were called seneschals), who, as "arms of the king", kept watch over the greater vassals and were in immediate control of the lesser vassals of their bailiwicks. The financial administration was centred on the king's chamber, justice was dispensed in the king's courts, where the all-important lawyers gathered to discover and administer the law in the name of the king as a royal prerogative. From the time of Louis IX the highest royal court was the *Parlement,* settled permanently at Paris. The operation of the Treasury was entrusted to Italians, Lombards or Florentines; as foreigners they were entirely dependent on the king's goodwill. The Church was completely subordinate to the Crown and in fact thoroughly "gallicanized", long before this state of affairs was made plain to the world by the attacks on the papal Curia launched by the University of Paris and the French king.

During the last quarter of the thirteenth century the basis of royal authority was radically transformed by the introduction of the Roman Law concept of sovereignty. The state had hitherto been regarded as the private possession of the king; now, however, royal authority was seen as something abstract and impersonal. The modern state had arrived. Crown lawyers trained in the school of Montpellier, together with other officials with a legal education, formed the nucleus of an administrative corps which increasingly took over the responsibilities of government. The king as an individual receded into the background. As time went on more and more of these officials were drawn from bourgeois circles, from the affluent, thrifty, educated bourgeoisie of Paris, anti-clerical and strongly royalist. They were an invaluable support to the monarchy. Philip Augustus foreshadowed this development when on his departure for the Crusade he entrusted his last testament to the custody of the city of Paris and appointed six burgesses to act jointly with his council in safeguarding the economic interests of the kingdom during his absence.

Philip the Fair was perhaps the first French monarch to dissociate himself from the day-to-day running of the country's business. His most audacious actions—the attack on Boniface VIII, the liquidation of the Templars (a most shameful affair motivated by the king's financial needs), and the removal of the Papacy to Avignon—were successfully carried through because he had the nation and the state at his back: solid ranks of lawyers, officials and bishops, and behind them the mass of the people. He was the first king to summon the *Etats généraux* as an assembly representative of the clergy, the nobility and the bourgeoisie. In form this body resembled the English Model Parliament of 1295. But the Estates General of France differed essentially from its English counterpart. It was the organ of royal policy, providing the king with cover and support in his conflict with the

Pope and the Templars and, later on, with money to defray the expenses of the Flemish wars.

It was in royalist, bourgeois, anti-papal Paris that John of Jandun and Marsilius of Padua collaborated, between 1324 and 1326, in writing the *Defensor Pacis*. The setting was appropriate; it was at Paris that the intoxicating idea of using man's reason to create a rational society was beginning to take shape, among officials, professors and townsmen. The *Defensor Pacis* was the most extreme, the most pregnant, of all attacks yet launched on the Pope's claim to supremacy; it also set out arguments in favour of a purely secular state.

John of Jandun taught at Paris at much the same time as Meister Eckhart; a thorough-going Averroist, he made a a sharp distinction between faith and reason, theology and knowledge, Church and State. John assigned a subordinate status to theology, and advised believers to abandon their efforts at reconciling faith and reason, which only exposed the inferiority of faith. He shared Marsilius's view that the political independence of the Church should be brought to an end in the interests of social harmony. The promotion of "the good life" was the concern of the state.

Marsilius of Padua, physician, lawyer, philosopher of the Averroist school, and like so many of his Italian compatriots a passionate opponent of the Papacy, was described by Pope Clement VI as the "greatest heretic of the age". Marsilius saw the state as a creation of human reason and human will. No reliance could be placed in the laws of religion, with their talk of "truth" and "falsehood". The state must be based on pure reason and rationality. The highest authority reposed in the state itself, and within the state it was the "people" who ruled; and among the people the more reasonable part should govern. All legislative power resided in the people, and princes could be deposed by them. The people should protect the persecuted: Marsilius claimed complete liberty of conscience and worship as a right and wanted to see "heretics" and unbelievers defended from any form of coercion. Marsilius's ideas for reforming the Church ran directly counter to the policies and practices of Avignon and the Papal Church, and amounted almost to a return to primitive Christianity. For Marsilius Christ's gospel was a gospel of freedom. The people should take the Church into their own hands, elect priests and bishops and lead the Papal Church back to the way of apostolic poverty. The canonists' theory of papal overlordship was the product of *hubris* and fantasy. The clergy should be kept strictly to their sacerdotal functions, the dispensing of the sacraments and the celebration of the liturgy; everything "secular" was a matter for the state and the people.

An English translation made in 1535 of the first printed edition in Latin of the *Defensor Pacis* (published in 1522) had some influence on England's breach with Rome. The development of England in the Middle Ages was largely determined by her continuous warfare on two fronts, against Rome and against the French (a battle fought out on French soil). On two occasions, in the twelfth century with the establishment of the Angevin Empire and again with the Hundred Years' War, it seemed that France and England would unite into one great Western Empire under the leadership of the English king. The English coronation rites, still in use, remind us of what lies at the root of royal power in England: a primitive magical belief in the king's saving power combined with the king's close and direct control over the Church.

Even in pre-conquest times there had been a close alliance between kings and bishops. Kings often took up residence in episcopal palaces, the boundaries of kingdoms and dioceses often coincided. When the king went to war he left the bishops to govern his kingdom. William the Conqueror, with the assistance of Lanfranc, his Archbishop, gained control over the Anglo-Saxon Church; once this supremacy was secure, the Norman kings looked to the Church for support and guidance, especially on matters of Anglo-Saxon tradition. Henry II greatly enhanced his royal dignity by securing the canonization of the last Anglo-Saxon king, Edward the Confessor. This example was quickly followed by Frederick Barbarossa, who in 1165 engineered a similar honour for Charlemagne, through the good offices of his puppet anti-Pope.

Henry II touched for scrofula just as the French kings did; he was "hallowed", "the Lord's anointed" (Peter of Blois calls him *sanctus*), and "King by the grace of God" (a style used continuously from 1172). Although reinforced by anointing and coronation at the hands of the Church, the king's hallowedness was something deeply rooted in primitive popular beliefs, and this helped to make the Norman kings readily acceptable to the people at large. Popular trust in monarchy as the incarnation of the nation's welfare sustained the kings of England through all manner of historical catastrophes. Henry VIII's virtually unopposed self-elevation as head of the Church of England to the complete exclusion of Rome was in line with the great tradition of English medieval monarchy, unimpaired by the efforts of powerful church leaders, native and foreign, and the weakness of certain individual kings. The unique position of the King of England rested squarely on the unshakeable confidence of his people in the office of kingship, a belief which also had the blessing of the higher and lower clergy.

Whilst still Duke of Normandy William the Conqueror had already shown himself a strict master in his own land, both of knights and of clergy. He treated England as his conquest, to be shared among his warriors. William came to England with some six thousand men, four thousand of them knights, rather less than two hundred barons, and the rest mercenaries. The vulnerable Anglo-Saxon foot-soldiers, whose weapon was the battle-axe, were weary from much recent fighting elsewhere and were finally mown down by the Norman cavalry and bowmen after a battle lasting from morning to dusk. After 1066 many Anglo-Saxon noblemen fled to Scotland; others went overseas, some even as far as Russia and a few to Byzantium, where they entered the service of the Emperor.

The new King of England had a castle built for himself in every shire; Pevensey and Hastings were the first to be built. His example was followed by the Norman baronage, who made use of their castles to defend their estates and keep their people in subjection. The new rulers of the Church, bishops of Norman birth, were energetic as the builders of austere and massive cathedrals, impressive emblems of power. The first Norman cathedral was Durham, built between 1093 and 1133.

The Anglo-Saxon population found the new regime harsh and vexatious. The "crown" attached itself to the land like a parasite, sucking up its resources. The almost unlimited power of the post-Conquest kings created fear and misgivings even among their Norman vassals, in danger of losing their fiefs by arbitrary distraint and disseisin. Henry II, who was constantly on the move, imposed his will on the country by appearing everywhere in person. Even the rear-vassals, that is, the most insignificant men of his great vassals, were bound in direct allegiance to the king, which had the effect of making the greater baronage less dangerous than might have been expected.

William the Conqueror was the most powerful feudal ruler of his time. The famous Domesday Survey, initiated by a Christmastide royal council held at Goucester in 1085, surveyed "the land, how it was peopled and by what sort of men" and is in effect a careful inventory of the kingdom's human and material resources. But even while the Norman kings were perfecting their control, the old Anglo-Saxon sense of freedom still remained alive and was not without lasting effect on the new aristocracy and the new monarchy. It is perhaps surprising that this fruitful interplay of two apparently contradictory tendencies should have been possible in a country so firmly in the grip of its Norman conquerors. From it there emerged the England of the future, a free nation, proud of its traditions and the source of those vital principles, constitutional, legal and social, which were to be the foundations of modern western democracy.

William the Conqueror had retained the Anglo-Saxon shire and borough courts, placing them under Norman control. To emphasize the legality of his position as the lawful successor of Edward the Confessor, William confirmed Anglo-Saxon customary law (the law dispensed in the local courts) and "the ancient rights and customs" of the English Crown. Two important royal rights were the levying of the Danegeld (a tax on all landed estates) and the right to enforce the King's Peace, which made all private warfare unlawful. Henry I (1100–35) appointed itinerant justices to travel through the shires and hold royal courts there. In England the man who stood at the head of the shire, the sheriff (*vice comes*), was never anything but a royal official, unlike his French counterparts, who turned their counties into dynastic principalities. The English shires thus retained their official character and made an important contribution to the development of self-government and, ultimately, to that of Parliament. Henry I established a separate department in his household to deal with finance, which, as it grew, made the Anglo-Norman kings the most considerable financial powers in Western Christendom. Twice a year, at Easter and Michaelmas, the sheriffs had to render account at the Exchequer for their receipts and disbursements. The reckoning was made on the famous chequered cloth. A record of these transactions was entered, county by county, on the Great Roll of the Pipe, the annual roll of the Exchequer accounts, one of which has survived from the time of Henry I (1130–31); from the reign of Henry II the series continues without interruption until the time of William IV, when this method of record-keeping was finally abandoned.

Henry II (1154–89) must be numbered among the most determined and far-sighted architects of royal authority in England. As ruler not only of England but also of a domain in France which stretched from the Pyrenees to the mouth of the Seine, Henry had a good knowledge of Latin and of a number of vernacular languages (Provençal, Italian, Northern French). His acquaintance with English seems to have been small, but he knew how to govern and how to calculate (in every sense). In 1166 he instituted a statistical enquiry (the *Cartae Baronum*) into knights' fees. The object was to discover which barons had enfeoffed more knights than were needed to discharge their feudal obligation of knight-service; it was discovered that there were altogether 6,500 knights' fees, although the Crown itself only claimed 5,000. In 1170, after the Inquest of Sheriffs, some of the older earls and barons who had held this office were replaced by royal officials; a revolt which occurred soon afterwards, possibly provoked by this action, was easily suppressed. Henry II was the father of the English Common Law, that is of law dispensed by the royal courts and carried up and down the country by the King's itinerant justices. Further aids to the enforcement of law were the sworn jury and the extended use of royal writs, instructions from the King to his officials to initiate proceedings and empanel juries. Every free tenant in England was entitled to seek the protection of the Common Law in defending his property against the illegal encroachments of greater lords. In 1179 we hear mention of the Grand Assize, an alternative to the older method of trial by combat; this was a jury of knights summoned to declare the facts about rights to land.

The judicial methods of the Angevin kings are an eloquent revelation of the extent to which the royal authority drew on irrational sources, of how much it relied on the royal freedom to act on impulse, arbitrarily, even ferociously, without losing the benefit of that level-headed and rational appreciation of law which the Angevins themselves contributed. This unusual and constructive combination made it possible for the king to choose between two courses: he could treat a case *mera voluntate*, in virtue of his own power and personality and according to his own will, for which he was unaccountable, or he could act *per legem*, according to the law, in his high court. After three generations, this dichotomy had induced a state of open schizophrenia, a split in the public character of the king.

This cleavage is particularly evident in the cases of Henry II and John. A contemporary, Peter of Blois, describes how Henry admitted in a conversation with the Abbot of Bonnevalle that he was torn between a desire for order, law and right and the promptings of the unruly demon in his nature which urged him to deeds of brutality and violence. Wrath and displeasure (*ira et malevolentia*) were legitimate royal traits. Fullness of power belonged only to kings capable of inspiring fear, the fear of God and the fear of wickedness. It was the wrath of God that manifested itself in the wrath and displeasure of the king. Henry II (who threw himself to the ground and bit the carpet in his rages) said on more than one occasion: "The displeasure and wrath of Almighty God are also my displeasure and wrath." "By nature I am a son of wrath: why should I not rage? God Himself rages when He is wrathful."

In the long run the English nation benefited as much from the demoniacal, self-destroying strength of its kings as it did from their deficiencies and want of self-control. Henry II, a man of immense ability, died broken and embittered in the knowledge that even John, his favourite, had joined his other sons in conspiring against him. Henry's last words, "Shame, shame, on a defeated king", ring out like a prologue to a Shakespearean History. With ruthless application Henry had built up a state in England: when John, unstable, faithless, but also immensely able, had been overthrown by his great adversaries, Philip Augustus and Innocent III, the country wrung from him the great charter of English liberties, Magna Carta. In practice, however, the "country" was a group of ruffianly and conservative barons, who in June 1215 surprised the King (perhaps actually at Runnymede) and forced important concessions from him; they were not representative of the English people in any simple meaning of the word. Similar concessions were being extorted at much the same time, or rather later in the thirteenth century, from feudal rulers in Hungary, Spain and Poland. A reactionary wind blows through Magna Carta, a document which embodies the group egotism of a hard-headed, self-seeking feudal aristocracy, who judged that the time was ripe for humiliating an already weakened monarchy and arrogating to themselves a number of its rights.

Yet when all is said, men are justified in celebrating Magna

Carta as one of the great declarations of political freedom. It was solemnly confirmed by each successive king right down to the end of the Middle Ages; it prepared the way for the constitutional monarchies and constitutional states of modern times, and even today has not lost its aura. The despatch of one of the five copies bearing the King's seal to the United States by battleship during the second world war was more than a gesture.

The clause of the Charter primarily responsible for its reputation as one of the great landmarks on England's road to self-government is that which runs "No free man shall be taken or imprisoned or deprived of his estates or outlawed or exiled or in any way impoverished, nor will we go against him or send any one against him, except through the legal judgment of his equals or the law of the land" (Clause 39). The essential fact emerging from this is that the King is under the law. Magna Carta is founded on the principle of legality: all political and constitutional decisions are judicial decisions. And the King must no longer give judgment by himself, but with the advice of the magnates of the realm and according to the law of the land. In typically English fashion, Magna Carta sets out no theories, no ideals of government; nothing could be further removed from the declarations of freedom and independence thrown up from the murk of the French Revolution. Magna Carta is concerned entirely with what is concrete. Specific rights are demanded, the freedom of the Church, the rights and privileges of London and other boroughs, protection for alien merchants and the right of the magnates to assent to taxation.

In only one place is this wholesome moderation exceeded, in the clause demanding a standing committee of twenty-five barons to control the King, with the right of organizing resistance against him if a complaint made to any four such barons claiming that the Charter has been infringed is not immediately redressed on being brought to the notice of the King or his deputy.

In actual fact no one in 1215 had any intention of abiding by the provisions of the Charter, neither the victorious barons nor the humiliated King. Innocent III condemned it in no uncertain language as an unlawful act of rebellion against a royal government. However, in the revised version promulgated in 1225, it became the foundation-stone of political and legal order in England, and was frequently confirmed in the course of the next three centuries.

The thirteenth century saw the rise of the English Parliament and the final transformation of England from a feudal kingdom into a "community of communities", under the rule of the greatest of English medieval kings, Edward I (1272–1307). His predecessor Henry III (1216–72) spent a considerable part of his reign under tutelage: between 1216–27 as a minor, and at various times between 1258 and 1265. During the time when he conducted affairs himself he clashed with the magnates and came out the loser; Henry's preference was for southern French culture, his Poitevin favourites, and Gothic architecture. However, the peace treaty he made with France was epoch-making in its effects on European diplomacy. Although a truce had been concluded with the French after the death of John in 1216, it was not until 1259 that a treaty was concluded in Paris which ended the century-old war between the houses of Plantagenet and Capet. Henry surrendered his claim to Normandy, Poitou and other lands and received Gascony as a fief from St Louis. Thereafter relations between France and England remained peaceful until the two countries were again plunged into the abyss by the outbreak of the great Hundred Years' War, 1339–1453, although there were some preliminary rumblings in the last years of the thirteenth century.

It was during the forties of the thirteenth century that important meetings of the King with magnates and high officials were first given the name "parliaments". Originally "parliament" meant simply a parley of any kind, as for example between the kings of England and Scotland. Any assembly might be so described. As an institution, the English parliament developed from the King's Council, that gathering of magnates and bishops, to which officials were later added, which discussed important matters with the king and decided tricky points in dispute. The "great peace" was observed during a parliament, which was under the King's special protection; the magnates came to it unarmed. During the reign of Henry III a revolutionary band of barons under the leadership of Simon de Montfort declared themselves the government of the country—in parliament. Edward I, "the English Justinian", a king with a passionate interest in law and whose legislation and government were under his personal direction, succeeded in making his royal parliament a forum for the open airing of conflicting claims among the leading sections of the community and for their resolution by lawful process. Parliament became the place where the king asked his people for money, troops, and more money; these demands were countered by "petitions" presented by the barons, the knights, the burgesses and the boroughs. The estates were intent on their "rights", the king on making parliament an instrument of government. The claim that they had the right of appointing royal officials figured largely in the petitions of the barons, who wanted to see the main officers of the Crown, chancellor, treasurer and justiciar, chosen in parliament, and backed up their claim by demanding that parliament be kept in constant session, instead of assembling when the king thought fit to summon it. To counteract this constant and growing pressure from the magnates the king sought the support of lesser men by summoning to parliament first the "gentry", the knights of the shires, and later the burgesses, the representatives of the towns.

The important and unique role of the gentry in English constitutional development can scarcely be exaggerated. On the Continent, particularly in France, the lesser aristocracy failed to establish themselves as a separate estate, but in England the gentry won a unique role for themselves. The gentry and the burgesses of the towns formed a single "estate", which in the fourteenth century gradually developed into the "Commons". Even though the separation of parliament into two houses, upper and lower, was accomplished only in 1352, the "Commons", with royal support, were increasingly successful in making their voice heard; formerly their role had been one of tacit acquiescence. The "Model Parliament" of 1295 is an important landmark in this evolution. The parliament summoned in that year to give counsel and provide money for the wars against France and Scotland was composed of clergy, barons, two knights from each shire and two burgesses from every borough. "What touches all must be approved by all" was the maxim cited in justification of this enlarged attendance. Europe's advance towards political freedom and the beginnings of Western democracy were largely due to the uninterrupted and tenacious struggle for their "rights and liberties" waged by individual magnates, lay and spiritual, and by separate groups, such as the English gentry and burgesses.

The reign of Edward I was a great age of legislation in England, only equalled by the reign of Henry VIII and the great ministries of the nineteenth century. Edward's laws were "statutes", given in parliament. Their primary purpose was to establish existing law and custom in permanent and systematic form. The majority of Edward's statutes are concerned with feudal matters. Pope Nicholas IV complained that the "king's clerks", who conducted the royal administration, refused to obey Papal orders. These men who staffed the royal service were well aware of their collective importance; they had been trained in episcopal or lay households, or had been through the universities. A number of them were appointed to bishoprics.

Edward I did much to promote English trading interests. In his financial transactions he relied heavily on Italian merchants and bankers. As Duke of Aquitaine he was a great patron of urban foundations: over 140 *bastids* were established during his time. Edward was a statesman of European stature; yet there was another side to him, which deserves to be remembered. By expelling the Jews from England in 1290 he set a bad example followed later by France, Spain and other countries. The first king since the Conquest to bear an Anglo-Saxon name, he was feared and hated outside England's borders as the "Hammer of the Scots" and the conqueror of Wales, which he subdued in two savage compaigns. He created his son Prince of Wales, a title from 1343 customarily conferred on the heir to the throne. It was during his reign that the English nation—or English nationalism—was born.

The long-drawn-out tragedy of Scottish resistance to the English, of which the issue often remained in doubt, and the equally stark tragedy of Ireland both fall outside our period. However, it is relevant to our main theme to comment on the antagonism towards the Celts shown both by the Anglo-Norman aristocracy and by the mass of the English population, and to mention a few important factors in the problem. Resistance to the English monarchy and government in these Celtic lands was concentrated in their churches; it was the clergy who incited the people to rebel. The English kings were forced to replace native bishops by their own appointees, and in this they had the willing assistance of the Papacy, long resentful of the autonomy of the Celtic clergy. The English kings scattered castles, cathedrals and monastic foundations up and down the conquered and rebellious countries.

The English looked upon the Celts as barbarians. A clerk

in the entourage of Archbishop Pecham, writing *circa* 1282, claimed that the Welsh were the remnant of the Trojans, cast adrift among the wild wastes of Cambria by diabolic intervention; they had abandoned themselves to a life of quite unspeakable promiscuity, brigandage and wicked idleness. This devilish race would long ago have been destroyed and swept off the face of the earth had it not been for the excessive clemency of the English kings, who allowed themselves to be deceived by the assumed and treacherous penitence of the Welsh and refrained from pressing home the advantages won on their frequent and necessary punitive expeditions. Gerald of Wales, on the other hand, writing a century earlier, remarked that the English were a people destined by nature to servitude.

The Welsh were a nation of herdsmen, nomads of the simplest type, free to move as they would and take their possessions with them; they were attached to their freedom, imaginative, and full of the joys of song. They were attracted neither by the sedentary life of the Anglo-Saxon peasantry nor by the organized stability aimed at by the Normans, and resisted both impartially. In directing popular hatred against the unfortunate Welsh, Irish and Scots, the English drew on a vocabulary of execration of which any modern propagandist might be proud. Equally ruthless were the techniques used to compel surrender. In 1282 the head of the great Welsh leader Llewelyn II was impaled on a lance on the Tower of London. The Scottish "rebels" of 1306 were savagely dealt with. Knights were hanged, bishops put in irons and imprisoned, the Bishop of Glasgow at Porchester, the Bishop of St Andrew's at Winchester, the Abbot of Scone in the castle of Mere in Wiltshire. Wooden cages were built for the female relatives of Robert the Bruce, who had allowed himself to be crowned King of Scotland. The Scots were later to take a grim revenge on the English monarchy and its "Church of saints" for this violation of their Church and territory. The English king and the English bishops of the seventeenth century had no more implacable enemies than the great Scottish Puritans.

The reign of an earlier Welsh king, Llewelyn the Great (1195–1240), was a golden age of Celtic culture, literature and bardic song. This renaissance of popular culture during the thirteenth century, at a time when national hatreds were intensifying among the peoples of the British Isles, draws attention to a phenomenon characteristic of the rich complexity of European development, both in the Middle Ages and later. This age of rising nationalism and mass hatreds, when one's nearest neighbours were automatically described as dirty dogs, filth, devils and heretics, was also an age which saw the outpouring of popular emotion in vernacular literature. What was happening in the twelfth and thirteenth centuries was not unlike the awakening which came to the peoples of Central and Eastern Europe in the nineteenth century, when attempts at creating a "national literature", for the Poles, Bohemians, Moravians, Hungarians, Croats, Serbs and Russians, went hand in hand with nationalism itself, stimulated from the outside by the infecting zeal of German romanticism.

French vernacular poetry may be said to begin in the early twelfth century with the *Chanson de Roland*, in which "anti-Saracen" feeling is strong. From Suger, Abbot of St Denis and "father of Gothic", we learn that other enemies were considered just as odious: the Germans were barbarians too, and their massacred corpses fit only for throwing to the wolves and ravens.

This combination of creative activity (which draws on the resources of love) with deadly hatred is a specifically European trait, exposing man in all his grandeur and wretchedness.

CHAPTER 15

VERNACULAR LITERATURE

THE stormy seas of popular emotion, with its mounting waves of nationalist feeling, reached in the later Middle Ages still greater heights of hatred and love, despair and expectation. The Hundred Years' War which started in 1328 intensified national feeling among both French and English and created on each side a "community of hatred" (Perroy) in face of the enemy. English national feeling, already hostile towards Rome and Avignon, towards papal claims and towards Scotland and the rest of the Celtic fringe, was now reinforced by hatred of the "wicked French". The chroniclers of both camps, Froissart, Jean de Bel, Mathieu d'Escouchy and Thomas Basin on the French side, John of Reading and Thomas of Walsingham on the English, provide unmistakable evidence that "nationalism" was leaving its mark on the progress of the war. The intensity of French animosity was further strengthened by the distinction made between "Good Frenchmen" and collaborators, those who sided with the English during the occupation. It was just such men, and there were bishops among them, who asked the Maid of Orleans: "Does God hate Englishmen?"

As Europe contracted, the nations were thrown in on each other. The climate became tense, at once heated and chill. Friction and isolated outbreaks of bad feeling were nothing new. The Crusading chivalry of England, France and the Empire had long bickered together in the Holy Land, Frenchmen and Spaniards had come to blows on the roads to Compostela, Italians, Frenchmen and Catalans had quarrelled as trade rivals in the Levant, as had Germans and Scandinavians in the North Sea and the Baltic. But the words *patrie* and *nation* now acquired a harsher ring. In Spain a number of "nations" fiercely clung to their separate identities,

Catalan, Aragonese, Castilian, Navarrese, Portuguese, and all had a common pride in being Iberian in the face of French and Germans, the aristocracy of Western Europe and the merchants from the North.

It was the Germans who first brought national feelings to life among the French. The expression *furor teutonicus* coined by Lucan in the first century AD was revived as an indictment of "German savagery and barbarism". The Englishman Walter Mapes takes pleasure in relating how Louis VI abused an envoy of the Emperor Henry V by calling him *"tpwrut Aleman"*. "This was certainly a great insult and a cause of much resentment." This term of abuse, which occurs elsewhere (and in other forms, *troup alemant* and *"Ptrut, Sire"*, for example) was the medieval equivalent of "Boche". The same basic themes recur in the *Chanson de Roland,* in the writings of Suger of St Denis and in the political propaganda of the French kings which, starting in the late twelfth century, kept roughly to the same line for the next two hundred years: the French nation is culturally superior to all others, it is the only nation of true believers and the lawful heir of Charlemagne, the French nation fights God's battles for Him on earth, all its wars are Crusades. The *Chanson de Roland* when recited by a *jongleur* to the troops on the field of Bouvines had the same stirring effect as the Marseillaise.

John of Salisbury, a man whose ear was always close to the ground, reports on the contemptuous attitude towards the French shown by German students in Paris in 1138, who openly mocked the French and their "unwarlike" king. German national pride, much in evidence in the reign of Frederick Barbarossa (1152–91) at the peak of the Hohenstaufen era, was deliberately worked upon by imperial propagandists such as the Chancellor Rainald of Dassel, as part of their campaign against the "kinglets", the contemptible petty kings of western Europe. This campaign was directed chiefly against the French, who claimed to be the heirs of Charlemagne whereas it was of course the Germans who were the true Franks, custodians of the Holy Empire. The play of *Antichrist,* which originated perhaps at Tegernsee *circa* 1160, develops its eschatological theme by showing the French betrayed by their excessive intellectualism, their *subtilitas,* into the service of anti-Christ, and actively preparing the way for him. The German *Minnesinger* who inherited the mantle of their Provençal and northern French predecessors extolled the virtues of German manhood and womanhood in the language of the people. Walther von der Vogelweide's *"Ich hân Lande vil gesehen"* has been described, by no means inappositely, as "the medieval German national anthem": "From the Elbe to the Rhine, And again to Hungary . . ." There is a complete absence, however, of any aggressive note; the mood is rather one of meditation. Germany, the Holy Empire, is a kingdom whose battlements face inwards, an interior kingdom. We shall trace later the progressive spiritualization of this German popular and national sentiment under the influence of German mysticism, an influence not unlike that exerted by Spanish mysticism in the sixteenth century as it sought for America, the "Indies of the soul", *las Indias de Dios,* in the soul's inmost depths.

In the event, the full blast of German popular hatred was never trained upon the West. Relations between the Hohenstaufen Emperors and kings and the kings in Paris were for the most part amicable. On at least eighteen occasions German and French knights met in friendly battles on the jousting field, and German and French *Minnesinger,* Heinrich von Veldeke and Guiot de Provins, met as brothers. It was no accident that Germany became the only place in Europe where the great French art of the late twelfth and thirteenth centuries met with an instantaneous and positive response, just as there was a close connection between the scholasticism of Paris and that of Cologne.

It was the people living to the East who were the main objects of German mass hatred and hysteria, a legacy of hate which has bedevilled Germany's relations with her eastern neighbours down to our own times. Not long before the outbreak of the second world war a German historian noted that the great majority of the many medieval campaigns launched by the Germans against their eastern neighbours were failures. This observation is of some interest, especially when set beside the opprobrious language used by German ecclesiastical chroniclers when speaking of the Slavs. Their attitude was clearly similar to that adopted by other peoples, equally on the defensive, towards Negroes: the Slavs, as it were, were "stinking niggers" (stinking with evil), despicable creatures like frogs and worms. For Adam of Bremen it was axiomatic that no one married his daughter to a Slavonic "dog", not even if he were the son of a baptized prince. The Slavs did not fail to retaliate: in the twelfth century Cosmas of Prague, recounting an episode of the early eleventh century in his *Bohemian Chronicle,* comments on the German attitude of innate superiority towards the Slavs and their language. Bernold of St Blasien wrote in his chronicle (*anno* 1077) that the Czechs pillaged other people to satisfy their baser natures; Arnold of Lübeck characterized the "Bohemians" as "depraved by nature, despicable in their actions". Helmold, parish priest of Bosau, writing of the Poles in his *Slavonic Chronicle* (it goes down to 1171), pigeonholed them with a formula long current among the Germans as a general description of the Slavonic character: their bravery was beyond doubt, but "they are remorseless murderers and robbers, who spare neither churches nor monasteries", and had an insatiable lust for plunder. The Slavs were faithless, they were a depraved and perverse nation and their land a dread and desolate province.

The war on the eastern front was fought with harsh and inhuman savagery. It must be remembered that in the later Middle Ages the West looked on this war as something of a sport, an annual outing for the nobility from all parts of western Europe; each year English, French and Flemish knights flocked at the invitation of the German Military Orders to join their German and Central European colleagues for the "Season", the annual campaign against the Slavonic peasant populations of what were later to be Russia and Poland. This international element was particularly a feature of the fourteenth century.

From early in the tenth century the Wends and other Slavonic tribes resisted the invasion of their lands by the *deus theutonicus,* the "German God" imported by German lords who were eager to convert the Slavs at the point of the sword and subject them to German rule. An anecdote added by a twelfth century clerk of Merseburg to the *Life of Henry II* illustrates in what suspicion the Germans and their God were held; a blind man of Wendish descent refused to seek a cure by touching the Emperor's holy relics, since he thought that no German would ever help a Wend. Rome, and Roman Christianity, were detested in Eastern Europe in so far as they were German importations. When the Polish, Czech and Hungarian Churches (for centuries the Hungarians were stigmatized by the Germans as "monsters", "barbarians") set themselves to break the spell of Rome they became the champions of their peoples' resistance to German overlordship.

However, as we have so often found, these animosities

were not in practice incompatible with a state of peaceful co-existence. Between 1000 and 1230 eleven Bohemian dukes and kings married the daughters of German princes, and scions of the house of Przzemyslid married into the German aristocracy. Despite numerous decrees prohibiting mixed marriages and community of bed and board (not to mention language), an aristocracy of mixed German and Slavonic descent nevertheless came into being; this aristocracy was responsible for the rise of Brandenburg-Prussia and even in the nineteenth and early twentieth centuries still showed traces of its dual ancestry. In the Middle Ages the lower orders of German society, peasants and townsmen, lived quite happily alongside the indigenous population in the Germanized eastern lands, Poland, Bohemia, Moravia and Hungary.

The trend towards nationalism as it developed in the later Middle Ages destroyed this earlier harmony. Popular resentment at the dominance of German prelates and German princes, at everything which stood for Rome, now became articulate in the Czech intelligentsia, which was growing in strength and numbers in the towns and universities. "God loves Czechs no less than He loves Latins." This bold remark came from Thomas of Stitny, a scholastic forerunner of Hus, who as early as 1409 was brought before an ecclesiastical court at Prague charged with "the expulsion of the Germans" from the University. The Council of Constance condemned Hus to death for the crime of having incited the Bohemians against the Germans by his preaching. The execution of Hus at the stake made him a national martyr, victim of a double act of treachery on the part of the "wicked West": for the Emperor had gone back on his guarantee of safe conduct, and Rome had shown herself the enemy of those who sought their salvation in the vernacular tongue and their refuge in the nation, their beloved and "holy" nation.

Anguish, anger, sorrow, burning hatred and burning love presided over the birth of the national literatures of Europe. The growth of languages implies the growth of nations. The people came alive as their languages gathered strength in opposition to the Latin which was the trademark of Rome and of the universalizing culture of professors, clerks and officials. For the poets of the twelfth century Latin was still heady and florescent, an "open" language. In the later Middle Ages it was decadent, both as a

literary language and as the language of common understanding, a pedantic and arid medium used only by specialists. In contrast, the first jubilant outbursts in the vernacular,
inspired by full-blooded love and hate, seem immeasurably
superior to the word-spinning of a Latin which was becoming narrow and crabbed. Even in its adolescence, that is,
during the twelfth, thirteenth and fourteenth centuries, vernacular poetry plunged boldly into the depths to probe the
tender places and cavities concealed in the popular soul.
The peoples of Europe were beginning to seek their salvation in their own tongues. It has only recently become
possible to see this process as a whole, taking in all the
many levels where life was germinating. A truly comprehensive view must range from Iceland to Verona (the "Bern"
of the German heroic epic: "Dietrich von Bern" was Theo-
doric the Ostrogoth), from the England of Langland, Chaucer
and Wyclif to the Prague of Hus and the early Czech
translations of the Bible, from French popular poetry of the
thirteenth century, with its uncompromising anti-clericalism
and anti-feudalism, to the inner kingdom of the suffering
German soul in the poetry of the German mystics.

Let us begin this brief sketch in the extreme north, in
Iceland, *"ultima Thule"*. Here the great legends of gods and
heroes we call the Sagas had been written down by the
middle of the thirteenth century, the work of unknown
writers and of Snorri Sturluson (1178–1241), a man
active in affairs and a historian. The Sagas provide us with a
unique and impressive self-portrait of the Germanic peoples
of Europe in the centuries of the migrations and the early
Middle Ages, showing them at war with themselves and with
their gods, always in conflict, man against man, man against
woman. It would be quite wrong to dismiss these legends
about the Icelanders and the old Germanic gods as an archaic
survival, valueless as evidence about conditions in the Middle Ages proper. It must be remembered that the *Nibelungenlied*, the great German heroic epic, was given its final
form by an Austrian writer in the late twelfth or early thirteenth centuries, and that it reproduces all the themes to be
found in the northern epics. The *Nibelungenlied* is the lay of
a lost people, and of how they were plunged into the abyss by
the hatred of a woman. One cannot fail to perceive that
under their thin veneer of Christianity the Germanic peoples
of Europe still kept alive the non-Christian elements which
for so long had been the source of their vitality. It was clergy

and bishops of the south-eastern corner of the Holy Empire who were the authors of the epic and created a public for it. More than one chronicler tells how a preacher could immediately arouse a soporific congregation with a reference to "these ancient tales". And this despite the fact that such parsons as appear in the epic are assigned inglorious or insignificant roles (as was also the case in the courtly epics). Hagen of Tronege throws a priest overboard without ceremony; in the courtly epics, as in real life, priests were hurriedly brought in whenever their lord's plans called for some religious rite. The epic is shot through with ungovernable hatred, tremendous and unbridled passions, swelling anger and overflowing love. There is perjury, treachery, endless fighting. Just as the Icelandic Sagas are full of women too strong for comfort, laughing to scorn the weakness of men less than their match, so here we have Brünhilde tying Gunther to the post of their marriage bed.

It is useful to keep the Icelandic social setting in mind. This was a land of Vikings, free warrior-farmers and traders of Norwegian descent who had occupied the country (then settled only by Celtic hermits from Ireland) in the ninth and tenth centuries, refugees from the growing power of the Norwegian monarchy. There was a governing aristocracy of *godar*, men who in their own halls were king, lord of the manor, priest and judge in one. The Althing, the assembly of all free men under their 144 chiefs or *godar*, which met in summer at Reykjavik, was established in 930. The oldest of Europe's popular assemblies, and the oldest "parliament", the Althing continued almost without interruption until 1798. In 1000, by a thoroughly democratic procedure, the Althing agreed to the introduction of Christianity into the country; one result of this voluntary conversion was that the attitudes and beliefs of the preceding era were taken over into Christianity, or else survived independently. Written records came into use in Iceland in the early twelfth century. Laws and customs were written down, chronicles compiled and the old legends, still very much alive among the people, were preserved in written form.

The Icelandic Sagas are stamped with a deep pessimism untouched by sentimentality; the Nordic heart is the seat of rugged emotions, of hatred on the grand scale. The world, the gods, the sea and man himself are harsh and cruel, beyond comprehension and yet subject to laws more adamantine than themselves. Perhaps we should learn to look on those early medieval crucifixes, where the ponderous figure hangs imprisoned by its own weary weight, as an echo of the hanging of Odin. There is a song in *Hávamál* ("The Words of Odin the High One") describing how Odin hanged himself on the world's tree to discover the runes:

> "I know that I hung
> On a wind-swept tree
> Nine nights long.
> Spear-wounded
> Odin-consecrated
> Myself an offering to myself
> On a tree
> Whose roots are known to none."

On that tree, Odin, the crucified god, in his mortal wounds found the "staff of life", the magic runes. Here poetry is born, in the discovery of words of power, saving words which deliver from even the deepest anguish, from the anguish of God and the anguish of men. This is in itself a powerful symbol of the birth of folk poetry as it happened among the young nations of Europe, a tremendous archetype of the birth of words of healing from the midst of great suffering.

The most impressive portion of the Elder Edda (the oldest collection of sagas of gods and heroes, probably more or less contemporary with *Hávamál*) is that known as "The Prophecy of the Seeress" (Voluspá). Voluspá (she found her incarnation, one might almost say, in such medieval visionaries as Hildegard of Bingen, Brigit of Sweden and Catherine of Siena) sings the history of the world from its beginning to its end. She tells of the first times, and of the Golden Age which ended with the coming of the Norns:

> "That was the dawn of time, when Ymir lived;
> Then was no sand nor sea, no salty waves,
> No earth beneath nor heaven above,
> But an empty nothing, and nowhere grass."

She tells of the first internecine wars of the gods, and the wars of the gods with giants and dragons. Her gaze reaches into the beyond, into Hell:

"I saw a sunless hall,
North-facing on a dead man's strand,
A poison-dripping roof above,
A wall of worming snakes all round;
There waded through its marshy wastes
Wolf-like and murdering men;
There Nithogg suckled on damned flesh,
The wolf gnawed human flesh: need you know more?"

The history of the world is a judgment of the world.

"Brothers in combat bring their own deaths,
Brothers' sons break up the clan.
Wicked is the world and evil is wantonness,
The time of the sword, the time of the axe, sundering shields,
Tempest-time, wolf-time, until the world be gone
Not one will spare another."

Gods and men go down in a welter of battle, the earth dissolves in a universal conflagration. But afterwards will come "a new Heaven and a new Earth", or, as the northern prophetess has it, the time when

"Once again will those wondrous
Golden banquets spread the grass
As once before they were.
The unsown earth will yield its fruit,
Worse becomes better: Balder enters his own again.
Höder and Balder dwell in Sieghof,
The gods rejoice in Valhalla.
Need you know more?"

"Need you know more?" The great northern sybil had her answer from a brother prophet speaking from the soil of Etruria, the land whose ancient sons had known how to conjure the dead and who understood the horrors of Hell and the delights of Heaven regained. The prophecy of Voluspá is a kind of sacred shorthand; its impact is somewhat similar to that of early medieval sculptures such as one finds at Schöngrabern in Lower Austria, where the entire history of the world from the Creation through the Fall to Christ and the Last Judgment is condensed into a few sacred signs, magic symbols and shapes.

Dante's *Divine Comedy* was forged in the fires of love and

hatred. Of the seventy-nine individuals Dante consigns to Hell who are mentioned by name or whose identity is clearly indicated, thirty-two were Florentines and thirteen Tuscans from other cities; he met with only four of his fellow-townsmen in Purgatory and only two in Paradise. Florence, so dear and sweet, had expelled him and condemned him to death. Dante was a life-long emigrant, and his poetry, like so much Italian poetry from the time of Petrarch down to the twentieth century, was poetry born of exile. But to speak of Dante's love-hate relationship with Florence is to adopt a one-dimensional view of his anger and resentment, of his love for the Church, for the Empire and for Italy. Dante's creation was born of his bitter appraisal of the whole contemporary situation. Dante had his own view of the consequences of Papal and French policies, the policies which had led to Anagni and the removal of the Papacy to Avignon: dishonoured Italy was made a house of shame, Christendom was savaged by the wolf's tooth, and all because ambition and the lust for power and worldly possessions had driven the Papacy from the time of Constantine to Boniface VIII and brought the Church down into the abyss. The Holy Empire of the Roman Emperor had been reduced to impotence and debility by the folly of the Popes, by the pretensions of Emperors such as Frederick II, and by the sins and weakness of all Christendom.

Dante's mission was to proclaim his apocalyptic vision of the coming redemption. Carlyle recognized in him "the voice of the ten silent centuries" and one might indeed say that when he took up his pen to sing of Hell, penitence and redemption, Dante made himself the mouthpiece of the wrath seething among the inarticulate, and the spiritual brother both of persecuted Franciscans and other visionaries and of free-thinking "left-wing" Aristotelians. Dante's boldness was quite extraordinary; there is scarcely a "heretic" of his times whose message he ignores. He has Thomas Aquinas in Paradise singing the praise of Suger of Brabant, the master of Paris whom the orthodox hated and feared. The *Divine Comedy*, authentically medieval in its mingling of opposites, brings together the worldly wisdom of heathen antiquity, the astrological lore of Dante's own time and material derived from Arab and Jewish philosophy (Dante got some of this knowledge from his Florentine Jewish friend, Immanuel Ben Saloman). Dante defends the recently condemned Templars: there are fulminations in Heaven against

Pope Clement V, that pliant tool of the French king who liquidated the Templars by administrative decree. He also defends the much-persecuted Franciscans, hounded down by the Popes of Avignon because they clung to their ideal of poverty. His chief target is the *ecclesia carnalis*, the Curial Church, now become the French king's whore, corrupted by the ambitions of the Popes and by the intemperate ideological claims of the canon lawyers.

Dante's constructive purpose was to set Christendom on the right road to the apocalypse. In the "last days" the Church would be refashioned into a Church of the spirit. Beatrice, symbol of light, and the incarnation of this Joachimite-Franciscan vision of a spiritual Church, proclaims its victory by her triumphal entry into Paradise. On earth this new springtime, the "second Easter" of mankind (to use Dante's own expression), is ushered in by the descent into Italy of the Emperor Henry VII. When he is fighting on this narrowly political front Dante casts aside all dissimulation. His *De Monarchia* is an overt attack on the theory of papal overlordship formulated by the canon lawyers. For centuries this treatise was kept on the Index, and Emperors of later centuries who were in conflict with the Papacy found it an invaluable prop to their case: Erasmus prepared a new edition for Charles V.

But when Dante fights on the inner spiritual plane, when his targets are theological or ecclesiastical, such frankness is impossible. It is then that he clothes his ideas and opinions in symbols, those artistically devised figures, numbers, word-plays and analogies which are now so puzzling. This was a technique already elaborated by Provençal poets (some of whom had fled to Italy in the thirteenth century) and by numerous other heterodox spirits. "Nicodemism", *minetiz-zazione*, long remained the chief means of expression available to poets and heterodox thinkers in a closed society (such as that which offered Dante the choice between exile and death at the stake), used by men who dared not voice openly their opinions on the existing political, ecclesiastical and theological situation. Cervantes' Don Quixote, the "knight of the green mantle", belongs to the same tradition, and it by no means died with him. The great poet was driven to adopt such devices from sheer necessity, not from any whim of self-concealment or a desire to be purposely "obscure". Only an elaborate deformation of his material permitted him to say truthfully all that was laid on him to say as the mouthpiece of a thousand souls doomed to silence.

Dante's immortal work brims over with ideas censured as "heretical" or non-orthodox by the Popes and leading theologians of the day who also looked with disfavour on apocalyptic prophecy. All this is clear enough today; what is also clear—and it is a key to the rich variety of medieval life—is that the *Divine Comedy* is a work of such catholicity that it dares to bridge the most daunting chasms. In the breadth of its comprehensive vision the most irreconcilable of opposites and adversaries are united (enemies sing each other's praises in Dante's Paradise). The poet's anger never turns to insensate rage: rather, it is the motive power which drives him on through Hell and Purgatory until at last the radiant fire of Paradise puts out the darkling flames of earth and Hell. Love, order, and salvation are man's aims and duty, and he will find them in a spiritual Church refined in the fires of history, a Church under the discipline of God and on earth under the protection of the Emperor.

On April 30, 1921, six centuries after Dante's death in exile at Ravenna, Pope Benedict XV in his encyclical *In Praeclara* paid homage to the genius of the poet; and in the same manifesto addressed to the whole Church, he repeatedly cited with praise the *De Monarchia*, that work which for so many centuries languished on the Index.

We have journeyed from Iceland's fire and ice to the fire and ice of Hell and the great Florentine's vision of humanity reborn. It is time to glance briefly at another axis of vernacular self-expression, that running from West to East. The close connection between the vernacular literature of England and Bohemia was first established in our period and was continued for some time afterwards. The elevation of English into the language of poetry and of Holy Writ was largely connected with what was happening far outside England, in Italy and Rome. William Langland (1332–76) was a devout admirer of St Francis, honouring him for his poverty, his humility, his love of the soil and all created things. The Mendicant preachers, who first came to England as missionaries, cherished the common people to an extent uncommon in England since Anglo-Saxon times, seeking by their preaching to stir their hearts and unloose their tongues. The brief account just given of Dante emphasized his role as spokesman of the Spiritual Franciscans. The Langland of *Piers Plowman* is a more gentle spirit, closer to the soil, concerned not with the fate of Emperors, Popes, kings and theologians, but with the simple folk, peasants and beggars, married couples and young girls. He is at one with Dante, however, in his conviction that love alone, the love of the Son of God, can set man on the right road.

Links with Italy and Italian poetry were a continuing influence on English poetry from the time of its first blossoming in the fourteenth century. Chaucer (*circa* 1340–1400), whose *Canterbury Tales* are peopled with the whole range of English characters, may perhaps have been personally acquainted with Boccaccio and Petrarch, whose work he introduced into England, some of it in his own translation. Since that time the music of Italian song has never failed to ring sympathetically in English ears, and this is true not only of the poets and composers of Shakespeare's day but also of our own contemporaries—Benjamin Britten has found inspiration in Michelangelo's sonnets and in the art of *bel canto*. Dante, as we have seen, set up Italian as the language of salvation in opposition to Latin, which symbolized the domination of the Curia and the canon lawyers. Wyclif's sermons and the translations of the Bible made by him and his Lollard followers belong in the same context. In many parts of Europe the sway of Latin, that "alien" tongue, the trade-mark of the Roman Church, was being challenged by the translation of the Bible into the vernacular, as proof that this despised and suspect medium could—indeed should—proclaim the good news of the Gospel directly to the people.

Biblical translation was the training-ground of the vernacular languages; here they were fashioned and brought to maturity to express the religious and political self-awareness of the peoples of Europe. The fruitful relations between England and Bohemia, fostered by dynastic marriages and the presence of Bohemian students in England, had an encouraging effect on the Czechs. The young preachers and professors of Prague took fire from Wyclif and his following; the efforts of Thomas Stitny to make Czech a literary language were inspired by English precedent and Hus was directly indebted to Wyclif for a number of his ideas.

Vernacular literature in France started to break away from the courtly and clerkly traditions of Latin poetry at the end of the thirteenth century. This new popular literature was anti-idealistic, anti-courtly, anti-feudal and anti-clerical. It was the people who now carried on the polemical warfare against Popes, kings and courts which, until they were crushed under the weight of ecclesiastical censure in the thirteenth century, had been waged by troubadours and *trouvères*. Rutebeuf, the most considerable French poet of the thirteenth century to write in the vernacular, already stands out as spokesman of the people. He lived and worked in Paris between 1245 and 1280, writing to earn his bread, always indigent but always carefree, something of a card, but a card of talent: in short a remote ancestor of Villon. He identified himself with the common people of Paris in their troubles, their anxieties and their pleasures. He shared their faith and was loyal to their king, St Louis; he attacked decadent and degenerate friars, whom he saw as the enemies of the people, and in this he resembles Rabelais.

The most striking and incontrovertible evidence that a great change was taking place in the intellectual climate about this time is provided by that ambiguous work the *Roman de la Rose*. This is the only piece written before 1300 which retained its hold over the affections of the French public down into the sixteenth century; in England echoes of it are to be found in the *Canterbury Tales* and in Shakespeare (in Sonnet XI, for example).

The earliest part of the *Roman de la Rose*, composed *circa* 1236 by Guillaume de Lorris, who came from Orleans, is a late-flowering bloom from the stem of courtly poetry, tender and breathtaking in its beauty. The young poet dreams he is in a walled garden in Maytime. There he finds the god *Amor* surrounded by joy, youth and liberality. He sees a rose and yearns to possess it: she is the virgin of his dreams, the glass of purity, tenderness and innocence of heart. Here the first part breaks off. Forty years later Jean de Meung took up the tale, adding another eighteen thousand lines. This bourgeois *littérateur* attacks orthodox scholasticism and courtly ethics with a cold cynicism which is not without a pedantry of its own. Chastity is an illusion: sex, not Eros, rules the world. "Nature", the principal personage in this lavishly mounted polemic disguised as a "romance", demands that men free themselves from the hypocritical conventions of society and of superstition of all kinds. Jean's work breathes a sturdy optimism and is consciously hostile to the great ones of this world and to the theological Establishment. The "heresies" of Jean de Meung came within Bishop Stephen Tempier's condemnation of 1277, but this in no way hindered the rapid dissemination of his work.

French, rather than Latin, now became the chief medium for ironical comment, raillery and scholarly invective; in addition the vernacular literature of the later Middle Ages in France is also characterized by a zestful enjoyment of life at all levels. After Paris the chief centre of literary activity in the thirteenth century was Arras, which boasted of a band of bourgeois "poets"—one might almost say *Meistersinger*—organized into an academy called the Puy, presided over by a "prince of the Puy". The Puy is known to have had more than 180 members at one time or another. There were similar organizations in Valenciennes and Toulouse. Their lyric poetry, often somewhat homespun, is satirical, serious and deeply felt, and is not without unmistakable under- and over-tones of anti-clerical and anti-courtly feeling. It reflects the sentiments of people who in their own fashion had consciously shared in the rise of a nation and in adding to its growing prestige in the world. This after all was the century which had opened with the French king's capture of the imperial standard with its imperial eagle on the field of Bouvines. In the last years of that same century the French king in his capital, Paris, was plotting the trial which would unmask and depose Pope Boniface VIII on grounds of heresy.

The circumstances attending the birth of German as a literary language, in the thirteenth and early fourteenth centuries, were entirely different. The mysticism of Meister Eckhart, Mechthild of Magdeburg, Tauler and Suso, was the answer of inspired and devout men and women to the spiritual destitution which threatened with the collapse of Empire and Church. The movement developed between the years 1260 and 1350, that is in the latter part of our stretch of the Middle Ages; for the first time the German people were offered a language which was suitable as a medium of education and for the expression both of speculative and philosophical ideas and of feeling. In the later medieval and early modern periods these German mystics exerted a far-reaching and varied influence, felt first in the Netherlands, then in France, Spain and England, and finally in Eastern Europe and Russia; it is still discernible in places far outside Europe. Eckhart's attraction for religious thinkers in India, China and Japan has been as powerful and real as it was for a number of French, Spanish and English *devoués* (it reached some Englishmen by way of Bohemia) between the fifteenth and the eighteenth centuries.

The great age of German mysticism and the developments in the German language which accompanied it ran parallel with the decline of the Empire and were a function of it. The years of the Interregnum, 1256–73, "the terrible years without an Emperor", coincided with the youth of Meister Eckhart. Between 1250 and 1265, Mechthild of Magdeburg was writing down her visions and meditations on "the fleeting light of Godhead in all hearts which are without falsehood". In these writings the reader is conducted through Hell, Purgatory and Paradise, all described as inner kingdoms of the soul. It is possible that Mechthild is identical with the mystic Matilda who accompanied Dante in Purgatory, leading him to Beatrice, and that Dante knew *The Fleeting Light*. Yet the response of the Germans to the political and ecclesiastical miseries of the thirteenth and early fourteenth centuries was very different from that of the great Florentine and of the men around Wyclif and Hus, all of whom attacked the problem from the outside, in the context of the political and ecclesiastical life of their countries. German mysticism was entirely inward, a delving into the "inner kingdom"; the mystics' all-in-all was a cosmos which was an inner kingdom of the soul.

Meister Eckhart expounded his methods like this: "When I preach, I usually speak thus: firstly of withdrawal, and that man should become free of himself and of all material things; second, that man should be again restored to that goodness which is God; third, that man should think of that high nobility which God has planted in his soul, so that through it he may attain to the wonderful life of God; fourth, of the purity of the divine nature—that clarity of the divine nature which is ineffable."

And this is the burden of the song of Mechthild of Magdeburg, dedicated to the brothers and sisters who come after her:

"The soul speaks with her God:
'Were all the world mine
And of purest gold,
And could I here remain at will eternally,
A queen most noble, queen most fair,
Richer than all, finer than all,
Yet would I count it all as nought!'

How much rather would I see
Jesus Christ, my best-loved Lord,
Honoured high in Heaven.
Think how men must suffer, who must languish long
without this sight.' "

This last line is sharply relevant to the situation in the Rhineland and the South-western towns of Germany, the main centres of German mysticism. This was indeed an area of spiritual famine, created by defective pastoral care and the resistance of the towns to the exactions of the Papal Curia and the authority of their local bishops. Urban resistance to Rome, particularly to papal tax demands, first declared itself in 1313 at Mainz; Cologne followed suit in 1330, the League of Rhenish Churches in 1335. The culminating point was reached with the anti-Roman manifesto of the League of Cologne in 1372. As in Dante's Italy, the political struggle for power frequently left a town or towns languishing for years under an episcopal or papal interdict, which meant that the clergy were forbidden to celebrate Mass and dispense the sacraments. Strasbourg had already spent ten years under an interdict a century before Meister Eckhart's association with the city. A number of German cities were put under an interdict as a result of the conflict between Louis of Bavaria and John XXII, who in 1329 condemned by Bull twenty-eight theses maintained by Meister Eckhart: these places included Erfurt, Eckhart's native town (three years), Ulm (fourteen years), and Frankfurt (twenty-eight years!).

The Empire was in ruins, its vast churches empty. But the void was not left tenantless. Numerous small groups sprang up whose aim was to lead a common life of devotion, secure in the peace of soul conferred by an inward and personal apprehension of God. Though often suspected of heresy, the great majority of these brothers and sisters in piety had no thought of separation from the Church; it was a combination of circumstances (the lack of pastoral care, the animosity of the higher clergy who were afraid that during their own period of enforced impotence their flocks would desert to these other shepherds, and the constant denunciations at Rome and Avignon) that drove them into precarious positions on the margins of orthodoxy and finally over the brink, to be swallowed up in successive waves of persecution. In the light of modern research it is difficult for us to draw a clear boundary between "heretical" and "orthodox" mysticism, between "Catholic" and "heretical" Beguines. These people, many of them women (the medieval failure to solve the problem of women's role was of great importance here), were caught up in the wake of persecution, often in company with other "brothers" and "sisters" who already belonged to the heterodox underground made up of the remnants of the Cathars and Waldensians, of Franciscans with "Spiritual" tendencies, and of Beguines and Beghards, who were in process of regrouping themselves and admitting fresh blood, such as the "Brethren of the Holy Ghost", the "Brethren of the Free Spirit", Lollards or Flagellants. Heinrich of Virneburg, who led the prosecution in person at the trial of Meister Eckhart, inaugurated his rule as Archbishop of Cologne with the execution of a number of Beghards, some by burning, others by drowning in the Rhine. Persecution of these brothers and sisters, whose only aim was to lead a life of dedication in the world, and whose language came very close to the mysticism of Meister Eckhart, came to a head in the years 1290, 1292 and 1306. The places affected were Basel, Colmar, Aschaffenburg and Cologne. There were further executions of Beghards and Brethren of the Free Spirit at Strasbourg in 1317 and again at Cologne in 1322.

The Archbishop of Cologne declared open war on both the Dominicans and Franciscans, regarding them as the inspiration behind these irregular religious movements. The Franciscans replied by denouncing the young Dominican intellectuals who had attracted attention both within their Order and outside it by their activities as the spiritual directors of Dominican nuns, as popular preachers and as speculative philosophers.

It was only after stubborn resistance, finally overcome by the direct intervention of the Pope, that the Dominicans had agreed to take on the spiritual direction of the women's houses belonging to their Order (at the beginning of the fourteenth century the German province had 70 houses for women as against 46-48 for men). It was from the acceptance of this responsibility that German mysticism was born, since it brought masculine intellectualism into fruitful union with feminine sensibility.

German mysticism put out its shoots in the shadow of the scaffold, menaced by the rumble of ecclesiastical censure and jeopardized by the sniping of envious clerics jealous of the young preachers' success. The mysticism they expounded had its centre in a duologue between the "heart" and the Godhead, the union of the soul, in its complete self-abandonment, with the Godhead. God, Christ, was reborn in a man's soul and from this reincarnation man became God.

The Europe which produced the philosophical boldness of Meister Eckhart and his fellow German Dominicans, Johannes Sterngassen, Gishelher of Slatheim, Helwig of Gelmar, Nicholas of Strasbourg, and half a dozen other scholars and friends of the same temper, could hardly be called narrow. Nor did it suffer from emotional atrophy. In this German branch of the great tree thought and feeling soared up together into the "space beyond the heavens" (to use the language of Plato's *Phaedrus*). The Platonist philosophical speculations of the Dominicans, which comprehended the whole of life, terrestrial and divine, were matched by the mysticism of Dominican nuns, with its roots in popular emotion.

The mystics' theme is that men should look for the kingdom of God within themselves. All the splendour of heaven and earth is to be found in the soul, the hiding place of God. God allows Himself to blossom and bear fruit within the soul, matching the degrees by which man sinks, under the weight of sorrow, pain and persecution; the inmost citadel of the soul is unshakable and invincible and its defences will stand where castles and churches (even though built like fortresses) have failed to give shelter. Eckhart himself dwells much on this tiny inner citadel at the heart's bottom; within it burns the flame of Godhead, light, fire, strength, the spark of the soul. It is an inextinguishable source of fire, linking man with God. "Cherish this flame and let God waken within you, in this fiery kernel of the soul." Devout men and women who were conscious of this indestructible bond linking the heart of man to God felt a surge of jubilation, joy and freedom which found its outlet in the creation of a literary language, the "mother tongue" of this inner kingdom of the soul and spirit. Although it can only be touched on briefly here, it must be stressed that the great religious literature of Germany was born in the Dominican nunneries.

Styling himself "secret emperor" of a "secret kingdom", Johannes Tauler, disciple and defender of Meister Eckhart, directed his message to the inarticulate pious laity, telling them to submit to a life of suspicion and shame, to persecution as heretics, even to death itself, and offer no resistance, casting everything upon God. Evil should not be resisted, whether in ecclesiastical or secular government: "Even if Pope, bishops and prelates preyed upon me like wolves, still would I bear it." A strangely transformed Francis of Assisi here makes his appearance, in the midst of German anguish and necessity. Tauler brought Eckhart's message home to the people; he and other preachers introduced it into the nunneries. The "inward-looking" man builds his Church and his Empire within him. The Church, the true bark of Peter, is that "inmost foundation of a man on which Christ rests".

German mysticism had the effect, accomplished silently, almost imperceptibly, of alienating men's souls from the "walled Church" (as Tauler called it) and from the Empire; it sent them on an inward migration which was to continue until the Reformation. The Church correctly assessed the great challenge and danger to itself inherent in the mystics' preaching of passive obedience; but by adopting unsuitable counter-measures, such as the posthumous condemnation of Eckhart, persecution, and the execution of individual mystics, it only succeeded in driving their ideas and spiritual methods underground. The transformation of the open Europe of the earlier period into the closed Europe of the later medieval and early modern periods is strikingly apparent in the attempt to exterminate German mysticism and all its offshoots, whether of the right or left, by training on them the great guns of Church and State. Gregory XI and the Emperor Charles IV solemnly proclaimed on June 17, 1369, their firm intention of eradicating heresy and of burning all books, texts and sermons written in the vernacular; Eckhart's writings were included in the bonfire. Church and State thus admitted that they were both of them too weak to separate the wheat from the chaff, and that both feared the awakening of the people and the nations. German mysticism, although driven underground, yet remained fertile; there sprang from its German poetry and song, both secular and religious, German philosophy and speculation. This is a literature of the "resistance", resistance to the ghost of the Holy Empire, to its heir the sovereign state, and to their allies, the official Church and the official faith. The flaw which separates the outer from the inner kingdom, power from spirit, politics from meta-politics, politicians from intellectuals, and which has been so tragic in its effects on German history, had here its point of origin.

At the consecration of Cologne Cathedral on September 26, 1357, Tauler preached a sermon on the theme of the true consecration of churches, explaining that this was a rite to be celebrated within "the inward-turning man". "Churches make no man holy, but men make churches holy." "Holy" Cologne was the largest, richest and most numinous of all the German cities, made glorious by its golden shrines and the relics of the Three Kings and the Eleven Thousand Virgins, proud possessor of uniquely magnificent churches (turned to dust and ashes by fire in the second world war): but Tauler and his spiritual brothers found nothing of benefit to man in all this routine and ritual of holiness. The real Empire and the real Church lay within. The future and the Kingdom of God belonged to the inward man, for whom the indwelling God, Father, Son and Holy Ghost, brought forth the fruits of the spirit, which are love and true freedom.

In silence, almost unremarked by the great world, a number of German Christians departed on an inner emigration, along paths where the fires and drowning floods of persecution could no longer reach them. Tauler's sermon on the occasion of the consecration of Germany's proudest cathedral raises a final question: what did the men of the Middle Ages —a period when virtually all art was ecclesiastical or religious —look for and achieve in their artistic creation?

CHAPTER 16

ART AND ARCHITECTURE

ANYONE with a dedicated and discerning eye can still see for himself what a wealth of contradictory and opposing forces went to the making of medieval Europe. Medieval art contains all those various elements whose conflict and harmony gave such a vital stimulus to the civilization which produced it. Features borrowed from the Sumerian and other ancient Eastern civilizations entered the European repertoire of forms by way of Romanesque sculpture and architecture, which also made use of primitive Germanic and Celtic styles. Some fresh features, derived from classical antiquity, Islam and Armenia, were added by the designers of French churches in the twelfth century. Medieval art also faithfully reflects the regional and social diversities of the age. About a dozen regional styles can be distinguished, each with its favourite forms of expression, and the various orders of society—monarchs, nobility, bishops, burgesses and common folk—all speak to us through their preferred and characteristic art forms. The world of imagination portrayed in medieval art comprehends monsters of pre-history, dreams of paradise, and infernal horrors of this world and the next. The bas-relief at Amiens which shows a noblewoman kicking her servant in the belly epitomizes feudal arrogance, the sixteen stone oxen high on the towers of Laon cathedral, built from stone hauled by their living brethren, is a tribute to the nobility of the animal world. The essential features of the different ranks of human society, the essence of the arts and sciences, all are captured and preserved, whilst devils and angels abound. Woman is present under all her guises, as Queen of Heaven, saint, peasant, nun, and she-devil with a toad at her naked breast. The masculine roles are usually those of judgment and authority: God is shown as a man judging heaven and earth, and in His Incarnation; man is shown as king of heaven and of earth and in the armour of knighthood; but there are peasants, and serfs too, and plain sinners. This is a candid art, and, true to its folk inspiration, does not shrink from the expression of intense love and hatred. It is quite uninhibited in that it portrays heretics and anti-Christ, and dangerous and detested enemies of the more mundane level, Saracens and Slavs. Contemporary anti-clericalism and anti-monasticism are faithfully reflected, for example when monks are presented in the guise of greedy wolves devouring the sheep, the laity; this kind of comment is most conspicuous in the sculpture of Italian cathedrals. Anti-Semitism also found vent in art, and Jews are shown as pigs. Though there was nothing sentimental about medieval art (this generalization does not entirely hold for Gothic, as will be seen later), its unambiguous austerity was at times capable of great tenderness. In an age when reconciliation at the political and social level was neither possible nor desired, it was perhaps only in art at its most sublime that at least a semblance of harmony was achieved. The artist who fashioned the two companion sculptures "Synagogue" and "Church" at Strasbourg has lavished more sympathy and beauty on "Synagogue" than on her victorious sister. The Naumburg master whose apostles have the features of Slav peasants gave them a dignity equal to that of the proud German noblemen whose effigies adorn the choir. Art was capable even of bridging the great gulfs which separated Western Europe from Byzantium and both from Islam. Arab architectural forms and techniques of building appear in southern France, Italy and Sicily, while a twelfth century book of the Gospels made in Brunswick, far away in the north, is remarkable for its faithful reproduction of Suras from the Koran in the Kufite script. As for Byzantine influence, its tremendous power was felt in successive waves from the ninth century onwards.

Is it then legitimate to speak of reconciliation through art, to claim that in its artistic achievement the different and opposing worlds of medieval civilization reached a genuine co-existence?

There is much in favour of an emphatic affirmative. For example, this theory provides us with a possible explanation for the recurrence as sculptural themes of figures drawn from the ancient past, Odin and the Fenris-wolf, demons and evil spirits, heroes of the Sagas (Dietrich of Bern, for example) and from Arthurian legend; it also accounts for the introduction of classical deities into Christian edifices. For the most part this happened without conscious contrivance; the same process was at work in architecture, with the adoption of classical and extra-European forms and motifs as the basis of freshly thought-out designs. But when we think of those medieval designers whose conscious subjugation of their material was intended as a service to their God and a monument to their own mastery, it is clear that we can no longer speak of reconciliation. With the victory of Gothic, a "tyrannical style", a new province was established in the world of art, whose language was to become an architectural *lingua franca*, valid throughout Europe. Its earliest propagators were the kings of France and the Cistercians, and lay and ecclesiastical princes everywhere were quick to follow suit. This victory was yet another symptom of Europe's impending decline, evidence of the transition from the eclecticism of an open Europe to the closed Europe of the later Middle Ages with its regimented Church and State, concerned above all else with uniformity: one form, one face, one power. Even so, older traditions survived alongside Gothic, and not only in Germany, where they even took on new life in the thirteenth century, when Gothic was at its peak. Nor was Gothic everywhere the same; English, German and Italian Gothic diverged from the French prototype, so much so that all they had in common was a certain resemblance in structure. In Italy and Provence the birth and growth of Gothic were accompanied by a classical revival, the movement known as the "Proto-Renaissance". Moreover, even the gaily-decorated world of later Gothic had also its grotesques, descendants of the Romanesque monsters; they remind us that bad fairies must always attend the birth of beauty.

The real discovery of Europe's Romanesque art (the Romanesque period runs roughly speaking from the mid-eleventh to the thirteenth centuries) dates only from the decades between the two world wars. Now each year brings the discovery of fresh Romanesque wall paintings, formerly obscured by later layers of paint, and of sculptures and capitals removed in the course of renovations to the fabric. The only comparable case is the discovery of the prehistoric cave paintings of France and Spain and of countries outside Europe. The two discoveries are not unrelated. It is fascinating for anyone familiar with modern art that medieval Europe, so familiar to us from thousands of documentary and narrative sources, still sustained an organic connection with the great forms of primitive art common to all continents. In Romanesque art primitive forms and primitive images received plastic expression; here are to be found archetypal visions of the world's decline and end, visions akin to those of the *Song of Voluspá* and of Dante. In the twentieth century it takes a stout heart, strong nerves, and an alert and unprejudiced mind to derive any benefit from an encounter with this great Romanesque art, so impressive in its use of space, columns, sculpture and imagery. For mass and volume Romanesque can compare only with the art of Mesopotamia, Egypt and early Greece and the primitive art of America, Asia and Africa; these qualities are almost entirely lacking from European art between the thirteenth and nineteenth centuries. The monuments of Romanesque are no mere curios, quaint objects to be given a cursory glance and then dismissed with a slick judgment (judgment, in fact, is entirely out of place); they elude the trigger-happy photographer, whose efforts are all too aptly described as "snapshots". What they demand is fear, awe, distance and detachment, patience and silent perseverance, until at last the beholder is brought to a genuine confrontation with the object of his contemplation. We shall come slowly to a proper realization of the elemental power of this art as we concentrate on the basic significance of its forms and means of expression, its handling of space, its use of columns and other forms, its images and the value it attached to stone and colour.

The Middle Ages invested space with a directly metaphysical quality. An enclosure was a vessel to contain what was holy and divine, it united the heights and depths, God, the saints and the dead. Medieval men preferred to build their churches near or over running water (for example Paderborn cathedral), for water was holy, a direct means of communication with the womb of the world where it lay in the depths of the earth. In the ancient world men had done the same, as the foundations of the Greek temples at Paestum still remind us. Space was essentially feminine, a sacred cave, a sacred womb—in fact the womb of "mother Church". Even in the Bronze Age men recognized the feminine character of an area dedicated to sacred rites; an enclosure such as Stonehenge was part of mother earth, quickened to new life through penetration by the fructifying sun. Sacred enclosures protected the dead until the time of their rebirth, for enclosure meant security. The Romanesque church was the stronghold of God, a sure defence against all evil powers and wicked men.

Feminine space was bounded by masculine stone. There are still many regions, in Europe and elsewhere, where people ascribe sacred virtues to stone, such as the power of conquering death and increasing fertility. In the eleventh, twelfth, and to large extent even in the thirteenth century, people lived in houses and hovels made of wood. Only the house of God and His saints was built of stone. Today it is as difficult for us to appreciate the awe inspired by the sight of buildings made from this rare, this unique substance, as it is for us to share the impression of grandeur and size felt by contemporaries as they saw these edifices rising up from the surrounding wooden hovels. When these churches were first built they really were large, overpowering in their immensity; nowadays they are lost among other tall structures and ignored by a public whose appreciation of size has become blunted by the sheer bulk of modern building.

Space, stone and immensity were all attributes of holiness; they were raised to a still higher power by the superimposition of towers and the presence of columns. The tower of a Romanesque church (where the bell was lodged) was the fortified outpost against the devil of some angelic task-force, often commanded by the Archangel Michael. Columns housed the tree of life and were hallowed things; to damage them was a most serious offence, as may be discovered from the *Lex Baiuvariorum*. It was admitted that they were mortal, yet they were capable of working miracles. Their function was to serve in God's house as lesser load-bearers in the service of a greater, the victorious Christ-God. The men who decorated these columns did so in rapt devotion, in a spirit of love and dread. Their capitals tell the tale of man's redemption, pointed by figures drawn from ancient mythology, from the saga-heroes of folk history and the legends of the saints. These columns are richly varied. There are some with animal motifs, others from which a human form gradually emerges, forced into shape by a dynamic inner momentum, others again where the spell of primitive terror has been finally shaken off and the mature human form is revealed in the round, with only a betraying twitch in a garment to reveal the memory of ancient and confining powers. When all these are considered together, it can be seen that there is a connection between these Romanesque columns and the birth of man as an individual in the full-scale humanistic statuary of Gothic.

Romanesque churches were drenched in colour. Walls, ceiling (for a long time still made of wood) and columns all blossomed in various hues, ochre, green, blue and violet being the colours preferred. The effect might be further heightened by tapestries on the walls and the golden splendour of light streaming from eight-spired chandeliers, as from the eight turrets of the heavenly Jerusalem. In the words of the introit of the Mass for the consecration of a church, "*Terribilis est locus iste. Vere est aula Dei et porta coeli*": "This is a place of awe. Here is the court of God and the gate of Heaven." And the Emperor of Heaven, Lord of justice, Lord of the living and the dead, Lord of good and evil spirits, invited the faithful believer to enter in, to do Him service and take part in a celebration, a banquet.

One of the commonest ground-plans of the Romanesque church, the four-square basilica consisting of a nave and two aisles, had a long ancestry. Used by the Egyptians for their throne-basilicas, it was introduced into the northern and western Mediterranean by way of the Hellenistic kingdoms and took on a new lease of life in the Roman Empire, where it was employed for imperial palaces (the Flavian palace on the Palatine, the Villa Hadriani at Tivoli, Diocletian's palace at Spalato), for the *praetoria* or official residence of Roman generals in the provinces, for law-courts, synagogues and the meeting-halls of various cults. In the Romanesque Middle Ages it was used to build the court of the King of Heaven, a stronghold both spiritual and physical, since it provided a refuge in times of invasion and civil war. Some of the Carolingian churches are known to have been built on this plan: the monastic church at Fulda, 791–822, the earliest version of Cologne cathedral, *circa* 800, Centula, otherwise known as St Riquier, which was started in 790, and Corvey and St Gall in the ninth century. In more peaceful times it was also used for city halls, places where the citizens assembled and where decisions were reached on important religious and political issues; these are to be found chiefly in Italy.

There were of course other plans. In some churches the nave and aisles were nearly equal in height ("hall-churches"); others were built on the central pattern, in imitation of Santa Sophia at Constantinople and its many western daughter-churches. Village churches were built in their hundreds, simple edifices in solid stone with a single undivided nave and a tower. But for all their simplicity these churches have a look of assurance; they are tranquilly self-contained, deceptively simple in the even distribution of their mass, secure in the knowledge that they sheltered God and the means to salvation. Such churches were being built everywhere in Europe between the ninth and the thirteenth centuries. Many of them are still to be seen in the byways of Central Europe, in the remoter Swiss valleys, in Bavaria, the Tyrol and northern Italy. They were built by the peasants, with the help of the patron to whom the land belonged.

The larger Romanesque churches were built by religious communities, in France and Spain by the Cluniacs, in Germany by the congregation of Hirsau, and were designed to attract pilgrims. Bishops were also building, and competed with the monks in grandeur and wealth of invention. The Gothic era brought new patrons; the French monarchy and the royal bishops, new religious congregations such as the Cistercians and the Premonstratensians, new Orders such as the Franciscans and Dominicans, and the city fathers of the new towns. With this development the "democratic" hall-church was supplanted by buildings devised on a hierarchical plan, in which monks, cathedral dignitaries, bishop and king all had their assigned place and the laity was kept firmly apart, separated from the choir by a screen.

In the Carolingian period Europe knew nothing of "national" styles of architecture. Palaces and churches in the Carolingian style might be found in any part of the Empire. It was around the beginning of the eleventh century that certain basic regional and national types of structure began to emerge. Thus we can say that St Michael's at Hildesheim is "typically" Saxon or north German, the chancel of St Martin's at Tours "typically" French. This process of diversification reached its height in the open Europe of the twelfth century.

Romanesque art can be divided roughly into two main regional types, the Mediterranean and the Northern. The former included Italy and southern France, the latter England, northern France (the Ile de France and Normandy), Burgundy, Flanders and Germany. In art as in other spheres there was a much greater contrast between northern and southern France than between northern France and Germany. Burgundy fell somewhere in the middle. Langres and Vézélay, the great pilgrim church where Bernard of Clairvaux preached the Second Crusade, inclined to the north, Autun and Cluny III to the Mediterranean. By Cluny III is meant the third rebuilding of the great mother-church of the Cluniacs, which was reconsecrated in 1130 and finished only with the completion of the west end in 1220. Destroyed in the French Revolution, this was a church of enormous dimensions, with a rosette of chapels radiating from the chancel apse. These monastic churches were designed as reliquaries on a gigantic scale and as a worthy setting for the great pomp of monastic liturgical ceremonies; they were capable of accommodating vast crowds of pilgrims. The naves were divided lengthways into three, five or even more aisles, with towers to crown the numerous inter-sections formed by the transepts. Pilgrims entering the church were confronted with elaborately sculpted portals depicting the horrors of the Last Judgment and the bliss in store for the elect.

The barrel- and cross-vaulted churches of Burgundy (Cluny was an example of the former, Vézélay of the latter) stood midway between the Norman method of con-struction and the southern schools. Norman techniques are in many ways an anticipation of Gothic: the segmentation of the wall area into bays made fully-fledged rib-vaulting a practical possibility, since selected portions of masonry could bear the thrust. In the North men strove towards the articu-lation and disengagement of their solid mass of masonry; in the South it was emphasized for what it was and chained so firmly to the earth as to give the appearance of a single block of stone. The interior of such a church is like a cavern hewn from the rock, its exterior is topped by a massive superstructure of barrel-vaulting and cupolas. The Roman-esque churches of Aquitaine, Anjou and Saintonge were of this frowning, heavily-domed type, Poitou had splendid hall-churches (like Notre-Dame-la-Grande at Poitiers), and there were even more lofty examples in the Auvergne, at Toulouse (St Sernin) and at Conques (Ste Foi). These churches were situated on the pilgrim route controlled by Cluny which led to Santiago de Compostela, to the oratory of St Michael on Monte Gargano and to places such as Conques in France itself. In the Auvergne there developed the custom, which originated in the tenth century, of parading the effigies of the saints round the countryside. These fetish-like images, resplendent in gold and hieratic in their staring passivity, provoked mixed feelings of awe and indignation in northern clerics who witnessed the spectacle.

Southern French Romanesque had its share of the horrific, as the portals of Moissac and Souillac bear witness. But it could also draw on the limpid charm of southern, oriental and classical art. Roman models were openly adopted, as in the magnificent west portal of St Trophime at Arles and at St-Gilles-du-Gard. Some exquisite small churches were built in the South, churches whose classical outlines seen rising gently from the red earth of the vineyards and the olive groves are irresistibly reminiscent of pagan temples. The classical simplicity and tenderness so many travellers have admired in that Tuscan jewel, the church of San Miniato above Florence, are equally to be found in these Provençal sister-churches. Between Cahors and Angoulême the domed churches of Aquitaine give the Gallic skyline a distinctly outlandish, oriental air; St-Front at Périgueux, like St Mark's at Venice, is a copy of the Church of the Apostles at Constantinople. Other domed churches are Cahors cathedral and St-Etienne-de-la-Cité at Périgueux.

German Romanesque, although it produced nothing so exotic and colourful, nevertheless developed forms and regional variations of its own. There was a readiness to accept and adapt Western (principally French) ideas, particularly on the part of the Congregation of Hirsau, who made Cluny their model in architectural as well as religious matters. It was Cluny II, not Cluny III, that was the decisive influence here. Built on the basilica pattern, these German churches have steeply-rising naves and a tautness of construction which hurry the eye forward to the chancel in the East; the masonry is austere, the columns classical in inspiration, there are towers at each end, and sometimes also over the crossings. Although echoes of Hirsau are to be found all over German territory, regional styles continued to flourish in Lower Saxony, Westphalia, the lower Rhineland, Alsace, the middle and upper Rhineland, Bavaria and Austria. Lower Saxony was the seat of the Ottonian dynasty and the home of "Ottonian" art, in the eleventh century still second to none in Europe in monumental quality, an art of truly imperial proportions. The churches of this region were built according to the metrical system, that is to say there is a rhythmical alternation of columns and piers running the length of the nave. Impressive examples of this imperial style are provided by the abbey church of Quedlinburg, St Godehard's in Hildesheim, the Church of the Virgin at Halberstadt and the cathedrals of Lübeck and Hildesheim. The hall-churches of Westphalia (St Patroklus in Soest, for example) may be cited as examples of a totally different idiom. These are real "mother-churches", gravid, earth-bound, built by men of peasant stock who were conscious that mother earth and the mother of God held them equally in thrall. The building of these churches was probably much influenced by the chapel of St Bartholomew at Paderborn, built in 1017, which has many Byzantine features.

The influence of both Byzantine and Roman provincial architecture can be seen in the spaciousness of the central areas of the trefoil churches of Cologne, which are related to the domed churches of southern France. The oppressiveness of the great mass is alleviated from the outside by dwarf galleries, a typically Rhenish *jeu d'esprit*. In German Alsace there was an increase in French influence from the twelfth century onwards. In Bavaria, while Regensburg took its inspiration from southern France, Freising had more in common with northern Italy, notably a ponderous style of building and the employment of decorative motifs and sculptural themes which are echoes from the period of the migrations.

Churches built with two choirs, churches with two transepts, emphasis on *Westwork* and symmetrical chapels are all typical of German Romanesque. The duplication of the choir and the emphasis on the West end should certainly be regarded as having a religious-political significance. In a Roman basilica all attention was directed to the East end, with its concentration of tower and altar, choir and clergy. The German designers, by drawing equal attention to the West, created a symmetry of powers; the East end, the preserve of the clergy, was balanced by a West end which had its own choir topped by one or more towers. *Westwork* was already a feature in Carolingian times; it was from the West that demons and evil spirits threatened and in the West that the Archangel Michael held the fort. But it also had symbolical significance as the seat of the Emperor (in the Emperor's gallery), so that Michael became by association the supreme protector of the Empire. There was nothing fortuitous in the fact that "Romanizing" reform movements tended to suppress this pleasantly archaic feature. In Germany attempts were made during the twelfth century to reinstate *Westwork* as a concrete contribution towards restoring the shattered equilibrium of *regnum* and *sacerdotium*, Empire and Papacy.

The double choir, which was without precedent and was never imitated elsewhere in Europe, was a constant feature of German architecture from the late eighth until the mid-thirteenth century. The Ottonian ground plan was still being used for new foundations even in the time of the later Hohenstaufen. It is probably an over-simplification to see the eastern choir purely as the symbol of monastic renunciation of the world and superiority to its demands and the western choir purely as the symbol of independent imperial authority. But it must surely be conceded that the urge to balance these two polarized forces, to create a tectonic equilibrium within the church itself between the spiritual and temporal authority, between the central cluster and its longitudinal extension, had its inspiration in the German conception of the Holy Empire as a partnership between Pope and Emperor.

The three "imperial" cathedrals, Speyer, Worms and Mainz, are of unparalleled majesty. When alterations and additions were made to Mainz and Worms in the twelfth and early thirteenth centuries, the Ottonian foundations were preserved, so that we have two massive structures confronting one another at East and West. Groups of towers and flanking turrets, dwarf galleries around the sections of the choir, resolve the ponderous mass and help to create an impression of proud and serene elegance. Speyer, the oldest of the three, was built by the Salian Emperors of the eleventh century (Conrad II, Henry III and Henry IV) and remodelled during the twelfth; it is also the most austere and the most impressive. Speyer is a massive citadel, not only of the Emperor of Heaven but also of the terrestrial Emperor and his episcopal lieutenants—Benno of Osnabrück and Otto of Bamberg helped in the building. It is also a tribute to human belief in the virtues of sacred stone (the western wall is about twenty feet thick!) and the power of mass subdued: here reigns majesty and dread, forcing the faithful to their knees. Here sovereignty is made concrete.

In its initial form Speyer was pure architecture, making its effect without recourse to reliefs such as are found at Worms and Mainz from the twelfth century. There the earliest sculpted figures are of animals; human forms appear only around the year 1200. Then man is shown wrestling with the powers of evil: Daniel with two lions, Samson as lion-killer, a lion getting the better of a man wearing a spiked cap (evil engulfs those not armed by Christ). The scenes on the tombstones of two archbishops of Mainz, Siegfried von Eppstein and Peter Aichspalt, which show tiny kings being crowned by giant ecclesiastics, belong to a later, post-Romanesque period, after the collapse of the Holy Empire, as do the imperial portraits at Speyer.

In the twelfth and early thirteenth centuries the magical world of Romanesque sculpture extended from northern Italy as far as Norway. As in vernacular literature, ancient powers were waking to fresh life as monsters and demons, heroes and devils joined combat on capitals, fonts and portals. Feelings of dread and the fear of Hell were living realities in the mass soul, and art offered a means of exorcism. This terror is what lies behind the animal-decorated column in the crypt at Freising, a representation of Odin and the Fenris-wolf; apocalyptic scenes such as are found on the north portal of St Jacob at Regensburg; the Romanesque work on the great door of St Stephen's cathedral in Vienna. Other examples may be found at Schöngraben, in the Grossmünster at Zurich, in the castle chapel of St Margaret at Nuremberg, at St Peter Turmfries in Hirsau, on the famous font of Freudenstadt, and on the portals of early twelfth century Norwegian churches, which illustrate amongst other subjects the saga of Sigurd.

In the world of Romanesque ornament and sculpture, monsters and monstrosities which were part of Europe's Celtic and Germanic inheritance mingle with a riot of horrendous themes and figures of Oriental origin, coming from Asia, Mesopotamia, the Steppes, ancient Sumeria, Coptic Egypt, Armenia, Georgia and Syria. Their very profusion shows how great was the hold of anxiety, hatred and brutality over the popular soul, and how much it stood in need of constraint and exorcism. Exorcism is to be taken quite literally; the practitioners of folk magic (still not extinct) and the men who made these sculptures tied knots to fend off evil. Knotted columns were much favoured and are to be found in the interior of churches and at the entrance; they were also used in private houses. Columns decorated with lions and other beasts served a similar purpose. An impressive example of this exorcising urge is provided by the pier of the doorway at Souillac, where monsters are shown locked in a Laocoön struggle with men and the kinder beasts. In France modifications of this motif were introduced at an early date as saints took over the task of warding off evil: thus the pier of St Peter's in Moissac has apostles as well as lionesses. In the Gothic cathedrals the animals have been eliminated altogether and their place and function assumed by statues on the central pier. In fact, in Gothic the more extreme monsters and terrors have either been banished or humanized, even when the subject illustrated is the Last Judgment. Great Romanesque sculpture, on the other hand, is dedicated to the task of exorcizing and confining terror, and this is particularly true of French Romanesque. The Christ of French Romanesque sculpture sits enthroned, the dread Lord of the Last Judgment, surrounded by no less dread figures which are symbols of the four evangelists. Even the Pentecostal Christ of Vézélay is a God of terror, and at Moissac Christ has become an Oriental despot. In the most sublime examples of French sculpture God incarnate and His angels have become ecstatic, trans-human, awe-demanding figures; one sees them at Vézélay, Autun, Angoulême (on the gable of the cathedral's western façade), Beaulieu and Moissac. Gothic sculpture has an entirely opposite effect, as though providing relief from intolerable pressure; its loss in numinous and magical power is balanced by a gain in "humanity". This willingness to pay so high a price is a key to the triumph of Gothic.

That this price was indeed high can be seen at a glance, by comparing the Gothic murals, with all their grace and ready appeal, with Romanesque wall-painting. True, even Romanesque painting is not without its humanistic and harmonious features, probably the result of Cluniac influence, which in turn derived inspiration from contact with the classical South, the Mediterranean, Rome and Ravenna. At Berzé-la-Ville, for example, the whole company of Heaven inclines in a beautifully composed symphony before a Christ in splendour, clothed in the majestic garb of Cosmocrator. This is aristocratic art. Against it can be set frescoes of an entirely different sort—though both descend from a remote common ancestor, the prehistoric cave paintings. In small parish churches scattered up and down the country one finds wall-paintings which are ecstatic, prophetic, apocalyptic, throbbing with magic; here monsters of the deep are conjured up and exorcized. To this category belong the illustrations of the Apocalypse at St-Savin-sur-Gartempe (probably mid-twelfth century), which are perhaps modelled on a Saxon manuscript of the Carolingian period, and the *psychomachia* (war of the virtues and vices) of the crypt at Tavant; among the subjects is one which in the later Middle Ages acquired a distinctly religious-political significance, the labour of Adam and Eve. The priory church of St-Gilles at Montoire has a dominating figure of Christ enthroned on the rainbow, a gigantic and potent figure; the church of Notre Dame at Montmorillon has an enormous figure of the Virgin, the Woman of the Apocalypse; at Vic the several scenes seem caught up in one sweeping movement, as the Three Kings ride to pay homage, the apostles gaze open-eyed in terror upon Christ, and Christ Himself turns with terrifying intensity towards Judas, who hurls himself at his Master to give his betraying kiss.

German Romanesque sculpture, painting and goldsmiths' work were very different. Until the early twelfth century, when primacy in this art passed to France, German sculpture was second to none, and even then the German craftsmen retained their skill in mastering a wealth of forms and continued to produce much fine work. During the early twelfth century their style of sculpture inclined to the impressionistic, and was not far removed from the delicacy of painting. Later the moulding becomes more robust and monumental, as artists sought to give power and dignity to their creations by an effect of self-contained solidity. This transition can be traced through a series of monuments: the grave-stones of the abbesses of Quedlinburg, the tablet of Archbishop Friedrich of Wettin in the cathedral of Magdeburg, the figures of Christ and an apostle from the gallery at Gröning, the marble reliefs of an ambo in the chapter refectory at Magdeburg (*circa* 1160–80, angelic forms bearing the Beatitudes), the choir-screen at St Michael's in Hildesheim and the church of the Virgin, Halberstadt. The first fully rounded figures are to be found at Brauweiler near Cologne, in an altarpiece of the Madonna between two saints, which shows the three figures standing together in an attitude of perfect tranquillity. The supreme example of Rhenish Romanesque sculpture in stone is to be found at the cathedral of Trier, and represents Christ enthroned between the Virgin and St Peter. The best-known of German Romanesque sculptures is in bronze: the lion of Brunswick, deservedly popular as a lively and convincing compliment to Henry the Lion, the most powerful prince in Germany next to Frederick I. Compared with this king of beasts, Henry and his wife as they appear in effigy on their tombstones in Brunswick cathedral look mild and peaceable.

Twelfth and early thirteenth century crucifixes of German workmanship are an eloquent expression of pain and dignity, of suffering and the conquest of suffering. No longer an autocrat enthroned on the Cross, unbending even in death, Christ is now shown dying a real death, His tortured body distorted by its agony (this is particularly characteristic of Swabian and Rhenish work). But the great Ottonian tradition was not entirely abandoned, as may be seen from the crucifix of Walsdorf (*circa* 1200), a bigger than life-size copy of an Ottonian model.

The art of working in gold came to Germany by way of lower Lotharingia, the region of the Meuse. German smiths fashioned caskets, shrines, reliquaries and altarpieces which still blaze with gold and gems and enamel. Nicholas of Verdun's altar at Klosterneuburg, the shrine of the Three Kings in Cologne cathedral and the shrine of the Virgin at Aachen were all completed between 1180 and 1230, almost a century before the school of Roger of Helmarshausen was at work, and must be reckoned among the most precious of medieval works of art.

Some six or seven regional schools can be distinguished among German illuminated manuscripts of the twelfth century. The most important was that of Salzburg, the seat of an archbishopric and an outpost of Byzantine art. The Salzburg Bible of Admont and the convent Bible of St Peter's, Salzburg, are so rich in colour and imagery that these "giant Bibles" are justly ranked among European masterpieces. Mural painting reached an equally high level, as may be seen in the frescoes of Kloster Nonnburg and the work of Meister Heinrich (*circa* 1220) in the West gallery of the cathedral of Gurk. Here at Gurk is depicted the entire history of the world from the Fall to the time of Christ, together with a life of the Virgin, executed in a manner which comes closer to that of an abstract drawing than to the older, more plastic, painter's technique. The only colours used are blue, red and green. All the emphasis is on the majesty of God and the splendour of Heaven, to the complete neglect of the Passion. This was a subject the Byzantines commonly avoided. At Ravenna, a city long under Byzantine control, a fresco depicting the Passion had been allowed to vanish away. Byzantium triumphed again in the splendours of this episcopally-inspired art at Gurk. The portraits of two bishops, Otto and Dietrich, show how thoroughly Heinrich had adapted himself to the prevailing atmosphere of the episcopal court, where he held an important position.

In the German lands of the Empire it was the bishops who led the way as patrons of art and architecture; even the imperial cathedrals of the Rhineland were their creation. There was no competition from the towns until the thirteenth century. In Italy, above all in Lombardy, it was the townsmen who built churches, to mark their rejection of episcopal control. The chroniclers emphasized the co-operative nature of the effort which went into the building of a cathedral, in which the whole population shared. Since possession of a large church or cathedral was an emblem of political and economic power, each town strove to outdo the next in the size and grandeur of its constructions. Scenes showing the merchant and craft guilds at work and other episodes of daily life occur not infrequently among the subjects illustrated (as at Piacenza and Borgo San Donnino), and were often complemented by frankly anti-clerical and anti-monastic figures, such as the wolf-monk of Parma, Ferrara and Verona. There was a distinct preference for churches of the "hall" type, used by the townsmen as a meeting-place for their councils and for assemblies of every sort (for example, St Ambrose, Milan).

While northern Romanesque remained the chief influence in the northern parts of Italy during the twelfth century, Florence and Rome were already becoming affected by strongly "Renaissance" impulses. There was a conscious adherence to native Roman tradition in face of the Byzantine flood which was encroaching on central Italy from both sides, from Venice in the East and from Norman Sicily and Greek southern Italy in the West and South. In Florence the classical tradition had never died out and it was now consciously fostered. In this so-called "Proto-Renaissance" of the twelfth century the Roman virtues of simplicity, lucidity and harmony were invoked against the "barbarism" of northern styles. In the fifteenth century there were Florentine purists who propounded their views as a fully-developed aesthetic theory, according to which everything "medieval" and "Gothic" was a perversion of the "purity" of antiquity. The conscious adoption of classical Roman motifs in Florentine architecture during the twelfth century should certainly be understood as a silent protest against the outlandish "barbarians" and their barbarous styles.

In Italy politics and art went hand in hand; artistic

creativeness helped to increase political prestige, and was exploited for this purpose by the Papacy, the towns and the nobility. Consider, for example, the much-debated mosaics in the Lateran, placed there by the Popes as a living reminder of their triumph over the Empire. When the city of Rome entered the arena as champion of classical antiquity, it initiated a lengthy struggle with the Papacy. Rome was no longer prepared to be regarded as a convenient pile of debris in which great secular and spiritual lords could quarry to their heart's content in search of stone for building their churches and palaces. A decree of the senate in 1162 made any injury done to Trajan's column punishable by death: this monument was to be preserved to the end of time "in honour of the church and of the Romans". People now began to collect antiques; Cardinal Orsini, for example, a contemporary of Frederick I, and Henry of Winchester, who visited Rome in 1151 in search of classical antiquities. The *Mirabilia urbis Romae*, a twelfth-century description of the marvels of Rome, was an early product of this Roman revival.

The thirteenth century saw the emergence for the first time of great art produced under papal patronage, in the tremendous creations of Pietro Cavallini (born *circa* 1250). In Cavallini's work Byzantine and Romano-Papal traditions are fused. His mosaics and frescoes in S. Maria Maggiore, S. Paolo fuori le Mura and the old church of Trastevere present us with a classically tranquil Heaven, serene under the rule of a "Christian Jupiter" and a Papal Christ (even Dante could describe Christ as "Jupiter supreme"). The apostles who look like senators in their toga-like garments are a worthy entourage for a celestial *Imperator*, whose terrestrial counterpart, the Pope, is surrounded by cardinals clothed in equal dignity.

This is perhaps a suitable moment to refer briefly to medieval notions concerning the use of colour, since it reflects the long survival of traditions associated with the late classical Emperor-cult. Whilst these traditions still held force (as they did until the thirteenth century), the artist was made to suppress his subjective ideas and impressions and keep strictly to the colour-schemes dictated by a protocol which invested each colour with an objective, symbolical and sacramental significance. The early Christians took over the system prescribed for the Emperors and imperial dignitaries: thus martyrs were always to be shown clothed in the white raiment of *candidi*, the "white ones" of East Roman imperial ceremonial, and Christ was to be robed in purple and gold, the colours of authority. The company of Heaven appeared in the colours appropriate to the state hierarchy of late classical times. The liturgical colours also had their origin in imperial court ceremonies; white, purple, gold (yellow), blue and red were the sacred colours. Colours used in this way were glowing symbols which proclaimed that all the attributes and powers formerly belonging to the Roman Empire and its Emperor had passed to Christ, as Emperor of Heaven, and to His terrestrial representative, the Pope. In the thirteenth century, starting with Innocent III, the Popes embarked on their great enterprise of rebuilding Rome as the city of God, governor of the cosmos, on earth; this implied that every new construction was to be understood as representing a rebirth of that imperial-papal Rome, whose splendour, as manifest in the basilicas of Constantine, already attracted the eye of every visitor from whatever part of Europe.

This "Golden Rome", which in the twelfth century sought to assert itself by the restoration of decaying churches, had a close rival in the wonder-world of Norman Sicilian and South Italian architecture, clothed in the splendour of forms derived not only from classical but also from Byzantine and Arab art. This richness was designed to show the world, and especially Rome, that the Norman kings were the rightful leaders of secular Christendom. Palermo, with its Cappella Palatina (completed in 1143), the proud chain of Norman cathedrals, Monreale, Palermo, Capua and Salerno, with Cefalù (1145) as its first link, the numerous castles and smaller fortresses (Zisa and Bari), did in fact arouse the wonder and admiration both of Christian Europe and of Islam. An Arab, Ibn Dschubair, was loud in his praises of the Martorana church at Palermo: "The inner walls of the temple are of gold—but that is too tame, they are a sheer mass of gold. They contain lozenges of coloured marble, the like of which no man has ever seen. . . . Suns of gilded glass raised on high and so radiant that they blind the eye bemused our minds so sore that we cried on Allah to defend us from them." The Arab ends his enthusiastic account with a pious wish: "May God in His grace and goodness grant that the call of the Muezzin may soon be heard sounding from the tower." As everyone knows, three centuries later this wish was granted in respect of the Byzantine churches in Constantinople.

In a sermon preached at the dedication of the Cappella Palatina in Palermo on June 29, 1140, Theophanes Ceramaeus paid a compelling tribute to its qualities: "In this house of God a truly great and royal mind has created his perpetual memorial, has laid, as it were, a strong foundation-stone to his palace. It is both grand and great, and gleams with a pristine beauty, sparkling with light, refulgent with gold, glittering with gems, blossoming in paint. It strikes afresh at every visit, as though seen for the first time, and the eye moves over its marvels with wonder and astonishment. The ceiling-vault is breathtaking, to contemplate it is wonderful, even to hear it described an experience . . ."

These marvels of a refined and luxurious art were made to be admired, to be "seen". Here we have the beginning of the cult of the "aesthetic", a frank and conscious enjoyment of visual beauty, whose physical and magical aspects gave equal satisfaction. A great gulf separates this art from the Romanesque of the more northerly cathedrals and churches, whose impact was "felt" rather than "seen". They were sacred places, and the chroniclers who describe them succinctly in terms of their size were conveying accurately their effect on the faithful.

The Apulian churches of the Romanesque family are large and impressive by any standard. Many have huge, cliff-like walls on their eastern side, as at Bari, Bitono and Giovinazzo, which has two eastern towers. These and the others, Manfredonia, Lecce, Otranto, Canosa and Monte Sant' Angelo, still stand out as aliens in an alien landscape. The castles which were the Hohenstaufen inheritance from the Norman kings of Sicily have the same effect, Castel del Monte, Lagopesole, Melfi, Gioa del Colle and Lucera.

Frederick II made these castles the incarnation in stone and significant proportion of his classical vision of *imperium*. His castles and his public buildings in Sicily were a talisman against the power of papal Rome and the independence of monks and townsmen. When Frederick's power was broken one of his craftsmen fled to Pisa, which was still loyal to the Emperor, and took from it his name, Nicolo Pisano. It is clear from his work that Nicolo had a close knowledge of classical sarcophagi, and his stone pulpits in the baptistery of Pisa and in Siena Cathedral are the first medieval monuments of this kind to rely on classical form and classical proportions.

Although the Italians adopted some features of Gothic,

they used them for the embellishments of structures still consciously or unconsciously subordinated to the requirements of classical form. The great Giotto (*circa* 1267–1337), who was caught up in the artistic frenzy produced by the life of St Francis, combined three styles, Gothic, Byzantine and Italian. His frescoes in the Arena chapel at Padua mark the beginning of a new era in European painting. The frescoes of other more or less contemporary Italians, Cimabue, the two Gaddi, Andrea of Florence, Vardo di Cione and Andrea Orcagna, and the Sienese school of Duccio di Buoninsegna, Simone Martini and the two Lorenzetti belong to the autumn of medieval Italy. These are strong paintings, satisfying to the eye, at once astringent and precious, and alive with all manner of memories and influences. Some are impersonal; others are boldly stamped with an individual vision, the hallmark of a distinct personality. Here is Italy as Dante saw it, a garden of mankind in full flower. This luxuriant growth owed nothing to the might of a sturdy young Emperor or to the authority of the Popes, who had summoned their artists away to distant Avignon. It sprang from the vitality of numerous native and competing talents, fostered by the towns, by the great urban dynasties and the guilds, who lived in constant rivalry, if not in open warfare. The springing abundance of forms and styles to be found in Italian art between 1260 and 1350 is a striking and accurate reflection of the great inner turbulence of Italy at this time, as the number of its principalities and city-states multiplied.

This creative diversity, characteristic not only of Italy but also of Romanesque art everywhere in Europe, was now confronted by a strongly disciplined style of architecture, an "engineer's" art in which technique is everything: Gothic. Romanesque variety was firmly thrust aside under the coercive power of this new and advancing system. Gothic originated in the Ile de France, the French royal demesne, which in artistic matters was the most backward region of France: it contained that Paris whose barbarism had so appalled Eleanor of Aquitaine. Here there was still a void unencroached upon by those Romanesque churches which elsewhere in France luxuriated in a richness of turretry and façade, in choirs wreathed with a rosette of chapels, a cheerful mélange of diverse styles and forms.

The ascetic purism of the Gothic style could come into being only in a vacuum, in the unrewarding soil of the French royal demesne and under the guiding hand of a hard-headed talent for organization. Suger of St Denis, who was anxious to build a new church worthy of the sacred dynasty he served, came of peasant stock and had just such a talent. He was able to enlist six powerful ecclesiastics as allies in his enterprise, peers of France and loyal and wealthy vassals of the crown: the Archbishop of Rheims and the Bishops of Laon, Langres, Chalons, Beauvais and Noyon. Since these churchmen were united in their hostility to the lay aristocracy this alliance had also its political aspect. The political setting in fact played an important part in the origin of Gothic. Suger the royalist was counsellor and friend to both Louis VI and Louis VII and on occasion acted as regent. He favoured an *alliance cordiale* with England and the Pope against the Emperor and the Germans. He built his abbey church of St Denis as a model of what the church of a *Rex Christianissimus* (the style is his own) ought to be.

Suger, a new-style Mayor of the Palace, supervised everything down to the smallest detail. He selected the finest timbers from the forest, arranged for the transport of suitable columns by ox-cart over considerable distances, was himself chief overseer of the building and of all the craftsmen employed, masons, goldsmiths and painters, and the proud author of a solemn account of the dedication in 1144 (*Liber de consecratione ecclesiae*). The day of consecration was a red-letter day for the West: it saw the birth of Gothic. Nineteen bishops and archbishops consecrated the altars (a Gothic cathedral might have thirty altars and more), King Louis VII, the Lord's Anointed, with twelve knights played the part of Christ and the twelve Apostles. St Denis, the archetype of the Gothic cathedral, became, as intended, the supreme witness to the sanctity of Capetian kingship. Paris, Chartres, Rheims and Amiens all faithfully followed their model, down to the galleries of kings and the echoing of sculptural motifs.

St Denis was the first abbey church in the Gothic style, Sens the first Gothic cathedral, the western façades of St Denis and Chartres the earliest examples of Gothic sculpture. They were the work of three men, Henry, Bishop of Sens, Geoffrey, Bishop of Chartres, and Suger himself, men united by the ties of friendship and their common outlook on politics and ecclesiastical affairs.

But what started as an individual effort soon became a collective enterprise. St Denis was Suger's unaided work and was financed by the contributions of a comparatively narrow

circle of lay and ecclesiastical vassals of the Crown. The rebuilding of Chartres Cathedral between 1194 and 1220 (the
western façade was completed earlier and escaped destruction in the fire of 1194) belongs already in the much wider
context of the growing tide of French nationalism; the
cathedral builders were building themselves into a nation.
Noblemen, townsmen, merchants and peasants all shared in
the burdens, both literally and figuratively. The cover of the
cathedral obit book shows the Virgin with bishops, knights,
burgesses and peasants on her left hand, kings, queens, burgesses and peasants on her right, and this was a just and
fitting tribute. Chartres, like many other Gothic churches, is
dedicated to the Virgin, mother of the people and the nation. Rich gifts came to Chartres from Celtic Brittany—
Peter of Dreux, its Duke, made a particularly munificent do-
nation—and the city itself came to have a prosperous and
influential Breton community. The Gothic style, in which
"material" considerations were paramount, was a medium in
which the imaginative and practical talents of the Celts could
unite.

The cathedral was the property of the Chapter, who earned
a considerable revenue from its altars. The annual income
of the Dean alone has been calculated at £250,000 (2,300
livres tournois). The fame of the Chartres fairs, held on the
four great festivals of the Virgin, attracted a crowd of pilgrims and their money. Merchants set up stalls within the
precincts of the cathedral, strangers to the town slept by
night under its portals and in parts of the crypt, craftsmen
loitered within the church by day, hoping that someone
would give them work. Even food could be bought inside
the church, and although the Chapter at one time had to
forbid the sale of wine in the nave, they set aside part of the
crypt for the purpose.

These mundane remarks may seem out of place in a discussion of an architectural masterpiece whose magic has
kindled romantic yearnings and genuine piety in so many
beholders. The Chartres of Henry Brooks Adams and Charles
Peguy surely deserves something better. But Gothic, and
above all French cathedral Gothic, was just as important for
its technical excellence, as a feat of engineering, the product
of a cool and calculating intellect, as it was for its spiritual
quality: here God was worshipped most highly in His attributes of light, measure and number.

"When He prepared the heavens I was there: when He set

a compass upon the face of the deep." This passage from the Book of Proverbs (viii, 27) is strikingly illustrated in a *Bible moralisée* of the mid-thirteenth century: God, as architect of the universe, measures the world like a geometer, compasses in hand. There is nothing mysterious about the unparalleled success of Gothic; a new technique and a new approach to art were yoked to a spiritual vision heavily preoccupied with "technology", with mathematics and geometry. This is something particularly relevant to our own times.

The men of the thirteenth century accorded their great architects as much respect and admiration as did the men of the Renaissance. The documents listing his revenues and privileges make it clear that the anonymous architect of Chartres was a layman. Pierre de Montreuil and Hugo Libergier, the architects of Rheims and Amiens, are proudly commemorated in their grave inscriptions, worked into curious labyrinths on the pavements of their cathedrals. The members of this new class of professional engineers and technologists were conscious of their skill and qualities, and their self-awareness expressed itself through the creation of the earliest genuinely international organization. Lodges of free masons were set up wherever a Gothic building was in progress; and the masons went to build wherever they were invited.

None of the basic elements of the Gothic style was a new invention. Modifications of the Armenian pointed arch and the rib-vault, an Arab invention, were in use in Europe from the end of the tenth century. The Gothic pointed arch is of Anglo-Norman origin; the earliest examples of it are to be found at Durham (late eleventh century), Winchester (after 1107), Peterborough (1118) and Gloucester (between 1100 and 1120). Despite the many unique contributions made in Normandy itself to the evolution of Gothic, no completely Gothic building was erected there until after its annexation by Philip Augustus. The cathedral of Le Mans, the capital of Maine, was originally designed in the Romanesque style, even though the earliest Gothic cathedrals were already in being; it was only after Maine had been annexed to the French crown that the Chapter decided on a Gothic construction for the choir, a decision which resulted in one of the most perfect examples of the style. Southern France resisted Gothic, and it was not until about 1250, after the subjugation of the Midi, that Gothic began to spread there. Admittedly, from the mid-twelfth century the French pointed arch was being introduced into Germany, Spain, Italy, Scandinavia, Hungary and Portugal by the international network of Cistercian houses, some 350 in all. But Cistercian Gothic retained certain basic Romanesque qualities and kept close to the freshness, purity and *naïveté* of its beginnings. For a long time to come this Cistercian Gothic would have a greater appeal for the less sophisticated peoples of Europe than would the subtle, autocratic, artificial construction characteristic of the French royal cathedrals.

"Architecture is applied geometry." This definition of Gundisalvo's (*circa* 1140–50) found general assent among medieval writers and architects. A Gothic cathedral is a mathematical work of art constructed with numbers, lines of force, and rays of light. The first essential was to enliven the inert mass of the walls. This was initially achieved by the fourfold articulation of the wall-masonry into arcade, gallery, triforium and clerestory. In the rebuilding of Chartres the number of divisions was reduced to three, and when the nave of St Denis was rebuilt in 1231 the triforium was incorporated into the clerestory. Treated in this way the walls of the cathedral became panels of light seamed by lines of force. Such a structure gives the illusion of floating downwards from celestial heights, bearing aloft its canopied vault. The Romanesque church is unequivocally ground-based, God's citadel on earth; the Gothic church is a vision of paradise, the heavenly Jerusalem. Gothic expresses that delight in making spiritual things visible which so possessed the men of this period, combined with a typically French view of paradise (this recurs over the centuries in many different forms, for example in Watteau). And the whole is infused with that sheer pleasure in technical skill which delights in every fresh opportunity for experiment, regardless of risk. Eager to outbid one another, the architects and engineers allowed their enthusiasms and obsessions to run away with them. The piers rose higher and higher, the shafts became more and more slender. The first disaster occurred in 1284 at Beauvais, where the vaulting of the choir built between 1247 and 1272 proved to be too lofty.

Although inherent in its structure, such excesses were avoided in the classic Gothic cathedral. The basic scheme provided for a spacious chancel with an ambulatory and radiating chapels, and for the articulation of the nave in the way already described. The steeply-rising mass of masonry was made secure from the outside by the use of buttresses to carry the weight of the vault. These buttresses were divided into sections, as in bridge-building, and this built-in scaffolding was adorned with little turrets, crockets, finials and statues. Technical mastery had provided an opportunity for further embellishment; and skill and delight in decoration were both merged into the still greater satisfaction of having achieved a complete creation.

The visiting throngs were sucked inside by massive doorways which were surrounded on one side by scenes from the sacred history of France, descending from Jesse through Christ, Clovis and Charlemagne, and on the other by representations of the judgment and redemption of the world and the coronation of the Virgin. The clustering ranks of statuary, kings, saints and damned souls, point the way to the interior of the church, where the eye is greeted by a wealth of light. Suger himself praises the commanding majesty of light as it shone through his church, "the wonderful and uninterrupted light of most sacred windows, pervading the interior beauty". It is a false romanticism which associates Gothic with "mystical" obscurity and gushing sentiment. These were cathedrals of light, in which everything should be bright and clear in obedience to the laws of the spirit and of engineering by which the whole was governed.

The Platonism of Chartres, the Augustinianism of Bernard of Clairvaux, the purism of Cîteaux and of other related movements all contributed to the formation of this code. The twelfth century theologians of Chartres were obsessed with the magic of mathematics, that ligature which bound God and the world and made them one. The harmony of the cosmos revealed itself in the secret of numbers. The secret of numbers contained the secret of music and of light. Light was "spirit incarnate", the creative principle. Beauty is truth made visible (by the power of light), the lustre shed by cosmic and divine order in its self-revelation. Anyone who could correctly measure and calculate light and number could also be a partner, as craftsman and executant, in the divine harmony.

It was in Suger's Paris that St Denis, the apostle of the Gauls, had finally been identified not only with the New Testament Dionysius the Areopagite but also with the fifth century mystical writer whose work was the main source of medieval metaphysical ideas about light. And it was on this authority that Suger felt justified in creating his new church as a magnet to draw the faithful towards eternal reason, towards the Godhead who is light, reason, clarity, unity and purity.

The artistic impact of the Gothic cathedral, which was intended to be total, was designed to affect the faithful in precisely this way and to lead them gently on towards illumination. Here was no place for horrors and demons, for death and his terrors. The invitation to man to refashion and transform himself should be couched in gentle and human terms. Nevertheless, Gothic had its own form of tyranny. As von Simson has observed, compared with Noyon, which has all the variety and richness characteristic of the open twelfth century, Chartres is austere and impersonal, a unit bonded together by exact proportion. Chartres is already dominated by number, unity, plan and a rigorous purism, which robs it of vitality: and it was this that set the tone for Gothic Europe as a whole. Anyone who today visits a dozen Gothic cathedrals in rapid succession is likely to feel disturbed by their technical and spiritual uniformity.

It requires a high degree of sympathy to appreciate as a whole that great symphony in three movements, each more richly orchestrated than the last, which brought French Gothic to its peak of perfection. The first movement, *circa* 1150, includes St Denis, Notre Dame in Paris, Laon, Noyon and Senlis. The second "classical" movement, *circa* 1200, is made up of Chartres, Amiens, Rheims, Rouen and Bourges. The last movement, which had its beginnings around 1250, is dominated by the "diaphanous" churches, Beauvais, the Sainte-Chapelle in Paris, St Urban in Troyes, Clermont, Limoges and Rodez. The Sainte-Chapelle, built by St Louis in the space of only three years (1245–48), is in effect a glass shrine: the walls have been completely engulfed by the fifteen huge windows, which depict altogether 1,134 scenes. Here is evidence that a lucid understanding, in sovereign command of all the available artistic techniques, could produce a vision of paradise, a world of faery and fantasy. The Sainte-Chapelle, a miracle of virtuosity, reminds one of the chiaroscuro and marvels to be found in the courtly romances and Celtic legends.

While the technical artistry of the Sainte-Chapelle compels our admiration, there is a greater and more familiar comfort to be found in the smiling serenity of Gothic cathedral sculpture, seen at its best at Rheims, Bourges and Amiens. The "Golden Virgin" and the figure of Christ known as the *Beau-Dieu*, both at Amiens, speak to us of a redeemed mankind, a humanity inwardly set free. The lions and dragons, vipers and basilisks crouching at Christ's feet are dwarf creatures, on the scale of lapdogs: and the Christ who extends His arms in blessing is perfect man, human and entire. But is He also perfect God? The Gothic which gelded the monsters of Romanesque and reduced them to mere grotesques had lost the power of filling men with the fear of God. There was nothing fortuitous in this. Neither the spirit of Greek metaphysics which illumines so many Gothic cathedrals and at Chartres has become a theology, nor the new lay technology, firmly rooted in the physical world, recognized the potency of "the Powers". These showed their face clearly enough in the trials commonly conducted outside the West portals, where books and men were burned. The Gothic tendency to play down death and evil and to conceal terror under fair forms and a gentle countenance is perhaps most clearly evident in the famous "angel pillar" of Strasbourg. Here the angels of the Apocalypse and the four evangelists are combined in a unique and moving harmony which culminates in the figure of Christ in judgment; and the angels seem to invite us to a terrestrial feast held in Heaven.

In Germany early examples of Gothic style are to be found at Bamberg, Naumburg, Marburg, Cologne, Freiburg, Regensburg and Vienna, but it does not emerge on the full scale until *circa* 1240 with the building of St Elisabeth's church at Marburg. In Westphalia, where southern French influence was strong, Gothic churches of the hall type soon became common. Elsewhere in northern Germany high-naved churches, austere and full of light, were being built of red brick. Examples of this brick Gothic could be found at Lübeck (the *Marienkirche*), Wismar, Rostock, Stralsund, Copenhagen, Malmö, Danzig and as far east as Riga, Revel and Dorpat.

French example stimulated German sculptors to the adornment of their cathedrals. The work they produced, both for the exterior and the interior, particularly the piers, ranks among the highest in the history of European art. "Church and Synagogue" and "The Death of the Virgin" at Strasbourg, the portrait-statues of the benefactors at Naumburg (typical representatives of the East German nobility), the arresting "Last Supper" in the gallery of the same cathedral, which brings us face to face with the lesser orders since the disciples are given Slavonic features, are unique in their nobility of form and power of characterization and expression.

The refined and courtly classicism of French Gothic sculpture was enlivened in Germany by a more aggressive, at times more naturalistic, approach, in which the emphasis is all on expression and movement. Apostles and prophets on the choir-screen of Bamberg engage one another in a battle of words—clearly no quarter is being given or asked for in this very German exchange, at once friendly and acrimonious. St John is given the appearance of a revolutionary peasant-prophet, an anticipation of the real-life peasant leaders of the fifteenth and sixteenth centuries.

The tempestuous Germany of the later Middle Ages, when the masses had lost confidence in the shielding power of Church and Empire, provided an outlet for grief in the *Pietà*, a poignant and shuddering expression of maternal grief which echoed the cry of all mothers who mourned their murdered children. The Italian *Pietàs* of the Renaissance, including Michelangelo's great group, are directly descended from this German Mother of Sorrows, for example the *Pietà* of Bonn (*circa* 1300). Southern Germany, the home of mysticism in the later fourteenth and early fifteenth centuries, developed several new devotional figures and themes during this period, for example the *Johannesminne*, the tender portrayal of John, the Beloved Apostle, reclining on his master's breast, in which the grief is all turned inward, purified by the softness of the medium, which was very often lime wood.

It is worth sketching briefly the triumphal progress through Europe of Gothic, the *opus Francigenum* or French style as the Germans called it. French architects worked far afield, in Spain, Portugal, Germany (Master Gerard, the designer of Cologne, probably originally came from France) and in Scandinavia. Etienne de Bonneuil was invited in 1287 to Uppsala as "Master of the Church Work", and the Emperor Charles IV, whose wife was Blanche of Valois, brought Mathieu d'Arras to Prague in 1344 to design the new cathedral; he lived to complete some nine chapels and was succeeded as architect by a German, Peter Parler. The design of Prague was based on the cathedral of Narbonne; St Stanislaus at Cracow in Poland followed a French plan. French Cistercians were active in Hungary, and after them came Villard de Honnecourt and Jean de Saint-Die, who built at Klausenburg and Kaschau. Gothic was developing into a European *lingua franca* just at the moment when the nations and the national languages were starting to go their separate ways. For the Jews, Gothic art provided what was almost a "Third Testament", a combination of the Old and the New: while the kings of Judah rode in triumph across Gothic portals, the Jews of contemporary Europe were being persecuted with increasing vigour. The *Elegy of Troyes* (written after 1288), a translation into French (but written in Hebrew characters) of a liturgical lament commemorating the burning of thirteen Jews at Troyes, epitomizes the ambiguity of their position: the Jews were being assimilated and rejected at one and the same time.

Whilst medieval Europe declined towards its autumn, Gothic ornament remained in a region of perpetual spring; it quivers with tender young shoots and blossoms, proliferates in pristine sylvan tracery. There is a bloom on the human countenance, the animals of field and woodland seek out human company, all creatures live together in peace and friendship. While wars and civil wars were raging, while populations were dwindling catastrophically, the Gothic cathedrals opened up vistas of paradise and of a world which was God's garden on earth. Even the Last Judgment breathes the hope of supernal peace, and the Archangel Michael presides over his fateful balance with a gentle, dreamy air, a youthful hero abstractedly meting out blessing or damnation.

The Europe whose nobility were killing each other on the battlefield was offered the vision of a genuine aristocracy held up by Gothic sculpture, whose human forms have an innate nobility of body and mind. There can be no doubting the close spiritual kinship which links Theodore of Chartres with Margraf Eckhart of Naumburg, Alphonso the Wise and Queen Violante in the transept of Burgos with their French and German cousins; and even Charles of Anjou, who might be thought an unpromising subject as an example of nobility since he murdered the last of the Hohenstaufen, as he appears in the Capitol at Rome seems a worthy member of this great European family of peers.

This universality is typical of the earlier Gothic. The later Gothic of the fourteenth and fifteenth centuries gave positive expression to national differences. These were the centuries when south-eastern Germany and eastern Europe really came to life. The Hapsburgs introduced Gothic into Austria, where in the later Middle Ages it developed into a luxuriant growth, particularly in sculpture, whose wealth of forms has only very recently begun to be appreciated.

It has been said that the characteristic feature of English

Gothic is its decoration. This is true of all its three phases, which follow one another smoothly, Early English (1170–1250), Decorated (1250–1350), and High Gothic-Perpendicular (after 1350). Norman England took French Gothic in its stride and adapted its elements to native use in characteristic fashion, at once imaginative and calculating. The result is that no English cathedral could ever be mistaken for a Continental building. English Gothic is adept at assimilating what is alien whilst rigidly adhering to its own code, a code full of violent contradictions and paradoxes. French Gothic found its earliest imitations in England, for example the choir of Canterbury (1175–85), which is the work of a Master from Sens. After this initial stage native ingenuity took charge and produced some perfect examples of the style, as at Lincoln and Salisbury.

With Westminster Abbey (1245–58) there was a return to French Gothic, followed by some exercises in High Gothic at Exeter, Ely and Lichfield, from which there was an easy transition to the Perpendicular style, which influenced the style known on the Continent as Flamboyant. Through all these phases English Gothic continued to develop according to its own laws, which became more clearly revealed at each step.

The English cathedral, at once city church, abbey church and monastery, was a huge and complex unit containing a whole range of separate enclosures, any of which could stand by itself. The scheme of decoration alone united the separate units, the vaults and bays, choir and nave, retrochoir, Lady Chapel, additional eastern transepts. The individual parts have a harsh, steely quality, like the figures of English cathedral sculpture. There was an early introduction of the pointed arch to articulate the walls, which higher up were reintegrated by arcading and criss-cross rib vaulting. It was largely as a result of this splitting up of the mass into separate slender linear forms that the dominating impression left by these actually very lofty buildings is one of breadth rather than height. These English cathedrals do not float; they are planted firmly on the earth, conscious of their authority and of what they represent. The visitor must be content to pass from one enclosure to the next and abandon the hope of a comprehensive view. Norman harshness is combined with a dry and tortuous imagination which calculates its effects. Planned down to the last detail, these English cathedrals remind us that English mathematicians and canon lawyers played a leading role in the Europe of the thirteenth and fourteenth centuries. The essential structural feature of the English cathedral is neither the arch (as in France) nor its mass (as in German Romanesque and even in early German Gothic) but the line, the network of lines of stress, which has its affinity with the chequered cloth of the royal Exchequer. The Perpendicular style, a trellis-work of slender wands, was implicit in English Gothic from the beginning.

English cathedral sculpture is best represented by its tombstone effigies, solemn, dignified, somewhat stiff, aloof from the world: the knight in the Temple church of London, Richard Swinfield in Hereford Cathedral, a lady on the tomb of Edward III in Westminster Abbey. The English schools of manuscript illumination are less inhibited in their use of line, more human and humanistic, altogether more sensitive. Here there was a great Anglo-Saxon tradition to build on, culminating in the Winchester school.

It has been said that Norman England never took Continental Gothic seriously, but simply borrowed from it at will to create something completely "un-Gothic". Yet it could hardly be expected that the England of the Plantagenets and their heirs would take to the building of French cathedrals, those power-symbols of the cult of the "most Christian king". Nor did the French vision of paradise and the magical faery of the Sainte-Chapelle have any great appeal for the harder-headed Anglo-Normans. But the existence of the proud and commanding range of English medieval cathedrals is proof that the land which was governed until the late fourteenth century in French and by a French-speaking ruling class, and which had brought the full force of its native powers to bear on the task of appropriating French architectural forms to its own purposes, could offer a formidable challenge to France, the mother country not only of Gothic but also of medieval English learning and culture.

When looked at side by side, it can be seen that, while close in form, the Gothic cathedrals of France and England are far apart in spirit; their handling of space is different, and so is the inner core of their structure. That conflict and convergence of France and England which did so much to lead Western Europe to self-discovery and self-assertion in the later Middle Ages are made visible in these cathedrals, this community of sisters, mothers and daughters, this clan of warring siblings contending for supremacy like Brünhilde and Krimhilde outside the door of Worms Cathedral.

BIBLIOGRAPHY

Note. This list is intended as a guide to further reading. Some titles (mostly in foreign languages) which appear in the bibliography of the German edition have been omitted, and additional works in English have been included.

CHAPTER 1

The Cambridge Mediaeval History, vols. v, vi, vii and viii, 1926–36.

C. W. PREVITÉ ORTON, *The Shorter Cambridge Mediaeval History*, revised by P. GRIERSON (Cambridge, 1952).

R. H. C. DAVIS, *A History of Mediaeval Europe from Constantine to St. Louis* (London, 1957).

E. PERROY, *Le Moyen Age. L'expansion de l'orient et la naissance de la civilisation occidentale* (*Histoire générale des civilisations*, vol. iii) (Paris, 1955).

F. L. GANSHOF, *Le Moyen Age* (*Histoire des rélations internationales*, vol. i) (Paris, 1953).

J. HASHAGEN, *Europa im Mittelalter* (Munich, 1951).

O. HALECKI, *Borderlands of Western Civilization: A History of East Central Europe* (New York, 1952).

R. W. SOUTHERN, *The Making of the Middle Ages* (London, 1953) (Grey Arrow Edition, 1959).

F. B. ARTZ, *The Mind of the Middle Ages* 2nd ed. (New York, 1954) (extensive bibliography).

M. SEIDLMAYR, *Currents of Mediaeval Thought, with special reference to Germany*, trans. D. BARKER (Basil Blackwell, 1960).

K. PFISTER, *Die Welt des Mittelalters. Geschichte-Weltbild-Kunst* (Vienna, 1952).

D. HAY, *Europe—the Emergence of an Idea* (Edinburgh, 1957).

W. R. SHEPHERD, *Historical Atlas* 8th ed. (New York, 1956).

C. McEVEDY, *The Penguin Atlas of Mediaeval History* (London, 1961).

L. J. PAETOW, *A Guide to the Study of Mediaeval History* (London, 1931).

C. P. FARRER and A. P. EVANS, *Bibliography of English Translations from Mediaeval Sources* (New York, 1952).

CHAPTER 2

M. BLOCH, *La Société Féodale* (Paris, 1939–40), English translation by L. A. MANYON (London, 1961).

J. CALMETTE, *La Société Féodale* 6th ed. (Paris, 1947).

S. PAINTER, *French Chivalry. Chivalric Ideas and Practices in Mediaeval France* (Baltimore, 1940).

O. BRUNNER, *Land und Herrschaft* 3rd ed. (Brünn-Munich-Vienna, 1943).

O. BRUNNER, *Adeliges Landleben und Europäischer Geist* (Salzburg, 1949).

F. L. GANSHOF, *Qu'est-ce que la Féodalité?* 2nd ed. (Neûchatel, 1947), English edition: *Feudalism* translated by P. GRIERSON (1952).

F. M. STENTON, *The First Century of English Feudalism* (Oxford, 1932).

A. TUULSE, *Burgen des Abendlandes* (Vienna-Munich, 1959).

The Cambridge Economic History of Europe, vol. i, *The Agrarian Life of the Middle Ages*, ed. J. H. CLAPHAM and E. POWER, 2nd ed. (1953).
(See especially Chapter VII by F. L. GANSHOF, "Mediaeval Agrarian Society in its Prime").

P. BOISSONADE, *Le Travail dans l'Europe chrétienne au Moyen Age V-XV siècles* (Paris, 1921).
English edition: *Life and Work in Mediaeval Europe* translated with Introduction by E. POWER (London, 1927).

A. VARAGNAC, *Civilization traditionelle et Genres de Vie* (Paris, 1948).

R. GRAND, *L'Agriculture au Moyen Age* (Paris, 1950).

D. M. STENTON, *English Society in the Early Middle Ages*, Pelican Books (London, 1951).

P. DOLLINGER, *L'évolution des classes rurales en Bavière depuis la fin de l'époque carolingienne jusqu' au milieu du XIII siècle* (Paris, 1949).

G. VERNADSKY, *Kievan Russia* (New Haven, 1948).

G. VERNADSKY, *The Mongols and Russia* (New Haven, 1953).

C. VERLINDEN, *Histoire de l'Esclavage en Europe médiévale:* Vol. i (Ghent, 1955).

E. PERRIN, *Le Servage en France et en Allemagne* and G. VERNADSKY, *Serfdom in Russia*, both in *X Congresso Intern. di Scienze Storiche Roma 1955, Relazioni III* (Florence, 1955).

E. PERROY, *Les crises au XIV siècle* (*Annales* iv, 1949).

Selected *Political Writings of St Thomas Aquinas* ed. A. P. D'ENTREVES, 1948 (for Aquinas' views on liberty and serfdom).

CHAPTER 3

C. DAWSON, *Religion and the Rise of Western Culture* (London, 1950).

G. SCHNÜRER, *Kirche und Kultur im Mittelalter*, 3 vols.

(Paderborn, 1927–29), French translation (Paris, 1933–38).

G. LE BRAS, *Etudes de Sociologie réligieuse.* Vol. i: *Sociologie de la Pratique réligieuse dans les campagnes françaises* (Paris, 1955).

E. DELARUELLE, "La pietà popolare nel secolo XI" (written in French), *X Congresso Intern. di Scienze Storiche Roma 1955, Relazioni III* (Florence, 1955).

A. FRANZ, *Die Messe im deutschen Mittelalter* (Freiburg, 1902).

B. SMALLEY, *The Study of the Bible in the Middle Ages* 2nd revised ed. (Oxford, 1952).

H. HEIMBUCHER, *Die Orden und Kongregationen der katholischen Kirche,* 3rd ed. (Paderborn, 1933–34).

C. BUTLER, *Benedictine Monachism,* 2nd ed. 1924 (and see the same author's edition of the *Rule of St Benedict,* 3rd ed. Freiburg, 1935).

D. KNOWLES, *The Monastic Order in England, 943–1216* (Cambridge, 1940).

G. DE VALOUS, *Le monachisme clunisien des origines au XV siècle* (Paris, 1935).

P. GUIGNARD, *Les Monuments primitifs de la Règle Cistercienne* (Dijon, 1878).

G. G. COULTON, *Five Centuries of Religion* (Cambridge, 1923–1950).

i *St Bernard, his predecessors and successors 1000–1200* ii *The friars and the dead weight of tradition, 1200–1400* iii *Getting and Spending* iv *The Last Days of Medieval Monachism.*
(Although far from impartial, this great work is a rich mine of material illustrative of mediaeval religious life in nearly all its aspects.)

G. G. COULTON, *Life in the Middle Ages Vol. I: Religion, Folk-lore and Superstition* (Cambridge, 1928). (Alternatively see the one-volume edition, *A Mediaeval Garner* (London, 1910).

Carmina Burana, ed. A. HILKA and O. SCHUMANN (Heidelberg, 1936–1941).

CHAPTER 4

The Cambridge Economic History of Europe, ed. J. H. CLAPHAM and E. POWER. Vol. ii: *Trade and Industry in the Middle Ages* (1952).

H. PIRENNE, *Economic and Social History of Mediaeval Europe,* English translation (1936).

F. RÖRIG, *Die europaïsche Stadt und die Kultur des Bürgertums im Mittelalter,* ed. L. RÖRIG (Göttingen, 1955).

W. HEYD, *Histoire du commerce du Levant au Moyen Age,* French translation by F. RAYNAUD of German original (1885–6, repr. 1923).

L. SALVATORELLI, *L'Italia comunale dal secolo XI alla metà del secolo XIV* (*Mondadori Storia d'Italia illustrata* Vol. iv) (Milan, 1940).

Y. RENOUARD, *Les hommes d'affaires italiens au Moyen Age* (Paris, 1949).

E. CARUS-WILSON, *Mediaeval Merchant Venturers* (London, 1955).

J. LESTICQUOY, *Les villes de Flandre et l'Italie sous le gouvernement des patriciens, XI–XV siècles* (Paris, 1952).

R. S. LOPEZ and I. W. RAYMOND, *Mediaeval Trade in the Mediterranean World,* illustrative documents with notes and introductions (Columbia University, *Records of Civilization No 52,* 1955).

K. PAGEL, *Die Hanse,* 2nd ed. (Brunswick, 1952).

S. D. GOITHEIN, *From the Mediterranean to India. Documents on the Trade to India, South Arabia and East Africa from the Eleventh and Twelfth Centuries* (*Speculum* xxiv, 2, pars 1, 1954).

L. R. NOUGIER, J. BEAUJEU and M. MOLLAT, *Histoire universelle des explorations* Vol. i: *De la Prehistoire a la fin du Moyen Age* (Paris, 1955).

B. N. NELSON, *The Idea of Usury* (Princeton N.J., 1949).

U. TIGNER HOLMES, *Daily Living in the Twelfth Century.* Based on the observations of Alexander of Neckam in London and Paris (Madison, 1952).

CHAPTER 5

E. GILSON, *History of Christian Philosophy in the Middle Ages* (London, 1955).

E. R. CURTIUS, *European Literature and the Latin Middle Ages,* English translation by W. R. TRASK (London, 1953).

J. DE GHELLINCK, *L'essor de la littérature latine au XII siècle* (Brussels-Paris, 1946).

J. DE GHELLINCK, *Le mouvement théologique du XII siècle,* 2nd ed. (Louvain 1948).

C. H. HASKINS, *The Renaissance of the Twelfth Century* (Cambridge, Mass., 1927).

G. PARÉ and P. TREMBLAY, *La renaissance du XII siècle. Les écoles et l'enseignement* (Paris, 1933).

P. RENUCCI, *L'aventure de l'humanisme européen au Moyen Age. IV–XIV siècle.* (Clermont-Ferrand, 1953).

R. W. SOUTHERN, *The Place of England in the Twelfth Century Renaissance. History* xlv, 1960.

J. G. SIKES, *Peter Abailard* (Cambridge, 1932).

E. GILSON, *Heloise and Abelard,* English translation by L. K. SHOOK (London, 1953).

N. A. SIDOROWA, *Die Entstehung der frühen städtischen Kultur in Frankreich* in *Sowjetwissenschaft, Gesellschaftwissen schaftl.* Abt. iv (Berlin, 1951) (A Marxist interpretation of Abelard).

E. GILSON, *The Mystical Theology of St Bernard,* English translation by A. H. C. DOWNES (London, 1940).

N. M. HARING, *The Creation and Creator of the World According to Thierry of Chartres and Clarembaldus of Arras* in

Archives d'histoire doctrinale et littéraire du Moyen Age (Paris, 1955).

H. LIEBESCHÜTZ, *Mediaeval Humanism in the Life and Writings of John of Salisbury* (London, 1950).

F. J. E. RABY, *History of Christian-Latin Poetry*, 2nd ed. (Oxford, 1953).

F. J. E. RABY, *History of Secular Latin Poetry in the Middle Ages* (Oxford, 1934)

A Scholastic Miscellany: Anselm to Ockham. Edited and translated by E. FAIRBROTHER (Library of Christian Classics X) (London, 1956).

The Letters of St Bernard of Clairvaux. Translated by B. S. JAMES (London, 1953).

JOHN OF SALISBURY, *The Statesman's Book.* Translated by J. DICKINSON (New York, 1927).

JOHN OF SALISBURY, *Memoirs of the Papal Court.* Translated with Introduction by M. M. CHIBNALL. Nelson's Mediaeval Texts (Edinburgh, 1956).

JOHN OF SALISBURY, *The Letters of John of Salisbury*, ed. W. J. MILLOR and H. E. BUTLER, with an introduction by C. N. L. BROOKE. Nelson's Mediaeval Texts (Edinburgh, 1955).

CHAPTER 6

On Byzantium:

J. M. HUSSEY, *The Byzantine World* (London, 1957).

G. OSTROGORSKY, *History of the Byzantine State.* English translation by J. M. HUSSEY (Basil Blackwell, 1956).

A. A. VASILIEV, *History of the Byzantine Empire 324–1453* 2nd ed. (Madison, 1952).

R. J. H. JENKINS, *The Byzantine Empire on the Eve of the Crusades,* Historical Association Pamphlet (London, 1953).

On the Crusading Idea:

C ERDMANN, *Die Entstehung des Kreuzzugsqedankens* (Stuttgart, 1935).

C. ERDMANN, *Forschungen zur politischen Ideenwelt des Frühmittelalters,* ed. F. BAETHGEN (Berlin, 1951).

Papers collected under the title *L'ideé de Croisade* in *X Congresso Intern. di Scienze Storiche Roma 1955, Relazioni III* (Florence, 1955):

P. ROUSSET, *L'ideé de Croisade chez les chroniquers d'Occident.*

M. VILLEY, *L'ideé de la Croisade chez les juristes du Moyen Age.*

P. LEMERLE, *Byzance et la Croisade.*

S. RUNCIMAN, *The Byzantine Provincial Peoples and the Crusade.*

A. CAHEN, *L'Islam et la Croisade.*

S. RUNCIMAN, *The Decline of the Crusading Idea.*

On the Crusades:

S. RUNCIMAN, *A History of the Crusades*, 3 vols. (Cambridge, 1951–4).

K. M. SETTON (general editor), *A History of the Crusade*, vol. i, *The First Hundred Years*, ed. M. H. BALDWIN (University of Pennsylvania Press, 1955).

R. LOPEZ, *Les influences orientales et l'éveil economique de l'Occident* (*Cahiers d'histoire mondiale* i, 1953).

On Western relations with the Far East:

H. LUBAC, *La Rencontre du Bouddhisme et de l'Occident* (Paris, 1952).

A. MOULE, *Christians in China before the Year 1550* (London, 1930).

C. D. DAWSON, *The Mongol Mission.* Narratives and Letters of the Franciscan Missionaries in Mongolia and China in the thirteenth and fourteenth centuries. Translated by a Nun of Stanbrook Abbey (London, 1955).

CHAPTER 7

(The list given for Chapter 5 will also be found helpful for this Chapter). The Anglo-French culture of the twelfth century:

R. R. BEZZOLA, *Der französisch-englische Kulturkreis und die Erneuerung der europäischen Literatur im 12 Fahrhundert* (*Zeitschrift f. roman. Philol. lxii*, 1942).

R. R. BEZZOLA, *Les origines et la formation de la littérature courtoise en occident 500–1200* (Paris, 1944).

A. KELLY, *Eleanor of Aquitaine and the Four Kings* (Cambridge, Mass., 1952).

P. RICKARD, *Britain in Mediaeval French Literature 1100–1500* (Cambridge, 1956).

J. S. P. TATLOCK, *The Legendary History of Britain* (Berkeley, 1950).

Courtly Love:

C. S. LEWIS, *The Allegory of Love* (Oxford, 1936).

M. C. D'ARCY, *The Mind and Heart of Love. Lion and Unicorn: A Study in Eros and Agape* (London, 1945).

The Art of Courtly Love of Andreas Capellanus. Translated by J. J. PARRY, *Records of Civilization* (Columbia University Press, 1941).

Troubadour poetry:

A. JEANROY, *La poésie lyrique des troubadours* (Toulouse-Paris, 1934).

A. JEANROY, *Histoire sommaire de la poésie occitane, des origines à la fin du XVIII siècle* (Toulouse-Paris, 1945).

F. BRITTAIN, *The Mediaeval Latin and Romance Lyric*, 2nd ed. 1951).

A. J. Denomy, *Concerning the accessibility of Arabic influences to the earliest Provençal troubadours* (*Mediaeval Studies* xv, Toronto, 1953).

C. Dawson, *The origins of the Romantic tradition* in his *Mediaeval Religion* (London, 1934).

K. Vossler, *Spanien und Europa* (Munich, 1951).

The Grail and the Arthurian cycle:

The literature on this subject is vast. Reference may be made to two publications:

A Bibliography of Arthurian Literature, compiled by J. J. Parry and M. Schlauch, published by *The Modern Language Association of America,* New York, and *Bulletin bibliographique de la Société internationale arthurienne* (Paris).

The following may be found useful as an introduction:

J. Marx, *La légende arthurienne et le Graal* (Paris, 1952).

R. W. Barber, *Arthur of Albion: An Introduction to the Arthurian Literature and Legends of England* (London, 1961).

French courtly literature:

P. Zumthor, *Histoire littéraire de la France mediévale VI–XIV siècle* (Paris, 1954).

G. Cohen, *Tableau de la littérature mediévale. Idées et sensibilités.*

German courtly literature:

H. Spanke, *Deutsche und französische Dichtung des Mittelalters* (Stuttgart, 1943).

F. Heer, *Die Tragödie des Heiligen Reiches* (Stuttgart, 1952–3).

G. Ehrismann, *Geschichte der deutschen Literatur bis zum Ausgang des Mittelalters* 4 vols (Munich, 1932–5).

F. Ranke, *Gott, Welt und Humanität in der deutschen Dichtung des Mittelalters* (Basel, 1952).

Gottfried von Strassburg, *Tristan.* Translated by A. T. Hatto (Penguin Classics, 1960).

CHAPTER 8

G. Tellenbach, *Church, State and Christian Society at the Time of the Investiture Contest.* English translation by R. F. Bennett (Basil Blackwell, 1940).

H. Grundmann, *Religiöse Bewegungen im Mittelalter* . . . (Berlin, 1935).

H. Grundmann, *Neue Beiträge zur Geschichte der religiösen Bewegungen im Mittelalter* in *Archiv für Kulturgeschichte* xxxvii (1955).

D. Obolensky, *The Bogomils* (Cambridge, 1948).

A. Borst, *Die Katharer* (Stuttgart, 1953).

F. Niel, *Albigeois et Cathares* (Paris, 1956).

R. Nelli, C. Bru and others, *Spiritualité de l'hérésie: le Catharisme* (Paris, 1953).

P. Belperron, *La Croisade contre les Albigeois et l'union du Languedoc à la France* (Paris, 1942).

Z. Oldenbourg, *Massacre at Montségur*. English translation by Peter Green (London, 1961).

N. Cohn, *The Pursuit of the Millennium* (London, 1957).

O. Karrer, *St Francis of Assisi. The Legends and Lauds*. English translation by N. Wydenbruck (London, 1947).

J. R. H. Moorman, *The Sources for the Life of St Francis of Assisi* (Manchester, 1940).

P. Mandonnet, *Saint Dominique, l'idée, l'homme et l'oeuvre*, rev. ed. M. H. Vicaire and R. Ladner (Paris, 1937).

E. W. McDonnell, *The Beguines and Beghards in Mediaeval Culture* (Rutgers University Press, 1955).

W. D. Morris, *The Christian Origins of Social Revolt* (London, 1949).

CHAPTER 9

The Islamic contribution:

G. E. von Grunebaum, *Medieval Islam*, 2nd ed. (Chicago, 1953).

F. Rosenthal, *The technique and approach of Muslim scholarship* in *Analecta Orientalia* xxiv (Rome, 1947).

De Lacy Evans O'Leary, *How Greek Science Passed to the Arabs* (London, 1949).

A. J. Arberry, *Sufism. An Account of the Mystics of Islam* (London, 1951).

E. Lévi-Provencial, *Histoire de l'Espagne musulmane*, 3 vols (Paris, 1944–53).

History of the Universities in the Middle Ages:

H. Rashdall, *The Universities of Europe in the Middle Ages*. Revised ed. by F. M. Powicke and A. B. Emden. 3 vols (Oxford, 1936).

L. Halphen, *Les Universités au XIII siècle* in his *A travers l'histoire du Moyen Age* (Paris, 1950).

H. Grundemann, *Vom Ursprung der Universität im Mittelalter. Abh. d.Akad. d. Wiss., phil-histor. Klasse* ciii (Berlin, 1957).

Lynn Thorndike, *University Records and Life in the Middle Ages* (Columbia University Press, *Records of Civilization*, 1944).

Medieval Intellectualism:

G. Cohen, *La grande clarté du Moyen Age* (Paris, 1950).

J. Le Goff, *Les intellectuels au Moyen Age* (Paris, 1957).

H. Fichtenau, *Mensch und Schrift im Mittelalter*

J. B. Pike, *Frivolities of Courtiers and Footprints of Philosophers* (Minneapolis, 1938). (Anthology of illustrative texts.)

For biographies of individual scholars, with full bibliographies, see:

G. Sarton, *Introduction to the History of Science*, 5 vols (Washington-Baltimore, 1929–48).

CHAPTER 10

(See also bibliography for Chapter 5.)

G. Leff, *Medieval Thought: St Augustine to Ockham* (Pelican Books, 1958).

F. van Steenberghen, *The Philosophical Movement in the Thirteenth Century* (Edinburgh, 1955).

P. Boehner, *Mediaeval Logic: An Outline of Its Development from 1250–c 1400* (Manchester, 1952).

F. C. Copleston, *Aquinas* (Pelican Books, 1956).

P. Mandonnet, *Siger de Brabant et l'Averroisme latin au XIII siècle*, 2nd ed. (Louvain, 1908–11).

F. van Steenbergen, *Siger de Brabant d'après ses oeuvres inédits*, vols xii and xiii of *Les Philosophes Belges* (Louvain, 1931).

For a Marxist interpretation of medieval nominalist thinkers see:

E. Bloch, *Avicenna und die aristotelische Linke* (Berlin, 1952). and H. Ley, *Studie zur Geschichte des Materialismus im Mittelalter* (Berlin, 1957).

Paris after Aquinas:

G. Lagarde, *La naissance de l'esprit laïque au declin du Moyen Age* (Paris, 1942–6).
(See especially Vol iii, *Secteur social de la Scolastique*.)

L. Baudry, *Guillaume d'Occam, sa vie, ses oeuvres, ses idées sociales et politiques* (Paris, 1952).

M. H. MacLaughlin, *Paris Masters of the Thirteenth and Fourteenth Centuries and Ideas of Intellectual Freedom* in *Church History* xxiv (1955).

CHAPTER 11

G. Sarton, *Introduction to the History of Science*, 5 vols (Washington-Baltimore, 1929–48).
(Extensive bibliographies for individual chroniclers and historical philosophers.)

W. Kaegi, *Chronica Mundi. Grundformen der Geschichtsschreibung seit dem Mittelalter* (Einsiedeln, 1954).

V. H. Galbraith, *Historical Research in Medieval England* (London, 1951).

R. Vaughan, *Mathew Paris* (Cambridge, 1958).

Otto of Freising's *The Two Cities*. Translated by C. C. Mierow, Columbia University Press *Records of Civilization* (New York, 1928).

Otto of Freising's *The Deeds of Frederick Barbarossa*. Translated by C. C. MIEROW, Columbia University Press *Records of Civilization* (New York, 1953).

F. FOBERTI, *Giocchino da Fiore e il Gioacchinismo antico e moderno* (Padua, 1942).

D. DOUIE, *The Nature and Effect of the Heresy of the Fraticelli* (Manchester, 1932).

CHAPTER 12

G. SARTON, *Introduction to the History of Science*, 5 vols (Washington-Baltimore, 1929–48).

LYNN THORNDIKE, *A History of Magic and Experimental Science*, 4 vols, 4th ed. (New York, 1947).

A. C. CROMBIE, *Augustine to Galileo* (London, 1952).

M. CLAGETT, *Some general aspects of Physics in the Middle Ages in Isis* xxxix (1948).

A. C. CROMBIE, *Robert Grosseteste and the Origins of Experimental Science* (Oxford, 1953).

C. ROTH, *The Jews of Medieval Oxford*, Oxford Historical Society (1951).

R. CARTON, *L'expérience physique chez Roger Bacon* (1924).

R. CARTON, *L'expérience mystique de l'illumination intérieure chez Roger Bacon* (1924).

R. CARTON, *La synthèse doctrinale de Roger Bacon* (1924).

F. SHERWOOD TAYLOR, *The Alchemists* (London, 1952).

G. W. COOPLAND, *Nicole Oresme and the Astrologers, A Study of his Livre de Divinacions* (Liverpool, 1952) (gives French text and English translation).

E. ALLISON PEERS, *Fool of Love. The Life of Ramon Lull* (London, 1945).

CHAPTER 13

S. GRAYZEL, *The Church and the Jews in the Thirteenth Century* (Philadelphia, 1933).

G. KISCH, *The Jews in Medieval Germany: A Study of Their Legal and Social Status* (Chicago, 1950).

C. ROTH, *History of the Jews in England* (Oxford, 1941).

H. G. RICHARDSON, *The English Jewry under Angevin Kings* (London, 1960).

G. VAJDA, *Introduction à la pensée juive du Moyen Age* in *Etudes de philosophie mediévale* xxxv (Paris, 1947).

G. G. SCHOLEM, *Major Trends in Jewish Mysticism* (London [re-issue], 1955).

A. LEHMANN, *Le rôle de la femme dans l'histoire de France au Moyen Age* (Paris, 1952).

J. LECLERCQ, *Leçons de droit naturel* Vol. iii: *La Famille*, 3rd ed. (Namur, 1950).

M. BERNARD, *Speculum Virginum. Geistigkeit und Seelenleben der Frau im Hochmittelalter* (Köln-Graz, 1955).

CHAPTER 14

H. MITTEIS, *Der Staat des hohen Mittelalters,* 5th ed. (Weimar, 1955).

K. HAMPE, *Das Hochmittelalter, Geschichte des Abendlandes von 900 bis 1250,* 4th ed. (Münster-Köln, 1953).

G. BARRACLOUGH, *The Origins of Modern Germany,* 2nd ed. (Oxford, 1947).

P. E. SCHRAMM, *Herrschaftszeichen und Staatssymbolik,* 3 vols (Stuttgart, 1954–6).

R. FOLZ, *L'idée de l'Empire en Occident du 5ᵉau 14ᵉ siècle* (Paris, 1953).

A DE STEFANO, *La Cultura alle Corte de Federico II Imperatore* (Palermo, 1938).

G. MASSON, *Frederick II of Hohenstaufen* (London, 1957).

J. HALLER, *Das Papsttum, Idee und Wirklichkeit,* vols ii and iii (Stuttgart, 1950–3).

A. FLICHE, *Innocent III et la Réforme de l'Eglise* in *Revue d'histoire ecclésiastique* xliv (1949).

T. S. R. BOASE, *Boniface VIII* (London, 1933).

G. MOLLAT, *Les Papes d'Avignon,* 9th ed. (Paris, 1943).

W. ULLMANN, *Medieval Papalism. The Political Theories of the Medieval Canonists* (London, 1949).

W. ULLMANN, *The Growth of Papal Government in the Middle Ages* (London, 1955).

M. SEIDLMAYER, *Rom und Romgedanke im Mittelalter* in *Saeculum* vii (1956).

E. W. KEMP, *Canonization and Authority in the Western Church* (London, 1948).

R. FAWTIER, *Les Capétiens et la France* (Paris, 1949) (English translation by L. BUTLER and R. J. ADAM *The Capetian Kings of France,* London, 1960).

F. LOT and R. FAWTIER, *Histoire des institutions français au Moyen Age.* Vol. i: *Institutions seigneuriales* (Paris, 1957). Vol. ii: *Institutions royales,* 1958 (in progress).

G. DIGARD, *Philippe le Bel et le Saint-Siège,* 2 vols (Paris, 1936).

V. MARTIN, *Les origines du Gallicanisme,* 2 vols (Paris, 1939).

G. W. S. BARROW, *Feudal Britain: The Completion of the Medieval Kingdoms* (London, 1956).

S. B. CHRIMES, *An Introduction to the Administrative History of Medieval England,* 2nd ed. (Oxford, 1959).

J. E. A. JOLLIFFE, *Angevin Kingship* (London, 1955).

E. KANTOROWICZ, *The King's Two Bodies. A Study in Medieval Political Theology* (Princeton, 1959).

J. B. MORRALL, *Political Thought in Mediaeval Times* (London, 1958).

EWART LEWIS, *Medieval Political Ideas*, 2 vols (London, 1954) (Documents with commentaries).

A. P. D'ENTRÈVES, *The Medieval Contribution to Political Thought* (Oxford, 1939).

A. GERWITH, *Marsilius of Padua*, 2 vols (New York, 1951–56) (with a translation of the *Defensor Pacis*).

G. LAGARDE, *La Naissance de l'esprit laïque*. Vols iv–vi (Paris, 1946).

CHAPTER 15

K. G. HUGELMANN, *Stämme, Nation und Nationalstaat im deutschen Mittelalter* (Stuttgart, 1955). A fine collection of texts illustrating national animosities.

P. KIRN, *Aus der Frühzeit des Nationalgefühls* (Leipzig, 1943).

M. DEFOURNEAUX, *Les Français en Espagne aux XIe et XIIe siècles* (Paris, 1949).

G. TURVILLE-PETRE, *The Heroic Age of Scandinavia* (1951).

The Saga of Gunnlaug Serpent-tongue. Translated by R. QUIRK and edited by P. G. FOOTE. Nelson's Icelandic Texts (Edinburgh, 1957).

The Prose Edda of Snorri Sturluson: Tales from Norse Mythology. Translated by J. I. YOUNG (Cambridge, 1954).

H. R. PATCH, *The Other World According to Descriptions in Medieval Literature* (Cambridge, Mass. 1950).

K. B. MCFARLANE, *John Wycliffe and the Beginnings of English Non-Conformity* (London, 1952).

G. PARÉ, *Les idées et les lettres au XIII siècle. Le Roman de la Rose* (Montreal, 1947).

G. S. LEWIS, *The Allegory of Love* (Oxford, 1936).

J. M. CLARK, *The Great German Mystics: Eckhart, Tauler and Suso* (Basil Blackwell, 1949).

J. M. CLARK, *Master Eckhart: An Introduction to the Study of His Works with an Anthology of His Sermons* (Edinburgh, 1957).

L. MENZIES, *The Revelations of Mechthild of Magdeburg (1210–1297) or The Flowing Light of the Godhead* (London, 1953).

CHAPTER 16

C. L. MOREY, *Medieval Art* (London, 1948).

L. RÉAU, *L'art réligieux du Moyen Age* (Paris, 1946).

E. MÂLE, *L'art réligieux du XIIe siècle en France* (Paris, 1922).

J. EVANS, *Art in Medieval France* (Oxford, 1948).

H. FOCILLON, *Art d'Occident. Le Moyen Age roman et gothique.* 3rd ed. (Paris, 1955).

P. H. MICHEL, *Romanesque Wall Paintings in France.* Translated by J. EVANS (London, 1950).

E. W. ANTHONY, *Romanesque Frescoes* (Princeton, 1951).

A. J. SCHARDT, *Die Kunst des Mittelalters in Deutschland* (Berlin, 1941).

O. GRUBER, *Das Westwork: Symbol und Baugestaltung germanischen Christentums* in *Zeitschr. des Deutschen Vereins für Kunstwissenschaft* iii, 1936.

H. WEIGERT, *Die Kaiserdome am Mittelrhein, Speyer, Mainz und Worms* (Berlin, 1933).

O. H. FORSTER, *Entfaltung und Zerfall des abendländischen Gottesreiches*. 2nd ed. (Köln, 1952).

G. H. CRICHTON, *Romanesque Sculpture in Italy* (London, 1954).

J. POPE HENNESSY, *Italian Gothic Sculpture* (London, 1955).

O. VON SIMSON, *The Gothic Cathedral* (New York, 1956).

J. FITCHEN, *The Construction of Gothic Cathedrals* (Oxford, 1961).

E. PANOFSKY, *Abbot Suger on the Abbey Church of St-Denis and Its Art Treasures* (Princeton, 1946).

M. AUBERT, *Suger* (Paris, 1950).

L. RÉAU, *Histoire de l'expansion de l'art français*, 3 vols (Paris, 1928–33).

T. S. R. BOASE, *English Art 1100–1216* (Oxford, 1953).

P. BRIEGER, *English Art 1216–1307* (Oxford, 1957).

F. HAEBERLEIN, *Grundzüge einer nachantiken Farbenikonographie* in *Römisches Fahrbuch f. Kunstgeschichte* iii, 1939.

K. H. CLASEN, *Die Überwindung des Bösen. Ein Beitrag zur Ikonographie des frühen Mittelalters* in *Neue Beiträge Deutscher Forschung, W. Worringer zum 60 Geburtstag*, Königsberg, 1943.

INDEX

Novgorod, 52, 80, 90, 91–2, 95, 97–8; cathedral, 17
Noyon, 74, 402
Nunneries, 63, 320, 373–4
Nuremberg, 89, 322, 388

Oceana (Harrington), 82
Ockham, William of, 231, 262, 271, 274–7, 295, 339
Odorico of Pordonore, 155
Oliverus Scholasticus, 145
On Husbandry (Walter of Henley), 47
On the Value of Man (Delmedigo), 317
Ophites, 185
Opus Maius (Bacon), 261
Orange University, 256
Orcagna, Andrea, 396
Ordeals, 59
Ordericus Vitalis, 279
Oresme, Nicole, 300
Origen, 146
Orleans, 84, 85, 102, 201; University, 255
Orosius, Paulus, 282
Orsini, Cardinal, 393
Orvieto, 221
Otranto, 395
Otto IV, Emperor, 187
Otto of Bamberg, 387
Otto of Freising, 61, 116, 123, 282, 284
Oviedo, 83
Oxford, 94, 169, 240; University, 252–4, 256, 276, 295

Pacifism, 142, 210
Paderborn, 380, 386
Padua, 77, 317–8; University, 244, 254–5, 277, 295, 296
Painting, 389, 390, 391, 396
Palencia University, 255
Palermo, 132, 240, 324, 395
Pallavicini, Uberto, 219
Pantokrator monastery, 131
Papacy, 32, 54, 61, 64, 116, 129–30, 139, 202, 212–16, 220–2, 241–2, 246, 249, 272, 297–8, 302, 325–39, 386, 393
Parens Scientiarum (Papal Bull), 249
Paris, 73, 77, 84, 89, 102, 148, 154, 160, 241; architecture of, 397–8, 402; University of, 241, 242, 243, 244, 246–52, 253, 255, 256, 257, 259, 261–71, 296, 297
Paris, Matthew, 280
Parler, Peter, 404

Parliament, 352
Parma, 78, 229, 392
Parsival (Wolfram von Eschenbach), 37, 196
Passau, 141
Pastorelli movement, 142
Patarene movement, 202
"Patrician treaties", 76
Paul III, Pope, 50
Paulicians, 205
Pavia, 243; University, 254
Peasants' Revolt (1380), 51
Pecham, John, 253, 295, 354
Pecs-Fünfkirchen University, 257
Peipus, Lake, 98
Peking, 153, 154, 155
Perceval (Chrétien de Troyes), 180, 183
Perfecti (Cather élite), 210–12
Périguex, 385
"Perscrutator" (?Robert of York), 296
Perugia University, 254
Petahiah of Regensburg, 313
Peter of Blois, 120, 345, 349
Peter of Celle, 120
Peter of Cluny, 240
Peter the Stranger, 306
Peter the Venerable, 116, 148
Peterborough, 399
Petrarch, 304, 365, 368
Petrus Johannis Olivi, 289, 290, 305, 338
Petrus Martyr, St, 219
Pevensey castle, 346
Philip II (Philip Augustus), King of France, 176, 195, 318, 342, 343, 349
Philip IV (the Fair), King of France, 83, 85, 89, 154, 297, 331, 332, 336, 338, 342, 343–4
Philip V, King of France, 319
Philip the Bold of Burgundy, 90
Piacenza, 229, 392; University, 254
Pian-Carpino, Giovanni de, 153
Pico della Mirandola, Count, 306, 316, 317
Piers Plowman (Langland), 53, 192, 367
Pilgrimage, 52
Pisa, 76, 78, 80, 101, 240, 288, 395; University, 254
Pisano, Nicola, 395
Pistoia, 77
Plagues, 70, 155
Plato, 19, 238, 295, 374
Plato of Tivoli, 240
Podestà, 81